WE'LL BLOW WITH THE WIND

Jean Brown

The Currer, 1958.

We'll blow with the Wind

JEAN BROWN

We'll blow with the Wind
Copyright © Jean Brown, 2008

First published by Palatine Books in 2008
an imprint of Carnegie Publishing Ltd
Carnegie House, Chatsworth Road, Lancaster LA1 4SL

www.carnegiepublishing.com

ISBN 13: 978-1-874181-59-0

Cataloguing-in-Publication data
A catalogue record for this book is available from the British Library

Typeset by Carnegie Book Production, Lancaster
Printed and bound by Athenaeum Press, Gateshead

For Margaret

Her caring for animals
is neither choice nor chore,
just who she is and nothing more.

Me and Margaret, 2008.

The Currer, 2008.

Foreword

by Geoffrey Smith

M Y FIRST ENCOUNTER with the Brown family and their farm, 'The Currer', came about when I read *We'll see the Cuckoo* which, by a stroke of good fortune was the first of four books I acquired written by Jean Brown describing life on a farm situated in the Yorkshire Dales. From the opening lines 'It is one song of a morning' to the final page 'But wasn't that what everything was about? That nothing would change! We only ever want things as they are!'my interest was so enjoyably stimulated I needed to know more of the Brown family and their doings. I made enquiries as to whether there were more books by the same author. There were fortunately four curiosity satisfiers so I have in succession read *We'll trace the Rainbow*, *A Song to Sing and a Tale to Tell* then the fourth, yet equally enjoyable, *We'll buy another on Monday*, a favourite expression of the author's father. Now there is a further book to enjoy. Written in a most readable, descriptive style they express a satisfaction with a chosen way of life and a caring for others which, in this modern world, is heart warming.

Growing up as I did in a small village tucked close up to the moor edge, situated between Swaledale and Teesdale, the books conjured up vivid pictures from my own childhood, with experience of a village school similar to that described. Since then the fragrance of mown hay or freshly turned earth has been replaced by the stench of exhaust fumes, the call of the curlew from the intake land or the song of a skylark on the moor edge for the roar of traffic. Even the seemingly endless call of innumerable cuckoos is no more a signal of spring's joyfulness; indeed this year far from seeing a cuckoo I never even heard one. Enough this to set me reading *We'll see the Cuckoo* for a second time. That this is proving even more engrossing suggests that a search for the countryside through the pages of a book becomes a discovery of tranquil beauty.

Not that the books are devoted to only farming life for Jean Brown was a teacher in a small village school and out of hours activities included Girl Guides with ventures such as camping trips to the Hebrides and elsewhere. Indeed the descriptions of those humour laced trips in *A Song to Sing and a Tale to Tell* suggest you can never enjoy the world properly until you have farmed the land, let the sea run in your veins, been tented under star studded skies and read Jean Brown's latest book *We'll blow with the Wind*. Add to that the other four volumes and you then have a complete picture, with the guarantee of a restful night's sleep resulting from enjoying a brief communion with the natural world.

Introduction

I F I AM TO CONTINUE this autobiographical narrative of ordinary people getting the maximum of fun out of ordinary things – and I think I should – I must get up before the cockerel. I'll continue for my own benefit and for Margaret, lest my already full memory box begins to let me down. There is a lot of talk, in my generation, of short term memory and I am far too busy to keep a diary!

In cold January, darkness does not lift till late and paying guests, needing breakfast, are few so there is a temptation to lie longer under the duvet. I must resist it. Having first checked the four large sheds, housing one hundred and forty cattle, and found all is well, I can now let my chattering pen loose again. Day-time is its sleep time and it performs best early and so do I.

I expected that if urged to write again, which I constantly am, the title of this would be 'We'll go the fields way' and that I should be recording frequent interludes when my sister and I would be finding the byways of our very beautiful countryside, in our newly purchased, veteran Land Rover dormobile. Instead it must be 'We'll blow with the Wind', the fickle element which has always chartered our passage regardless of the way we have trimmed our sails. It blows almost perpetually on our hilltop, sometimes comfortingly calm, occasionally frighteningly strong. It has lived here longer than we and is wiser so let it be.

Outside the farm entrance is a different world from the one my generation grew up in, the one in which I taught children at a village school and took hundreds of children to camp in the Yorkshire Dales and on islands in the Hebrides. There has inevitably been some change in the way we farm and in the holiday accommodation we need to provide but, as far as is humanly possible, we cling to the customs and courtesies, the morals and frugalitiy of our up-bringing. These are the foundations on which has grown our happiness. We are all children of our time. My slot, the only one I expect to get in the endless spinning of the planet, began in 1930 and, as I see it, I was born at the right time and in the right place for me. Whatever happens now, after we have just crossed the threshold into 2008, can never change that.

You would have to go to some remote place to re-live my childhood. It was magic. There was nothing to tempt children indoors other than the delicious smell of their mother's home baking or the warmth of the blazing,

Margaret with five Atkins boys, July 2005.

open fire in the Yorkist Range when darkness came. There was no radio, television or computer game or the pile of brightly coloured plastic toys which currently offends. My brother Harry's cerebral palsy didn't prevent him joining me and our friends as we went out to play on daisied pastures in spring, in floral meadows in summer, to gather ripe blackberries in autumnal woodlands and to sledge down snow covered hillsides in winter-time. We were farmer's children, often barefoot, often alone bringing from afar, the dairy herd at milking-time. We were ever working, for chores were done by hand so we could always help. Singing was just a parental voice, crime an unknown word, curtains were drawn and men doffed their flat caps when a cortege went by and we really could depend on there being snow in the winter-time.

We, and all our juvenile friends knew a freedom which no longer exists for children today and we were richer by far.

All our lives seem restricted, now, by Health and Safety gone crazy and that wonderful freedom, so many young men died for, has been lost. Fortunately, for me, it lasted for as long as I needed it. I could take children, or even send them alone to the edge of a wood and, with a legal sheath knife could cut turf and roll back sods to build and light a fire, with birch bark and hawthorn twigs. We could feed it with beech and ash logs and, on shaven green sticks, roast sausages or bake flour and water dampers. We could take water from the stream, boil it in a paper bag and fry eggs (not those bearing a lion stamp) on an unwashed flat stone in the embers.

Today the door is shut on all that healthy fun. Early experience of space and trust has been lost. Is it possible that the knowledge of how to survive is also not being taught?

In the late forties we were trained in college, not to rear children eager to sit at the top of the educational ladder, but to impart the knowledge of how to climb it. We were shown how to discipline with a look whilst relating to each other as friends. For all those thirty years and more, Teachers, Guiders, Scouters and Youth Leaders were, within reason, allowed a freedom now no longer theirs. I am told emphatically that I would not be allowed to do today what all of us did yesterday.

I could no longer send children clutching my purse to buy something, needed for an activity, from the village shop. On an impulse, excited by the weather, I could not take them fishing for sticklebacks in The Cut, gather waterflags on the riverside, sketch in the church yard or to count the pews or the steps of the spiral staircase in the tower and finally drop a weighted plumb line to measure its height. To take them into town in the Land Rover, to buy the Christmas tree or their Prize-giving books, would now mean an application for permission. I could not have taken them on snow expeditions or to skate on the frozen tarn at The Tewits and there is no way I would have been allowed to take so many barefooted children to camp on island shores, forbidden to administer a paracetamol, if needed, or use elastoplast on a grazed knee.

I took them on trains and boats and on the back of a lorry. They slept two in a bunk and one on the cabin floor. They climbed the ben, with the crofter, to milk his cow and they brought untreated, warm milk to our store tent. They drank water from lochan and burn, ate fresh butter and crowdie and cream and returned sausages, dropped in the sand, back into the frying pan. They cooked on an open fire of peat and driftwood and swam daily in the green Atlantic and ailed nothing. They came home healthier, happier and have become, year by year, more confident, caring citizens.

There was a slot in history, albeit brief, when we could do all these things and, thank God, it was mine. If I am obsessed with numerical time, I must have inherited it from my brother, Harry, a mathematical calendar genius. As I write this introduction, the contents of *We'll blow with the Wind*, are yet to be written and it is all of seventy eight years since I was born and seventy nine since Grandfather bought The Currer. It is almost fifty years since we came to live in the ruin standing on its western boundary. It is twenty seven years since I retired from teaching and twenty eight since we converted the barn into holiday accommodation. I cannot believe it! Sadly it is many years since our parents died and seven since we lost Harry and I wrote *We'll buy another on Monday*.

Today is far from being the right time to be a farmer but, within our boundary, we try to retain old values of husbandry and confine today's mountain of paperwork to the over full desk by the wall. The fun of multiple workers in the field at harvest time, has gone but we have memories, each other and two dogs.

We began with 'a father, a mother, a sister, a brother and a baby so cunning and dear'. Now there is only the sister and the baby and both should be retired but it is not on our agenda. The future for all is unknown but, although different, the new century has filled this book with as many mini-miracles, extra-ordinary encounters, as much laughter, as many tears as the three that have preceded it. There have been as many near disasters, as many struggles with weather and work and as many different roads to follow. If you have read Cuckoo and Rainbow and Monday you may wish to make sure the magic of The Currer still works, that our optimism is still strong, our partnership secure, our luck still holding and our Guardian Angel still hovering. For that reason I am willing to use my pen and fill the early hours of winter and spring, to prove to you again that life isn't ordinary at all but a miracle from first to last.

Chapter One

'Life happens to you when you're busy making other plans.'
John Lennon

THE YEAR 2001 had been cruel. It had been the year when Foot and Mouth disease had devastated the farming community. It had horrifically reduced the animal population of many parts of our green island, the beauty of which depends on pasturing cattle and sheep. At the same time, virus free farms had become grossly overstocked when movement was banned.

From March to September the epidemic had threatened us, surrounding us and creeping ever nearer, but our Ark, with its close on one hundred and sixty animals, had out-witted the virus and a padlock on the entry gate had kept white coated, contiguous killers at bay. From within the cargo hold, we had struggled to feed and nurture but the stress had left us weak. Success was heavy only with relief for during the final fortnight we had lost our brother, Harry.

Oh, we were proud and grateful that he had lived seventy four good years in spite of being born with cerebral palsy, that for most of his life he had been active and healthy and that the final curtain call was swift and worthy of applause, but we were bereft. Our loss became an emptiness we will never fill. To Buy another on Monday, is possible with anything but a dear one and the fun we had with him can never be replaced. As real Yorkshire people, who always prefix relatives with the possessive pronoun, he was always 'Our Harry'. He was ours and we were his. He was the reason we did so many things, why we got up when we were tired, why we went out when the hearth was tempting, why every excursion was a journey of discovery and why routine was never boring.

The day of his funeral, on the 13th October, convinced us that Aunty Mary was right. The golden days of autumn, she assured us every year, when we were in Grange-over-Sands or Wales, were St Luke's Little Summer. Harry's funeral was on perhaps the most perfect day of 2001. It was utterly, utterly beautiful, warm with ethereal sunshine. When we looked up from the cemetery all we could see was the hilltop where our heavy, two year old bullocks were grazing, happily unaware that we still had no permission for their sale. Beautiful days can be so peacefully sad. We have learned, too, that 'the morn can tearless be' and that life can and must go on.

Summer.

Two weeks later we were able to sell our eighty heavy stores to a buyer in North Stainley. The good weather continued into November and we bought our annual intake of week old calves direct from the Dales' farms, east of the Settle Triangle devastated by the epidemic. We bought almost daily until we had twenty more than usual. The weather was beautiful and grass continued to grow. There was only a gentle breeze and none of the rains and fogs for which the eleventh month is renowned. The yearlings had plenty to eat and kept their distance from the steadings. For overstocked farmers this abundance of food was a blessing, the good weather a godsend.

That we dared to buy at all, if not exactly dangerous, was foolhardy for Margaret was suffering from a July fall. A wobbly stone, near the stile into the land we rented from George, had thrown her to crash against the wall and jerk her neck and spine. At first she thought her very black eyes showed the only damage done but it soon became obvious that the pain in her legs, the wobble of the thigh muscle, her inability to bear weight or stand still comfortably, were all a result of the accident. Before it she had been Yorkshire's healthiest woman, capable of knocking in fencing posts by the score and carrying bales of straw and hay by the hundred. I saw her struggling to stand in church at the funeral and was worried. I was bending under the weight of our ninety five year old aunt. She had lived with us semi-permanently since her sister, Aunty Janie, had died in 1975. She had sold her house in 1989 and come to live with us for good. She was no where near as agile as Mother had been at ninety four. She was a heavy lady we pushed in a wheelchair when out of doors but on that occasion she had flatly refused to go in it into the church. 'Four wheels are better than two legs,' she announced to all but when we most needed her to do so she would not entertain it!

Immediately the Government allowed us to sell the eighty, two year olds we recklessly bought ninety one calves admitting that we must be crazy. I was seriously wondering if, having put Harry's wheelchair up in the loft, we'd have to bring it down for Margaret. As usual, when we are scared, we were glad to have so much work that there was no time to think. We were glad we had bought automatic milk feeding machines, some years ago but there is no easy way of lifting half a hundred weight sacks of milk powder, high enough to empty and when bales can no longer be carried, they must be rolled which slows up feeding time alarmingly.

Nevertheless we had so much to be thankful for. We had escaped the Foot and Mouth. We had sold our bullocks and bought our calves though markets everywhere were closed. In spite of this we were marooned in the doldrums with no wind or tide to lift us off the sandbank. There was little, it seemed, to look forward to except work and winter and worry. We desperately needed something to float our boat, some wind of change to break the monotony of a routine without Harry.

One late morning towards the end of November, we pushed Aunty Mary, in the wheelchair to the Land Rover and heaved her onto the front seat.It had been her's since 1970. Her Divine Right. To get her in was a performance which had recently needed both of us. Margaret clambered across the driving seat and pulled and I balanced her on a stool. Then she put one foot on the station wagon step and I heaved, with my shoulder under her bottom. Always she would emit a volume of protests but she never would be left behind.

We were heading for the Land Rover specialist's for an MOT test but when we got there it was dinner hour so we had to wait, which was why I saw a very old Land Rover dormobile. Inside it was lovely but viewed from the yard it looked as if it had been in the Gulf War. It was for sale and on an impulse we bought it. Just like that. It was cheap but needed new doors and a coat of paint. 'Take your time,' we told David Simmonite. We envisaged great future joy in the spring. It seemed to offer so many possibilities. When Father was suffering from cancer we had hired a dormobile, not to sleep in but it had been day-time fun. The buying of this veteran vehicle saved our sanity during too long a winter, too anxious a new year.

Too long a winter! How many times have generations of farmers known too long a winter, too late a spring, too many cattle, too little fodder, too many aching muscles, too many days in January and a too tardy Dr Green?

We needed some spiritual medicine. We needed to move on. We were clutching at any means of survival. We wanted to be free but it was wishful thinking. We wanted the 'once was' and that can never be. We had a demanding farm and many animals. We had a thriving holiday accommodation business and we had Aunty Mary. Margaret was struggling not knowing what the end would be for both of us.

Our local policeman had retired and bought a dormobile and begun a round the world tour. We didn't want that, but we talked a great deal about what we could do with a mobile home. Harry would have loved it. He had the ability to enjoy almost anything. Aunty Mary wasn't interested but she expected to go wherever we went and for that trait we can only commend her for it meant she never held us back, though she never made any effort to preserve her mobility. Of course we could never take her and use the camper van for sleeping but it would make a lovely en route cafe. We could maybe go to Saltburn. We thought Aunty Mary would like that for it would be a trip down memory lane. She had spent many holidays there in the fifties, with her sister and our grandfather. Strangely she showed no interest. She wanted to go to the Hebrides. She loved the islands. She was sure we could handle her. We were used to it, she insisted.

Little by little the tide was floating our boat and Margaret thought it was time to do something positive about her physical health. The doctor had stared at her once, in August when both eyes were very black. We had taken Harry for his appointment and Margaret had laughed and said she wasn't the patient. The doctor had made the traditional remark about 'the other man'. He had made no comment on the way she was walking! We were far too busy, immediately after the Foot and Mouth, to decide what to do. So we did nothing.

Shortly before Christmas we had a visit from the FABBL (Farm Assured British Beef and Lamb) inspector. We had applied for this status at the beginning of the year but all farm visits had been put on hold because of the epidemic. The man came. He told us all was in order but that we would need to fence in our muck heap. Having done so and paid the inspection fee, we were awarded the coveted Symbol of Excellence. 'Call that nowt!' Aunty Janie would have said and Father's smile would have been a picture. The inspector told us that if we hung male holly in the shed we would reduce the incidence of any ringworm! It was worth a try!

In spite of everything we could only feel a sadness as Christmas approached. The reason was the slowly deteriorating health of George Winup. He and his wife, Dorothy, had been our caretakers when we went on holiday, ever since the mid-eighties. They had come twice a year and both loved it. George had been ill for some time having been diagnosed with cancer and we'd expected that he would go before Harry. We deplore the use of terminal. Life is terminal. Used with cancer suggests it is imminent and sufferers, so diagnosed, have lived for years. Margaret demands it be erased from the medical dictionary.

George had been in hospital at the time of Harry's death but he was home again, albeit slowly getting worse. There was little we could do to help except be thankful that we had been able to provide the two fortnights a year he had loved so much.

On Christmas Day we tried to behave as we always had, leaving the farm and taking a run up into the Dales. Always we would take the wheelchair and push Harry along some quiet waterfront. In 2001 we went to Bolton Abbey but we never got out of the Land Rover. We just ate our ham sandwiches with Aunty Mary and drove home. Had our 'get up and go' really 'got up and gone'?

With the festive season behind us Margaret immediately sought advice from a physiotherapist friend but exercise did not seem the answer. Jill gave her two sticks and they helped enormously, taking the weight and steadying the wobble. She then visited an osteopath whose clinic was near to where the Winups lived and we were able to call after each weekly session. George was remarkably cheerful, a role model to follow. Even the district nurses and carers fought for the opportunity to visit him. We were full of respect for him and for his wife but his disease finally won and in February his suffering was over. I seem to remember that there were daffodils dancing in the church yard sunshine. I may be wrong about that but the memory of many friends being there, to pay tribute to a fine man, is indelible. Father died in February, a long time ago and it is such a cold month in which to lose a dear one.

We had no help at all during the first months of winter. Our two wallers are dependent on good weather but when, in late February, our hay began to run out and we ordered another load, Tim Walker, our waller, came to help unload. There was a shortage of small bales, Mark, the haulier, said. Everyone was converting to big, plastic covered monsters, only moveable with a machine and a tractor expertise we did not have. At some earlier date the idea of a manitou had been aired. Margaret caused amusement over the cup of tea which always follows unloading.

'If we have to have big bales,' she said, 'we'll have to have a "man(a)tou".'

'That's right,' someone laughed. 'What you need, Margaret, is a man or two!'

Jill had concluded that Margaret's problem was an injury and the osteopath thought the same. It was impossible to tell whether any treatment was succeeding because hard work was undoing any good. Always, at the end of winter, farmers are suffering. We have many friends crippled with arthritis and awaiting replacements but Margaret had none of their symptoms. If she did not move she had no pain. Sitting, driving, sleeping she was fine. Weight-bearing was difficult. 'If I can just get through winter,' she said almost daily. Secretly she admitted to herself that she was also suffering from years and years of hard winters, late springs, busy catering summers and multiple calf-rearing autumns. She had never added being a carer to her list though some, rightly, find it a full time job. Caring for our family had been a pleasure but it had inevitably taken its toll.

With three hundred and fifty more bales, enough for a fortnight, we relaxed and hoped that we could put off Bed and Breakfast guests until Easter. Self-catering guests occupied that area at weekends and our cottages were mostly full so we prayed no one would ring for serviced accommodation mid-week. When one man did I lied, which was naughty. We would be using this slack time to decorate, I said. Decorate? In our condition? Nothing was further from the truth! We were tired. We'd been used to disturbed nights with Harry and Margaret always checked her calves during the night. Now Aunty Mary called us often and, let's face it, we really did need a rest from making breakfasts.

I did, however accept a booking from a lady from Scotland bringing her handicapped son, to the David Hart Clinic, to be fitted with a walking frame. On Thursday, the 22nd, she said. March seemed a long way off so I pencilled in the booking, bright red on the chart. We'll open at Easter. I decided. That's soon enough for Margaret, but I was thwarted.

On the 21st of February guests, who had been several times, rang to report the death of a relative, living near us, and to ask for accommodation on the 22nd, 23rd and 24th in order to attend the funeral. I could not say no and prepared the beds in three rooms. Two couples would be coming and both double bedrooms are upstairs but it occurred to me that the older couple might prefer not to climb the steps, so I also made up a twin on the ground floor. On the 22nd Margaret went down into the cellar, brought up more coke and lit the boiler for the central heating. I put a match to the fire and piled logs on the hearth. Here we go again, I sighed but the way we greet guests is forever welcoming however weary we may be.

The two couples came mid-afternoon and both chose to climb the stairs. They had a cup of tea and then carried in their cases before leaving for the home of their bereaved sister-in-law. It was nice to see lights again in our converted barn. I came in from the outside darkness, to pause a moment before the evening work. I felt more than a little guilty for I had turned away a man on the pretence that we might be spring cleaning when that chore was some way off.

It was about 6 p.m. and I was just getting Aunty Mary's tea when the phone rang and a Scottish voice said, 'I'm in the yard just outside your door. Och, I'm not sure about your dogs.'

Maybe I'm not as old as I think. My reflexes seem to be still working. I had made a gross mistake. Harry, whose knowledge of the calendar was perfect, would have been amused but even I, not so skilled as he, do know that, when it isn't a leap year, if March 22nd is on a Thursday so will be February 22nd. Thankfully, in this case, I need not admit my mistake or confess I'd coloured in the 22nd of the wrong month. We fall, like everyone else but amazingly seem to fall on our feet.

'Be with you immediately!' I said, as bold as brass and I hurried to open the Barn Door and to welcome her in with a smile. 'Do you need to get out the wheelchair?' I asked, outrageously displaying my knowledge of her reason for coming. 'Perhaps you could just carry your little boy in.' I'm an actress as well as a landlady and a farm hand! Oh boy, can I put on an act when necessary!

February is such a cold, bleak month to drive south to a hilltop farm but when she stepped indoors the fire was blazing, the logs aglow. I opened the door onto the downstairs twin I'd prepared, in case the older members of the funeral party needed it. 'Everything is ready for you,' I said with real confidence. The warmth was like a blanket. Towels were ready on the heated rail.

'It's really lovely,' she said.

It was not laughable. How could it be? Things which happen here seldom are which is why I stare with disbelief when my readers think my narrative is funny. They should be here at the moment of truth. In this case a poor man had to die and his funeral coincide, in order that a poor, stressed mother, bringing her handicapped child to the clinic, should not arrive to an icebox, an empty hearth and unmade beds. We have a guardian angel. Of that we become more and more sure.

'Phew,' I said to Margaret. 'That was near!' How shockingly out of practice we were, after the guest-empty year of 2001. It had taken it's toll.

In November we had bought several weaned calves from Newsholme Church Farm and Margaret had kept them separate in the yard shed. We had increased their number by transferring some strong Charolais, from the calf shed, at the end of February. One was a pest. There is always one. Animal or human. We were to experience both.

During March, weather permitting, we were able to let them out for an hour or two each day. A dusk return to base camp meant that the eighteen stirks were invariably distracted by a yard full of polished, shining cars. To turn them into their shed really needed two people but the weight of farming falls on Margaret. One evening, when I was busy with guests, she was attempting to guide them in alone. She is quite capable of doing so and cattle are easy to train to routine, but the naughty Charolais had developed an individual sequence and frequently insisted on inspecting cars before going to bed. Margaret desperately needed help for the shed door, if left open, was an invitation to the other seventeen animals to join in the game. Usually, when an animal realises it is alone, it panics and dashes back to join the herd. Not so the naughty Charolais!

Suddenly Margaret saw the Mistal Cottage door open and human help seemed available. She was wrong. The woman had a camcorder and was deaf to all cries for help. She would not stop filming.

'Oh, don't!' Margaret begged. 'Please! Just hold this door,' she shouted, but the situation comedy was too attractive to the holidaymaker. The opportunity to film a farmer, hopping about on two sticks, chasing a stirk in and among parked cars, might never come again.

There was no alternative but for Margaret to scream, 'Jean! Jean!' The loud cry for help penetrated the thick kitchen walls and I fled to the rescue. What is a problem for one is a piece of cake for two and the disobedient animal was returned to the shed. When we came indoors Margaret was trembling. 'I could have killed that woman with the camera! I could have been hung for her! I could cry buckets if I weren't so angry! How dare she? How dare she?'

I was shaken too. It was Margaret's first emotional anger at her disability, at the predicament which put farming in jeopardy. Again someone had found amusement in our antics and we hadn't a laugh in us.

However, never for one moment did we regret buying the dormobile. It represented the future. Maybe not an immediate one but so be it. We found a bungalow in the small village of Moorsholm, near Saltburn and that gave us something to look forward to. Then, unexpectedly, our cousins suggested they aunty-sit for us for a week in June, three couples doing two or three days each. This would enable us to drive up to Harris alone. We considered their kind proposal and decided to accept? We reckoned we had taken Aunty Mary on nearly sixty holidays since 1970. We could cope with a cottage at Moorsholm but not with boats and long distances. What was wrong in accepting help? We had not asked for it and it had been offered sincerely. Just Margaret and me on holiday would be to return to the freedom of the early fifties, the 'once was' we were eager for and we had this exciting mode of transport and accommodation. It was the beginning of recovery.

A load of hay lasts little more than a fortnight, at the end of winter. The steers are seventeen months old and the calves five months and all are eating us out of house and home. Reluctantly we decided we must experiment with big bales of which there was a never ending supply on the market. Buying calves at Robert Lofthouse's farm, in Addingham in the autumn, Margaret had admired his strong bullocks feeding from metal rings in his stockyard. They had constant access to food outside their well bedded shelter. The memory haunted her in March, when big bales seemed to be our only option.

Outside our two bullock sheds is a large, concreted yard leading to the lean-to feeding bay, adjacent to the barn. John had built this a few years ago allowing a number of our herd to be fed hay there. Bales could just be thrown from the barn, so lessening the number we had to carry to the bullock sheds. We could buy some big bale feeders, Margaret argued and

Tim took us, and Aunty Mary, to buy three from a sale yard on the opposite hillside. Then he went off to North Yorkshire and bought a second hand Kramer with a suitable grab to lift the round monsters and drop them into our new feeders. Our experiment could begin. He bought and delivered a load of haylage bales and, within a week of Margaret's decision, a new era had begun.

It had two flaws. The three new feeders were as many as the yard could take but the feeding bay was still essential to accommodate all our quite impressive herd. The manger, therein, could only hold small bales of which we had none so a big one had to be tossed onto a straw platform in the barn, torn apart by hand, and thrown loose into the long manger and that was awful. However spring was almost on the doorstep so we ignored mutilated hands and broken nails and got used to smelling of silage. The second problem did not manifest itself until we had heavy rain and the manure dropped by the feeding cattle, which had been dry, suddenly became a mire a foot deep. We were horrified. 'This won't do!' we said and prayed for the grass to grow so that we could call a halt to feeding and assess out situation.

We may have to wait for it, but Spring always comes. We were pondering in the barn, aware that its vast proportions looked like becoming obsolete and discussing how to erect a platform on which to drop a bale, to handle manually. An empty shed seemed unacceptable. Could it replace the yard, be a covered in eating area with the feeders out of the rain? A discussion with John, our contractor, was productive. He could remove the dividing wall between the barn and feeding bay and expose the long manger. The wall had been made only as a partition over which we had thrown the small bales. It had been made with railway sleepers slotted into iron uprights. They could easily be relocated to enclose one bay of the large barn to stack small bale calf hay, should we be able to buy any. Having exposed the long manger, John would widen it to big bale size and put another iron feeding fence on the barn side so that cattle could feed simultaneously from either side. Eureka! Of course John did not come to do it until October, or was it November? That was normal for John but he is always in time and his workmanship is to be recommended.

When Spring really did come, the bigger cattle were shut out of the sheds and into pastures where they would stay all summer. The calves, now quite big, were re-located to the bullock sheds, returning at night and learning the accommodation they would begin to use at bringing-in time. Teaching is a big part of husbandry and parenting.

Easter holiday makers were all self-catering and when the end of the festive week came so did Emilie, the youngest member of our much loved French family from Lyon. The slide back into the evening meal lark was made easy because she was here and could take Margaret's place throughout her stay. It was also easy because our first guests were some who had come annually for nigh on twenty years. They were Philip Oakes and Bill and Margaret Warner from Kent.

'This is our first evening meal since October 2000,' we told them. We didn't say that, after eighteen months and after losing Harry at the washing up, we were shy of starting again. The Foot and Mouth had drawn a line under one life and, though we held the rubber, hoping to erase it, it proved to be indelible.

'Well, you've not lost your touch,' they said. Emilie and I became quite big headed and, in the kitchen, repeated, 'See, we haven't lost our touch!'

Next day we had a hiccup. We were expecting a couple from Yugoslavia bringing a child to the David Hart Clinic. We regularly get people doing this from abroad, from Malta, Montenegro, France and Greece. We have a mother from Belarus bringing her daughter twice a year with the help of a charity. All bring victims of cerebral palsy to be fitted with a frame which helps them to walk. These from Yugoslavia had ordered an evening meal but had not given an arrival time so I had used melon as a starter and made a casserole and a trifle, none of which would spoil if they proved to be late. They were and the Kent trio were finishing their cheese and biscuit course when they arrived.

Their friend had brought them all the way from London and spoke their language. The father came in and inspected the warm, ground floor bedroom with its spacious ensuite. He returned to the taxi and sent in his wife who, in hesitant English, explained to us that her husband didn't like the accommodation. It was not comfortable enough, he had said.

To be confronted with dissatisfaction is seldom and always a shock. 'It's alright,' I said gently. 'I don't mind. You can go to the hotel.' I silently hoped that they would and crossed my fingers. The three from Kent, who'd been satisfied for twenty years, sat open mouthed and Emilie went into the kitchen and said to Margaret, 'Poor Jean'.

This was a punch line often used. Harry had invented it for a totally different reason. He liked the second cup poured from the tea-pot. The first was too weak for him and, each time, he'd wickedly said, 'Pour Jean(s)' and pushed my mug under the spout. Poor Jean had to have the weak one and the command became a condolence, eagerly stored in Emilie's vocabulary, ready to be brought out every time the opportunity arose.

The lady from Yugoslavia returned to the car and their chauffeur could be seen phoning the hotel. There was room but the price was too high so they began to unload their cases and they came indoors. My heart sank into my boots.

'Do you want your meal?' I asked. They did and they enjoyed it.

The man and child went into the bedroom and the wife spent the evening learning English in the sitting room with the other guests. How I loved them, Philip, Margaret and Bill trying so hard to help the lady enjoy herself.

Next morning the lady asked me to phone for a taxi. Saying they had no money and must go to the bank. I could imagine the taxi driver's response if he were asked to park somewhere whilst two foreigners trotted along the High Street. He would not be prepared to wait so I gave the lady some coins and a £10 note and I crossed my fingers that they would return in the evening and they did.

The child, I never managed any of their names, went home at the end of the week with a fitted walking frame and a more hopeful future. His mother put in our Visitors' Book. 'It was lovely to stay in your house and eat your food.' Sometimes you lose but mostly with a little help from your friends, you win!

I cannot let this opportunity pass without emphasising that we credit our guests with 51% of our success. They made this place what is has continued to be over decades and we are extremely grateful.

Anna came. She was with us from April to August and was a veterinary nurse in the practice we have used for over seventy years. We got a special welcome every time we went into the surgery. Also, on the plus side, it always gives me pleasure to be on the receiving end financially. Usually it is we who pay the vet! It is also a pleasure to have someone nice who stays a long time. They become family.

Only occasionally do we feel to have had a massive overdose of people and that we could retire from that section of our work pie-chart and feel that we have had an excellent sufficiency and not be hungry for more. When people ask me if I miss teaching children I certainly take that view. I loved it, but it's over. I can happily be an onlooker, rarely stressed when politicians make a mess of things. Given the opportunity I would no doubt tell them what to do, even as I sometimes advise adults on parenting and disciplining for I am essentially a teacher! Possibly they think I don't know, as five year old Alison did when she suspected that I did not know what was happening in the school yard.

We took Emilie to Bolton Abbey, one of her favourite places. We paused, on the way, to picnic at Beamsley and she wanted to climb the Beacon. She managed it easily. She, like us, had a summer ahead which promised adventure. With her parents she planned to walk from Lyon to Santiago de Compostella in Spain. It would take her parents three months and she would join them and spend all her summer holiday walking. We have never been free to do anything like that but would have once been game. Even a long life can be too short.

Margaret faired less well. She could barely manage the first leg of the climb and her poor performance haunted me and no doubt worried her. Before Emilie returned to France we went over to Simmonites to inspect the progress of our dormobile. We were eagerly looking forward to enjoying whatever it had to offer and we were more than pleased with it's new look.

It had new doors and was immaculately painted Land Rover green. We still did not urge a quick delivery, not having sorted out our big but full garage. We needed to move the corn bin and it still had some corn left in it.

I did however name our new vehicle THE DORM'OUSE and Emilie went to the Library in search of a picture of the minute creature and I bought some sticky letters at B&Q. We were cocker-hoop! We were sure it would be ready for us to travel in it, to Saltburn in May. We would be able to practise using the kitchen equipment by making coffee on the promenade. Restoration of it was costing the earth but we'd never spent extravagantly on ourselves before so we did not feel guilty. This purchase had been necessary to aid our recovery.

The Lloyds had filled the house on a self-catering basis over Easter Week. It was the first of many times they have repeated their visit. Then came a month when we were well and truly back in the business of serviced accommodation, breakfasts and evening meals daily. Trade was not as dependable as it had been before the Foot and Mouth and we surveyed our chart, with its increased number of fully self-catering groups, with relief. The swing in favour of this was as acceptable to us, weary as we were, as was the coming week in May and a promising mobile home holiday future. Margaret was finding standing at the Aga and the washing up sink worse than feeding cattle. The score and more years of evening meals would maybe have to end. As often as possible at any rate.

Since July, nine months earlier, there had been nothing more important to me than Margaret's persistent disability. The Foot and Mouth had not attracted my attention more. Nor had Harry for he was not the keystone that Margaret was. Her injury had the potential to alter our lives completely. Our presumption is always that the body will heal itself, given time and we did not know where to find that illusive commodity. Pulled muscles, strained tendons, torn ligaments are all part of farming. Go to any cattle market and you will notice that bowed legs and bent backs are the norm and that walking sticks are not brought to encourage cattle but to support the handler and fend off frisky cattle which approach more quickly than work-worn farmers can avoid. Rest was maybe needed but the holiday in Saltburn would not be easy with an immobile, ninety-six year old aunty.

'Do you know, Aunty Mary,' Margaret said one day, 'I haven't had a holiday since 1975 without someone over eighty being with us?' The old lady was in her usual and replied, as ever, 'Well, you're used to it!' Poor Margaret, it won't be very long before I fit that category!

After Harry's death we began to have very broken nights with Aunty Mary. She excused herself in her usual manner, but we weren't really used to responding to her kind of attention. Harry had only needed rolling back into bed and covering. We could almost do it with our eyes shut and go straight back to sleep. Attending to Aunty Mary was a half hour job, by the end of which we were fully awake. I frequently returned to my bed wondering whether it was worthwhile taking her on holiday at all. She showed no interest in Saltburn. She probably would not recognise the place nor remember she had been when we returned. The camper van was still at Simmonites and we began to think it might be better if we used our old, well known Land Rover for this trip to the North Yorkshire coast. A mobile home would be a constant reminder to Aunty Mary, that we were going to go to Harris without her.

The truth was we would have much preferred to take her with us. We never actually look forward to leaving land or house, guests or animals, in another's care and have always preferred to take dogs and family with us and to be able to relax. For thirty years she had been a happy family member, going where we went, doing what we did. Not all OAPs are so accommodating. She never voiced her luck or her gratitude but she wallowed in the respect of the Hebridians and basked in fame for island hopping at ninety five is no mean feat.

We were leaving one abnormal responsibility behind. The swallows were back from their African winter and one had chosen to build its nest in the duck hole. Each morning I let out the ducks by lowering their drawbridge from which they have access to the pond. They hear human approach from a distance and become wildly excited before anyone can climb the fence and undo their exit. They almost fly down their slope and whoever releases them must dive out of their way. But that nesting swallow was quicker than they. The draught of its wings disturbed my hair each morning and it was always a shock even if expected. At dusk, when the ducks were tempted back into their beach hut, with their evening meal, we had to presume and hope that the swallow was back on the nest but we did not know for sure until her lightning flypast confirmed it next morning.

Speed is necessary in our household and I am good at it. Too good perhaps. Long, long ago Father named me Hellfire Jack. Maybe Aunty Mary's quieter life never did demand that she hurry. Now it was almost impossible to get her anywhere on time. Always she blamed us. I do believe she thought it was my fault she had grown old. She certainly said everything else was. I'm used to taking the blame. Margaret invariably says, 'Where have YOU put ...?' 'What have YOU done with ...?'

Since middle-age Aunty Mary had periodically visited a chiropodist and, as befits a lady of her generation, she had a fortnightly visit to the hairdresser's for the shampoo and set of her permanent waves. The lady who did this was tolerant but the gentleman who did her feet was not. On the very last time I took her to the foot surgery, we were a quarter of an hour late and he was quick to agree when I suggested he take the money and we make another appointment. I explained the awful job I'd had to get her there at all, even her hearing aid had been forgotten. He calmed down and said, were he to do her feet he'd be late for every customer all day.

'Would you like a home visit in future?' he suggested. 'I could come next Tuesday?' I was so relieved. He turned to Aunty Mary and shouted close to her ear, 'Your appointment is next week, Miss Smith,' and Miss Smith turned on me and said, 'See, you got the wrong date. I knew. It's your fault!' and the good man hit her with his soft Appointments Book. We laughed, of course. I could win a trophy for that!

You have to get used to a lot of things if you are caring for the average elderly. Our excellent role models were Mother and Father and Harry, all of whom had grown old behaving as they always had. Perhaps everyone does, really and that, unless you are careful, just less likeable characteristics show up more. Stella Stowell was staying with us and said, 'I'm going to grow old nice. Nobody has any patience with cantankerous old ladies, at home or in care.' The stark truth is that there will soon be a lot of old people! They had better be nice

I think we all should have the experience of caring for both species of the previous generation. We had a double dose of it for we also had Aunty Mary's friend who was in her 100th year. We used to pick her up every Sunday and take both to the chapel and pick them up after the service. It was an outing Harry enjoyed for he found both very funny. Collecting Hilda became more difficult when bollards were put at the end of her cul-de-sac, preventing us from turning round in the playground of a school for special needs children. This meant we had to park two streets away. Aunty Mary could not have walked so far but her senior friend could if there was no alternative. One Sunday morning there was, for the Main Entry gates were open and, with relief I drove in and stopped on the inside of the bollards and collected Hilda from her home only a few yards away. She was, as usual, waiting impatiently, for being on time was her law but is not always possible in our busy life. 'You are late,' she said as she always did. But there was no rush for I was parked almost on her doorstep. It was easy! I jumped back into the Land Rover and drove back to the gates which, to our dismay, were now shut and padlocked. We were prisoners. We had no wheelchairs so we could not escape on foot.

The ladies wore expressions of complete disgust. I decided I must find a caretaker with a key. I knocked up a sleeping neighbour who told me the caretaker lived a mile away. He hadn't a car but walked down every Sunday to feed the school cat. He knew the name and together we found the phone number. There was nothing we could do but give the caretaker time to walk home, then call him and wait for his return. When he did, he wasn't annoyed at all. The oldies in my car had no sense of humour but thankfully he had. They blamed me for not being able to go to chapel and were miseries all afternoon.

Forgive me for wandering down memory lane but there is one other incident I am sure Harry would want me to recall. We were taking Hilda home one tea-time, after she had been with us for a long weekend. I needed to call at the supermarket and, thinking she might want to take home some food, I pulled into the car park and asked, 'Can I get you anything, Hilda?' I was even more accommodating than that. 'You can come in with me if you like,' I suggested. She wanted neither so, with relief, I went into the store alone.

I had barely disappeared when the two old ladies, sitting on the back seat, decided they did want to go in after all but they could not open the passenger door. They were determined and battered on the window to attract a passing man who put his head to the window, presumably seeing one very wizened centenarian and one plump nonagenarian hammering to get out. He turned to the front seat window saying, 'Are they allowed?' but seeing a handicapped laughing man took to his heels and fled. Harry was still laughing when I returned and, my goodness were the oldies mad!? Harry had often referred to the sitting room, when Hilda was here, as the Eventide Home and he would repeat the conversations he had overheard. Sadly, with his death, we had lost the main generator of so much of our fun but we had a warm chuckle when a guest told us she had taken a grand-daughter to see an old lady who was a hundred and the child had been wide eyed and had said, 'And did you begin at one?'

Chapter Two

In April I open my bill, In May I sing night and day.

T HE ADVICE I HAVE ALWAYS GIVEN to parents is that the most important thing to teach children is how to solve problems, how to use knowledge and skills to achieve results. To iron out the wrinkles avoids having to do major surgery.

When Aunty Mary came to live with us permanently, in 1989, we wired a bell from her bedroom to ours so that, if she ever needed us, she could ring. She never did. She was not ill or incapable of looking after herself, as we had supposed, when she had become afraid of even the four days a week she was alone. Seven years on, when she was ninety and much later rising, we'd bought a cordless bell so that it could live on our bedside table at night and be brought down into the kitchen when I got up. She never used it even if she needed to. Instead she sat on the bed getting colder and more and more cross with us for not coming. Sometimes she would go to her wash basin pushing her wheelchair. Though it be only 4 a.m. she would begin to dress. She wasn't senile, just determined not to ring. In fact she was a very healthy lady, needing no medication, just choosing to use her legs less and less. We told her repeatedly that all she had to do was ring the bell but she never did.

We noticed an obvious wear and tear on our stairs and corridor carpet for we were constantly running up and down. The installation of the wheelchair lift for Harry had disturbed it and it was getting more and more shabby but, even should Aunty Mary live past the hundred mark, we were determined to wait. Her wheelchair was pulling it every which way. A new carpet was out of the question.

We had finally decided not to use our dormobile for Saltburn, even if it were delivered on time. We'd never test driven it. Only Margaret had ever been in the driving seat and that had been to enable the height to be adjusted so that my diminutive sister could see out of the windscreen. I washed the old station wagon and swept the rear of winter hay and straw and litter which naughty picnickers leave after parking their cars at the road entrance. I put Aunty Mary's case on her bed and most of what she needed to pack. However she appeared to have no intention of doing so. She always left it to the last minute but we had reached that moment and she made no effort, saying it wasn't tomorrow that we were going. In the end I had to do it for her. Mary, Mary quite contrary was frequently apt.

We were just about to get into the laden Land Rover and leave for holiday, when the phone rang. 'We are just coming over with your dormobile,' said David Simmonite, the garage proprietor.

'Oh, no you're not,' I replied, 'and don't say, "Oh, yes we are" because we are already heading for the Land Rover and in a few minutes we'll be gone!' Our life is a pantomime all the year round.

'It's maybe as well,' David said. 'This classic has leaf springs and might not be as comfortable for an old lady and you'll have to get used to the non-powered steering.' If we had not been so keyed up at the start of a holiday we may have found this remark disturbing but we never gave it another thought.

It was to be our first holiday without Harry. Though the Land Rover was full the roof rack was not needed and our well-fitting Bowness cover looked like being forever redundant. We heaved Aunty Mary into the front seat of our well-known vehicle and Meg, in the back began to bark, as she always does. Danny never did but Meg thinks she is the ignition. We should have stopped her but she made Harry laugh and we are skilled in deciding what is important and what is not. We were not as relaxed as at the beginning of previous holidays when, to get to the top of our road was long enough for the holiday spirit to have entered all of us.

We had driven to the east coast several times before but I don't think we had ever taken the fields way through the Hambleton and Cleveland hills. In the first half of May, was there anywhere more beautiful? How can anyone criticise north-country farmers? Their cattle and sheep are landscape gardeners beyond reproach. North Yorkshire is beautiful at any time but the May blossom was like drifted snow on the hawthorns and the chestnuts looked like Christmas trees so festooned were they in candles. There were bluebells everywhere and, though the daffodils were over, their dandelion replacement was second to none. Along the road sides they bloom in such profusion they annually excite our applause. We used to sing in school, 'Daisies are our silver, buttercups our gold' but I challenge that. For quality and quantity the dandelion is king.

The Hambleton Hills enchanted us. Avoiding the main roads we explored the byways and the attractive villages, all three appreciative of the county we call home. We were missing Harry's query, 'Where is this?' every time we saw a village sign. We always would, but we were content and looking forward to an unknown holiday cottage to add to the score we have occupied.

The village of Moorsholm was idyllic, the gardens well tended and everywhere there were flowers. In front of our cottage was a beautifully maintained lawn, newly mown for our arrival. We viewed the up-gradient of the drive with a whisper of apprehension. To unload the elderly on a slope, is not easy and there were five steps to the path leading to the front door. They were well spaced and weren't really a problem and the bungalow was so suitable inside we did not grumble. It was perfect for a wheelchair but we left that in the Land Rover. Why bother with what was not really needed? We were immediately at home, being seasoned holiday cottage people and next morning three happy ladies had the joy of breakfast outside on the patio. What more could we want?

The north east coast was pleasant enough but somehow the beach seemed inaccessible. Most of the remote, UK beaches we have visited have been empty but wheelchair friendly. Many have been Land Rover friendly, too. All of us love being at the water's edge. In Saltburn the season had not begun. There was building activity on the promenade and the beach cafes, open on Sunday, closed again on Monday and did not re-open until the next weekend. Not able to get car or chair onto the beach restricted us to the promenade wherever we went, north or south of Saltburn. It was Aunty Mary's holiday so we weren't prepared to leave her, even if Margaret had been able to stride out. I think that, during that week at Moorsholm, I really saw her disability and didn't like what I saw. Watching her playing with the dogs on the beach, I saw she was struggling and when we walked them through the village, before bedtime, there was none of the active, younger sister I was used to.

Sitting in an armchair in the comfortable cottage she was fine. We re-read the manuscript of *We'll buy another on Monday*, ready for me to take to Lancaster on the 24th of May, to leave it with an interested publisher. I never record immediately preferring to have a period of understanding between event and pen. There are plenty of opportunities to correctly date an incident, for an accommodation letting-chart is above our telephone. Last year's remains underneath it and if that fails to jog my memory there is always the receipts and expenses account books, bank statements and the herd book with its births and deaths and days of store cattle sales and calf buying sessions. As we have little or no social life, our engagement calendar has only dental appointments and Margaret's thrice a year hairdresser's visit. As September approaches it has the fortnightly Cattle Sales but, on December 31st, it can be thrown away having no further use.

I see more and more of Father in Margaret. Every day, like him, she said, 'Yeh, I'm a bit better today than I was yesterday!' but she remained dependent on sticks. At the end of 2001 we had felt grounded and we knew we hadn't yet pulled up the heavy anchor. We believed we would, given time. We'd see the cuckoo, we'd trace the rainbow, we'd be ready to buy again but it wasn't happening as quickly as we had hoped.

As expected, Aunty Mary didn't really remember Saltburn but every day we jogged her memory. They'd had such happy times, she and Aunty Janie and Grandfather. Daily she repeated how one day he had fallen and given them such a shock and each time we said, 'Remember something happy, please!'

We noticed that occasionally she was confused about who was on holiday with us asking if we'd told Mother we were coming and being sure that her other two nieces were in the back seat of the car. Nevertheless she was doing alright. We were sure she was enjoying her holiday. She was a holiday lady and must have had many more than others of her generation. I don't think any one of them had not been a pleasure. We explored the North York Moors for the first time and spent two afternoons in the quiet village of Sandsend. Mother would have labelled the holiday as uneventful, not normal for us. She would have been proved wrong.

On Thursday we planned to stay in Saltburn for the day promised to be hot. We breakfasted and were heading down the two steps from the front door, very carefully for the manoeuvre was tricky. I was hanging on to Aunty Mary's right arm, one step lower than she and Margaret was steadying her from above. 'Step down,' I ordered but she was already leaning on me and was over balancing. Margaret couldn't hold her heaviness but did manage to lower her gently. I fell onto a nearby bush and she slowly sank on top of me. 'Whoops!' we all said simultaneously.

There appeared little harm done. I wriggled from beneath her and, being so near the steps we were able first to hoist her onto the lower step, then onto the top one and then to pull her up. We walked her to the five, well spaced ones and got her into the Land Rover. We spent a lovely day in the Valley Gardens. We managed to get her into the wheel chair and, after a picnic, back into the car to return to the bungalow without a problem. We did, however, take the wheelchair into the cottage and when we inspected her ankle we saw that it was quite swollen.

On Friday morning, our last day, we again got her into the car but this time we let her stay there and came back to Moorsholm early. Next day we headed for home, a successful holiday over. 'Didn't we do well,' we thought.

Nearing home we had to pass our local hospital and, on an impulse, we called into Accident and Emergency. Aunty Mary's leg was X-rayed and a broken fibula was identified. We took her home with a pot leg, more immobile than she had ever been.

She thrived on her new found celebrity status and for a week or two was quite confused. She told one guest that she had only been in hospital one week but, little by little the confusion went and normality returned. At Moorsholm I had slept in Aunty Mary's bedroom and, on our return, Margaret put a mattress on her bedroom floor. All the previous week in Moorsholm she had not wakened me in the twin bed beside her and neither did she wake Margaret. She sat on the edge of the bed getting colder and colder so, after two days Margaret recognised it for what it was, an utter waste of time and comfort. We had to solve the problem some other way before we left for Harris. Things had to go as smoothly as possible while we were away and we were going in less than a month's time.

We engaged the help of the district nurse and the male physiotherapist who came to bring a zimmer. Aunty Mary liked gentlemen and appeared to be listening intently when he insisted she really must ring the bell.

'You've got a broken leg. You need help. The ladies will do anything for you. You will get so cold sitting on the bedside,' he coaxed. She smiled. She was a charmer but not an obedient listener.

A social worker rang to tell us we were due for help. Aunty Mary could go for Respite Care. We told her that we'd accepted relative-relief but we said the night care problem was worrying us. We had every disability facility in the book, leftovers from Harry's last years. We had a wheelchair lift, a commode and a shower chair and a floor level shower. We had an hydraulic bath seat and hand rails all over the place. We had a bedside bell but that she would not use.

'Get a baby monitor,' she said, 'then all she has to do is call you.'

I went straight to Boots chemist's and, weathered and grey-haired, I went to the Mothercare section for my purchase. I'm sure the sales lady grinned so I hastily said it was to be used to monitor a ninety six year old lady with a broken leg! A guest, who was a grandparent, showed us how to plug it in and we said, 'All you've got to do Aunty, is call.' But we hadn't misinterpreted her non-compliance. Others thought it was a question of 'couldn't' but we knew it was 'wouldn't'. She did not call. The tragedy was that if we spoke to her without remembering to turn it off, everybody heard the over loud conversation downstairs. The wallers had hysterics one morning, having elevenses at the kitchen table. There is comedy in almost every situation if you have a short fuse.

I was dusting the windows in our sitting room extension, the area Mother called the New Do, when the draught of my duster disturbed wind chimes hanging between the mullions and I knew what to do. A friend had bought them one Christmas but our front door is always being opened by people or dogs or the wind, which blows almost perpetually on our hilltop. We could not stand continual chiming so had hung them as far out of the draught as possible.

I unhooked them, found a wooden stand I knew would be just right and I hung them very near her bedside. Eureka again! Every time her legs came over the bed edge they jangled and the monitor amplified the chimes. We could now, perhaps, concentrate on our fast approaching holiday.

I am sure all previous Mays had not been completely free of night disturbance. There had been more than seventy of them. We had done a lot of May camping, in the mid-nineteen hundreds and I must have been wakened many times to attend to children and tents. We have had many May holidays when our departure has meant an almost sleepless night and an early rise. I'm sure we had broken nights with Father when he was ill and with Mother when it was her turn and, more recently, I remembered

School Party.

being constantly up and down with Harry. But it wasn't until the May of 2002, when Aunty Mary's chimes alerted us often, that we ever heard the cuckoo singing all night. He just cuckooed continuously. His message was welcome. We had survived the winter and we were climbing out of the Slough of Despond. We hardly dare say to him, 'Alright, we've heard. Now please, please go to sleep!'

Before we could even begin to think about our coming holiday there was a four day Special Needs School holiday to cope with. We could not really do anything until that was over for we were doing the cooking and there were twenty children and five members of staff.

How to cope with so many is not a problem for, as a relative Fish and Chip Giant once said, 'Anybody can fry chips if there is a queue!'

The children were very appreciative of our traditional menu. I have always believed the introduction of choice, in a school dinner menu, to be wrong. When I was teaching there was none and the children ate everything. We have never offered choice in our dining room but everyone loves to have our evening meal. One of the teachers asked a twelve year old what he had eaten that he had never had before.

'Carrots,' he said, 'and peas and custard and ginger pudding and chocolate cake.' Fancy that! Nearing teenage and never having experienced basic food. How sad can that be?

Children are noisier than they used to be and they ignore adults. I have noticed that in supermarkets. Mother says, 'Don't,' and her child takes no notice or says, 'Why?' Perhaps they always did to parents but now they ignore and question their teachers. I stand right back. It is not my job any more and I do not interfere. Perhaps it would be more honest to say I try not to interfere but sometimes when I do, I know it to be risky. Why do I think they will obey me and not their teacher when she tells them they must go out of the kitchen? Maybe because even as I speak I am guiding them to the door and shutting it behind them!

On their last evening I had baked two large sponge puddings, each capable of feeding a dozen. They had enjoyed their soup and eaten their main course and the plates had been removed. I carried in the first of the two puddings but children were sitting at one table only. Half the class had disappeared.

'Where are they?' I asked.

'They are watching Coronation Street,' their teacher replied.

'Well, just call them back,' I said and went back to the Aga to get the second pudding. Returning with the steaming dish, I was surprised to find them still watching TV. 'Won't they come?' I said and the poor teacher shrugged his shoulders in defeat. Interfering is not really risky because children haven't changed. Adults have just lost confidence. I walked quietly into the room and switched off the television and shepherded them back to the table and they ate their pudding.

'If you come to my house, you do it my way,' I said gently for in college, in 1948, I was taught I must speak no louder than you can say 'lovely'.

Teachers are blaming poor parenting but I believe children can still learn many ways of behaviour. We used to expose them to as many environments as possible teaching them how to behave walking the narrow country lanes, crossing the High Street in town, taking the footpath through the church-yard and entering our church nave or climbing its tower. We taught them there is a way to behave in the houses of others, in the shop, on the bus, at the hospital, on the canal bank and in the swimming pool. If we had children we knew behaved unsuitably at home, it did not mean that behaviour was accepted elsewhere. When teachers are transferring blame and accusing parents, I disagree. Every situation is different and at five, Joan my infant teacher, said almost on admittance, 'Johnny, that is not allowed in school'. The sad thing is that children do not accompany adults frequently enough, these days and you do not learn how to live from your peers.

The amazing truth is that children still do not like to disappoint adults they respect. Our young guests were embarrassed by their behaviour and to make amends they were extremely helpful clearing the table and some even brought me some of their sweets.

'I like your food!' one said. Children also know how to butter you up with praise!

'Your house is nice,' said another.

'I like it here. I don't want to go home,' they said, one after the other. 'Can we come again?'

When they left next morning they thanked us and hugged us and said they'd had a wonderful time. Shortly after that Health and Hygiene ruled out farm holidays as too risky and closed many of the Special Needs Schools. Believe it or not, the Guide Movement had to say no to camping on land on which there had been animals within the past three weeks. Whatever would I have done?

Margaret found standing at the sink washing dishes most difficult. The chore, after every meal, served to those twenty five of the school party, was destroying any good done by the relaxing Saltburn holiday. 'I think we should enrol at a fitness class,' she said. 'Are you game?'

So we went to the big, newly built one in town and asked for a brochure. The receptionist took one look at Margaret and said, 'You'll need a doctor's certificate before we could enrol you.'

'Don't do that,' advised the osteopath. 'Go to the swimming baths.' So we went down to the Leisure Centre and renewed our pensioners' passports and went swimming. Margaret's recovery was as important to me as it was to her so I sang, 'I'm sticking with you, for I'm made out of glue. Anything you want to do, I'm doing it too!'

Margaret told the osteopath that she feared she would not be able to walk any distance on the tempting Harris beaches. 'Any distance' was an over statement. She could hardly walk at all. 'I'll lend you my folding bicycle,' said the kind lady and brought it for a trial. Riding it meant all weight was on the saddle and it was a doddle. Being the opportunists we are, we went straight to the local cycle shop and bought two folding ones which we hoped would fit into the new dormobile, still in the mechanic's garage. We went up onto the green lane connecting us with Bingley and I wobbled at first for I hadn't ridden since college days, when I used to borrow a friend's cycle and ride to Fountains Abbey or up Wensleydale to West Tanfield and Masham. I was over fifty years younger then! We behaved like visiting children in the farmyard, cycling round and round when there was no danger of spectators.

Our beautiful Land Rover caravanette was delivered just ten days before we were to go north. Ken brought it. Others drive much faster than we do and he voiced a little concern. We might find, as he had, that the leaf springs offered a less comfortable ride and he reminded us that there was no power steering. 'I'll take you up the road,' he said.

I jumped into the front seat and Margaret climbed in behind me. Ken put his foot on the accelerator, as men do, and at every bump in the road I left my seat and Margaret threatened hysteria. We hadn't indulged in real abdominal laughter for some time. It was medicinal. Ken looked worried and we hadn't a care in the world. Not a qualm. Nothing would puncture

Aunty Mary and Hilda.

our inflation. The holiday was going to be magic. We were going to be young again. We were going to ride the sun!

We paid the staggering high sum for the hours of labour the makeover had needed. We'd lived without extravagance all those many years. This was our first indulgence. We ignored the hole in our bank balance. Harris, here we come! We bought the necessary insurance. We had to take photographs of our purchase because of its incredible age, and we sent them to our insurer with pride. It looked like something from a rich man's collection. Then we bought the necessary road tax disc but we were too busy to test drive it.

At the beginning of June, Hilda celebrated her 100th birthday and, a few days later the local chapel held a Welcome Hour party for her. We made our first attempt to hoist a pot-legged, old lady into the Land Rover and took her early to the hall, whilst the tables were still being laid. We had prepared for this event and the moment we returned home we exchanged one vehicle for the other. It was time, belatedly, to test drive. Margaret is the better of the two so she was in the driving seat as we went gently up the hill and over the cattle grid. The minimal discomfort of the old-fashioned springs was easily ignored.

Tentatively finding the gears and gingerly exploring the dash board we went the fields way to Otley, gaining confidence with every mile. Our destination was the home of Olga Beardwood, a friend who, until the death of her husband, had spent the summer months in a caravan at Horgabost, on Harris. They had done this year after year and now, after a long absence, she was flying back to attend the Golden Wedding of John and Mamie MacKay who had been their hosts for many years. She was flying on the day after our departure but would arrive before we did. We had told no one, not even Olga, that we were going for there were too many ifs and whens and hopefullys but, with newly gained confidence, we told her and said she could announce our expected arrival and tell them we had our own accommodation. We crossed our fingers. You can't do more than that.

'Come and look at what we've got,' we urged her. 'What do you think of that, now?' My, were we big headed? Teenagers not pensioners. We knew she was an authority on caravans and we were relieved when she approved.

'It's lovely,' she said.

We hadn't been back to Harris since 1999 and she hadn't been for much longer than that and we were almost giddy with excitement. It doesn't take much to please us. We were Luskentyre people and she belonged to Horgabost where John's boat is moored on pure white sand and the island in the bay is Taransay.

'Call that nowt,' we bragged, showing her the convenient cooking facilities we had never tested, the seat conversion to beds, the picnic table, wardrobe, sink and cupboards. Everything was perfect. 'The roof goes up for headspace,' we said but we had never tried to operate it. We just hadn't had any pre-holiday time but all our guests and Olga our friend were unanimous in assuring us that we were going to have a lovely time.

We could not tarry. Welcome Hour parties are fairly short lived and we had to collect Aunty Mary. We could not abandon her until cousins were installed and the morning of our departure had arrived.

Margaret had one more visit to the osteopath and I drove her there in the dormobile. It was like driving our 1965 Land Rover. We'd soon get used to it.

Our euphoria was short lived. Pre-holiday preparation used to be concentrated on camp equipment, rucksack contents, routes and reservations. That pleasure was all in the past. Preparations now are not on how to go, but how to leave everything safely behind. We re-housed the dormobile in the garage and concentrated on the house, the holiday accommodation, cattle and Aunty Mary. Had anyone said to us, during that last week, anything about our holiday we would have said, 'What holiday?' We were not too concerned about leaving her. Michael, our youngest cousin, was married to a doctor. You can't get luckier than that and Aunty Mary was hobbling on her pot leg as far as the cloakroom loo. Dorothy would come as usual but this time she would live in the Mistal cottage with all her show collies. She would monitor the cattle, call for professional help, if necessary and give extra care to Little Toughie who had survived neglect, when born during the

Foot and Mouth era. He was now on the road to recovery after Margaret's belated recognition of a copper deficiency. Having put that right the little man only needed some loving care. For some unknown reason Dorothy was to christen him Sweet Pea but to us, ever since we had dragged him out of the calf-trailer, following our November purchase, he had first been Poorly-getting-better and then Little Toughie. Sadly we only name sickly calves, blind ones or monsters. Occasionally one is called Pest. We would never call one Sweet Pea!

We should never have bought several of the calves we did that ill-fated, post Foot and Mouth, November. The vet authorising movement should not have allowed sale, but if you are ill, be you animal or human animal, the best place to be is at The Currer. Little Toughie was doing alright.

On the day before leaving I hung the curtains in the dormobile, threw in sleeping bags, a change of clothes, pan, kettle and some food. There was a time in our history when this would have been done meticulously. Those days are gone. Margaret stocked it with dog food and finally we carried in the folded cycles. We were only semi-organised.

Cousin David and his wife Joan arrived from home on the south coast, to take over the first three days of caring. We were more than grateful. I remember little of their ordination, only that I was fairly sure they would cope.

Next morning Margaret came very slowly and carefully down the stairs saying silently, 'I must not fall. I must not fall. I must not let Jean down. We need this holiday!'

Chapter Three

The answer, my friend, is blowing in the wind.

O UR DEPARTURE NEXT MORNING had the unreality of a dream. We hadn't left Aunty Mary behind for thirty three years and had fully expected that when we did there would still be three of us, the younger generation, H. J. and M. That was never to be and there were only the two of us and nothing was real.

We had left relatives we hardly knew, caring for Aunty Mary at The Currer. She had been sulky and had not said she hoped we had a good holiday. Our cousins we had known as children, when the family had been close, but they had long since gone their separate ways, married and raised children. Two or three times a year they had come to The Currer to see Aunty Mary. We would never have left her in Respite Care.

We always had bi-annual misgivings at leaving house-guests and animals, even in experienced hands. That feeling, on the morning of the 20th June 2002, was the only normal one. Almost everything else was surreal. That I got into the driving seat, for the first well known lap of our journey, was normal. When a map isn't needed I drive, when it is Margaret takes the wheel. It was scary, only my second time adjusting the seat and identifying knobs on the dashboard. Everything was still to experience. Ignoring the fact that we had kitchen facilities, we had filled a big flask. We hadn't, ourselves, tried to raise the roof, we had never tested the calor gas, experimented with the bunk beds, tried the lighting or drawn the curtains across windows that would never be so clean again.

Had anyone asked our expectations, when we bought the dormobile, we would have said we anticipated excitement and freedom; to be overwhelmed with the novelty. Instead we were stunned. We could not identify with the situation. Some would classify our status as Third Age. Enrolment at any such organisation would have been instantly accepted on age grounds. Perhaps others would say we were longing for a second childhood. Rubbish to both. The truth was we were just tired out and we must be constantly aware of it on our long journey all the way to the distant Outer Hebrides. The joy of Harris at least would be normal. We'd recapture excitement there, surely.

I drove to the centre of Keighley, stopped at the War Memorial traffic lights and slipped out of gear. With the return of amber, I tried to engage

Land Rover dormobile.

first gear and could not. I panicked. I could not get any gear at all. Margaret leaned over and tried unsuccessfully and the green light disappeared. I could not find the hazard light knowing those behind were getting impatient. I tried the gear again and it worked simultaneously with the second green light. Sweating with effort and relief, I pulled onto North Street and neither of us spoke till we had left Skipton behind and were heading for Wharfedale. At Threshfield Filling Station I drew in front of the pump to refill our tank. That is always Margaret's task whilst I, who hold the purse, go to the kiosk. Then we change over.

Margaret said, 'It swallows petrol!' It did not matter for we would have no Travel Lodge expenses, nor cottage rent, but we'd have to remember to re-fuel before heading into the Highland Outback where filling stations are few. Margaret tried to get into first gear and couldn't. 'What's wrong with it?' she said in exasperation. A car was behind us was waiting to take our space as Margaret struggled. At last it worked but not before she was sweating as I had been. We drove on through Kettlewell and Buckden in shock. We needed a coffee and, having left Hubberholme behind, we pulled onto the sheep grazed verge in a state of nervous exhaustion. We opened our mega-flask and drank and ate. We were not yet ready to be proper caravanette people, not ready to light the calor gas and play the Dorm'ouse game. Then we walked slowly alongside what may well be Yorkshire's clearest stream. Wharfedale is so beautiful. I don't really know what the dogs were thinking but I'm sure they must have been intolerant of our speed. We walked as if 'dead lice were dropping from us', to use one of Mother's outrageous descriptions. Margaret was using two sticks and we were very tired. I felt angry for her. It wasn't fair.

She and I had been given, by cousins, this week of freedom and her July fall, nearly a year ago, was still making her life more than difficult.

We felt more fettered than ever before. We had gallivanted on Hebridean beaches for half a century. First alone, then with hundreds of happy children who, at first, had not been able to outrun us. More recently we had leapt to the edge of the ocean pushing wheelchairs, throwing balls for enthusiastic dogs, not as agile but not all that slowly, considering how work worn we really were. Yet here we found ourselves, using our freedom to wobble along the edge of this Pennine stream like two veterans of some bygone struggle

An elderly couple, walking far more quickly than we, overtook us from behind. They stopped and enquired, 'Is that your dormobile on the roadside? We've got a caravanette. That's a gem of a Land Rover. Is it a classic?'

'1973,' we said, 'Re-sprayed, of course.'

'Someone has made a perfect job of it,' said the man. 'It's a beauty!' They waffled on about their touring experiences in The Dales, The Lake District, The Peaks, and their summers in Scotland and Wales. 'Every weekend,' he crowed. 'We never miss an opportunity.'

Whatever had we bought a dormobile for, we wondered? For once, at the most twice, a year? We had thought we could maybe loan it to friends who found holiday-making too expensive. We hadn't bargained for it being so slow and heavy and so hungry for petrol. Nevertheless we were cock-a-hoop with our Upper Wharfedale encounter and, getting back into our palace, I found I had no difficulty at all with the first gear. 'Scotland here we come,' I said. We were smiling. We hadn't yet started to laugh.

We paused for lunch at a picnic place on the B6472, beyond Lazonby, a favourite spot where Aunty Mary would decline to get out but Harry demand to sit at one of the tables and enjoy the fresh air. Always the multitude of honeysuckle bushes offered a profusion of flowers and a scent to die for. Friends had expected that now we would dine out, as most people do, that we would have a pub lunch and an evening meal in some restaurant. Not us. We had packed sandwiches and we ate some of them outside Lazonby, as always but now strangely alone. Danny went on a smelling tour and Meg chased blackbirds begging crumbs from our generous fingers.

We were quiet. Harry had laughingly said that life without him would be boring. Too right! We looked at each other and remembered Matthew, the small son of one of our Guides. His family had been taken, for a treat, on a canal barge at Skipton. It is a dull experience for an active boy and he had whispered to his mother, 'What am I supposed to do?' With no tray to carry to Aunty Mary either, we looked at each other and said simultaneously, 'What are we supposed to do?' This new life would take some getting used to. It was an uncanny moment.

An hour later we really did laugh. The road from Lazonby to Brampton was practically deserted but ahead of me there was a strange tandem. A cyclist was pedalling down the centre of the road and behind him was his other, smaller half, a five year old. The rear of the contraption was swinging from side to side and there was no way I could pass. I bet anything the father was singing loudly, 'Daisy, Daisy!'

I dare not hoot for fear of startling the duo and causing an accident so I trailed it slowly and then drew into a passing place and turned off the engine. We sat resigned to a pause in our journey and whilst we waited not one car came from behind nor did one approach. Ten minutes later I pulled back onto the road. Surely the bicycle-made-for-two would have reached its destination. It is so pleasant driving along an empty road, heading for the Scottish border, when the sun is hovering in the south west.

Suddenly there appeared again, ahead of us, the circus act. Surely it could only be a clown practising his act and the miniature on the rear wheel must be a monkey. Coming up behind we could see it was a child but the man at the handle bars was still driving down the centre of the road and as deaf as ever. This time, when I pulled onto the verge we collapsed with laughter. 'Our vehicle is wrongly named. It should be Genevieve,' we laughed.

Perhaps I now know why people think the life we live and the anecdotes in my narrative are funny. Ordinary life is funniest of all. Writers of comedy lost it when they tried to manufacture fun. Leave whatever will be, as it is and reader, listener or spectator will find there is laughter round every corner.

We were to spend the first night at East Riggs, near Annan on the Solway Firth. I can write that without difficulty but to say it is always a problem. One wet playtime I was playing a game we had invented. We laid a green plastic map of the British Isles on the classroom floor. We could chalk in place names and erase them with a damp cloth. A child, with a blackboard stick, pointed to places inland or on the coast and hands would fly. Someone pointed to the west coast border. Andrew leapt from his knees and shouted 'The Swalloway Frith.' Thirty years on and I still have to think lest I make the same mistake.

We had chosen to make our first stop at East Riggs where Mrs Hamilton and her husband live. We had never met but she had shown interest in my books and written to me. Always, with family, we had driven straight through on our way to Dumfries. This time we called and spent such a pleasant evening with them. She was just back from a holiday in Austria and we were on the threshold of ours on Harris. We had a great deal to talk about and it was after midnight when they escorted us down to the edge of The Solway. There was no moon but the water mirrored light from somewhere magical and we pulled our dormobile onto the bank and said a grateful thanks. Their welcome had been without precedence.

They had brought us over a mile down a road which ended abruptly at the water's edge. It was a strange and eyrie place alongside two fisherman's cottages, one at least of them was empty. There were wheel marks on the bank suggesting that cars frequently parked there and we had the assurance of our friends that to do so was usual but, for our first night in the dormobile, it was a little scary. Two other cars came down. One turned and went. The other disappeared into the undergrowth. We were slightly uneasy which was strange considering we live away from people and have often pitched our tent in an empty wilderness. In our immaculate mobile home we felt rather vulnerable on account of the fact that there was no get-away. We told ourselves not to be silly. We have no fear of open spaces but there must be some genes in our make-up, inherited from those who built castles. Every mediaeval room has two doorways so that, should intruders enter, there is an escape route. Come to think of it we had planned alterations at The Currer so that all our ground-floor rooms have two entries. If we are indulging in the pleasure of eating a meal by the sitting room fire, and we hear someone approaching the main door, we can whip our plates out of the other door and no-one is the wiser. All our cattle sheds have two doors, one at each end and every manger has a safe get-away. The facilities are primarily for getting out of the way of animals, if necessary, but they would provide equal opportunities should an unwelcome human intruder appear.

Perched on the water's edge, we realised that the only way out was the way we had come in but we had Hobson's choice, none whatsoever. I don't think we ever switched on the lights. We had eaten well at the Hamiltons'. We crawled into sleeping bags where I was too warm because Danny was too close and Margaret was cold enough to pick up the newly washed dog mats to add extra insulation. She was even then none too warm, so wakened first and roused me.

'Let's go,' she said. It wasn't yet 5 a.m. but it was light and the wanderlust was beginning to excite us. Incredibly the remaining water in our flask was reasonably hot. We had a quick drink, returned bunks into seats and left The Solway safely.

Of course we had had far too little sleep. We have too much activity in our lives and an accumulation of early rises and late nights result in a backlog of tiredness. For years we have not been oblivious of our pre-holiday fatigue and that we have not been able to respect it as we should. In our hay-making days we were often bringing in the last loads after dark, before leaving in the morning. We have been hunting cattle that have strayed and herding them home, re-building fallen boundary walls and even farrowing pigs prior to leaving. Travelling by train was a godsend for we could relax and sometimes sleep. Only the engine driver had to have his wits about him. When we began travelling by car and safety became our responsibility, we sometimes paused for a sleep at the car park outside Kirby Lonsdale. To do so was increasingly necessary when we entered the holiday accommodation business.

No-one should drive when liable to fall asleep. For that reason we paused before reaching our Clyde Ferry from Gourock to Hunter's Quay. We pulled

into a lay-by and slept again. For that reason too, we planned to sail to the
Outer Hebrides from Oban, taking the Water Way to Lochboisdale instead
of driving further to Mallaig. If we could let Caledonian MacBrayne do the
work, why not?

We found we were not doing much talking. We knew every inch of the
way to Inverary. Arriving there, Margaret knew exactly where to walk the
dogs and I knew where to buy something to eat and a cold drink. There was
too much urgency to get to Oban before 2 p.m., for the three o'clock boat, to
experiment with our built-in kitchen. Greatly refreshed Margaret climbed
into the driving seat for the last lap of our journey confident, by now, of the
gears and getting more acquainted with the dashboard. We were too relaxed
with no-one to talk to, no land marks to point out. Normally I would have
been saying, 'That's Loch Awe, Harry.' 'This is the Pass of Brander.' 'Look,
that's where we normally put petrol in.' Instead I was trying hard not to
fall asleep. It was a very surreal 21st of June. Margaret and I were even
strangers to ourselves, making slow but adequate progress to the harbour
in Oban where the MV *Lord of the Isles* would be waiting. We hardly knew
who we were, where we came from, unbelieving of where we were going.
The islands had been magic for fifty years, magic with children, magic with
family. How wonderfully magic would they be during the next respite
week, one our relatives had made possible, we could only imagine. I could
hardly keep my eyes open. I never used to sleep while travelling. I had
never been comfortable enough. As a passenger, when there were seven
of us, I had been with the luggage in the back. When we were six there
was minimal space between two others on the back seat. Then we began to
take the dogs and, though we had become five, we had been pestered with
Lusky and Shep. Reduced to four we had Danny and Jess and only Aunty
Mary, on the front seat, ever slept. Now that throne, when not driving, was
mine and waves of sleep were engulfing me. All thoughts fled of home,
of cousins coping with Contrary Mary, of cattle littering the pastures in
their summer multitude, of Bed-and-Breakfast guests deserving the best
welcome possible and the goose sitting on too many eggs. We might have
died and soared to another plain, so strange was the dimension in which I
seemed to be floating.

I was dreaming, surely. I wasn't even upright. I was hanging as from a
parachute lopsided and Margaret was below me saying, 'Jean, I'm sorry. I've
blued it!'

How come? I hadn't felt a thing. I looked out of the windscreen and saw
that the dormobile was on its side and people were running towards us
shouting, 'Are you alright?'

Margaret was answering, 'Yes. I'm alright' and I repeated, 'I'm alright.' I
was dazed and unbelieving.

Margaret continued saying, 'I'm sorry, I'm sorry.' A man opened the

door but we couldn't get out that way. I struggled to release myself from
the harness suspending me above Margaret and scrambled to the rear door.
The dogs were all over me and, when someone opened it, they leapt out
and Meg climbed the banking. Men tried to catch her but only Margaret,
following me out, could do that. One man turned off the engine and a lady,
from a cottage across the road, came to say she had phoned the emergency
services.

The car following us was full of very helpful Australians. They had seen
what had happened. Traffic had been travelling at less than thirty miles an
hour through Taynuilt and Margaret had followed the bend on the outskirts
of the village. Relatively unused to the non-powered steering she had not
righted her wheel sufficiently enough to follow the kerb and had strayed
six inches onto the sheep-lawned verge, horizontal with the road. That was
my interpretation. She is not sure. She thinks she was checking the time.
Initially she feared that she too had fallen momentarily asleep. I think not
for she had been immediately aware of her error and could have corrected
it easily if there had not been a 12' plastic drain pipe in her wheel track. It
had ripped the front, nearside tyre and the slow moving vehicle had been
diverted up the banking. Margaret described it as a Wall of Death! It had
been steep enough, vertical enough, to turn the dormobile gently on its side.
The manoeuvre had been so slow-motion it had not wakened me, no glass
was broken and no cupboard door had flown open. The vehicle was lying
almost undamaged off the road and traffic was moving freely. Surely, up
above was hovering our Guardian Angel.

The lovely lady from the roadside cottage, a Mrs Sheila Robertson,
shepherded us all into her living-room and made tea for the police, the
Australians, the paramedics and for us whilst our well behaved dogs sat
mesmerised at our feet. The Australians were nearly as shaken as Margaret
for they had seen the Land Rover fall on its side. Margaret had faced the
possibility of death but I had missed it all. I even felt refreshed after my
sleep, relaxed in the knowledge that no real harm had been done. There was
nothing we could do. As autumn leaves blow with the wind, so must we.
No one was hurt, no other vehicle involved. Margaret had even given the
dormobile off-road parking so that traffic travelled freely to Oban. Kindness
flowed from the lady, the touring Australians, the caring paramedics and the
police who pointed no finger of blame and left Margaret's driving licence as
clean as it had remained for forty years.

The car had been overturned and so had our role. It had always been that
of carers and organisers, of family and children, animals, holiday-makers
and everyday events. We had frequently been heard to say, 'There is no ME
in this equation!' We have always had to take a back seat. Where personal,
occasional luxury is the prerogative of most and where food and warmth and
comfort considered a human right, we have always come second. It has been

others first and Margaret and me last. It has never been a problem because we enjoy being in control and being a leader and have acknowledged that with it comes the role of being servant.

We have always watched, amazed, when group leaders of our holiday-makers choose the best rooms for themselves. So often our bed has been on the floor.

With the overturning of the Land Rover came the reversing of our roles. We have never known such caring attention. There was nothing left for us to do. A recovery vehicle was sent for, to pull ours off the verge and sit it upright on the road. In doing so they damaged it more than the accident had. Hearing it being dragged onto the gritted road was like hearing a good friend being tortured and we cringed when the starboard wing buckled. The recovery team was apologetic. The plastic drainpipe was undamaged but the tyre had been ripped off the nearside wheel hub and the axle had been twisted. Otherwise not a window had been broken, every door would open and the engine responded. However four wheels were necessary and there wasn't a thing we could do other than accept it, and the lift our benevolent, Taynuilt lady offered us to Munro's garage in Oban. We could not thank her enough. We waved her goodbye and things were back to normal for us. We had to take control.

Margaret whispered, 'WE ARE NOT GOING HOME. Do you hear me. I'm not going home!' She made the decision but it was for me to implement it. We couldn't go to Harris for the Outer Isles boat had left the quay and was well on its way across The Minch. Everyone was so accommodating.

'Yes, you can use our phone,' said Mr Munro.

'Certainly,' said the AA when we asked them if we could leave the dormobile in Oban for a week before being taken home. 'You go and have your holiday,' the man ordered.

'Yes, we have a room for tonight,' said the receptionist of The Kelvin Hotel, on the harbour front. 'Of course we'll take your Collies!'

'I'll take you down to the hotel,' said Mr Munro.

'To the quay, please,' we said, unloading one small holdall, a hamper of food and two folding bicycles.

'Leave them with the freight in that shed,' said the harbour master. 'They'll be put on the boat in the morning.'

We went to a kiosk and phoned our Tiree friends and told them what had happened and that we'd missed the Harris boat but were prepared to sleep in their cow shed if necessary. Hughie's two holiday cottages were occupied but not his caravan. He said it was too old to let to holiday-makers but we said it would be fine.

We phoned home. All was well. We said we'd missed the *Lord of the Isles* and were heading for Tiree instead and then we phoned Harris and told them to tell no-one of our accident, in case the news reached home before we did and to say how very sorry we were that we would not be coming, that year, after all.

Then we went to our hotel with our dogs, went to our room, made a cup of tea and ate the rest of the ham sandwiches we had made at home, only yesterday. It seemed a year ago. Then we went out, into Oban. The smell of it was like wine. How do I know for I never drink it? Why did I think it was wine when it smelt of sea and salt and fish? We walked the dogs along the southbound road towards the Kerrera ferry and remembered taking Guides across to picnic there before boarding the old *Claymore* for a night in berths. In those days vehicles had to be winched on board but then there was sleeping accommodation. Now, when cars are driven on there are no passenger berths, a tragedy had we still been able to take children. It, and a host of other changes, would have put paid to our annual invasions of The Hebrides.

The other facility we used, when bringing children to camp on the soft machair of islands in the sun, was British Rail. It was still available. We went down onto the quay and behind us, adjacent, was the station and suddenly the future was simple. The answer was blowing on the wind. Driving up had not been easy and it had had no real purpose. We could have got on the train in Keighley, as we used to, that morning instead of leaving yesterday. We could always hire a caravan on any island and after a blissful holiday we would not have to drive all the way home again.

The station was empty of train or travellers but it was full of memories. I felt that if we went onto the platform we would see our six skips of equipment ready to travel with us to Tiree next morning. Our regret at being unable to go to Harris was softened with incredible gratitude. The worst fear ever, had been that of an accident because of tiredness. It had happened causing no harm to anyone and had brought us to the railway station. It had taken the expensive purchase of a dormobile and an accident which had written off the beautiful classic machine, to show us the way our future must go.

Later we sat in the hotel bedroom talking quietly, which was unusual for Harry had been deaf and so was Aunty Mary and both wanted to listen to everything. If the latter could not hear she was sure we were talking about her.

Margaret kept saying again and again, 'I'm just relieved. We won't take risks any more. We've known so many times that we were too tired. Thank goodness we don't need a car any more.' It was becoming obvious that Danny and Meg would follow us to the ends of the world and behave.

The train would be the answer. I slept all night. Margaret's was disturbed with flashbacks of the accident but the night could not be long. We had to board an early-sailing boat and had to make sure our bikes came out of freight storage. All I could think of was that we didn't have to drive all the way home.

For so many family holidays we had driven from road to quay and onto the boat. In the bowels of the ship we had entered the lift and travelled in it to the corridors and smells of bar and cafeteria. On our legs, for the first time in nearly thirty years, we recaptured the thrill of embarkation. The early morning air was full of the tantalising smell of salt water, fish and sea breeze and we walked up the gangway with a remembered feeling of freedom. To be on foot is so preferable to being on wheels, whatever Aunty Mary might think!

We hadn't expected this holiday to be so memory provoking. If the boat had pulled in at Tobermory, I would have expected to see our pile of bark strippings waiting to be hoisted into the hold. But the boat no longer sails into the harbour and the multi-coloured hotels and shops, along the sea front, could only be seen from a distance. I may also have expected to be met by Johnny Kennedy, his lorry and bus but instead we were greeted and transported to Salum, by Donald Brown. Not the boy we used to know but the greying man, Hiawatha, waving to us from the shore, from the Regions of The West Wind.

For six days it was to blow us in front of it, wrestling with us on our return, teaching us that to go with the Wind of Life is recommendable. On such a flat island everything blows horizontally and in a straight line, even the washing there does not get entangled as it does at The Currer. Amongst the hills, debris is blown every which way. Perhaps that is why blowing with the life-wind has been so exhilarating and exciting and why we needed to be, for a short time, where the wind was blowing in one direction, making sure we got the road ahead right.

We were exuberant cycling on the hard, flat beaches of Tiree, helped by the same boisterous breeze which had accompanied all our island holidays, so many of which were with children, in the often longed for once-was. His Excellency swept the dry, silvery particles of sand before us and what little flotsam the June tide had left during the night. He chuckled with glee because we had appeared with cagoules to billow, hair to send awry and cheeks to redden.

On such a flat island an angry wind must feel frustrated and hasten to the Mainland unfulfilled. On Tiree there is little with which to frolic. There are no trees, or windmills and few cliffs to throw breaking waves against. There are no umbrellas to turn inside-out or urban litter to chase. The wind surfers and the sea birds cope with it, turning even its rage to advantage. The washing on the line floats horizontally on the constant current providing little or no fun at all.

For a never to be forgotten six days, that element we both love and fear, treated Margaret and me as playthings on the beach. It was definitely more amused than belligerent. Why not? There is surely comedy in a couple of elderly, women farmers who, because of our hilltop home, have never, even

Margaret, Tiree.

as children, had bicycles yet were enjoying the new experience to the full. On the single track roads Meg followed the rear wheel of Margaret's cycle and it was up to me to pause frequently and wait for Danny, our sniffer dog. From Hughie's caravan to the Salum beach is no distance and once on the hard sand, with the wind behind us, we could exceed our normal speed limit but never, ever, could we compete with Meg. She sprinted to the water's edge, almost airborne, surprising any unsuspecting oyster catcher. Chasing them became her favourite pastime. First one bird and then another tormented her, tantalisingly low, yet always out of reach.

The wind blew us towards Vaul but forced us to dismount on return. Before it we were young and ecstatically mobile, increasing even our maximum speed. Returning we had no alternative but to walk and push. Amazingly Margaret was finding that walking beside the bike, leaning on the handlebars, was not a problem. Wind failed to deter Meg, either way. She streaked across each of the island bays like a close-to-the ground black arrow and watching her almost caused wheeled accidents.

A non-scientific study of the wind intrigues me. I could easily go with a belief that it is a deity who is a teacher-carer-disciplinarian, who demands and rewards. I could believe we are little more than the article of disposable litter, holding the wind's attention for a short time in eternity. Like litter we are carried joyfully high, dropped in the void, rescued and revitalised, forced to struggle over the obstacles, free ourselves from marram grass entanglement, to follow, to rest and to get up again, to weary, to resist the tide and finally to be buried in the sand and forgotten.

I have recently been watching the television Time Team, digging human remains and villages from the sand, on the Island of Barra. By buying this word processor I have made it unnecessary for a future Team to exhume me or my family. I certainly did not intend to chronicle my life, and expose my thoughts, in such detail when I first began to write about our camping experiences, in 1976, for the wanting-to-know parents we left at home. Finding the sequence of events so interesting I have a continuing urge to share them accurately with whoever wants to read. I am not interested in make-believe. Doing so has been like following a woodcraft trail. What fun we had in our youth, laying or following a readable trail. In woodland we had twigs to make arrows and crosses. Grass and bracken we could knot or bend to indicate direction. Stones we could place, one on the other and show a change of route with an added pebble. When laying the trail it was important to recognise that, where there was an intersection, the wrong turning might be chosen so, to make doubly sure that the tracker would not go astray, a few yards along the wrong road a cross would be scratched or a line of four stones laid across the way. I believe the Trail Blazer of Life does that. If you have made a wrong judgement He stops you, if you take heed, and prevents you from making too big a mess of things. Our accident at Taynulit was our Trail Layer saying, 'You've taken the wrong turning. Go back and start again.'

It is so important to have thinking times in one's journeying. Six days were not enough for all the thinking we had to do.

In retrospect, most of our holidays have been perfect because of the joy we have given others, children, friends and family. Now pleasure came from watching the joy of our dogs. We thought about the others who had accompanied us over the years. Shep, in the 1970s, was an anxious dog worrying at the water's edge if Maragaret ventured among the breakers. Lusky was in his native environment having been born in Luskentyre, Harris. He was a teaser who would take a ball and drop it in the ebbing tide. 'Throw it and I'll catch it and carry it for you!' was Jess's contribution. 'I won't drop it.' Neither would she! But Danny always played ball properly, unless he chose to sniff among the sand dunes, for the repugnant smells of decaying seaweed, sheep and cattle dung or, best of all, a stinking carcass.

Meg? Oh, Meg is best of all for she needs no entertainment and we are older and really like to sit and be entertained. Meg remains an expert at that. We sat for two hours at Balephuil, where the crystal stream falls from the machair onto a clean bed of pebbles and finally crosses the exquisite, white beach before entering the Atlantic. There are two miles of sand but, other than us, there was no-one.

For two hours Meg played in that stream or dug holes in the sand, more content than the happiest of children. We sat and watched. Danny, on completion of his nasal investigation, dug himself a bed and slept. It was wonderful.

Though she grows old along side of us, we will never forget that, in 2002, Meg was the tonic we needed when we wakened from a dream. She helped us get real about life, which was necessary. On our return, there would be ever increasing demands from Aunty Mary and Hilda and a solution must be sought for Margaret's problem legs. Farm-wise it would be naive of us to think that the aftermath of Foot and Mouth was left behind, or that the injured holiday trade needed no revitalising.

But on Tiree there was Meg! Happy leaping Meg! Capable of fantastic speed. Independent Meg, almost flying the two mile length of Gott Bay from Ruaig to Scarinish, disturbing the salt water in her chase of whichever sea bird led the way. Her speedy return left a trail of widely spaced footprints in the sand. She threatened to knock us down with the exuberance of reunion, showering us with her a gift of water and sand. Seeing her approaching we braced ourselves for her arrival.

Beautiful Meg! She is a classic Collie. Her image can be bought in expensive china shops or framed from a picture gallery. Her tail follows her like a bridal train. When we took Emilie, our French Teenager, to the coast she said, 'When I go to the seaside I build sand castles.' Meg did not want to play with us. She wanted no help in her efforts to dig to Australia. Devoted Danny looked at Margaret with his adoring brown eyes and said, 'I'll play with you, Margaret.' She obediently threw the ball and he retrieved it and dropped it at her feet. I was aware that bending to pick it up was difficult and that she gave up before Danny wished. For six days we talked about Meg to each other and to islanders. We talked to islanders a lot. We are farmers and they are crofters and we have so very much in common.

We spent long, soul-restoring hours on the beach and evenings sitting in the comfortable caravan, watching the sun go down into the depths of Salum Bay, as we always had with children. From the bay window of our mobile chalet we could watch Hughie's sheep and suckling herd. One Saler heifer deposited her wet, black baby beneath our window. We slept on the comfortable couches in the window bay, ignoring the bedrooms and neglecting to draw the curtains so that the morning sun could be our alarm clock.

This was how it used to be in the fifties and early sixties except that our sleeping area was then a little white tent with its door rolled back. Between then and 2002 we shared a host of treasured memories. Contentment had returned and with it, I realised, I must not crave youthful agility for age has a great deal to offer. Come to think of it, those few holidays Margaret and I had spent alone, had not been wildly energetic either. Our five private holidays, with only two of us and no dogs, had not been exhausting. How many were the times we had slept on the sand dunes, or a loch side and wakened sunburned on one side only? We had enjoyed an idleness which, five decades on, we had regained. Contentment was growing like a mushroom.

For many, to holiday is to wine and dine on some foreign shore, ticking off places on a frequently fingered atlas. I neither criticise nor envy them. Chris Calvert, now living in New Zealand, wrote in the sand, 'Tiree is the place for me' forty years ago. In 2002 I totally agreed. For teenagers it was the edge of paradise and for we whose aching bones require space and peace, silence and infinite beauty, only an Hebridean island can fit the bill. Neither I, nor Margaret, will ever tire of a repeat.

There are few chapters in my life I would not care to experience again. I could manage the sad times, the hard times, the struggles and the constant, constant work. Even the accident had a positive side, to soften its blow if not to recommend its second viewing. It was an unexpected human encounter with friendly, caring people and a timely warning we would not ignore.

'It can't happen again. We will not ever drive so far again and nowhere when we are so tired,' Margaret said with relief but we have proved a thousand times that you cannot predict the future. Circumstances can alter things.

There was, however a negative experience we never want to repeat which, with hindsight we could have avoided. We should have gone home by train and let the dormobile travel alone. Never again do we want to be taken home, from Oban to Keighley, in a recovery vehicle. I was petrified almost the whole way and Margaret lived in fear that her school mistress sister would chide the driver. Actually I would have done so had I dared. The one bringing us from Oban to the outskirts of Glasgow seemed sensible enough and we, and the dogs, were in the seats behind the driver well secured with safety belts. He abandoned us at a service station, outside Glasgow and we waited a long time for the vehicle which would take us the rest of the way. Earlier we had phoned home telling cousins that we'd had a breakdown and were coming home by recovery. Sitting on a grass verge, in the Services' car park, close to our invalid dormobile, we phoned again to say we might be later than planned. All was well there. No-one was perturbed so we sat, not very relaxed, on the grassy verge and waited almost an hour.

When the recovery vehicle came it was we who were perturbed. There was no space behind the driver. When we'd put the dogs into the Land Rover and he'd towed it onto the trailer, he motioned for us to get into his cab and sit in front of the enormous windscreen. Had our feet had eyes they, too, would have been able to see out.

'I can't find the safety belt,' I questioned the driver.

'Safety belt?' he said. 'There isn't one!'

I have been told safety belts are not necessary in cabs of heavy vehicles. That may be true but we'd escaped injury a week ago, because we'd been wearing belts and we were nervous. The driver was a real chauvinist. He assured us we'd be home in record time. 'Straight down the motorway!' He was over seventy, he said, and driving all the time. He'd brought some horses home from Ireland that morning. The worst bit of this journey, he said, would be when we left the motorway and joined the A65.

We had no real reason to mistrust his driving for even with only one hand on the wheel, whilst the other was permanently attached to the gear shaft, he remained in control. The steering wheel frequently managed on its own whilst he pointed out landmarks he was sure ladies would know nothing about.

'Did you drive up this way?' he asked and chortled when we said we hadn't. 'Don't you use the M6? How long did it take you? Good Lord!'

He delighted in travelling in the middle lane, passing traffic with undoubted skill. We were petrified! Margaret need not have feared that I would interfere. Had I done so he'd have gone faster, I'm sure. I thought I'd never been more frightened but when he pulled off onto the A65, came the real nightmare. He was still driving with one hand on the wheel. He was still driving as fast into the empty blackness of midnight.

Had Margaret or I been driving, we would have pulled off the motorway and sighed with relief. The journey from Kirkby Lonsdale to The Currer left us both nervous wrecks. Our driver was determined to immediately drive all the way back to Glasgow.

'Do stay overnight,' we encouraged him over a cup of tea round the kitchen table. 'We've plenty of beds. Drive home in the light.'

'No. I've another job in the morning,' he boasted. We thanked him. He had, after all, brought us home safely. Physically. I'm not sure about mentally! Whether he got home safely we will never know.

Chapter Four

When care is pressing you down a bit,
Rest, if you must, but don't you quit.

W E WERE HOME. We unrolled our sleeping bags in the sitting room
and slept on the floor. Vaguely we heard Aunty Mary's wind chimes
alert our cousins, Barbara and Kathleen, but we did not respond. We heard
footsteps cross her bedroom floor. Later we would take over that role again
but there was, we suspected, a long road ahead for us and we did not hasten
to begin the journey. We felt in control. Every experience makes one wiser.
We knew the brief era of the dormobile had ended. The expectation had
exceeded the reality. Provided the dogs were train-happy, all would be well.
The beautiful Land Rover would be towed back to the garage. We did not
regret our brief encounter with it. It had floated our boat and shown us the
way. Once again our Guardian Angel had accompanied us. We must try not
to put him to the test quite so dramatically again! Luck is a fragile thing not
to be expected every time.

Aunty Mary had never seen the dormobile before our departure and, if
she saw it crippled on our return, she did not comment. It was difficult to
tell if she even remembered we had been away. We suspected that she was
far more alert than she let on, that she heard and understood more than she
would admit but we felt it wise to keep our counsel, also. There is a lot to
be said for a quiet life. We slipped easily into our normal routine, her pot
was removed from her leg and we were able to hoist her into the front seat
of our old Land Rover and wither we went so did she.

If 'four wheels' were her choice, they began to be compulsory for
Margaret. To count the adult herd, every two days, is often a two mile walk.
That was out of the question. It had been possible to cycle on a Tiree beach.
To do so on a rough, Pennine hillside pasture was impossible. Every two
days, all three of us went on the count. It was not unpleasant but it emphasised the fact that Margaret's injury was dominating her lifestyle. Every time
we drove across the floral pastures we still call the meadows, we saw with
pleasure the continuous rebuilding of our drystone walls. The project had
been resumed after the Foot and Mouth halt. How beautiful they looked.
Villagers walking by congratulated the men, and so they should, but our
old lady only saw those walls still in ruin and never failed to comment. She

grew more and more negative, a trait not previously found in our family. Seeing her in the front seat, the two men always said, 'Are you alright Aunty Mary?'

Her reply was as ever, 'Half left!' but she was indeed alright. She was a lucky lady but wild horses would not have made her admit it. Her diary did, however, when we eventually read it following her death. She made a daily entry and, though brief, each began with the word 'went'. Too true. That lady went somewhere every day for longer than anyone I have ever met. Her gratitude, never voiced, leapt from the diary in a single, daily repeated word.

If Margaret could not walk to do the count, something must be done or everything she had worked for, all her life, would have to go. 'I am going to the doctor!' she decided. Everywhere members of our generation are suffering from arthritis and it is too easy to jump to the conclusion that leg pain is such. I have to admit that a lifetime of walking and working has given me a slight hobble, too. A visiting doctor guest, years ago, said, 'You've got a hip op coming.'

'Rubbish,' I laughed. 'All farmers walk droll.'

Margaret has toiled far more than I have and carried thousands of bales in excess of me, been impaled against the wall and trodden on far more times than I have. She has had pulled muscles and torn ligaments galore. We had taken Harry to the doctor shortly after Margaret's fall, whilst she still had two very black eyes and instead of saying she was injured, I remembered only that she said to him, 'It's Harry. Not me,' and that he had made the usual remark about the 'other man'.

She really was admitting her plight when she decided to make an appointment with the doctor and he immediately jumped to the conclusion that it was her hip and recommended no more than eight paracetamol a day.

She was adamant that the problem she had was totally due to the fall and I was a witness. Until that unfortunate trip, on the wobbly stone, she had been arguably the fittest person in the locality. Just before her fall she had hammered in more than fifty fencing posts round the area we call the 'wet lands' in the Dyke Field. She had climbed and crawled under, could run fast and jump high. She could beat me to the ground. Now it was I who had to do those things and I was a poor substitute.

She asked for an X-ray and it showed some wear and tear but there was no mention of an operation and no comment when she insisted she had no sitting or sleeping pain. She only had difficulty when she was weight bearing. She made an appointment for a second opinion and we went for this privately, to a consultant who seemed only to look at the doctor's diagnosis and agree with it. He ignored the fall and the irregularity at the base of her spine, which she'd had for decades. He dismissed her occupation and the fact that, unlike our friends who were suffering from constant pain, she had none except when she put weight on her legs. Then it felt like a nerve pain and her limbs looked and behaved as if partly paralysed, loose, like a puppet with too long leg strings. He offered her proof. He said he'd give her an autumn injection and it was only early summer.

'I'm going to Settle!' she declared, once again in the control seat of hopeful recovery.

When the vet cannot solve an animal problem we have so often turned to homeopathy. Frequently we have experienced success. The Settle Practice also has a human clinic and Margaret made an immediate appointment. There had been a recent purchase of a machine which scanned the body, locating the source of the problem and highlighting others. Homeopathy is all about treating the whole person. I expected the scanner to concentrate on the hips but it did no such thing. Where the trouble really lay, the lady user said, would show a crimson colouring of the skin. Margaret could not see but I could and the only appreciative reddening was at the neck. I was most impressed. No-one had suggested the crashed head could have jerked the neck and injured the nerve centre, because neither doctor nor surgeon had taken the fall into consideration. We seemed to be getting somewhere at last. The homeopath also diagnosed extremely low energy levels and problems with toxins. Another machine was used to recommend treatment and we drove home with the usual collection of squirts, which appear ridiculous but so often work. We were happier and more confident than we had been for some time.

Our visit had been on a Friday. On Saturday evening Margaret's big toe began to swell and on Sunday morning it was three times the size it should be and she could not walk at all. We panicked. I pushed her in a wheelchair to the Land Rover and we went straight to Casualty.

'My goodness. You've got chronic arthritis,' the doctor said. 'It's going to be very painful. Paracetamol won't be strong enough. I'll give you something better.' He handed her some pills. 'These won't be enough. You'll have to go to the doctor to get more.'

I pushed her back to the car and we were disheartened to put it mildly. It was already long past mid-day. She took the recommended dose and, with its help, we got through the evening chores. The future looked bleak and uncertain. We had hoped that the moment we could no longer farm was a long way off. The end of holiday catering seemed in jeopardy too. Usually, faced with a problem we try to sort it out immediately. This one was too outrageous to even think about, so we put it under the carpet and went to bed.

Next morning, incredibly, the swelling had gone, and the pain, and one foot looked exactly like the other. We could not believe it. Margaret put a phone call straight through to Settle and told the practitioner what had happened.

'Oh good!' was the immediate response. 'That's fine. Just what I wanted.'
I'll say no more for I do not pretend to understand toxins and their need to
be obliterated. How a machine could send them scurrying to a big toe, I have
no idea and where they went from there is beyond my comprehension. All
I know is that there had been no arthritis, presumably, and there was never
any need for further doses of the strong painkiller. Perhaps we should have
told the doctor who would receive the hospital report but we were suddenly
too busy with guests from Spain.

The visit to Settle was the turning point on a long slow road to improvement. The magic of that first incident was just the first jump onto the lowest
rung. The climb up the ladder of recovery depended first on a rejuvenation
of those depressed energy levels. No-one could be more determined than
my sister. She left no opportunity untried, to remain able to rear animals,
she being who she is.

We thrive on variety. One week we have Brownies from Harrogate. We
love that. Brown Owls can control children today, just as satisfactorily as
they did almost a century ago. Notices for the Sixes go up on the walls
and windows. Wherever they want to go, they walk. It's great. I even go so
far as to say today's youth problem is because responsibility for discipline
has been taken away from our Infant Teachers. Children of that age can be
controlled without punishment. Parents cannot be trained but teachers have
a three year course in their profession. Yet they are no longer coping. Brown
Owls are and Cub Akalas.

After guests have gone, we have to adjust to our next intake. Margaret
calls it changing gear. We also have to change our speech. With the party
from Spain we had to slow down our words. Another thing Aunty Mary
is right about, we are used to people with little or no English. This party
numbered seventeen. They were coming to Barbara Sykes's, Sheep Dog
Experience, on Baildon Moor.

When she phoned to ask if we could accommodate seventeen I expressed
doubts. Using one cottage, I could still only provide seven rooms. If there
were families and bunks could be used, I'd manage. She said there were
children in the party and between us we sorted it out. We seem to be able
to provide a kaleidoscope of opportunities to solve most of our accommodation puzzles. She said they would also want an evening meal. I had one
other family, from Derbyshire, self-catering in the Loft Cottage and they
had a German Shepherd dog and the Cowells were here, in a ground-floor
bedroom because Janice uses a wheelchair.

We hadn't had any call to get used to people bringing pets from abroad
and we stared, open-mouthed, when the large party from Spain arrived,
accompanied by some very vocal dogs. There was a procession of cars and
as they drew into the yard, the dogs saw each other and Danny and Meg,
and went barking mad. Seventeen equally noisy people came indoors. It

was a floor show for the Cowells. Everyone enjoyed a noisy evening meal. It is quite a spectacle when nineteen people dine round one table but it was normal for The Currer, in 2002. What was far from normal was the after dinner spectacle in the yard, when our guests produced folding seats and sat in a circle with their leashed and chattering dogs. It looked like I imagine Crufts might do!

I was clearing the table when the wife of the leader of the group, came to me carrying a very small dog. She pointed to it and said, 'Sleep bedroom?' We have always allowed a well behaved dog in a bedroom even though ours, when on holiday with the Land Rover, have always slept in the car. Because many guests want to bring their dog, to allow them to do so means we are never short of customers.

The pooch was very small. I whispered so as not to be overheard, 'Well, it's only small.'

'No, no,' the lady almost shouted. 'We all bring dogs bedroom!'

'All of you?' I gasped. 'How many dogs have you got?'

'Only twelve,' she answered.

There was a continual doggy conversation going on outside.

'No-one will get any sleep,' I complained.

'Yes, yes,' she was sure. 'They will be polite!' and they were. I worried about the Cowells but they found amusement and thought the whole charade hilarious. There are such strange goings-on at The Currer!

It was a relief, on the following Saturday, to admit a group who would fill the house and self-cater. It gave us a freedom we definitely appreciated. July is the month for cutting thistles and Margaret used to sit for hours on the quad bike, pulling the flail mower, whilst I hacked away at the sidings, with a thistle sickle. We think the mower is a male machine. A string has to be pulled to start the engine and it nearly always needs a man to do so. Especially the first time, after almost a year of non-activity. I'm sure it is not strength, just knack which is needed. Margaret sometimes succeeds. I never do.

One Sunday we hitched the mower onto the quad and Margaret drove into the paddock for a trial run, whilst I filled a flask and prepared Aunty Mary to accompany us. It was arrogant of us to think that we could start a mower engine which had been unused for a year but, with no resident men we have to be blatantly so. We tried simply ages to start that engine and were about to give up, and cancel Aunty Mary's outing on the hill, when Tim drove down the lane. He never comes on a Sunday. Our luck was in. Margaret mowed the paddock and we forced our old lady up the step into the Land Rover and, in procession, drove to thistles unaware of their fate. The mower's engine sprung immediately into life for a second time, without male persuasion, and work progressed without a hitch. Then came lunchtime. The engine rested, too, and a contented trio supped and dined. When work was to be re-started the engine refused. We took turns, pulling at that unresponsive string with female incompetence. We'd been cutting thistles near the boundary and a group of ramblers came along the green lane and stood watching our struggle.

One man called out, 'Are you the lady who writes the books?'

'We are the ladies who can't start this engine!' I called back.

'I'll do it,' said the man and clambered over the wall. We are also ladies who have been known to say we wouldn't have a man given but when we need one, amazingly one turns up.

One such day I will never forget though the month and year evade me. We'd required more petrol for the quad and mower and, as it had turned out, for the Land Rover, too. We had got as far as the top road, with our cans in the rear, when the vehicle had stalled and we'd seen, with horror that the gauge was showing empty. Aunty Mary had said it was our fault and rightly so! I'd left them and had hurried towards a cousin's, carrying one of the cans, but their door had been locked and their garage empty. My only alternative must be the bus to town and a mile walk home carrying a full can. But, such is my luck, I'd returned to the road and a car had pulled up in front of me, driven by a friend, currently resident in Leicester, coming to call on us.

'Where are you going?' his welcome Hebridean voice had asked. I'd hopped in and had told him my emergency and we'd driven into town, filled my can and returned to the stationary Land Rover. Then we'd all gone home and had eaten a meal together. Donald Campbell, a vet born on Tiree, had once been practising in Keighley. Who needs a resident man when one invariably turns up at the right moment?

A lady friend did at the beginning of August. She phoned first, as befits a friend who is well acquainted with our busy life. Margaret had just walked in the bearer of problem news. Two goose eggs had hatched that morning and, for some reason, the mother and the other geese took to one gosling and rejected the other. This was a situation we had never come across. Margaret had had to pick up the one being attacked, for they were out for the kill. She'd put it in a box and brought it into the kitchen. That was the moment when the phone rang and Hazel said, 'Are you in? OK I'm on my way up.'

'Hazel's coming,' I called to Margaret who, had left the gosling near the Aga and was off back again, across the yard. She turned and her face was a picture. 'Hazel,' she said. 'Hazel will rear the gosling!' Too true. This friend of ours has reared many a feathered friend. She has ducks galore on the mill dam now part of her garden. She took the gosling, called it Bonnie and brought it back, weeks later, fully grown. Rearing babies by hand is time consuming and, by doing this for Margaret, Hazel was a godsend. She had been my companion for over a decade of taking children to camp in The Hebrides.

Hazel's gosling.

With a self-catering group doing our job for themselves we had some free time so we took Aunty Mary to St Ives, the parkland on our boundary and pushed her wheel chair along the wooded path round the lakeside. We felt to be on holiday. We persuaded her to buy us an ice cream at the resident trailer and she delved in her purse and gave us £1 emphasising how inflation has soared since she came to us, leaving us to do the domestic buying. Next day we drove to Bolton Abbey taking with us another wheelchair and Hilda and her niece and on the 12th of August it was possible for both of us to take Aunty Mary to the hairdresser's. It had become increasingly necessary for there to be two of us to handle our old lady from car to chariot. On this occasion we should have phoned to cancel and pay, because Diana, our only cow, was on the point of giving birth to her fifth calf. She always found the annual labour very stressful leaving most of the hard work to us. Her last calf had been a huge Aberdeen Angus bull, called Lord Harry. It had taken both wallers and the two of us to calve her. On this occasion we had asked the AI man for a smaller breed and the calf, now due, was to be a Saler and, hopefully, easier to calve.

Tim was walling close by and we expected to visit the hairdresser and be back in time, so we just alerted him to keep a watchful eye on the lady in the maternity ward and we took the risk. In the event we could not have done more if we'd been at home. The birth had been quick. Tim had been there. When we arrived home, the baby was already born and had been well and truly licked.

Margaret was anxious for it to stand and feed and we tried to disturb it and hoist it onto its feet but without success. 'It's got a hole in its head!' she gasped suddenly. 'Look at its forehead. I could put a finger into its brain.'

We had never seen anything like this before. Human skulls have to be pliable to make their birth possible. Presumably the same applies to calves but this was a definite hole. It wasn't one recently made. There wasn't a speck of blood. Just a hole in the skull, a peephole even the hair did not hide. We didn't like it. When we finally got the baby on its feet, there was no way we could direct its mouth to the udder. The calf thrashed around, going headlong into a wall. We were glad when its legs buckled and it collapsed on the straw.

'It's blind,' we concluded. We had had blind calves before and they had learned to cope remarkably well but this beautiful baby had too many problems. Viruses and germs were shunted all over the place after the Foot and Mouth. Much later, talking to a vet, he suggested it might have been a form of spina bifida caused, maybe, by Diana having contracted BVD (Bovine viral diarrhoea) which had not been noticed. We were to experience other pre-natal defects, caused by this virus, in bought-in calves during the years that followed. Throughout that first week it became obvious it was not a problem even a vet could overturn. Had we sent for him his advice would have been to put it to sleep immediately but we could not do that whilst its mother loved it so. Margaret milked her and we tried to feed it the necessary colostrum and we prayed it would not hurt itself too much when it thrashed around. We cringed every time it got up, knowing what would happen, trying to cushion it with our bodies against the cold, stone walls. It was a week we do not want to remember so this account is brief. Whilst we waited for nature to take its course, we went to Gisburn calf market and bought two baby Limousin heifers, one week old, and placed them in the pen. Diana, who normally suckled any calf given to her for adoption, ignored them completely but nursed her own continually. To feed them we had to put her in the crush and restrain her. We did this twice a day, having to force her to allow those bought-in babies to feed, but we had to take milk from her by hand to bottle feed her own.

For the first week the baby was strong enough to get up and flounder. To watch was unbearable but, even as human parents are ever hopeful that their handicapped child will thrive, so we hesitated, praying for a miracle. Then the baby began to have fits, became too weak to rise and the worst was over.

We do our level best to prevent animal suffering. There is no more caring a farmer than Margaret but nature can be cruel and prayers are not always answered in the way that we would wish. We do our best, also, to keep tragedy away from our guests believing that to read it exists, is better than to witness it. We could not keep the birth of this baby a secret from those already here. They had been awaiting the magic moment, hoping to be still here when it happened. They were as upset as we were. The event they had looked forward to was not merely a disappointment, it was awful. Telling children a new sibling is on the way, has always frightened me. Things don't always go as they should. We also go to great pains to disguise a sudden death. We have to accept that, as part of our job, but we do not want a holiday to be spoiled. I have seen Margaret cover a dead calf with straw so that it could not be discovered by calf-orientated children.

I know of one occasion when a steer was brought in, looking a bit off-colour, during late autumn. Margaret already had a couple indoors for early wintering. A few days later, without warning, the steer sat down and died. Its head had been thrown back and Margaret reinstated it so that it looked asleep and those who looked in the shed had no idea.

When Diana's baby died there could be no cover-up. All were relieved, glad it was over. We left the calf in the shed until Diana finally walked away. She never did take to the adopted family properly. Indeed, though we forced her to feed them, the real adoptive parent was an over-age bullock, enjoying a summer he would never have had if a haematoma, below his shoulder blade, had not rescued him from a normal autumn sale. The buyer of the whole herd of two-year-olds, when the Foot and Mouth crisis was over, would have taken this animal too, but Margaret will not sell anything imperfect, even though times were abnormal. The haematoma kept disappearing and reappearing all winter. Every time a sale would have been possible, the sack filled with blood again. As each opportunity to sell was lost, the bullock got a new lease of life and the BSE thirty month deadline came and went. From then on the animal could not enter the food chain so Margaret said, 'What the heck. He might as well have another summer. Grass costs nothing.' So he had had a life extension and when Diana and her new family were let out of the shed to join him, he undertook care of the little ones. It was lovely to see him, sitting with one on either side, playing Dad.

Things have a habit of going in threes. Eighteen months will pass and we do not go to a funeral or send a carcass to the knackers yard. Then, whoops, one, two, three. Exactly a month after the birth of Diana's baby, we had a very bad storm. The heat of summer resulted in thunder following lightning so quickly and so noisily, we were all in shock. But it passed and cattle which had been startled and had clustered, spaced themselves out again and grazed as if nothing had happened. It was at the following morning count that a tragedy was discovered.

The nine month old steers and one Friesian heifer had sheltered from the storm at the foot of the Five Acre. This was obvious. The grass was flattened and cow pats littered the area. Up against the wire fence lay the Friesian heifer. Dead. Margaret first saw it from a distance. When an animal is alone something is wrong. Cattle are herd animals who are stressed when separated. One alone is ill, or lame, or dead. This one was the latter, a burnt line under its belly explained all.

We were upset. The more so because it was our only heifer. Born a twin, a freemartin, it had been destined to be shot. Its brother had been among fourteen calves bought from a softie farmer, when all cattle markets were closed. He didn't want to shoot it and Margaret is a softie, too. So she had bought it and reared it. We were doubly distressed because, though freemartin heifers are infertile, it was a girl. We live in a male dominated environment. Most farmers are men. Contractors and buyers are men. Increasingly women are entering the veterinary profession but mature ones are still male. Almost all our animals are male for we buy bull calves. Two of our three cats are toms and only once has a load of hay been driven by a lady driver. So we cherish little girls when they stray into our kingdom. We loved Bess and Skye and Jed and Floss, and Jess and Meg our more recent female canines and we love Diana and any daughter she has. Though the Friesian heifer had never been named, we loved her and to find her dead, through lightning, was a horror story which became a problem. How were we, two rather old ladies, going to get her home ready to be taken away.

We do not have qualms about handling anything dead. How to do so is our problem. Perhaps it is because our maternal grandfather's family owned the Town Hall Livery Stables, in town, and therefore organised funerals and transported the dead. Maybe we have inherited genes. We had first to go into town for our cupboard was bare and we had evening meals to serve. All the way home, in whispers, we were discussing how to get the carcass home. We dare not let Aunty Mary hear for she would say, 'I knew you'd get IT!' IT being Foot and Mouth. She was always asking if we had got IT yet and, although we said no, would not believe the epidemic was over. Our gate had been locked the previous summer. It was no longer so but she never failed to say, 'You haven't locked it.' So we whispered and when she was safely home beside the fire, we went outside and hitched the quad trailer onto the station wagon, took two planks and oodles of rope and set off hopeful of success. Margaret said, 'Did you ever hear of anything so ridiculous as two old ladies with nothing else to talk about but how they are going to bring home a dead animal, without anyone seeing?'

Having said we protect guests from the horrors of our profession I will not describe to my reader the performance of the next hour. The remover, when he came, said the awful smell and swift decay was due to lightning death. Flies had moved in quickly and an infestation of maggots caused him to drive away without the carcass, as he had others inside. We liberally sprayed and awaited his return with an empty van. Who'd be a farmer?

There was a third event to come before things calmed down. Occasionally Margaret briefly wondered what she was going to do with the enormous, three year old bullock. We could not possibly keep a huge animal all winter, that was only suitable for the Over Thirty Month Scheme. Margaret knew that one day she would have to say to him, 'I'm so sorry but you'll have to go. I've kept you 12 months longer than I should. I can't any longer.'

Soon bullocks one year his junior would have to go to the fortnightly store sales. Before bringing-in-time, he'd have to go. She just continually put off the event and tried not even to think about it.

We had a houseful of guests and were returning from doing the necessary shopping for the late Summer multitude. We smiled, as we drove down the road for Diana and Co were grazing the verges. She was apart, as usual, and the babies were with Dad. They were a quarter of a mile from the shed in which they slept but it was not Go Home time. 'He's so lovely!' Margaret said of the hefty male. 'So gentle. What can I do? It's going to break my heart.'

We had shopping to unload, tables to lay and the evening meal to prepare. Cars belonging to those who would eat it, were already parking in the yard. Before dusk, the ducks must return to their manor house lest the fox choose one for his supper. He must eat and we are predators too, so are non-critical but he can go elsewhere. He's not having my ducks. I walked down to the pond and, with my back to the sheds, I climbed the fence and encouraged them to safety and wedged the door. I re-climbed the fence, this time facing the sheds and I noticed that the Diana quartet had come home. They had hesitated on the threshold of the open door and the huge bullock was on the floor. I hurried to investigate and found him to be quite dead. He had not collapsed. Supposing the beautiful china Jersey cow, in our glass cabinet, had been accidentally knocked over without breakage, it would have looked like that bullock. He was just like a fallen domino. I couldn't believe what I saw. I went to the kitchen, where Margaret was clearing away vegetable peelings, and said, 'The bullock has just dropped dead!'

'He's what?' She couldn't believe it either. We went out together to the stock yard.

He'd been alright an hour ago, eating at the top of the road. Margaret said. 'He must have heard me and decided no way was he leaving alive.' She said this with sadness but with relief. It may cost the earth to have the vet inspect and to have the carcass taken away and there would be no OTMS government hand-out, but we didn't care. There was another reason to be grateful to that animal. He had come home to die and not done so on the road. What a palaver it would have been had he trapped all those cars parked in front of the farmhouse. Amazingly, not one of our guests noticed, when they drove out next morning. They would certainly have told us if they had. Thank goodness that was number three and things quietened down. I can tell you we had had enough.

A new project was necessary. The wallers sorted out the fallen stones around the huge rock where, centuries ago during the Civil War, Thomas Fairfax's men had built a lookout. There the view encompasses the Pennine dale down which the winding river Aire is said to write its name. Almost any day without mist, or the now infrequent fog, Ingleborough, one of the

Three Peaks, can be seen on the western horizon. When we were children the round lookout was standing four feet high, on top of the rock. We played in it, hiding from companions, pretending we were scouts watching for the approaching enemy. We know, only by recorded history, that in our meadows there was a military entrenchment and we have picked up the occasional heavy gunshot, smaller than the marbles we played with on the tarmac. I suppose it was generations of the children of yesterday, who gradually reduced the lookout walls, tumbling the remaining stones at play. The rock had remained bare for decades but investigation proved that most of the stones were there. Each one had been cut on a curve so that, when built, the structure was round. Many of the stones lay at the foot of the rock but generations of farmers had used others to repair the field wall which shares the rock, using it for the corner. When we had been negotiating the conditions of our membership of the Countryside Stewardship Scheme, the rebuilding of the lookout was one necessary clause. There is no longer fear that children will again play in it and, bit by bit, demolish it. Not whilst computer games remain the current obsession. Nor whilst parents imprison them away from imagined danger.

Only the elements are the destructive forces of the new millennium. When re-assembled the lookout appeared as it did when first built and is likely to stay that way. It is not as high for some stones have not been located, but we are proud of it.

Whilst we can only be sad that children are now indoors, playing with mobile phones and watching television, because parents fear they will be molested if let out, the bonus is that they no longer harass us. We never catch them trespassing in the sheds, playing on the mow, making dens out of bales. We do not have to chase them from throwing stones into the duck pond or to disturb them damming up the stream as all children used to do. Even holiday children are shy of dirt and animals.

The only other evidence of civil war is in the farmhouse. Between the mullions on the north front, were vertical iron bars which we removed in 1958. We no longer need to fortify our homestead. The holes in the sills and lintels will remain as proof, if need be, for future generations.

The view of the valley, above what we used to recognise as the snow line, is relatively unchanged since Fairfax days. The scattered farms on the hillside have been there since before the Civil War and the intakes from the slopes of Ilkley Moor are centuries old. But the floor of the valley has suffered from urban sprawl and, today's monstrosities called industrial estates. Flat roofs of corrugated tin are an insult to the landscape. Our ancestors, without planning officers, managed to build in harmony with it. The mills of yesterday are fine monuments to previous generations, worthy of re-use as residential palaces. Sadly we are not only killing the planet we are ridiculing it with exposed, un-camouflaged concrete and tin.

The summer had been extraordinarily wet. At one point we had so much rain the duck pond overflowed and Margaret hurried to see that the river across the stockyard, was not flooding the sheds. She always anticipates that it will. I remember writing, 'Wet, wet, wet,' on a letter to a friend.

The deluge which occasionally causes the duck pond to overflow, suddenly appears from underground, halfway up the dry valley of Lower Hollow Pasture, one of the eight fields rented since 1990. I love field names dating back to the Middle Ages. We never use this one for all our rented fields are just referred to as 'George's.'

In 2002, when it was dry it was very hot. One such day I was taking a short cut behind the small fir plantation, near the house, when I came across a black stirk frothing at the mouth and gasping for breath, just outside the paddock gate. The rest of the young herd had strolled into the next field and this one had conveniently stayed behind, close to the gate. At least that is what other people might think. I prefer to believe an animal comes home when it is ill. It happens too often for coincidence. If its condition develops a distance away, it invariably stays within sight of Margaret's binoculars and comes home to safety and medical help without any resistance. Though this one was virtually on our doorstep, Margaret feared it might be too late. She had treated all the calves against worm several days ago. The Pour-on kills, or paralyses lung worm and this allows many of them to fall back into the air-sacs. The treatment itself, though rarely, may lead to fatal pneumonia. Though extremely ill, very slowly our calf got better, but it remained a patient much longer than most.

Margaret had several appointments at Settle. It was a lovely day- trip, each time, for Aunty Mary. We never went on the A65. At Gargrave we followed the road towards Malham and turned west at Kirby Malham taking the scenic route over the high ground. Everything they suggested, Margaret took on board. The treatment, using the extraordinary Russian invented machine, seemed to be having effect. The pressure of August became intense with holiday makers and September brought the annual cattle sales. Neighbouring farmers, even the market staff, offered to help us gather in the more than eighty head of cattle for sale. They could see that Margaret was not able to leap about chasing them in. She politely refused all help. She never has any intention of chasing cattle. 'I'll send for you if we can't manage,' she said, thanking them for their concern. She believes, and practise has so far proved, that she and I, (who don't mind being shouted at), can handle our own cattle without stressing them or us. Each day the herd decides when to come to the water trough. It moves as one quiet stream of Angus and Limousin black, Belgium Blue white, Charolais brown and white faced Hereford, towards the waterhole. This migration can be seen from any south facing window of the house. We watch patiently for their daily trek. The only thing which will delay or even prevent them coming, is heavy rain causing puddles enough for them to water elsewhere. When they head for the waterhole, we climb up to it also and open the adjacent gate into the road. Eager for something new, they all wander through and down into the stockyard. Gotcha, without any fuss! We've done our share of bringing in cattle with difficulty, before we could afford to fence the road and before we had the water trough and took water from the town mains. All that was now years ago and ever since we have had no trouble. With her particular brand of skill, Margaret sorts a third of the herd into a shed and the others are allowed out. Cattle are naturally curious, love open gates and these traits can be turned to advantage. We did accept one offer of help. Tim came to help Milford, our haulier, drive the bullocks into the wagon. He had begun to do this the previous year, following the Foot and Mouth epidemic, when seven loads of cattle were moved within twenty four hours. The vet had warned Margaret that she must, on no account enter sheds with such big animals. What does he really think she does the rest of the year? We find that the young vets ignore the fact that Margaret has been a farmer since before even their parents were born. Neither did we refuse help with the washing-up after breakfast. Our guests did that and we were grateful.

Throughout the busy selling season, when to go to Settle would have been impossible, the homeopath came to The Currer. When another course of treatment, in Harrogate, was suggested Margaret agreed. She was notice-ably improved and the big question of the moment was should we buy or not buy a new intake of calves.

A family from Australia booked into the Mistal cottage, for two weeks and didn't even stay overnight because the children saw a spider and went berserk. We appreciate that spiders in Australia can be dangerous but we have never had anyone leave because of an English one. No matter how we protested that there was no danger, no matter how we assured them they would encounter our variety anywhere, in any home in this country, they could not pacify their screaming children. They went and we never heard what happened and we had an empty cottage for two weeks!

For the new treatment, suggested by the homeopath, Margaret had to attend a clinic in Harrogate. The appointment was late afternoon and we would not return in daylight. We hate driving in darkness and fight shy of searching for an address in an unknown town, so we took the soft option, called in a friend to stay with Aunty Mary. We left the dogs, went by train and then hired a taxi. It was a local rail service stopping at every station to Bradford, where we had to change trains for Harrogate. They were both full, both noisy and mobile sideways as well as forwards. Crossing lines in Bradford, upstairs and down, and listening to the announcements of arrivals and departures, we felt a sudden panic. Determined as we were never to drive again all the way to Oban or Mallaig, our return to The Hebrides depended on us, and on our dogs, being happy by rail.

'They'll never cope with this!' we were almost sure. They had never needed to be on a lead. They live on a farm, never tethered, never going beyond the entrance gate except in the Land Rover. They had never been on an urban street, let alone walked through a crowded, noisy city. They had never been on deck when we sailed or seen the turbulent Atlantic a few metres below.

The lady at the Harrogate clinic was optimistic about Margaret's health.

'Yes,' she encouraged. 'Be positive. Go and buy calves!'

Few people knew how important this news was. I don't think, for a moment that the lady had any idea what a monstrous job rearing calves is. Twenty two years ago, I had given up teaching because it was the only way we could go on farming. Now all the onus was on Margaret, the farmer. If she couldn't continue then our way of life would alter dramatically. We are becoming two old ladies and all we want to do is rear cattle. We have a love affair with week-old calves, strapping teenage stirks and beautifully fit steers we hate to part with come September. We have no hobbies, as such, no addictive reading habit, no computer mania, no compulsive desire to shop, eat out, or extend our garden. We don't want to go to Coffee Mornings nor do we wish to join societies. We are never tempted to go on coach trips or cruises. There was only one answer.

'Let's go for it!' decided Margaret. 'Are you game?'

I was, so we went three times to the mart. Due to the annihilation of so many milking herds, calves were few and not very robust. It was a matter of take it or leave it, bull or heifer. We had never bought heifers but when there is no choice you stock with what is available at the time. We would not feel it financially, until autumn 2004. It's a funny business ours. If we stop, when do we stop? We were already making accommodation bookings twelve months ahead and every calf-buy has a shelf life of two years. We are committed. Obviously we can't stop so there you have our answer, all you who persist in asking.

A farmer from Cowling rang to say he had a Limousin bull calf and did we want it, so we went over Slippery Ford to collect it. The man carried it out and shoved it into our trailer where it bashed about in a very lively manner. We would have to use cunning if we were to transfer this scared calf, from the trailer into the shed. It is at such a time we wish one of us, at least, could reverse that trailer. Neither can so we have to improvise. By opening the collecting pen gate and swinging back one yard gate, we can make a passage to the entrance of the enclosed area and twin doors, one into the bottom bullock shed and one into the calf shed. This improvised passage is large-bullock proof and we have no problem transferring big cattle from one shed to another. With the installation of a sheep hurdle, we have often brought a stirk further, into the garage and through to the yard shed. It would be easy to reverse this system, we argued. All we needed to do was

Calves!

to unload the calf into the garage and down the passage into the calf shed. It would be simple! Fortunately we do not have male spectators when we cope with not being able to back the trailer.

No larger animal would have attempted to jump the 3ft 6in sheep hurdle from a narrow passage but that tiny animal needed no manoeuvring space to leap. Like a tennis ball it cleared the 'net'. We were taken by surprise and our eyes shot simultaneously to the paddock gate. It was shut. By closing the yard gate forming the passage we had the calf trapped in the spacious paddock. Had it been drivable, or catchable and light enough to carry, as the farmer had done, it would have been easy to let it through the ten foot north door of the calf shed. It was none of those and furthermore it was determined to show off its high jump capability. On the east side of the paddock is the not very productive orchard. By that I mean we do not harvest much fruit but the nettles do very well. The calf took one look at us and charged in my direction, almost up-skittling me. It leapt over the sheep netted fence, regardless of the barbed wire, into the jungle of nettles in the orchard. By this time it was in a state of frenzy. We tried to open the well-tied gate but the binder twine was weathered and the knots would not loosen. In any case the calf had re-jumped the fence and was heading towards the north and a wall we had every reason to believe it could jump. I beat it by a hair's breadth and it shot back over the fence and careered once more among trees and nettles in the orchard. There was no way we were going to succeed. The poor little thing was petrified.

'Let some of the others out,!' Margaret shouted. It was a gamble but, should the new calf get into the field and have access to a hundred and eighty acres we would never find it again. So I opened the gate and a score of quieter calves spilled onto the concrete forecourt of their shed. Seeing others of its kind, the frantic calf jumped back to join them and we eased them all back into the shed with the wayward one in their midst. There is nearly always a way if you can think of it soon enough.

As he had promised John and his competent team came to convert the barn manger ready for big bale feeding. Not one of his three sons is less able than the rest. We were beginning to envy those with strong, healthy farm orientated children following in their footsteps but have realised that, had we had our own, they would have reached the half century mile stone and it is grandchildren we needed to do the heavy work. To hand over to the next generation, one must do so earlier, the Queen being no exception. The conversion was relatively simple but a lot of concrete was needed for the floor. When it was finished we could have held a barn dance inside. That's just what we would have done thirty years ago. We would have hunted up an accordionist and a piper and brought Scotland to Yorkshire.

People do not listen to us when we talk about our husbandry. Those who ask questions do not wait for the answer. I am sure we speak clearly and coherently. I hope I taught children to speak in a way they could be understood. So often, nowadays, I have to ask, 'What did you say?' not because I could not hear but because, universally, speech is poor. We have so many from abroad we have to automatically separate our words. I am sure an overnight journalist, who asked so many questions, never listened at all and that the article she wrote for a national newspaper had been already written and gone to print.

Her errand in Yorkshire had really been to find out what it would be like to be a farmer's wife. There was to be a television reality programme called, 'The Farmer Wants a Wife.' Hundreds of applications had been received from ladies wanting to enter into such a relationship. This young journalist introduced herself as a real city girl, like most of the applicants, but she did not tell me her profession or her assignment. The following day was to be spent with Barbara Sykes, the competent shepherdess across the valley. As we cater for scores of those going on the sheep dog experience, it never occurred to me that she was a journalist.

Dorothy brought us the article when it appeared. The writer, it says, anticipated a preview of an idyllic life in the countryside, occasionally tending a sick bird, dressed in a floral pinny and leisurely making beef and ale pies with meat from cattle her husband killed. She had stayed in a farmhouse B/B on Haworth Moor, (our home is not on Haworth moor) where it was so bleak, so like Wuthering Heights, she hardly slept for fear she would hear and see a small hand scratching on the window pane.

She described me as a dairy farmer. Does she really think bullocks give milk? Having just bought over sixty calves, most of them baby bulls, I had taken her down to the calf shed.

I buy them, she says, 'rear them, love them, get them pregnant, milk them then, er! kill them.' (Presumably for the steak and ale pies.) The public understanding of the farming profession is way off course.

So many people say that I must be glad I am not teaching, that I may well have commented on this before, several times. Again people do not understand. A teacher always wants to teach. More so if they think things are going wrong. Of course I would welcome the opportunity. It is sad that when you are young you think you can change the world for the better. When you are old and know you could, the opportunity is no longer there!

The 2002 calves were difficult to rear. We had bought fewer simply because they were not there. We lost two of the sixty one before Christmas. The festive season was becoming more and more meaningless with the family shrinking. Even Hilda was in hospital. So often she had spent Christmas at The Currer and had accompanied us on our trip up the Dales in lieu of turkey and all that seasonal fare. We took Aunty Mary for a brief outing across the other side of the valley through Morton. We went west to Brunthwaite and dropped down steeply into Silsden. Then we went to the hospital to spend some time with our centenarian.

The two oldies scarcely spoke to each other. Hilda's voice had become so feint and Aunty Mary's hearing was not aided by the device resident in the dressing table drawer. 'Don't leave me with Mary,' Hilda had often said and Aunty Mary, unkindly and repeatedly, had said that to be left with her friend was purgatory. The older generation can be so extreme. She also said it was purgatory to go to the hairdresser's and to get into the bath! At ninety six she not only assumed the divine right to do what she wanted but also to say whatever came into her head. Fortunately, as she so frequently told us, we were used to it. Also it was possible to engage a hairdresser which could come to the house!

Chapter Five

Keep busy at something. A very busy person never has
time to be unhappy.

Robert Louis Stevenson

WHEN CATTLE HAD BEEN BROUGHT IN, just before Christmas, we
had begun feeding big bale haylage and had to admit it was easier.
For one thing fodder, not fully made into hay, is more nutritious so we could
stop feeding corn.

However it did introduce a stress into our lives we had avoided for
over twenty years. To be dependent on someone else, at least during the
winter months, was something Father had repeatedly urged us against.
Independence, in farming, eliminates some of the stress. When a successful
harvest had been dependent on him and Margaret, only the elements could
let them down. With technology came the hired baler and it was frightening
to wait for his arrival whilst rain clouds gathered above.

So, Father had recommended Margaret rear more cattle, graze the
meadows and buy in hay, harvested elsewhere and that we had done for
over twenty years. For all those summers we could unload and stack the
small bales and handle them for feed and bedding without any help. We
were independent. We were in control.

Forced, due to a market shortage of small bales, we'd had no alternative
but to blow with the wind and convert to plastic covered monsters and their
well hidden contents. Never in a month of Sundays could we ever regain
our winter independence. It was, yet again, a miracle that the wallers were
only three-quarters of their way through the decade of The Countryside
Stewardship Scheme and that Tim was a master of the craft of Kramer
driving, big bale harvesting and manipulation. Our gratitude was immense
but our loss of independence occasionally causes the stress we have so often
tried to avoid. It is essential that, by hook or by crook, we must purchase at
least one load each, of small baled straw and hay so that we have an emergency hoard we can handle. And for as long as is possible, we must keep
our independence in the holiday provision area, helped as we are with the
current trend for groups who want to self-cater.

So much of our modern anxiety is caused by technology and I look back
with nostalgia on the relatively carefree days when we lived without it. It
didn't matter, then, if there was snow in the winter because we didn't have

a car. Our horse and wooden-wheeled milk float never had a low battery, a puncture or a failing gear box. There was no worry about an electricity cut because we had tilly lamps and there were no harassing Health and Safety laws. No one needed Yakult because the bugs necessary for immunity were left in the unpasteurised milk.

There were, we had to admit, what Aunty Mary called the 'ads and disses' of the new era. All winter Tim left the wall building every three or four mornings a week to fill the mangers. Every morning Margaret let the bullocks out into the stock yard with access to the sheltered accommodation, now offered by the barn and feeding bay. With the sleeping area empty, during the day, it was safer for me to lay straw than it had ever been and Danny no longer needed to protect me from frisky bullocks, a job he had enjoyed. It was delivered in big round bales which could be rolled. As we did so they unravelled, spreading a carpet. The only problem was they came without plastic covering and were too ungainly to stack indoors so, in wet weather, it was impossible to keep the top ones dry. Eventually we bought rectangular bales, possible to stack indoors but frighteningly large and unrollable.

Every evening the cattle gathered, full and sleepy, at the shed doors and were let inside. They came in gratefully, until the smell of spring grass floated temptingly over the gate. Then they became giddy with anticipation and were easily spooked. The operation was better done without spectators and definitely easier without help. Every offer was refused. It takes time to perfect new ways but we were getting there.

Rearing the new intake of calves was difficult. The recent epidemic was still sending shock waves in every direction. The national herd had not only been depleted, it had been moved about more than usual and regional germs had been scattered. The calves seemed less robust. One struggled to get up for some time and then sat down and stayed. We tried every which way to hoist it onto its feet but its legs were useless. It sat comfortably and ate everything put before it, but never attempted to get up. Had it been a pet dog, others (not us) it would have put it down, but most farmers don't do that. I don't believe for one moment that Margaret is alone in her hope that an animal will get better or die naturally. This calf didn't look like dying. It sat upright, guzzled its milk and ate its hay and corn eagerly. We tried to hoist it with a rope and pulley and we tried to sit it with its feet dangling over a bale. We were in poor shape, too. Margaret was coping but, with the added work-load, movement improvement had halted. In the end we gave up struggling with the calf. Margaret turned it onto clean straw twice a day and continued to satisfy its appetite. What would be, would be. We were too weary to anticipate. Then two calves got indigestion problems when stomachs became extended with gas. Usually it can be let out with a syringe needle but occasionally a vet must insert what is called a red devil. This allows a semi-permanent hole into the stomach so that gas can exit. Our

Big bale straw and haylage.

sitting down calf had begun to have the same problem and when the vet was sent for to see to the two stronger calves, Margaret asked me if we should be the money out and get a red devil in the one on the floor. Why not, I answered. In for a penny. Why not go the whole way and give it some of her human homeopathic leg squirt as well. So the little fellow got a red devil and a daily squirt and a tiny useless looking capsule and after seven weeks of sitting down he got up and continued to do so. He was soon walking round the pen, catching up with his peers. We believe in miracles. Often there is no other explanation. In spite of everything we love our work.

Our calf buy had been sixty instead of seventy so Margaret bought three suckled stirks from Tim and asked Milford to buy a few more at the market. She has always liked numbers and the land needs enough to graze it properly. He bought six at Selby and two at Otley, increasing our herd by eleven. Unfortunately they brought in a pneumonia bug which gave Margaret enough trouble to deter her from ever buying in winter again. There was a new antibiotic on the market, Draxxin, which proved to be a blessing. Today's medications are not cheep but do work.

January and February had become the norm for visits from those in Malta and Yugoslavia. At this early time of the year these parents bring their children to England and the David Hart Clinic. The Seric family made the long journey twice a year, mother, grandmother and handicapped son initially coming in July 2002. They had no English and used fingers to indicate the time they wished me to call a taxi. She'd put up six fingers on leaving in the summer and had expected me to understand that they would come again in January. I had been completely taken unawares. Without warning they had been in the yard, paying their chauffeur. I had hurried out into the darkness knowing I had nothing prepared. Fortunately New Year guests had gone and those following, in the ground floor cottage did not come until the weekend. There had followed accelerated action to re-heat The Mistal and make the three beds. I asked the Clinic, in future, to let me know when this family was coming. If they arrived unannounced in July it would be a disaster!

Simultaneously with all our farm work the holiday business continued but it, like everything else, was changing direction and of that we had no control. We can go to the cattle market to buy seventy chosen calves and come home supplied. We can take stores to the Friday sales and sell. About the bed and breakfast we can do nothing. Unlike Gladys Aylwood we cannot go out and drag in the lead donkey. Everything depends on someone out there, phoning or writing. They seldom do the latter these days. No wonder the Post Office is in distress! The phone may remain silent, a letter may not come and there is absolutely nothing you can do about it. Nor can you choose who comes. If they have not been before you do not know to whom you are opening the door. This diversification could never have been my sole profession for I like to make things happen and you can't do that in the holiday trade. Compared with being a farmer it is more like being a fish-erman. You offer bait. You throw out your advertising net and sometimes you catch a shoal and sometimes only a flounder.

The miracle of the eighties and nineties was that the 'ocean' around us was teeming with 'fish'. If it had continued into the new millennium I believe we might have been pushing up the daisies already. Now that there are fewer needing serviced accommodation and many groups wanting to self-cater, I do believe we can keep going for yet another decade. We had group bookings all over Easter and it was great. We wondered how we had ever coped with twenty for breakfast and evening meal, before cattle were turned out for the summer. We had been so full, those twenty Easters before the Foot and Mouth, that we, the family, were sleeping in the front room, Margaret and me on the floor! Tolerance had to grow in us like mustard and cress on the classroom nature table.

We wondered what had brought about this extraordinary change. It could be that British people are finding their own climate too cold and are flocking abroad. It could be that today's children prefer a swimming pool in the sun to a field of daisies, or that people listen to health scare prophesies from government, saying that, on farms, they will get salmonella, E. coli and BSE.

On the plus side, it may be that families wishing to unite, want more space to do so than the ordinary home can provide. Or it may be none of those things at all, but no other than our own Guardian Angel, taking care of us as always! Things have certainly changed in favour of us. Our work load in that field has lessened. We must be grateful though we admit it is not quite so much fun!

Easter posed no problem and, spring being just around the corner, we began to feel it was ages since we had had a break and that the autumn holidays we'd been used to, had been necessary. The May week in Saltburn had been pleasant but had ended in a broken leg. Aunty Mary had recovered from that. She still needed no medication. Everything encouraged us to take her away for yet another May holiday. It would make us feel easy about accepting aunty-sitters in June, whilst we went off by rail.

'Let's go to Grange-over-sands,' we said. We hadn't been since Mother died in 1990. We had booked a cottage, in 2001, at Witherslack, just a few miles outside Grange, but had had to give it away to a friend, Veronica. There was no way we could leave with Foot and Mouth on our doorstep. Now we could go, so we phoned the Grange estate agent, responsible for the reservations, and secured it for a May break. It was a bungalow and the friend, who'd used it in our stead, said it was wheelchair friendly. We began to look forward to the summer.

We told Aunty Mary and her response was as expected. She remarked, 'Well if that's what you want.' If only she had kept on her feet we could have taken her to the Hebrides, as we had for thirty years. As it was, getting her into the Land Rover was verging on the impossible. If she had kept even remotely mobile we would have been happy to take her north for, we had to admit, she loved it and it is always a pleasure to share what you love with someone who loves it also. But we admit, too, that taking away old people, when you are getting quite elderly yourself is, what Aunty Mary always described as 'no maughing latter.' We did not relish the prospect of leaving her at home again, even with relatives, which was why we were determined to give her a Grange holiday. We instinctively knew that for all of us the year ahead was not going to be easy and we had every intention of keeping 'right on to the end of the road,' as Father had taught. What we've begun, if we can, we finish.

Sadly she showed no interest in her coming holiday and I packed her case without her verbal instructions. We decided not to go until Sunday and told Dorothy we might return on Friday, depending on how well we were coping. Our old lady no longer knew what day it was. We strapped the wheelchair and commode into the back of the Land Rover, threw our two bicycles onto the roof rack and set off determined to take the fields way, at least as far as Settle. Grange is not much more than fifty miles away and we had all day.

The road was empty, just as we prefer it and the holiday spirit was alive in the vehicle, as it always is. All our oldies have loved being driven around the countryside. I'm not sure Margaret and I will take to being passengers. We prefer one or other of us to be at the wheel. We prefer Land Rover to luxury car and we don't like speed and detest the motorway.

We had got to within half a mile of Settle when a car approached and the driver slowed beside us. He told us the road was blocked due to an accident and that we should turn and go back to Kirby Malham. So much for the fields way! So we retraced our journey and arrived in Grange later than expected. It did not matter for our key was to be collected at The Spar, which opens 'Eight 'til late,' and on a Sunday, too.

As Veronica had told us, the bungalow and the pastoral view from it, was lovely. Inside it equalled the Moorsholm one in convenience. Unfortunately it was similar in that it had a two step entry. It is possible to get a wheelchair up one step but two are impossible. However Aunty Mary could still take her own weight. We had a stool in the Land Rover necessary to raise her high enough to be hoisted onto the seat. It was just the right height when placed alongside the bottom step, to widen it and provide more foot room. It was easier to manhandle her into the Land Rover than it was, once a day, to get her up those steps! The memory of the broken leg was still vivid. We dared not let it happen again.

The view from the kitchen window was magnetic. We prolonged our meal times in order to watch the routine activity of a dairy herd. We have a love affair with other people's cattle, too. The bungalow had a large, lawned garden which was being disturbed by the nightly visit of badgers. We never saw them, only the rooted up sods next morning.

We could manoeuvre the wheelchair anywhere within the house and it was safe to leave its occupant whilst Margaret and I exercised the dogs, the easy way, on cycles. Parallel to the A59 the old road runs as straight as a Roman one and is level and empty. It was only a quarter of a mile from the bungalow and every morning we cycled along it with childish glee. Those small folding cycles were useless on hills but on the flat were an early morning rejuvenation unique to the Brown sisters.

We had chosen Grange, once again, hoping Aunty Mary would feel at home in a place she knew. It had been our venue, year after year, throughout the eighties. It has a gem of a promenade for pushing wheelchairs and an ideally situated cafe, overlooking Morecambe Bay. In a way the holiday was successful for there was a place to park east at the railway station, or west at Cark Road and I am sure she knew where she was, though the bungalow was unfamiliar. The weather behaved, there was no need to fill a flask for the cafe proprietor soon recognised we only needed a little help with the wheelchair and hurried daily to our assistance.

Grange promenade is never crowded so there was no fear of collision with other pedestrians and those approaching are of the friendly variety who smile at, and chat with, anyone in a wheelchair. It caused us great amusement for, of everyone, Aunty Mary asked, 'Are you in our coach?' It was more than thirty years since she and Aunty Janie had gone on holiday by coach!

Margaret was vocally horrified at what had happened to the bay, since our last visit in 1989. Grass had grown on the mud flats, so profusely that sheep were grazing. In the space of a decade the coastline had changed. The tidal bore still came in twice a day, covering the grass momentarily then re-exposing it. Morecambe Bay had had a magic totally different from the white shell beaches of The Hebrides, but magic there had been and the growth of grass had taken some away. Margaret was spellbound and queried locals all week. I did not fail to notice that, with two sticks, she was walking the whole length of the promenade and never sending me back to the parked Land Rover, to drive it round and collect the two of them. After re-fuelling at the cafe, she could walk all the way back. She couldn't have done that, in Saltburn, a year ago. Progress was slow and might never be perfect, considering our challenging lifestyle, but it was forward not backward. People of this new millennium constantly say, 'Wow'. It says it all when I admit that, when I expel air, I say, 'Phew!'

We had a secret plan. Only a couple of miles from Witherslack lives one of my Guides who, before marriage, had come as caretaker of The Currer whilst we had taken holidays in the early eighties. Sandra is a very special friend who worked for more than ten years at our local Sue Ryder Hospice for very ill patients. Her happy family had recently bought a beautiful farmhouse at Levens, with a lovely Granny-flat for her parents. We asked her if she would care for Aunty Mary, one afternoon, so that we could go on a test drive of the railway, with Danny and Meg. She was more than willing. Aunty Mary did not query why or where we were going, visibly clutching our senior rail cards. She went happily with Sandra and her mother and we drove to the station. We were sure the platform of the tiny halt, on the Barrow Line, would be relatively empty and quiet. The train would not be full either, we calculated. We did not dwell on what we would do if the dogs panicked. They were used to leads only occasionally and they had never been asked to do anything like this before. The journey to Oban was alarmingly long and only a month away.

We parked on the attractive station forecourt. There was a buzz of conversation coming from somewhere but there was no queue at the ticket office. When we got onto the platform it was teeming with excited Junior School children obviously setting off on a school trip. They were not uncontrolled but they were many and exuberant, giggling and laughing. When the train glided in, the teacher held them back to allow us to board. Sheep dogs prefer to be in the rear but Danny and Meg deemed the safest move was to follow us onto the train, rather than turn into this mob of chattering children. Meg slipped under the seat and Danny allowed a multitude of legs to step over him. The children were carrying rucksacks and clutching information sheets. It was to be an educational visit. 'Been there, Done that!' I whispered to Margaret and we relaxed enough to laugh and, whilst we held our breath, the train pulled out of the station. We had booked a short return journey to Arnside, only a matter of minutes away. Our dogs did not panic when we struggled back down the corridor, nor did they try to bolt when the exit door offered a return to freedom. So far so good. We would know, before long, whether they would calmly get back on board for the return journey. Sitting for the half hour wait, on the empty platform, we prayed the train would this time be empty. It was not. It must have been a commuter one and, as it pulled onto the platform, it looked as if it might have standing room only. Nevertheless our beautiful animals climbed happily onto it. Empty seats were few and far between and Danny had to sit in the aisle and allow friendly passengers to stroke him. It was a test drive indeed! When the ticket inspector came neither he nor Danny objected and Meg, again under the seat, could not be seen.

'Yes,' we said to each other, with clenched fists and thumbs up. 'YES! We did it!' But we didn't intend to do it again until June when it would have to be for real.

We deviated, one day, from our routine drive into Grange and our leisurely stroll along the sea front for coffee on the promenade. We drove into Bowness but it was wet. The Lake District can be and it was with a vengeance. Even so the mountains and lakes of Cumbria are beautiful, the villages are idyllic and, rain or shine, there are ramblers to envy. Oh, to be walking alongside them! Finding a parking space, with ample room to bring a wheelchair alongside, is always difficult. In a brief gap in the deluge we transferred Aunty Mary into her chariot and contemplated the lakeside view of Windermere and the moored boats. No-one was risking a sail. I can't say I enjoy pushing a wheelchair among crowds. It is a disaster if someone unexpectedly stops in front and a heel is caught on the foot rest. We began to regret getting out of the Land Rover and did so fully when the heavens opened again and threatened to drown us completely. We dashed for the shelter of a cafe where we could pause over a coffee but, though the entrance had a double door, the proprietor initially refused to open the bolted, second half. She could see how old our invalid was and how torrential the rain, but said she wasn't allowed to open it wide. It was a management rule, she said. The rule concerning disabled access is very specific and a nightmare for some businesses but that cafe needed to make no adjustments other than lift the bolt, which dropped into the floor. We couldn't believe what we were hearing and I had to beg, and beg again to get access, getting wetter all the while. At last it was grudgingly given. Maybe the lady was overworked and harassed by tourists and weather. We tried to forgive her.

We were on the verge of feeling overworked and harassed, too and possibly nearing the end of our tether. As always, according to Mike our electrician, any stress will pass. Our outer clothing dried in sunshine on our way back to the car park. We abandoned all further plans to venture amongst crowds, confining ourselves happily to the promenade and the Main Street.

By Friday we were ready to go home safely and well. Packing is a

marathon task with several additional items of equipment, necessary whenever one takes disabled family members and two dogs. We threw the two
bicycles on the rack and felt exhausted. We made our final descent of those
precipitous steps, with infinite care, lowered Aunty Mary into her wheelchair and pushed her to the open Land Rover door. We placed the stool in
position and steadied her onto it. I supported her whilst Margaret ran to the
driver's seat to haul and I hoisted her 12 stone, floppy lump on to the front
seat. The activity was the usual success and we sighed with relief. A friend
once commented that we must surely have celebrated every success. She
was wrong. Whatever our success, in all the varied situations we have found
ourselves, we have greeted it only with profound relief.

We made room in the back and heaved the heavy wheelchair into the
narrow space between the cases. We climbed aboard. Eventually we would
relax but first we must drive down the Main Street, to the estate agents, to
return the key. Margaret was driving and I was poised to hop out whilst
she hesitated on the double yellow lines, for the brief minute it would take.
Immediately she was accosted by an over enthusiastic policeman and told
she could not stay there. I was only two strides away, already returning to
the car. Margaret pointed to our disabled parking card, visible on the windscreen and the wheelchair in full view in the rear, for a Land Rover station
wagon has windows all the way round.

'I'll have to book you,' said the officer. 'It's not the disabled person who
is out!' I was already back in my seat.

'Please,' I begged. 'The car park is right at the bottom of the hill. You saw
me get out. You know I haven't been a minute. You don't know how in need
of care we carers are.'

'Well, don't do it again,' was the ungracious retort. Sometimes we really
did need to feel to be understood. Our role as carers had been 24–7–365 for
a long, long time and, let's face it, we were tired. Only being busy ensured
our continuing happiness.

It was a relief to get home but we were greeted by shocking news.
Dorothy had just received a phone call alerting us to a serious road accident.
Two farming friends had, a few years ago, left Marley Hall Farm, on the
valley floor below us, and bought a farm on the A19, south of Easingwold.
For most of our nearing fifty years of living here, they had been good neighbours, always available if we needed help. The two brothers, ageing as we
were, sold their large house and the steep land belonging to it and bought
a more manageable property they could farm well into old age. Farmers
never want to retire. The move, for Joe and Billy Drury, had been a good one
until that day of our return when a man speeding at 80mph had ploughed
into them, killing the eldest, instantly. We were too shocked for words and
neglected to get Aunty Mary out of the Land Rover. We suddenly heard her
banging loudly on the car window.

Our next train journey was to York. We did not take dogs or Aunty. It was a very sad funeral. We were hovering near to rock bottom but Billy, the younger brother, was in a far worse predicament. We had been wondering how we would cope with everything ahead if something were to deprive us of our coming holiday. Suddenly we began to think whatever would we do if one of us was left to struggle on alone?

We didn't quite get back into our pre-holiday routine. A self-catering group came for four days and that meant no evening meals. Then it was Spring Bank Holiday and we were back under pressure. The period in Grange had weakened us but strengthened Aunty Mary. She resisted with more determination than ever before. The chimes were ringing on and off all night and we were up and down like yo-yos. Sleep deprivation lowers energy levels like nothing else. God help the relatives, we sighed. We feared they would really need some help. It never occurred to us that a time was coming when we would need it, too. We had cared for paternal grandparents, Father, Mother, Harry. It had been no problem. They were all liftable. Aunty Mary was heavy.

I suppose this is where our Guardian Angel intercepted again, for Aunty Mary, who was on no medication at all, suddenly appeared to be out of sorts. The doctor was called and we had a visit from the district nurse. We would not wish an infection on anyone and it did not prove serious but it was an introduction to her doctor and to the facilities available should they become essential. Aunty Mary's physical health had been exceptional. I'm not sure her mental health would have survived had she been told her previous doctor's diagnosis in 1979. Following her sister's sudden death she had hovered on the edge of breakdown and had spent most of her time at The Currer. She had been here during the prolonged period of snow which lasted almost all of the first three months of the year.

She had begun to move her mouth and click her tongue perpetually and on the day before Father died, Mother had asked the doctor what was wrong with her sister and he had said, 'She's got Parkinson's Disease.'

'Well don't tell her,' Mother had ordered. 'Whatever you do, do not tell her!' Mother was amazing. Small and more fragile than we, she had a hidden strength with which few could compete. We knew. We're are not sure that she was aware that we knew and sometimes fear we never told her.

And then Father had died during the night and there had been no access through the snow, for the undertaker or the hearse, and we had other things to worry about. The strange movement of tongue and lips had gradually disappeared. Aunty Mary had not had Parkinson's Disease. Dear knows what she would have had, if she had been told!!

Since then she had had no indigestion, no heart or blood pressure problems, no need for a water pill, no need whatsoever to allow herself to become immobile or so demanding. She was beginning to control us. We were getting hardly any sleep at all. In her chair in the sitting room, she slept whilst we worked and she kept us awake all night.

Very early, on the morning of Saturday, May 31st, she sat on the edge of the bed and refused to do anything. She would not go back to bed, she would not get up and dressed. Nothing. We wrapped her in blankets, we coaxed, we begged, we ordered but we couldn't move her. I think, perhaps, had cousin Michael's doctor wife been here, she might have noticed then, that this was a sign of a urine infection. Instead it went un-noticed. We called the doctor on night duty and he witnessed the struggle we were having and thought she should be taken to hospital, so that she could be checked over and maybe we could get some assistance. We thought the relatives might need it, so we agreed to her being a few days in hospital if it might help. We had just over a fortnight to sort something out. To go or not to go could not be decided. To have a holiday or stay at home, was in the balance and the latter was increasingly likely.

I went with her in the ambulance and she was indignant. Margaret followed us in the Land Rover. That night the electric light was turned off, at the top of the staircase, for the first time since electricity was brought to the farmhouse, forty four years earlier, except perhaps when our family went on holiday together. We slept like the dead.

The nurses said Aunty Mary could walk alone and that she had been playing us up. They said she wasn't ill and thought her confusion was rather funny. Daily she told us the lady in the next bed was our cousin Freda. She created all night and frequently had to be wheeled into the day room so that others might sleep. What was new? They didn't spot the water infection. It was Michael's doctor wife Fiona who did, when the two of them did their four day aunty-sit and we were on Barra.

Her two weeks in hospital gave us moment to sort things out but it was terribly time consuming. Everyone agrees that hospital visiting swallows the day. We found the daily journey almost impossible and vowed to keep Aunty Mary at home, come what may. It was far and away the easiest option. Changing from working clothes to clean, threading our way through traffic in the town, searching, searching, searching for a parking space in the crowded hospital grounds, was a nightmare and my heart aches for those who, sometimes, have to do it for years. Each day the hospital corridor got longer. The weather was hot and every afternoon we put our aunty into a wheelchair and pushed her into the sun. Margaret would bring the dogs out of the Land Rover so that they could be stroked. Then we would leave our aunty protesting that it was all our fault. We would hurry home, frequently to make evening meals for our guests.

Twice our cousins did the hospital run. Once to allow us to drive to Harrogate for Margaret's monthly appointment and once for us to entertain the residents from White Windows, Leonard Cheshire Home. The

Residents from White Windows, Leonard Cheshire Home.

opportunity to do so, whilst Aunty Mary was away, was too good to miss. These annual visits had begun in the late fifties, long before the barn conversion. Then we had toileted them on a commode in the front porch and had fed them in the beamed farmhouse kitchen, dear knows how. All moveable furniture had been evacuated and their wheelchairs had touched like sardines in a tin. They had been able to watch me lift the sizzling joint of beef or the roast turkey from the Aga oven and it had all been far more fun, and generated far more laughter, than today's convenience and space does. I dare not think what the fire officer would have thought of our wheelchair traffic jam.

It was a relief to get this annual event out of the way without domestic responsibilities. We also managed to build up some dangerous gaps in a boundary wall. We dare not leave it unsafe if we went north. We went on an exciting shopping expedition in case we did. We bought two small rucksacks and sleeping bags which, when rolled, took up no more space than a four pint milk carton. Margaret bought two folding, hikers' walking sticks. We parcelled up our two bicycles and sent them to Tiree in advance. They could stay there until next year if necessary.

One afternoon we had an unexpected visit from one of my pupils. We see so many children with handicap, caused by cerebral palsy and visiting the David Hart Clinic. I would love to be able to promise them the success story enjoyed by Craig, who could walk barely from desk to desk at five but with a career, a marriage and a lovely daughter, he has triumphed over every difficulty in his path. I will never forget him and he doesn't forget me and I am grateful beyond words.

Craig and Harry were survivors without the sophistication of modern help. We see children much more handicapped than they were, nowadays and it is a blessing that there are people like those at the David Hart Clinic. All those working with disabled, be they children or adults, are special and love their work but they can leave it behind when they go home and come fresh to it every morning. It is a blessing. Those who care for their family members are always on call. We have tremendous respect for husbands and wives, caring for a spouse in a wheelchair, disabled by multiple sclerosis, arthritis, accident or stroke, and who bring them here, on holiday, year after year. We watch children with cerebral palsy getting bigger and heavier and know that, if they do not walk, many problems lie ahead. But love and laughter accompany them all. Survival rates are higher nowadays and those who do are often very disabled and Harry's problems, and Craig's fall into insignificance.

We never thought of ourselves in carers' shoes because we weren't. Not really. Harry struggled and succeeded in being as near normal as possible and what you are born to you think as normal anyway. Perhaps our experiences enable us to view another's predicament with more understanding and applaud any device which gets a child walking.

Towards the end of Aunty Mary's two week period in hospital things were being set in motion for her return. Though we could cope with her at home, our relatives must have help or we would not leave. The NHS was considerate and quick to respond. We were interviewed by many careworkers and therapists. They came to The Currer and saw that we had every facility for coping with disablement. Our home is wheelchair friendly and there has been a wheelchair lift through the kitchen ceiling since it was first needed for Harry. Everywhere there are handrails, there is a downstairs toilet, an hydraulic seat into the bath, a wheel-in shower. All we needed was some help for the relatives not used to handling her. We have nothing but appreciation for the rapid response of the Home Care team.

So we were able not only to bring Aunty home but to prepare for the break we so needed. Cousin David and his wife came from Sussex on the day before our departure, giving us time to pass on knowledge of the necessary skills and routine. We did the last night shift. I got up early, wrote a letter saying that, if it were posted, we would be heading for the railway station. I printed it out twenty three times and addressed that many envelopes to friends on the islands. I posted them on the way to the station. I bought the tickets and followed Margaret and David, and the dogs, down onto the platform. I felt weak at the knees. We were going fantastically lightweight. One-day hikers would be carrying more than we were. Waves of nostalgia swept over me. I was back in the past, waiting for a train to take us to the Highlands and Islands of Scotland and we had nothing to do but look out of the window all the way.

Chapter Six

It's the blue islands that are pulling me away,
Their laughter puts the leap upon the lame.

WITH A STRANGE FEELING OF 'been here before' we clambered onto
the train with our two cattle dogs, as nonchalantly as if we were
seasoned commuters. In the early fifties Margaret and I had travelled north
by coach, because it was cheaper. Then for twenty five years, every summer,
the train had transported us and our scores of children. In the early days the
railway coaches had small carriages and corridors. The children loved that
and were disappointed when open compartments were introduced for they
preferred their privacy. So does Meg. On that first long journey, she secured
the space between two back-to-back seats and no-one even knew she was
there. Danny, the larger, older dog crawled between our feet, beneath the
table, with his head protruding into the passage. If we had feared that other
passengers might look disapprovingly on our canine companions, we were
soon reassured. Every passer-by stooped to pat Danny's silky, ginger-brown
head. Myself, I would not dare to stroke a doggy stranger, least of all on a
train, but everyone caressed Danny and he did not mind.

It was so, so lovely travelling by rail, no on-coming traffic, no tail of impatient drivers, eager to pass and inclined to hoot. We felt privileged to be able
to scan the amazing, north-country vista on either side of the track. Oh yes,
I would have loved the coach to be full of excited children and the guards
van to be piled high with rucksacks and kit bags. Or maybe just two, enormous packs, tent and cooking equipment, too bulky for the compartment.
There had been five occasions when Margaret and I had wandered alone.
However, we viewed our minute gear with pleasant amusement. What we
craved for was freedom and we were going to enjoy it to the full. It took no
time at all for our shackles to fall off. We have always enjoyed our commit-
ment to family, farm, catering, Guiding and teaching but, at that moment in
time, freedom was another kind of joy.

The Aire valley looks different from the train, though line follows road
much of the way, until Settle when it turns from the west to follow the North
Star without hesitation. Then over the fells, across the Ribblehead viaduct,
through the Blea Moor tunnel towards the pastoral half of Cumbria, to
Appleby and Carlisle. We had chosen an early, direct service, avoiding a
change at Carlisle but giving us a four hour wait in Glasgow. We were so

unsure of how the dogs would cope. Danny had a reputation for clinging to Margaret, earning him the name of Super Glue. We had simply no idea of what Meg might do, but just as she followed closely when we cycled, she now fixed us with the stare of acknowledgement. I, apparently, was leader of her pack and whither I went, she would follow.

We avoided walking through the city, teeming with people and traffic and leapt aboard a taxi to take us from Central Station to Queens Street and there we found a seat in the massive arena, in front of the platforms. Glasgow is the friendliest city in the UK and we had entertainment galore. We bought a coffee and ate our packed sandwiches. We watched the kaleidoscope of people, guessing their origin and destination, identifying them as workers or holiday-makers, witnessing their reunions and observing their frustrations. Every few minutes someone came to talk about dogs. It was an environment we were unused to but we thrived in it. A lady accompanying a handicapped girl, sat with us for a while. Americans photographed us and two inebriated youths gravitated towards us as did almost every child on the platform. If you want friends you travel with dogs.

It is necessary to choose the right half of the Highland train for, en route, the four coaches separate, one half going to Oban and the other two travelling to Mallaig. We left the station over-filled with tired passengers. Fortunately most were workers just going to the outskirts, to home and an evening meal. We were soon able to stretch our legs and delight in the slowly passing countryside which surrounds Glasgow. The city, seated as it is on the banks of the River Clyde, is also sitting on the doorstep of The Highlands. It was healing to be driven along each loch side, first Gareloch, then Loch Long and Loch Lomond without having to negotiate oncoming traffic, on roads which get busier every year. Whenever we looked at each other, we smiled. We had left our burden of responsibility behind and were determined to be at peace.

Arriving at Oban we left the station and found our dog friendly hotel. We had used it overnight several times and it had been a welcome haven following our accident. We were greeted by the boisterous landlord. The harbour was ablaze with the lights of the anchored ferries. We left the curtains undrawn and window wide open, unwilling to miss any of the pre-sail excitement.

Next morning, too early for the hotel breakfast, we collected our fare and boarding tickets and climbed the gangway. 'This is a God given holiday,' I was thinking. 'We must not waste one minute of it.'

Those with dogs on deck must sit in a special area outside the observation lounge. There was another couple with a smaller dog. They were seasoned island-hoppers, taking friends to Coll who had never been to The Hebrides. They were fearful lest inclement weather put them off. I told them of a Guide of mine, on holiday on South Uist, who had sent us a postcard. All it said was,

'Wild, wet, windy, wonderful!'

'Oh, I like that,' said the fellow traveller. 'I'll put that on my postcards if ever I need to.' There was no need that fortnight. The weather was glorious.

Our first week in Hughie's wee cottage at Caolis was luxury. We were soon golden with the dawn to dusk sunshine. We cycled joyously on the beach but borrowed a friend's old car to take us around the island we love so much. Tir nan orna in Gaelic. We left the one bedroomed cottage early every morning and did not return until night. Tiree is so flat it is almost all sky. Amongst hills of home, the heavens are no more than a roof but on the ocean the sky begins at sea level and completes a full half circle whichever way you look. Tiree is no more than a raft on the Atlantic and if, sadly, the brilliance of the heavens is being lost on the Mainland, by pollution and all that man-made urban light, the night sky of The Hebrides is near perfect. 'Two thousand acres of sky', is no exaggeration.

The islanders showered us with 'ceud mille failte', a hundred thousand welcomes. On foot we sauntered, by cycle we frolicked, by car we barely exceeded 20 mph. We met some seasoned caravanette owners who had parked their dorm'ouse at Balinoe but were using cycles to get round the island. It transpired that the lady was born on the same day, month and year that I was. An astrologist would have recognised something in our joint star charts, indicating our love of far-flung islands in the western sea. We tried not to wonder about the status quo at home and declared that we would not discuss it between ourselves or amongst our friends, but each one asked innumerable, concerned questions about Aunty Mary and The Currer.

The Currer? Where was that? Aunty Mary? Who was she? We were so far from reality we could have lived the dream always, if our friends had not continually reminded us. They all loved our old lady. They had found her very funny. Ellen had once said she'd recommend her as a stand-up comic at The Lodge Hotel. We phoned home and Fiona, the doctor, did not tell us that she had detected a urine infection, had sent for our doctor to prescribe antibiotics and that Aunty Mary was quite seriously ill. Had she done so, I am sure we would have returned and forfeited our week on Harris, once more. Instead we sailed on the boat heading for Barra on Thursday, the only day of the week it makes the crossing from Scarinish to Castlebay.

We had booked accommodation at the Youth Hostel there. Being ardent campers we had never before used a hostel. When alone, or in a three or foursome, we had carried tents. This was to be a first time, not as youths but as OAPs. Nevertheless we seemed to fit in with the younger generation, an adventurous group organising some Long Island challenges for competitors, running, climbing, walking and canoeing from north to south, down the Outer Isles. All new experiences are fun and, considering the fact that we head north each year, the variety holiday-life throws at us, never fails to amaze and triggers off this writing habit! I hope I am proving to other working people that, if they observe, their ordinary lives are full of the extra-ordinaire and minor miracles galore. The variety of a simple life is mind-boggling.

We made an easy breakfast in the hostel kitchen and then caught the bus to the Eriskay ferry. The island of Barra, of 'Whisky Galore' fame, is very small. Our journey was no more than six or seven miles and the sailing across to Eriskay is brief. It was our first step onto this island of song. 'Vair me o' rovan o', my school children had sung in BBC Singing Together and my Guides round the campfire and in island kitchens. With our family we had looked across the shallow water between South Uist and Eriskay but never crossed. Now, years later, a causeway has been built making a second ferry unnecessary. Having sailed from Barra, our journey from island to island could now be done on wheels all the way to Berneray.

A bus was waiting the arrival of the ferry and we boarded it along with a few other passengers, tourists I would imagine. We never think of ourselves in that category. 'Friends of the people', we have always been described by the islanders .

It had been a crisp. early Thursday morning sail and we were rosy and invigorated with the spirit of adventure. We were doing things together we hadn't done for a long time. It was not uncharted territory. The road was familiar and we were the same people but our packs were minute and the two cycles, posted to Tiree, now accompanied us. They had ample room in the boot of the bus but, having been told it only went to the Benbecula Airport, where we would have to transfer to a sixteen-seater mini-bus, we were not over confident that our next driver would be as pleasant as this one was.

We had a fifteen minute wait at the air terminal. Margaret went a short way to walk the dogs and I sought a Ladies' room in the foyer-cum-cafe. I never found the Ladies for need of it was forgotten when I had a one in a million encounter.

It was over forty years since Enid had been a County Cadet, training to be a Guider, in the Bradford based unit where I was currently Lieutenant. For a short while I had been busy with an expanding Sea Ranger Crew and Margaret had taken responsibility for the Guide Company. Enid had become her assistant accompanying our joint summer camp on Tiree in 1962. She had spent some time living in Shetland and, returning to the Mainland, she had lived in Glasgow, then Preston and was currently in Crook, County Durham. We saw her only at Reunion time but she had accompanied us on the Millennium Week on Tiree and that, presumably, had re-kindled her love of islands. There she was, coming across the terminal cafe floor with her husband, her mouth and arms wide open ready to embrace me. Seconds later and I would have been in the Ladies and she would have followed us to Harris, been on the island unexpectedly at the same time as we and none of us knowing. They were currently staying on one of the Uists, were sailing north on Saturday. It would be her first visit to Harris, staying at Scarista in a cottage owned by Angus MacKay, son of Mamie and John our long time friends.

We filled that fifteen minute pause, before our connecting bus came, as only long standing friends can. Enid's husband never got a word in edgeways. Margaret came, was amazed and hugged. Meg, who doesn't like either of us to even shake hands with another, got all agitated but Danny watched tolerantly, as always. The mini-bus came too soon and we were helped onto it, bikes and dogs and the driver was a gem and didn't complain. 'See you on Sunday,!' we shouted. 'See you at Luskentyre!' That may not seem quite the one in a million chance you were expecting but the story did not end there.

The mini-bus took us from causeway to causeway, across Grimsay, North Uist and to the Berneray ferry. The sail from there to Leverburgh, on Harris, was only handicapped by the fact that the observation lounge was up the steepest of iron steps which Danny refused to mount. It was not a major problem because there is a small, enclosed area below, with seats and a view but it is less preferable than the upstairs vista.

We have few complaints as travellers but Margaret is very vocal about the tinted windows on cars and buses. To see colourless islands is deprivation of the megga kind. It is so sad to travel from Leverburgh to Luskentyre and not see, in sharp relief, the green of the machair, the white of the beaches, the turquoise of the Atlantic and the pink of the acres of thrift growing on the shore line.

Once on the Harris bus, everyone knew us except the tourists. We were confident that the driver was well aware the latter could less appreciate his island behind tinted glass, for he frequently paused and made everyone new to the island, get out and urged them to take photographs.

We got off the bus at Horgabost paying our first respects to the family of Rachel MacLeod, a friend we'd known for forty years and who had recently died. Had the dormobile brought us safely to Harris, the previous year, we would have been in time to enjoy yet another year of her friendship. Though the Dorm'ouse had deprived us of that pleasure it had shown us a safer way for us to travel. We had to be satisfied with just talking of the friend who had been our island 'god-mother', our anchor and comfort for twenty years of camping and the friend of all our family throughout the twenty-three years that followed.

Norman drove us to the end of the road at Luskentyre, where John MacDonald's caravan awaited us. Approaching Paradise, I always find there is a lump in my throat. I am overwhelmed with nostalgia and, let's face it, with amazement that we should dare to bring so many children to such isolation. Youth dares do many things but we were no longer young when,

Horgabost, Harris, when we were seven.

in 1980, after twenty five years of this activity, we'd taken nearly sixty children, to be under canvas together for a full fortnight.

That first evening we visited John MacDonald. He was confined to a wheelchair, and we were worried because he looked so ill. Afterwards we went down to the beach where, daily we had supervised our swimming children. It is only a step away from the caravan. The tide was well in and the ocean was unusually turbulent for the time of the year. Before every wave broke it was a deep green monster with a foaming, white mane. There was a navy blue shawl on Taransay and the North Harris hills were etched in silver for, behind them, the sun had set in cloud. Had we first seen Luskentyre in this Arctic guise, we would never have dared to bring children. It was awesome, fearsome, wild and incredibly beautiful. If there were seals in the turbulence they were hidden and no water fowl strutted along the shore line. We shed our shoes and walked barefooted amongst the myriads of shell particles and found the rocky shelf where we had had so many campfires.

We sat speechless, crazily in love with the might of the Atlantic at our feet and aware of our human frailty, not feeling cold but licking from our lips the salt left by the spray, continually dampening our anoraks. Much later, when the midsummer light began to dim and the warmth of excitement turned to chill, we hurried to where the sand became orchid scattered machair and quietly opened the door of our caravan. We switched on the heater and filled the kettle.

Those who visit a different holiday venue every year must be under the illusion that those who return frequently, have no variety. This could not be further from the truth. Maybe you thought the million to one encounter on Benbecula was minimal, not worth the ink in this pen. If so, then listen to this.

In brilliant sunshine on Sunday morning, Margaret and I rose early and walked a long way, barefoot, on the Luskentyre shore. Margaret with her two sticks was doing fine. The beach was absolutely empty and we sat down, not on the rocks, or dunes or on the edge of the machair, but right in the very middle of the miles of white sand. Suddenly we saw an unknown lady running towards us. Our immediate reaction was to fear some islander had received a phone call from The Currer, recalling us for an emergency. However the unknown woman was smiling and incoherent in her excitement.

Two weeks ago, in the hospital ward, opposite Aunty Mary, there had been an old, very sick lady who had turned out to be the mother of my infant teaching assistant of more than twenty years ago. I had commented to her daughter, one visiting hour, that Margaret and I were hoping to go up to the islands for a much needed break. I did not know that Liz Wheatstone lived next door to a lady who had also been in the County Cadet Unit, at the same time as Enid. We had met once a month, over forty years ago and I had only kept the one connection, the one with Enid. This other lady had, in 1979, read my account of island camping, *A Song to Sing and a Tale to Tell*, and she and her husband had been tempted to visit Harris. They had returned year after year, they had loved it so.

Luskentyre, Harris.

Knowing that her neighbour, Eileen Thompson, was going north on holiday, Liz, my colleague, had said to her, 'Jean Brown is going up to Harris sometime soon.' Eileen and her husband had driven to Luskentyre on the very day Enid and we were planning to meet, not expecting we would be sitting 'where the tide visits untrodden shores' worshipping the God of the Open Air.

'It must be them,' she had said to her husband. 'It can't be anyone else!' She had begun to run. What a Charlie she would have felt if it hadn't been we who were sitting there! She recognised me but I not her. It was forty years and many, many people ago. That afternoon Enid and Eileen were re-united.

It was just one more unexpected miracle, a unique part of an extraordinary holiday. I only write these memoirs because I am so interested in my life's journey. Most of us lead ordinary lives but, even so, they take an interesting road if one has time and inclination to chart them. I am short of the one but cannot rest my pen. My life has been so full of small miracles I do not ever want to forget. I find that in front of my word processor I can re-live them and treasure each. You, my reader, are just incidental.

I am often asked to write but never why I do. I am not writing for others. Only for Margaret and me. This is not a story fabricated to please a reader. I would be incapable of that. I consider myself creative in our practical world but asked to be imaginative I would fail. I can only write it as it is. We live in the real world, not one of make believe.

Some say we, at The Currer, do not live in the real world at all. They say we are a community apart, that we can believe that all people are nice, that the common task is acceptable, and that little miracles are everyday occurrences because we live in a bubble, protected from foul language, alcohol and drug abuse. We have never known a dysfunctional family, deep depression or poverty of opportunity. That is true, but we are not blind or deaf as to what is going on elsewhere and would be the first to attempt to put right what is going wrong, but I am not writing about that. It is my life's journey I am writing about and it fascinates me. At my age I am interested only in the positive, in collecting and sharing words of wisdom. Here is one. An AA man said to me when recently called to home-start our reluctant vehicle, 'I upset no-one. Nothing is gained by making enemies!' I like it.

I do not expect other people to be interested in my life, even though it is of a kind which is disappearing and may soon be history. If it inspires them to evaluate and appreciate their own, it will be enough. Neither the human voice nor the camera can do what the pen can. And if because I wrote *A Song to Sing and a Tale to Tell*, Enid and Eileen could be reunited, on the beach at Luskentyre, forty years on, in brilliant sunshine, I am more than satisfied.

We were beginning to realise that it was fifty years since we had had a holiday when time did not matter. The islanders insist that 'when God

Reunion, Luskentyre beach, Enid, Margaret, me and Eileen.

made time He made plenty of it' but we seldom have enough and dash late
to everything. With children and family we had to partiality obey the clock.
On Tiree and then on Harris in 2003, I don't think we ever looked at it. The
sun shone from dawn to dusk and we have enough knowledge of the axle of
the compass and the orbit of the sun to be independent of it. We had always
had so much to do, feeding and caring for others, that we really appreciated
this 'having to do nothing'. It was almost like having life on another level,
on another planet. We had Sunday lunch with Farquhar and Catrina, called
for a chat with Margaret MacLead at Borve and then had an evening meal
with Enid and Tom, in their cottage at Scarista. Cooking in the caravan was
fast becoming an unnecessary activity. We realised we need not worry about
time until the boat home must be boarded and the train caught. Like the
seagulls, where we went and how long we stayed when we landed, before
becoming airborne again, mattered not one wit. What and when we ate,
or whether we ate at all was immaterial. Frequently it was decided by the
islanders, sometimes too frequently for a slim waistline. Nor did it matter
whether we went to bed the same day we got up. Neither would it have
mattered if it had rained, but it did not.

We had thought that Sunday had been perfect but have learned from
experience, that perfection can be bettered. 'Tomorrow, is another day!' and
the following Monday equalled it easily.

The sun had already risen from the regions north east of Stornoway, and
was hovering over the Cuillin of Skye, beckoning us as we cycled east, along
the single track road from Luskentyre. The King of the Heavens had had less

sleep than we and though he would be still high over the western horizon on our return, he would again be in front of us, welcoming us home to the caravan. Like us he was rising early and bedding down late.

The two miles to the road end are relatively flat and we cycled along, followed closely by Meg. Danny was to wait for frequently. He was an odd-bod and no mistake. This was his home territory. He was Harris born and spoke the Gaelic. The Luskentyre road is no wider now than it was forty years ago but in places, where there has been erosion, it is now much closer to the sea. With every incoming tide, a little more sand leaves the bank. Where it was once possible to pitch a tent, the sea now almost washes the road and must do so properly in a storm.

Reaching the bridge, spanning the peaty river which runs into the estuary, the verdant banks become little more than moonscape. No house is visible and sheep among the grey rocks are lost to sight. Only their Persil white babies, frisking and gambolling, catch one's eye. By June, the lambs on the Mainland pastures are nearly fully grown but the Blackface babies of the Highlands and Islands are born late. We, who only rear calves in November, love the spring babies of the island hills.

Frequently Meg disappeared to find herself a deep pool for her morning ablution. She is a water baby, almost always wet but her coat is so thick it never penetrates to skin level and a good shake seems to leave her dry and it is we who are frequently wet. Danny only submerged himself in a pool if it was a hollow in the sand and warmed by the sun. Meg's bathing is noisy. Surely a hippopotamus at play would disturb the water less.

We left the cycles by the roadside and flagged down the bus on its almost empty journey to the slipway at Leverburgh. We alighted at Seilebost, the location of so many of our family holidays. It used to be a much longer journey before the causeway was built. In the pre-shortcut days, the last four miles home seemed never ending with tired, but determined children. There is more traffic nowadays and island motorists drive too quickly for our liking, so we dared not cycle when a bus could transport us.

Katie Ann Morrison only recently gave up her job as postmistress, in the tiny porch of her bungalow. We could still cash our pensions there in 2003. To walk round the back of her house is to correctly anticipate the welcome we will receive. To cash pensions is a weak excuse for a pleasant visit. She was, of course, expecting us for she was one of the twenty three to whom we had sent a letter.

'Where are you going?' she said, seeing we had no car.

We were going to Seilebost school, to visit Rhoda, the headmistress. We wanted to see the seat we'd bought, on behalf of all our Yorkshire children, in memory of Rachel, who had driven the island school bus for so many years. It was such a beautiful day, we intended to walk across the bay to the spit of land on which stand the minute school and the headteacher's house.

'But first we must put the kettle on,' said our hostess. A strupak is always more than a cup of tea. It is a veritable feast, cloutie dumpling, pancakes and scones. These used to be richly spread with fresh butter and crowdie and cream but, sadly, there is no bovine population in Seilebost, and very few cattle graze anywhere on Harris. Milk comes in plastic bottles on the ferry. Isn't it sad? There used to be fresh butter and Jersey cream at The Currer, too, but Health and Safety rules insist that milk products, fed to guests, must be pasteurised. Eggs have to be stamped with a lion and surplus homemade cakes can't be donated to Retirement Homes. There goes a good way of life along with the rest of past joys and privileges.

Much later, the good lady accompanied us to the edge of the beach. It was exposed in all its glory for the tide was out. Barefoot and carefree we crossed the dazzling expanse, strolling, pausing frequently for the sea bed is interesting be you human or canine. There was no hurry. The sun had not yet reached its mid-day peak. We made the fascinating crossing of the bay, in shirt sleeves and shorts. Well bronzed as we were when we left Tiree, we were now a golden brown. A holiday is good for the skin as well as for the soul.

We had warned Rhoda to expect a visit so there was no need to introduce ourselves as we entered the school gate. We learned that others had been expected also. She had prepared a lunch for relatives intending to arrive at noon but who had phoned to say it would now be evening before they came. She had prepared generously for them. Soup was simmering on the hob and the kettle was boiling. Sandwiches had been cut and filled, cakes displayed and strawberries and cream at the ready.

The evening meal had also been anticipated. A chicken had been made ready for the oven. It was all too obvious that the lunch would be wasted unless we helped Rhoda to eat it. The soup was delicious, Danny and Meg helped to eat the sandwiches and who can say, 'no', when a headmistress insists you eat the strawberries and cream.

Then came the joy of viewing the schoolroom where just a handful of primary children learn about a world many miles away. It was my own environment, my village school profession. 'You are a lucky teacher,' I said, 'and they are lucky children.' I knew, for so had I been and such had been my children's primary school experience.

Before we left, Rhoda took our photograph sitting on the memorial bench with its inscription,

In memory of Rachel MacLeod, Lola,
from the Yorkshire children.

We left reluctantly but timed our leaving to catch the passing service bus, alighting at Northton. Here we were to call on Maggie and her two daughters. When we first met, Chrissie and Diane were children. Now they

Rachel's memorial seat with Danny and Meg.

are Care Workers looking after the elderly still in their homes. They are also Lady Farmers with a herd of Highland cattle. They were currently doing an evening call on John MacDonald. Catrina had suspected his problem was a urine infection and had insisted on a second dose of antibiotics. We were crossing our fingers, hoping it was having success little knowing that, at home, a similar scenario was in motion. There is an excellent team of Home Care workers on Harris and we seem to know them all. Fortunately a urine infection can be cleared with the use of antibiotics. We were to return home and find equal professionalism among care workers in our area.

Maggie and her daughters greeted us at the gate. It was the first time we had been without family or children. Always they had relieved us of our responsibilities. One had taken the arm of Aunty Mary, one had taken Harry and the third had taken both dog leads. Now it was our turn to be cared for. We felt like royalty. It was obvious and expected that Maggie was going to feed us and we have sampled her table so many times we know its excellence. Buckingham Palace can scarcely compete. 'Please, please,' we begged, 'let us go first to see Jessie and we've to call on the Scott-Forests. Then we will spend the rest of our time here.'

Jessie, too, had been our friend since we first went to Northton in the early sixties. Her daughter, Alice Ann, was one of the island Guides who joined us in camp. Jessie's husband, before his premature death, had found a farming affinity with my father and he had never hesitated to take responsibility for Harry.

We have never fathomed how the islanders get to know we are coming that day. By letter I had warned them to expect a visit but not the day nor the hour. Does the message arrive airborne on wind or wing, does it come in everyday croak from the corncrake or the baa-ing of sheep? Is it the heron that spills the beans or just the gossiping postman who sees us on his round? Who can tell. We suspect it might be Farquhar, the current coal man. Suffice it to say that, arriving at Jessie's, just a few doors away from Maggie's, we found the table set and the soup pot boiling. I caught Margaret's eye. 'Loosen your belt,' the silent message conveyed. The sensible thing to do would be to visit one person per day but our time is so limited and the distance between townships great. In all these fifty years of island hopping we have never persuaded the people to feed us sparingly.

'I am all ready for you,' said Jessie. 'I set the table this morning and made the sandwiches. But first the soup.' She should have used a qualifying adjective and said 'the delicious soup.' Soup, in Scotland is a meal in itself. So it is in Yorkshire at the family table. We call it stew and it is three times as nutritious as the starter we serve for holidaymakers. Scottish soup is full of vegetables and is served on a dish twice the size of a recognised soup bowl. It is a belly full of goodness and need not be, but always is, followed with sandwiches and scones, pancakes and cakes. Fortunately there is so much to talk about, eating can be slow.

Happy and very full, we strolled down to the post office to introduce ourselves to the Scott-Forests, incomers to the island, to whom we could

The newest arrival to Chrissie and Diane's herd.

say emphatically, 'Do not even think about feeding us!' As an English lady she was well aware of the wonderful generosity of her fellow villagers. Instead we all walked down onto the first of Northton's beautiful shell beaches. Our new companion had written saying she had read my books and wished to meet us. On the beach I told her we had once seen two enormous dogs, romping with their owner. 'That would be me,' she told us. Sadly the two monsters had been very old and had since died. She took us to the home of our late friend, Mary MacKay. Incomers live there now, who have two donkeys, the only ones we have encountered on the islands. Then we wended our way back to Maggie's for the feast we knew would be waiting.

Maggie, whatever the weather, has a roaring fire. We love it. We know that Maggie would be as caring for us as Rachel was, if need be, but all our dependents have gone. We first knew her when food on the island was homemade scones, crowdie and cream and bread was the variety almost black on top and bottom, unsliced and without side crusts. Every islander had hens and sandwiches were always chicken. Mother used to wish she could take strawberries for them from the Mainland, and salad vegetables from our garden. Forty years on and the mini- supermarket, An Clachan, at Leverburgh sells all of these. Maggie's salmon salad is a sight to behold and fresh fruit and cream always follow. We chatted and ate in comfort, by the glowing coals. Sadly little peat is now harvested. Harris used to smell of peat smoke. It greeted the ferry with as satisfying a welcome as any provided by the islanders. When it was time for the Home Carers to drive to Luskentyre, dogs and we were squeezed into the small car and, at the Luskentyre road end, our bikes were folded and rammed into the boot. Their transport hospitality goes all the way!

The sun was still hesitating above the North Harris mountains. We were in time to see it drop behind them in unbelievable splendour, as befitted a final curtain of an unforgettable day. We wonder if the next generation will know and sing, 'When you come to the end of a perfect day,' as we always do, albeit untunefully.

Guides, I'm sure, will still sing Taps. Where better than in Luskentyre? So we sang,

> Day is done, gone the sun,
> From the sea, from the hills from the sky.
> All is well, safely rest.
> God is nigh.

How I wish I could sing in tune. There's always tomorrow. A new day was born to revisit Scarista where, in the bungalow Aunty Mary called The Cloisters, there were new holiday residents but the door of the owners,

Mary Ann and Donald MacSween, was open in welcome. Aunty Mary, a Yorkshire woman, liked the close proximity of each room in the chalet, to the smallest one. 'They're all cloise t'toilet,' she'd said with gratitude, in the middle of the night. We have such happy and varied memories and every year we add more to the treasury.

We were managing quite well without a car. We alighted from the service bus at the road end, retrieved our bikes from the ditch and pedalled back to Luskentyre, our youthful enthusiasm brimming over. We'd been invited to have our evening meal with Kathleen and Bobby and toddler Kate, in their newly built house right on the edge of the beach at Luskentyre. It had been only at the planning stage, four years ago, on our last visit to the island. It had taken a long time to build and perfection showed in every room. We honestly believed it to be one of the most beautiful houses we have ever seen and we were full of praise for Bobby who had done so much of the work himself and for Kathleen who, we guessed, was behind the decor. Her father, Angus, had built his crofter's cottage, when he and Katie had married. The next generation are following suit and their contribution is almost majestic, without being imposing. The meal was excellent, too. The islands produce women of Master Chef ability.

But, sadly the holiday was nearly over. Angus parcelled up our cycles to take to the post and he took us to the road end for the morning bus from Tarbert to the Leverburgh slipway. It was a chilly morning and there was a stiff breeze when we boarded the ferry for Berneray and our return south, down the Long Island to Eriskay. We had come on this ferry a week ago and knew that Danny would not climb the metal ladder to the upper deck. It had not been a problem for there is the car deck mini-lounge and toilet for the disabled or elderly. We entered it immediately and found it deserted but there was a most obnoxious smell. No wonder every seat was empty. We were cold and are of the belief that you can get used to a queer smell if you have to. But we couldn't get used to that!

'It must be coming from the toilet,' Margaret said, hoping that just a flush would solve the problem. She opened the door of the fairly spacious vestibule and shut it immediately, speechless.

I am my mother's daughter. She would have had to look and so had I, taking no longer than a expellation of air and no intake before slamming the door. I have never seen anything quite so unexpected. Holding our breath we both dashed out onto the car deck. We knew too well what had happened but how remains a mystery. Boat toilets are flushed by pressure on a chrome button. There follows an energetic suction from below and everything disappears, presumably into a tank liberally dosed with chemicals. We have used chemical elsans on permanent campsites and have emptied them when full. In our early days of providing holiday accommodation we have put them in rooms for the handicapped, for convenience during the night. Emptying them is a job I'd willingly have given to any who'd offered but no-one, other than Margaret, ever did. My job was minimal compared with the job some crew member would have, clearing up the mess behind that door.

Something must have happened to the suction device and put its function in reverse. There had been nothing less than a volcanic eruption. Gallons of the contents of the tank below had been exploded. Chemically decomposing sewage and paper had been hurled onto walls and ceiling and was inches deep on the floor. The toilet seat had been blown off and was floating on the stinking mess.

We slammed the door shut and held our breath until once more out on the car deck. So often the problem is ours to solve, ten important two letter words being, 'If it is to be, it is up to me!' This one wasn't. Only a masked man and a hose pipe could have any effect. We were cowering on the freezing car deck when a member of the crew came by.

'Something's happened in the toilet,' we said and he looked at us with masculine intolerance. 'Women!' we guessed he was saying. He went in to investigate and shot out considerably alarmed. We were struggling not to laugh.

'Good God!!' he gasped.

'We didn't do it,' I said. In Yorkshire I would have said, as did five year old David, 'It warn't me,' even when it was, but the finger of blame was not being pointed. The sailor was concerned and advised us to go up the steps into the warmth but there was no way Danny was climbing the metal ladder. So the sailor brought us two deck chairs and we crossed the Sound sheltered by the windbreak of the car deck, freezing but chuckling. I seldom laugh at mass produced comedy- slapstick, possibly because we have so much real life variety and it is reality which is most amusing. I don't think the cleaner would agree. He didn't attempt to investigate further during the sail. He just locked the door. I went upstairs and put money in the machine and brought down some coffee.

Do the varied experiences of other people come in such rapid succession as ours? Is that why they continue to laugh at our escapades? Or do most people have a calmer life, where day follows day with similarity? We experience joy and sorrow, laughter and compassion, fear and confidence, chaos and tranquillity almost every hour of every day and it seems to have been that way always. The next episode can never be predicted. Who phones, who knocks on the door, who walks towards us, is as big a mystery as what a magician will take out of a hat. The only thing we can safely anticipate is that something, often bizarre, will happen soon.

Guests we had not met before observed, 'We haven't been here twenty minutes and enough has happened to interest the Warner Brothers!'

There was a time pause and a bus change on the outskirts of Lochboisdale and we were ready for a cup of tea but the driver said the only place to get one was at the hotel. We have two dogs and are not used to that level of social behaviour. Alighting within sight of the hotel, we were deciding we didn't require that sustenance when the driver suddenly said, 'The Charity Shop is still open. You'll get a cup of tea there.'

Sure enough, in the middle of nowhere, there was a second-hand sale, where we found an amazing welcome. The islanders on duty were about to close but were more than willing to make us tea, provide us with cakes and biscuits and to allow us to bring in our perfectly polite dogs. They were eager to talk. It was one of those wonderful island interludes. We have collected so many to store in our memory. Our hostesses made us welcome, as if we were celebrities, as they tidied up for closure.

Eventually we reached the Eriskay slipway and the ferry crossed the sound to Barra. Time was going like wildfire and there was no bus waiting on the jetty. The fear was that we were about to miss the only weekly boat to Oban via Tiree. It sails at 4 p.m. and if you are not there it goes. We enquired of the pier master but he was too busy and said he didn't know whether there was a bus or not. There was a party of youths with packs and tee shirts announcing 'I have climbed Everest', but there was no bus. We were beginning to panic having no time to phone for a taxi and there being no car in sight.

If we missed the boat we would have to retrace our steps to Lochboisdale and find overnight accommodation. We would be a day late at the hotel in Oban and there would be no train to Glasgow until Monday. At home Barbara and Kathleen were preparing to leave. Dorothy would have the mammoth task of coping with the departure of sixteen Shakespearian actors, and the big wash that would entail. It was our job, not her's. She would most likely have a dog show weekend! She usually did. But, at the very last minute the bus came. The driver was surprised we were dashing for the boat. Were we the only travellers ever to come from Eriskay and wish to catch the ferry to Oban? We, who always hope the vehicle goes slowly, be it on Island or Mainland, begged the driver to get us there on time. He did, but only just. We scrambled up the gangway with relief, as always for the journey to success is always scary.

The dogs were tired and we were able to tether them just outside the open door of the observation lounge, seat ourselves on comfortable uphol-stery and begin to think about home, something we had not done all fortnight. The sail was calm, the lounge all but empty. I brought mugs of the most delicious soup from the cafeteria and we drank them slowly, in comfort. Eventually the boat pulled into Tiree again, just seven days after we had enjoyed our holiday there. It could have been seven years, so far back in time it seemed.

As we sailed down the Sound of Mull, the sun went to sleep beneath the most beautiful of star studded bedspreads. When we sailed into Oban it was dark enough for the illumination of street lamps. The quay was ablaze and moored ferry boats were so ornamented with light we could have been approaching some southern coastal resort. We were back on the Mainland safely, homeward bound.

We dropped our minute rucksacks on the floor of the hotel bedroom and I said, 'Let's have a bath.' We belong to the generation used to one bath a week.

'You go first. Leave the water and I'll follow,' Margaret said. It is normal for us. The youngsters today waste too much water and power and surely must injure their skin with too much heat and soap! I go first. Age before beauty Margaret insists. I prefer to call it clean before dirty. This is true in winter-time when Margaret is a full-time farmer!

The ensuite was reasonably spacious but without a window. I had just lowered myself into the water when the lights went out and the darkness was impenetrable. It was never so dark at The Currer. Even before we had electricity we had always had candles. Margaret opened the drawn curtains in our bedroom and the light from the waterfront and the moored ferries, illuminated the room but, even with the bathroom door open, it was dark within. We got the giggles. I towelled and dressed fully and Margaret took my place in the bath whilst I went out onto the first floor corridor. It was dimly lit with the emergency light, triggered by the electricity cut. Two guests were on the landing. They came from Calderdale. He had been downstairs and reported that the proprietor was in a tizz. I know just what it feels like having been in that situation.

'It's just like Fawlty Towers on television!' the woman said.

We have often felt an affinity with Basil Fawlty! We eventually crept under the covers, with the curtains wide open and all the excitement of the lighted harbour at our bedside.

We had to wake early and breakfasts were not served until after the train left the station, so we were grateful that the power had been returned and we could make a cup of coffee before leaving. Oban is wonderful in the early morning even if the journey is now homeward. We hadn't phoned since leaving Harris. When there is no way of getting home any quicker, it is unwise to make enquiries! We think so anyway.

The morning air was crisp and tasted of salt. The train was almost empty. Across the passage was an elderly couple, from London, with a little dog as well behaved as ours. It transpired that they had relatives at Steeton, a mere five miles away from us. 'See you sometime in Keighley,' we called when we left them in Queens Street station.

We were met there by Ellen MacInnes, from Salum, Tiree and her sister Christine's husband, Matt. They had a sumptuous picnic for us and they led us to seats in St George Square. It was teeming with people. A huge stage had been erected for some annual festival. Although it was only midday, musicians were already active and the noise was tremendous. We are unaccustomed to volume. For two weeks we had heard only wind and waves, seabirds calling and the soft sound of the Gaelic. At The Currer there is only distant noise. We wondered what the dogs would make of this outpouring of musical exuberance. Amazingly they took it in their stride and followed meekly at heel when, later, we threaded our way along busy city streets to Central Station.

We had travelled hundreds of miles among dog-friendly people and were flabbergasted to find, on reaching our home station, that not one of the parked taxis would take Danny and Meg. We were about to walk.

'Let's just phone the firm we usually call for David Hart patients,' I suggested.

With final success we waited patiently and were amused when the driver spread a foot square piece of plastic on the front seat and really did think two, big collies would sit on it together all the way home. Margaret clambered onto the sheet with Meg cramped at her feet and Danny sitting on her knee, closer to her than he had ever been!

'Now for it!' we said. 'Let's see what awaits us at The Currer!'

Chapter Seven

You can stand on your head for a fortnight, if you have
to!

Grandma Smith, 1870–1942

W E WERE REARED ON THIS THEORY. If you have to, you can! Father
urged us always to 'keep right on to the end of the road', for it can be
reached. Though long and wearying it, in real life, does not 'wind upward
all the way'. Nor does it continue to plummet downhill for ever, because
you can only go so far down before it begins to rise again and, as an added
blessing, there are level stretches of the road. There are milestones too, where
you can rest and look at the map, crossroads where you can change direction
and, best of all, there are encounters. Others are travelling too and provide

> Good cheer to help you bear the traveller's load,
> And for the hours of rest that come between,
> An inward joy in all things heard and seen.
>
> Van Dyke

It is wise to remember, too, that the end of the road is never insight until
you have rounded the last bend.

I have recently been concerned in case today's children are not being fed
the proverbial sayings and wise quotations on which we, their predecessors
were reared. I do not speak the language of Pop Songs so may be missing
out on something. Maybe their lyrics have a wisdom my ageing ears cannot
interpret, so I cannot be their judge. All I know is that, untuneful though I
be, I have a song for every occasion, every hour of the day, every season of
the year, and every emotion. I have a prayer befitting every need and every
emergency. I have a quotation offering wisdom and comfort to share with
others, whatever comes our way and a song of praise, always on hand, to
warble my joie de vive.

If there is language, to be beneficial it must be rich, for words are peace-
makers, shock absorbers, stress moderators, laughter stimulants and a
child's memory box should be fed ad lib. If you have missed being taught
that 'you can stand on your head for a fortnight, if you have to,' a helpline
is unavailable when you most need it. If you take nothing else away from
these pages, remember my grandmother. But take my added warning.

Having been upside down for quite some time, for a while expect to have a headache and a stiff neck!

I think, perhaps, we love our home more than most. It has been our creation. Peeping through the keyhole you would have no difficulty in deciding whose house is this? Coming home to what we normally feel to be a sanctuary of our making, is one of the most difficult things we do. In order that we can become re-energised on the edge of nowhere, others, friends, lifesavers have lived our life in our house and the only thing which is recognisable is the string of problems with which they have had to cope. They narrate them immediately we cross the threshold, as if problems here are unusual and that their capability in coping with them is equally so.

As a rule we leave them with the minimum of tragic possibilities but life at The Currer is accident prone and whilst we have tremendous respect for our stand-ins, we think they are crazy to accept responsibility anyway. For an hour or two, we listen with sympathy to all their reports of near calamity. Returning in 2003 was worse than usual. Dorothy took Margaret aside to unload her tale of woe and the resident cousins bombarded me with an update on our old lady and the-twice-a day visit of the Home Carers.

Our fear had been that Aunty Mary would die whilst we were away and we hadn't wanted that. After a quarter of a century of housing holiday-makers we know that, so often, members of a family die whilst their loved ones are away. We have taken many phone calls and said goodbye to those whose holiday has ended abruptly. I am not sure that Aunty Mary ever really classed us as loved ones. Certainly she didn't greet us with open arms. I think she was very cross with us but she was alive. It was not she but Jasper, our 24 year old, white donkey who had died in our absence.

We would have greeted this news with disbelief but for the fact that his friend, Joe, the brown one, was standing with his head down, totally bereft. Donkeys mourn almost as a human would. He was utterly distraught. His friend had been unexpectedly ill. Strangers had forced Jasper back to the buildings. A vet had come and immediately Jasper was dead. Before long a removal van had taken him away and there was no Margaret to comfort him so he was not going to eat either. He didn't much care whether he lived or not.

We heard the rest of the mishaps experienced by The Currer residents, whilst we had been away, with little enthusiasm. Our caretakers always remind me of five year old Alison who repeatedly came to the staffroom to begin every report with, 'You don't know, Miss Brown.' We were back. We just needed to hold the reins and pick up where we had left off. We'd find another donkey to comfort Joe. We'd have to or lose him, too.

Aunty Mary had been quite ill whilst we had been enjoying a carefree holiday and had Fiona, the doctor wife of cousin Michael, not been here to insist on a second dose of antibiotics, we may have lost her too. It had been our fear. She didn't look very well and we were mightily glad to be home.

We said our grateful thanks and goodbyes to the many courageous people who had given us the opportunity to have such a wonderful holiday and we introduced ourselves to the Shakespearian theatre group, Chapter House, who were self-catering whilst performing at Harewood House. Homecoming is always difficult! This one was particularly traumatic.

Infants have a slant on life worthy of pursuit. Gillian had told me, nearly fifty years ago, 'I don't grumble, Miss Brown. I just get on with it.' So must we!

First we had to meet the Home Carers who had supported our relatives so well. We had thought that, on our return, we would be able to cancel their help but we never did. They were so cheerful and Aunty Mary liked them. There comes a time when even those as independent as we, must accept help.

We began immediately the search for a new donkey. The Shakespearian actors were replaced by some guests needing serviced accommodation and among them was a lady with a dog. She was very concerned about our distressed donkey and when we told her we were searching and that donkeys were very expensive, possibly that we would have to pay nothing short of £600, she was shocked. When she got home her dog wrote to Joe saying that his mistress could afford to help pay for him a new friend. There was a cheque for £300 in the envelope. It arrived simultaneously with our success in finding Bobby. Tim had seen the advertisement in a farmers' journal and had been with his trailer to collect him. The price had been only £350. We returned the dog's donation with many thanks. It was such a nice gesture and we did appreciate it, but we could not let others pay for our animals. Joe left his wailing wall and seemed happy, accepting Bobby as a friend in need.

Everyone loves the donkeys. Everyone brings carrots and apples for them and ignores our lovely cattle. To us the donkeys are free spirits, wandering wherever their fancy takes them, hardly needing us at all. We do not feed them titbits and only ever restrain them when the blacksmith comes to trim their hooves. They are neither friend nor foe. They have no purpose but to live and entertain our guests. They are nearly as wild as the fallow deer we welcome but could not tame, or the goats who are a law unto themselves. For a little while Bobby was a nuisance chasing dogs. There are many dog walkers on our land. He also pestered those who brought him treats so we had to put up notices which said, 'Do not feed the donkeys.' That made us unpopular for a time. After a few weeks Joe had taught him good behaviour and he has been no trouble since.

We, of course, love cattle. If donkeys, deer and goats are in the category of neighbours, cattle are family. We cannot understand why most of the people who come ignore them. As calves they are utterly dependent on Margaret for food and health, shelter and warmth and only become partially independent in adolescence. To see them leave the nest as adults would destroy us if we weren't off to the market to buy some more babies.

They were currently out at grass and causing us no concern but Aunty Mary was. When we returned we feared she was on a downward spiral. One night, during our first week home, she became worse. We'd had a problem with the lift and had sent for the specialist engineer. He had come very late and, quite honestly we, and the carers, thought it impossible to get her upstairs. She had slept once in the recliner whilst we had been away, when Fiona had thought she might lose her. So we left her where she was and I slept on the divan and Margaret on the floor of the sitting room.

Next morning the carers found a quite nasty bed sore on her heel and another at the bottom of her spine and told us to send for the district nurses. They said she must never sleep in the recliner again and that a bed must be brought down stairs. One of us could sleep on the divan in the sitting room alcove. We could take it in turns. They said she must lie down every afternoon, the carers must come at midday and again at four. A few days later they said she must have a hospital bed and an electric mattress and she must have a hoist to lift her in and out of bed. We insisted that the hospital bed should be taken upstairs. There was absolutely no reason why nights could not be spent aloft. We had a perfectly good wheelchair lift. The bed we had brought down could remain in the alcove for emergencies and afternoon siesta. But the delivery men could not get the hospital bed upstairs. It was massive and the wheelchair lift looked like being redundant.

So, too, the enclosed ensuite and double sized shower well, Brian was nearing completion in her bedroom. We were disappointed about this for it had been specially designed for her use, with all the necessary disablement gadgets. Our downstairs shower being in the domain of holidaymakers most of the time, we had deemed one in Aunty Mary's room absolutely necessary.

We struggled back upstairs with our rejected bed and allowed the men to carry the enormous, clumsy replacement into the alcove. From that day our front room became a hospital ward. The improvement in Aunty Mary's health became promising but she made no effort to move. Her twelve stone weight was still to be lifted every where. We avoided the use of the hoist for months, for it was humiliating. Aunty Mary's size was not extreme but it was a dead weight and floppy and alerted us, and it should others, to the disaster overweight people will face when age means they require assistance. Our carers came four times a day and if they hadn't been so cheerful, so wonderfully competent at their job, so happy in their profession, I think we would have gone mad. Even Aunty Mary enjoyed their visits. They knew what to say and she was ready with a regular answer.

'Are you all right, Aunty Mary?' they said on every arrival.

'Half left!' was her daily reply, or 'Once was!' was an alternative. Sometimes she would recite, 'It's not the cough that carries you off, it's the coffin they carry you off in!' She had a memory box full of quotations and poems.

Her masterpiece was the recitation of a letter sent to her grandparents in 1878, by a George Schoon, an employee on the local newspaper. She was never to persuade and her memory was perfect.

Dear Friends,

Your invitation kind is just the thing to suit our mind. There scarcely is another place, we so well like to show our face. You so remind us of the time when we were young and in our prime. Those days, alas, are gone forever, their like we'll see again, ah never.

Oft when at work I am intent, a moment's glimpse to me is sent of days that we together spent. I then, in fancy often roam those scenes about our native home, where oft we wandered out together, in pastures fair or blooming heather. To Bingley Altar or to Ilkley town, by River Aire through fields with flowers strewn, with you two just before or just behind, looking so loving and so very kind, as if a frown would never cross your faces, you seem to be possessed of all the graces. And time, I think, has proved it so to be for such another couple I never did see. Jane's face is a sign for all Dull Care to take itself away and live elsewhere.

Her hospitality so full and free, her table, when set out, is grand to see and yet she shyly will pretend to say, 'My friends, I'm sorry I hev nowt today'. This often would my good wife's mother tickle. She'd say, 'Now lass, th'art in a bonnie pickle. Think on, nah tha axes me when tha hez summat, then let's see. There really isn't room nah on the table top for thee to cram another cake or pot!'

Peace to her memory, she's gone the way we all must follow at no distant day. Caroline and I have now no parents left. May it be long before you are so bereft.

Last time I saw your father in the town, I noticed he was grey and venerable grown. I have not, for a long time, seen your mother, nor yet your George, your most illustrious brother, you're going to honour in your baby's name and I consider honour me the same.

But of these weary lines I'm sure you'll tire and tempted be to throw them on the fire. Well, to make it short, we'll do ourselves the pleasure of coming to see your little treasure. We'll Bradford leave by train at 10 a.m. and get to Keighley I can scarce tell when.

And now, hoping you are all in the best of health and gradually creeping on in wealth and that your lives will long and happy be and that we shall each other often see, I'll bring my rhyming letter to an end and when I write again I'll try to mend. I'm in a hurry now to get my dinner. Believe me,

Ever yours,

the same old sinner.

Increasingly we wish we had Aunty Mary on tape. I began to recognise so much of Grandfather Smith in her. He didn't converse properly either. 'Sit yourself down and walk about a bit,' he'd say or, 'I nivver saw yer, weer wa' yer sat?' We, as children, always laughed at him and so did the carers at Aunty Mary. She repeated things over and over again, and basked in their appreciation and welcomed their applause. It all helped to make things easy that could have been difficult.

Whilst we had been on holiday our, eighty year old cousin Freda had been in hospital and was currently in a convalescent home. Social Services had provided us with a sitter for two hours every week. This enabled us to do our shopping. We went together, one to drop out and one to drive and to hesitate on double yellow lines whilst the clock ticked away, mercilessly. We were to become time scavengers. Visitors to Aunty Mary were greeted with a request to hang on whilst we dashed to the boundary, to count cattle, to run to whatever needed attention. On one two hour respite, we went to the Care Home where Freda was and found her very unhappy indeed. She had no downstairs facilities in her own home. Wheels were being set in motion for alterations to be made and Home Care arranged, but in the meantime she was very tearful. We had no occupants of the Mistal, our ground floor cottage, that week so we said she could come to us providing her daughter came to sleep overnight. Our friends said we were crazy, or soon would be, if we had two invalids to care for. At the end of the week arrangements were still incomplete for her return home to the farmhouse, our joint grand-parents had occupied in our childhood. We brought her into a ground floor bedroom and our friends almost had the opportunity to say, 'I told you so!' We had carers coming four times a day and Freda had Health visitors and District Nurses coming to talk over the possibility of getting her back into her own home, making the necessary adjustments and ordering equipment. All the while we continued to serve breakfasts and some evening meals.

By the time Freda was able to go home, Aunty Mary was getting appreci-ably better but she still had the ulcer on her heel. Sadly Hilda, her friend, was dying. She had her 101st birthday in hospital and was never to go home again. When discharged she went into care and in July she died. We did not know whether to tell Aunty Mary or not but decided we must.

'I think I should go to the funeral,' she said unexpectedly.

'You don't need to,' I said, wondering however we would manage it. 'We'll go, you stay at home.' But she would not hear of it.

There are many steps into the village chapel but there is a second door which leads straight in on the level, through which I had pushed Aunty Mary for Hilda's hundredth birthday celebration. There was no problem, we were told. We could get in easily. The caretaker had the key. We knew, however, that we would not be able to get Aunty Mary into the Land Rover. We were advised to phone Dial-a-ride and a van, we nickname a

'popemobile', would come. Several of our guests have such vehicles. Social
Services gave me a number and I booked the hire. It did not come on time
and we were getting agitated. The phone rang and the driver, with very
poor English, said he was lost. Indeed he was three miles away and, having
a language difficulty, posed a real problem. Speaking very slowly I tried
hard to direct him here but I was not over confident that he would. We
must, at all costs, be represented at Hilda's funeral. We had never been part
of her family but she had been part of ours. We had taken her almost everywhere we went and brought her frequently to The Currer. Here she had
spent Christmas, New Year, Easter and Whitsuntide. She had expected us
to ask her, just as Aunty Mary had, ringing to say had we forgotten her if
we had been delayed. We were often late, due to last minute interruptions,
but to be late for her funeral must be avoided. When Hilda had been told, a
while back, by some outside authority, that she must not get into the Land
Rover, her life-line had been cut. She had been more capable of getting in
than Aunty Mary but with real family you can take risks. You can push and
shove and shout but with adopted family you must be careful and do as
you are told, obey all the rules. The routine of ringing her daily had never
stopped until she went into care. Initially Aunty Mary rang every morning
and Hilda rang every evening. When, through Aunty Mary's deafness and
Hilda's disappearing voice, they could no longer converse, and to do so
became 'purgatory', Margaret assumed the phoning role. I really believe
everyone should have a 'hands on' experience of the very old so that a
behaviour lesson is learned for when it is your turn! Perhaps, then, you will
be less demanding. Hilda had been vocally demanding. Aunty Mary's was
silence which spoke loudly indeed! Our nuclear family had never become
intolerant as they did.

Some of our guests were just leaving and Margaret begged a lift up to
the chapel in the village. There wasn't time to open the garage doors and get
out our own car. The congregation was beginning to filter in. A Dial-a-ride
van dropped a lady outside the gate and drove away. Margaret was witness
and ran after it shouting, but was not heard. Unable to do anything about
that, she went into the chapel and chose a pew near the side door. Then she
checked to see that it had been unlocked. It had not! The minister said that
only the caretaker had a key and he had gone to work. Not to worry, the
minister said, they would carry Aunty Mary in. Margaret nearly laughed out
loud at the very thought of our old lady agreeing to be carried in to any but
her own funeral! She was sure the minister would never have suggested it,
either, had he known her weight. But the likelihood of either she or me being
there at all, was getting smaller.

The lost driver phoned again and this time I managed to direct him but
he called again from the cattle grid saying there was no way he would come
down our road. I could see him there and it wasn't the Dial-a-ride it was the

Bradford Access Bus, a twenty seater, very low to the road. I took a deep breath.

'Low cars come down frequently,' I told him. 'Buses seating fifty come from Holland. Loads of straw and cattle wagons come safely and we are already late for the funeral!'

If I'd known we could not get into the chapel, I'd have cancelled the hire and let him go, but believing in better late than never, I insisted and we got there, very late! It would not matter! We could just creep in the side door without being seen. The door made an awful noise when I tried, unsuccessfully, to open it and the service halted whilst Margaret got up and came out to tell me and silence me. It was extremely embarrassing. I pushed the wheelchair out of the wind and we waited until the proceedings were over and the coffin carried out. I do not think Aunty Mary knew what was happening. I pushed her towards the hearse but she was unmoved and responded cheerfully to friends who came to her. They asked her if she was well and she said, 'Once was!' I prayed she would not say, 'It's not the cough that carries you off …,' which was so often her reply and which would have been highly inappropriate. My suspicion that she had no idea where we were, was confirmed that evening when carers asked her where she had been and she said she'd had a trip out to the park!

A member of the congregation whispered to Margaret, 'Wouldn't Hilda have been amused?'

Margaret answered, 'Certainly not! I'm afraid she would have been horrified!' For a hundred years Hilda's theme tune had been 'punctuality' and a sense of humour had never been one of her characteristics. Fortunately it is one of ours. However could we get through the day without laughter?

One useful tip came from this otherwise rather embarrassing experience. The real Dial-a ride van had brought Lily Best to the funeral and she was able to give us the correct phone number so that we could use the service on future occasions. We proved we could be driven to St Ives and left for a couple of hours, with time to push the wheel chair round the lakeside and then end up at the ice cream van. I'm not sure Aunty Mary really appreciated it for she still blamed us for not taking her in the Land Rover. We tried a different trip out when Emilie came from France, by hiring the 'popemobile' to take us to Cliffe Castle, in town. The heat of that summer was almost unbearable. The flowers, usually so beautiful in the castle grounds, were desperately in need of rain.

We asked someone to sit with Aunty Mary whilst we stole a day out, with Emilie, at Bolton Abbey. We tried to walk to the Strid but it was too far in the time we had. I hurried the others and walked so fast my ankles became quite painful and Margaret scolded me, saying I was taking life far too seriously. Being Hellfire Jack would get me nowhere. Fortunately we had no guests to feed for the group currently in, were self-catering. It was another visit by the Lloyds who love it so much they have returned often.

Emilie, at eighteen, was a tremendous help during the period of her holiday month. We realised we might not see her again for some time for university lay ahead and she had already assumed holiday jobs at the hospital in Lyon. Time, we felt, was accelerating. We must be growing older. We hoped it was far more noticeable in Emilie, tall and very beautiful, than it was in us slower and greyer.

An exciting project was under way on our summit. We have acres of flat land on our Pennine ridge, forming the southern wall of Airedale. Furthest away from the farmstead are the eight fields we still call the Meadows. Indeed hay was taken from them annually before 1980, except for the war years when government ordered that corn, must be grown. It was a nonsense, really, for corn crops cannot be grown at this altitude and be harvested before the sun cools and the days shorten for the autumn. Successive governments have more than enough to do without interfering in farming, education and medicine, about which they apparently know little.

Growing corn on a mountain certainly did not work. I have childhood memories of stooking the sheaves which would have to be fed unthrashed to the cattle. To make hay in September was to feed it mouldy in January. Similarly the unripened sheaves never dried out properly but to be uncooperative, during the war, was to lose your land. So we had sown oats.

Where the corners of four meadows meet, our skilled ancestors had dug out a hollow and lined it with clay before cobbling it. The bottom of the inverted cone is six feet deep and the walls are at a 45 degree slope. By some forgotten magic, this hollow was always permanently full of water and the feature was called the Dewpond. All this structure was invisible in my youth but, over many years of allowing crops to seed before harvesting, a growth of grass round the perimeter began to choke the reservoir and slowly, as it began to dry and more forage grew amongst the cobbles, the water disappeared and the pond was no more. The cobbles and the depth could now be seen but there seemed nothing we could do about it until our acceptance on the Countryside Stewardship Scheme was conditional that we did. Experts giving advice did not understand how it worked and said it must fill from drainage. That was not very bright of them for the pond is on the horizon and it certainly wasn't a tarn for the builders of it had lined it to prevent water draining away and, in so doing, had prevented it from rising. It remained a mystery, for those who came said it couldn't be just a collector of dew. I did however uncover an article in the reference library. It suggested the original builders first monitored the channel, up which the morning mist rose from the valley before hanging for a time on the hill, prior to dispersal. Throughout the nearly fifty years we have lived here, we have frequently wakened to find a lake of mist above the river, deceiving us that Airedale was really in the Lake District. We have watched the spiral of mist wend its way up the hillside and hover over the meadows.

The Dewpond.

Work began in the summer of 2003 and was completed in September. The expert of the project was none other than our own waller, Graham Foster. Together, the men cleaned out the overgrown hollow. They took out the cobbles, stone by stone to be replaced exactly as it had first been built and a new lining was laid. This time clay was not used. Plastic replaced it for time was important. When completely rebuilt it was an interesting sight, soon to be lost for, incredibly, in a very short time the pond, deep as it was, was filled to the brim. Magic!

Little by little the fallen walls were being erected and the farm was looking cared for. We were into the seventh year of stewardship and the 4500 meters would have been near completion had not the Foot and Mouth standstill lost us a year. We still had three left of the ten year project. Hopefully two would be enough to finish the marathon task. Ancient walls are bound to tumble. Deterioration in everything accelerates and it is wisdom to put a stop to it early, be it property, health, behaviour, global warming or whatever. An abandoned building is soon derelict, health cannot be neglected, naughtiness quickly becomes delinquency and once ice begins to thaw, it is gone.

When wood begins to rot it will no longer restrain cattle. The heavily fenced walls of our loading pen showed signs of the wear and tear of generations of two year old bullocks. The uprights were sawn telegraph poles and they had begun to wobble. A dozen years ago it would have restrained elephants but more than a thousand cattle had seriously weakened it. We were proud of the loading pen. It was conveniently sited against the west wall of the top bullock shed and animals were easily directed out of the shed and into the pen, even when the transporting lorry was in place. It was also built on an upward slope so that they must walk downhill before stepping onto the ramp which, because of the slope, was not so steep as it would have been from the level.

It is necessary to stay in any job for a long while, for perfection is not achieved instantly. We had, in the late fifties and sixties, loaded cattle from the stone barn, adjacent to our house and that had taught us the first priority. Load them from a downward slope. When we built the Dutch barn and converted the stone one we learned the second priority. Cattle will always enter a shed where there is fodder. We made sure the entry was on the summit of a slope. It was not until 1990 that we reached near perfection with telegraph poles and now they had begun to weaken.

Margaret asked John to replace the rotting timbers and he suggested motorway barriers which, being metal, would never need renewal. As usual he was doing it at the last minute, late August, ready for use when cattle must go to the end of the month sale.

We had more yearling cattle than usual after the overstocked year of the epidemic. Lest we run short of grass, Margaret let the big cattle down from the hill, for their last weeks before sale. John was busy reconstructing the loading pen when the phone rang and our neighbour at Roydfield, Dennis Rawson- Chad, told us that some of our two year olds had broken through the fence into his pastures, and had joined his herd and his bull.

Imagine our horror! Where they had made a break through was way down our mountainside, where there are hawthorns and bracken and a multitude of blackberry bushes. It would be almost impossible to drive them out and should we succeed, it was almost inevitable that Rawson-Chad's suckling herd and bull would accompany them. Glory be! We were already preparing the evening meal for fifteen people and John and his son were packing up their tools ready to go. I dashed out to insist they did not leave until we had got our animals back. As we were going to need more than just two strong men, I ran into the sitting room for reinforcements in the shape of Hayley, a fourteen year old guest who wanted to be a vet and her mother who didn't and we all hurried down to the lowest corner of our land and the tell tale broken fence. I felt my age as never before. Margaret seemed more agile than I was and it was she who went with the healthy Sugdens to round up our strays and I who stayed at the gap ready to turn them home. I widened it for cattle will break out through a hair's breadth but require a gateway to return. Dennis Rawson-Chad was waiting with the nine, soon to be sold, bullocks and, miraculously, they were alone. Not one of his suckling herd was in sight, nor his bull. To return them was not too difficult either, with two strong men, Hayley and her mother and a jubilant pair of dogs. I found the return climb wicked. My ankles were tired out. Just as they had been at Bolton Abbey. They have always been too thin and liable to sprain.

We made and served the evening meal and presumed the episode was over but our neighbour rang next morning to say there were 'hundreds' of our cattle on his land, hobnobbing with his suckled herd. How could we have been so stupid as to think only nine would stray? Usually it's all or nothing. This time there was Tim, walling in the low pasture, to come to help and we took with us a ten foot iron gate to replace the fence for several years to come.

This time separating them was more difficult and, having done so we very securely tied up the gate and headed back up the steep slope, mucky, scratched and torn. There has been such a lot of hawthorn growth in that area since my childhood. Bread and cheese, we used to call the edible leaves. It is uphill all the way back to the house but only the first bit is very steep and carpeted with brambles. With a job finished successfully one is allowed to pause and relax and view the dale with pleasure for, at that point the man-made scars are hidden. You cannot see the rapidly growing industrial estate with its acres and acres of tin, nor the hundreds of new houses crammed on the hillside above the canal. Nor can one see the town. There is only the spectacular view of the valley. Even the bypass is unobtrusive and the massive growth of the village of Silsden is too distant to offend.

We stood there, nursing our wounds and recovering our breath and our gaze fell again onto the pastures belonging to our neighbour and our jaws dropped with horror as we saw, below us, even more of our straying cattle. I was incapable of going back down that mountainside. I hovered watching whilst Margaret, Tim and the dogs returned. Had they had trouble, I like to think I would have followed but the strays were eager to join their own herd and were not to persuade with force, so I was never put to the test. The whole herd of two year olds came for water and, as you may suspect, Margaret counted them. Twice, before returning them to our own hill and securing the gates to keep them there. Strangely I had no further ankle trouble. I now know the cure. Should it happen again I will run twice, up and down that precipitous hillside and all will be well.

A few days later the newly reinforced loading pen had its debut and the first batch was sold. We followed the second load of the day in the Land Rover, for the first time without passengers. There was no Harry and we were now unable to get Aunty Mary into the front seat, so a friend came to stay with her. After the Royd Field fiasco the round up had been relatively easy and the selected stores had walked meekly, without stress, up the ramp and into the wagon. The loading pen was perfect. For the first time for me and for decades for Margaret, we bought and ate a Cornish pasty in the Market Cafe. It marked the beginning of a new era, a farming twosome. It was a new experience to be able to sit chatting to other stockmen. Alison, at the counter, was the mother of children I had taught, children now in their thirties. I laughingly told her I was carrying a small cushion to sit more comfortably on the hard seats of the auction ring. The cattle sold well and whilst we were waiting for the cheque to be processed, we stayed in the ring watching two year old cattle selling for a fair price and yearling heifers going for a song. Our intake the previous year, of new born bull calves, had been less than normal. We had bought a handful of weaned calves in March but our total was still low. Margaret took a risk and bid for cheap yearling heifers. I think we were eager for a new project to colour the monotony of our daily life.

Defining monotony is interesting in itself. Surely our life could never be described as monotonous. It varies by the hour but the routine of holiday-makers and carers, cheerful though both were, was beginning to get at us. An autumn holiday would have refuelled us but we had to be satisfied with buying some new heifers to provide the tonic we needed.

Most women shop for ladies accessories to satisfy their craving. What a funny pair we are that we prefer buying cattle. The newcomers settled down at once and we had new life in us. Margaret bought again at the next sale, four sturdy Angus heifers. They, and our own yearlings, were let up on to higher ground to join the remaining twenty six bullocks so that, by following the seniors still remaining, they could be taught the geography of the wider pastures. Margaret thinks this is a necessary part of educating easy-to-handle cattle. I must say she is successful. She can handle her cattle. There is no doubt about that!

When the final two year olds were sold the pastures looked reasonably well stocked and the sheds would be full over winter.

We were in control outside. Inside the Currer hospital ward it was a different story. The district nurses, try as they might, were having negligible success with Aunty Mary's heel ulcer. It began to have a gangrenous smell and we were horrified for guests frequently came to visit her. One was a male nurse from Norfolk and he wrote down some instructions advising the nurses of a better way. They were determined to be unbeaten and, quite quickly, the ulcer healed. Too quickly, in fact for the healed surface hid an infection. Aunty Mary's leg began to swell alarmingly and the nurses sent for a doctor we had not met before. He feared thrombosis but Margaret was sure it was just a buried infection and asked a visiting vet what his diagnosis would have been and he agreed with her. When our own doctor came, so did she and antibiotics soon reduced the leg to normal. We seemed to be allergic to problems but, one by one we were solving them, ticking the answer boxes.

With a semblance of normality in our old lady's health, we decided to insist she went upstairs to bed and our wheelchair lift was in use again. We transferred the electric mattress aloft and the hospital bed, no longer needed was taken away. Our every-other-day night on the sitting room divan became a thing of the past.

We had closed the gates on the meadows to keep the herd nearer home for the sale gathering and also because we had become nervous of the recently constructed dewpond. It was a new, potentially dangerous hazard where cattle were concerned. Margaret told the wallers to put a fence round it. I was glad because I knew my sister would not sleep if she thought she might find an animal drowned. I had seen more than one cow carcass floating in the canal, behind my school and it isn't a pleasant sight. So the dewpond became a feature but not an amenity. We'd rather the cattle came home to drink, anyway. In that way Margaret can monitor them twice a day, once on foot and once with binoculars.

Perhaps if Margaret had had less work, or lighter work, she would have fully recovered from that unfortunate fall. Lifting, carrying and calf- rearing, cooking, dishwashing and decorating, caring constantly for Aunty Mary and bringing many hods of coke a day, out of the cellar, gave little opportunity to do so.

We tried to lighten some of the duties with the use of the Land Rover. We no longer scorned those who checked cattle by wheeled transport. When teenage cattle were moved to the hill we could do this comfortably. The juniors had entered the senior school and, like all their predecessors, they loved their room at the top. All except one Limousin who suddenly went down with what can only be described as treble pneumonia. To have contracted this terrible, viral infection near home would have been a tragedy but to become so ill, so far from shelter was unusual and almost certainly would prove fatal. We found it panting and struggling for breath, its dripping, frothing mouth wide open, a mile away from our caring environment.

There seemed no way of getting it home other than in the calf trailer. We hurried home to attach it to the tow bar and, with an injection ready to use, we returned to the gasping animal. Dying it seemed to be, but it still had enough strength to resist. Try as we might we were unable to loaden it. We stressed it even more by trying and quickly gave in. Margaret managed the all important injection but that was all.

It was still alive next day and when the herd came home for water it came with them. Whether it managed to reach the trough but could not make the return journey, or sank to its knees before reaching its destination, we were unsure but, returning from town, we saw the herd on the hill and one black dot, a quarter of a mile from the water hole.

We hurried across the three fields expecting to find it dead, but it wasn't and we managed to heave it onto its feet and, very slowly, steadying it all the way, we finally got it through the gate, onto the road. There it could go no further. It sat on the tarmac and blocked the road. Knowing guests would be arriving we had to phone for Tim. Had the shovel been on the Kramer, Margaret would have managed but there was only the grab and that bit of technology, she did not know! We only ever send for help as a last resort.

Safely housed in the calf shed it began to recover. Life is an extraordinary, tenacious thing and it is an insult to the Almighty to label a disease as terminal. Margaret never ever does. She tries. It's who she is. We did not immediately return it to the herd so it was there to befriend the next casualty. The four sturdy heifers we had bought at market remained aloof. They were seldom with the herd, snooty in the extreme. They began to frequent the Dyke field into which we had expanded and built our bovine village. There is, at the west-end, a direct entry into the calf shed. Margaret was to be seen frequently with binoculars, monitoring the newcomers and one day, when all the bullocks were on the hill, this very feminine four were alone in the Dyke Field, close to the house, Margaret noticed one was very blown. Its belly was like a balloon and, somehow, the heifer must be brought in and the gas let out. We have known animals to die very quickly in this condition. Having four stomachs, a cow's digestive system is very complicated. Caught early enough Margaret can release this gas with a syringe needle but it was all too evident this was a job for the vet and a permanent red devil. I remember once seeing her rush into the kitchen, grab a small knife and hasten to a blown animal, just yards from the house. She would have punctured its belly, I'm sure, but on her return, just minutes later, she was too late.

This quartet was wild, its members strangers to The Currer. They were grazing in a six acre field with ungated access to one hundred acres of hillside.

Again I stress I can never comprehend why sick cattle invariably come in the vicinity of help. That the foursome was even near the buildings was a miracle. The animal was frothing at the mouth and scared out of its wits. To drive it anywhere, let alone into a strange shed, seemed impossible. Fortunately there were two male guests on hand and a friendly bullock already convalescing within. The three healthy animals fled, but the blown one went into the shed. It was an emergency and the vet was needed and came at once. Enough gas was expelled to ensure a lift-off had it been ignited but the animal was saved. Another of the four caused us trouble developing a severe cough so Margaret hastened for the wormer and dosed them all. Buying-in is a dodgy business not to be practised frequently.

Whatever the emergency, and there had been many since our return from holiday, we seemed to be coping. Life has so often proved it is dangerous to be so cocksure!

Chapter Eight

Give me a sense of humour, Lord.

W E WERE BRIMMING WITH CONFIDENCE. One of us sleeping
downstairs, every night, had been quite ridiculous when we had a
perfectly good wheelchair lift. We had sorted all this out in September and
felt ready to cope with outside routine. Calf buying time was approaching.
Margaret had continued only infrequent visits to Harrogate and said she
was fit enough and raring to go. We prepared the shed and sent for Stuart
Lawson to service the milk feeders.

We housed one self-catering group after another. It was amazing. There
were panic stations when changeovers came one on top of the other. The
thirty students from Holland were followed by the Wards who went out
on the morning that the whole place was booked for an elaborate Golden
Wedding.

'Here's to a new life! we grinned. 'The place is full, everybody is happy
and we don't have to feed them! Surely we can cope with the turmoil of
changeover! Who wants to make evening meals? Nearly a quarter of a
century is enough!'

Of course we hadn't completely escaped but serviced accommodation
was definitely on the decrease. A friend had prophesied we would keep
up the momentum for five years and we had fed people for twenty three.
We welcomed the increasing interest the public showed in group holidays,
family get-togethers and sleep-over celebrations.

Having already bought six Belgian Blue bull calves from a local farmer,
on the 23rd of the month, we went to the Thursday calf sales at Gisburn
and we bought forty one. We settled them in over the weekend and taught
them to use the feeding machines. We had a weekend group from Germany
attending a Martial Arts Course locally and they left early on the Monday
morning. The Lloyds were coming for half-term and were expected early
evening. We did as much of the changeover as possible, left Dorothy in
charge of Aunty Mary and went to the Monday Calf Sales at Otley, hoping
to top up our autumn number to somewhere in the region of seventy. There
were few animals and we only bought five. It seemed ridiculous to have to
ask Milford to transport a mere handful in his enormous loader, but we had
not taken our small trailer. We left giving him instructions to follow and we
arrived home early. Dorothy left, having done everything necessary. I had

asked the Lloyds to make their own beds. The pile of their freshly laundered sheets was on the dining room table, awaiting their arrival.

I wish I could stop being such a control freak. I am far too impulsive! I should have put on the kettle and enjoyed a cuppa. Instead I decided I could at least put the right number of sheets in each bedroom. I lifted up the heavy pile and crossed the hearth rug in front of the stone fireplace. It slipped backwards on the parquet tiles, for the first time in twenty three years, and I crashed onto the stone hearth. I remembered seeing a French boy, Henri, breaking branches on the corner stone and my demanding that he stop at once and take out the wheelbarrow he had cheekily pushed inside. I knew I had treated my thigh the same way Henri had that piece of wood. I am sure my face was as red with embarrassment as Henri's had been. Why am I so impulsive? I knew immediately I had made one big, big mistake.

I heard the arrival of the cattle wagon and Margaret opening the door of the porch. I shouted for help and manoeuvred myself, with difficulty, to sit on the hearth with my left leg outstretched. The pain was excruciating and I was filled with nausea and sweating profusely.

Margaret was furious, as she had every right to be. She shouted for Milford and they lifted me into Aunty Mary's wheelchair. I was ashamed and horrified. Our predicament was bad enough as it was with fifty two new calves, a steady flow of guests and a ninety seven year old aunt who could no longer move. Almost everything we needed to do required two! Together, she and Milford unloaded the calves, grateful that there were only five. Returning to me Margaret said, 'I can't possibly take you to hospital. I'll have to phone for an ambulance. You'll have to go alone!'

What a fine mess I had landed us in! My tail was well and truly between my legs. I was smelling richly of the calf market clothes I could not possibly exchange for clean. Any slight movement I made, I felt sick with pain. Thank goodness the Lloyds knew what to do.

I was transported by ambulance, on a stretcher and taken to A and E. Eventually it was my turn to be X-rayed and I was pushed back to my cubicle. The nurse came and said there was nothing broken. She handed me a mobile and I phoned to tell Margaret the good news that I would get a taxi and would soon be home. I made an unsuccessful effort to get off the stretcher and broke out into another sweat. I have never ever had pain like that!

The nurse was adamant. 'You definitely can't go home!' she said and returned to the doctor on duty. They looked at the X-ray again and, this time, saw a clean break of the femur. It was to keep me in hospital for eight days.

I re-phoned Margaret. 'I feel such a fool,' I moaned. 'I stink of calves. I can't move. I have no night attire.' I had sweated so. I knew the soles of my feet would be Wellington dirty. Someone picked off the streets would be cleaner. I had no soap or towel and could not have used them. I had been lifted from stretcher to bed and could not move. I had not had a bath since before we had bought the Thursday calves. I hadn't brushed my hair since early morning. There was bound to be straw in it. As my mother's daughter, I was far more worried about this than about my leg. Always anticipating she might have an accident, her practice was to be prepared yet in ninety four years she had never needed hospital care. I told the nurses more times than was necessary, that I had just come home from the cattle market. An opposition M.P. had recently asked, critically, on television, 'How difficult IS it to keep a hospital clean?' Very, I would say, with customers like me.

Poor Margaret! I knew she would be up and down all night with Aunty Mary, and with calves and that my predicament was all my own fault.

There was absolutely nothing I could do but let the nurses give the orders. I learned that when you cannot run away it is not all that difficult to conform. I believe today's children would soon be potty trained if introduced to it, like we were, before they can get up and walk away! I began to wish, as always, that Harry were still alive. He would have laughed! He had coped so well with his two short hospital stays and had enjoyed the brief experience so much he couldn't stop talking about it for weeks. He had feared I might not be able to manage, saying so frequently and laughing at the very thought of his independent sister being whisked away in an ambulance. Well, brother, you would have learned that I could cope. Like everybody else, I had to be patient.

Unlike Harry, however, who remembered every detail of his short stays in hospital, I appear to have had a mental blackout for I remember hardly anything and would have failed miserably at answering the questions with which he would have bombarded me. I would certainly have failed any senility test. I am continually being asked how I write in such detail about the life we lead. Do I keep a diary? No. Well, do I write as events happen? Not at all. Sometimes many months, even years pass before I pick up a pen. Some things I cannot remember. Where I put my glasses is one. What were the names of the last people to vacate the cottages or where I last saw the yard brush. No doubt, with increasing age, my memory will deteriorate further. I must say it let me down badly in hospital and Harry would have been very cross and disappointed.

I can't even remember the number of the ward I was in. I never knew who performed my operation. 'You must know who did it!' said the three ladies waiting for hip operations. I can't remember their names, either! They knew who their surgeon would be and the names of the cheerful nurses and the cleaning lady, so why didn't I?

I do remember being asked innumerable questions to which I answered no, so often it was embarrassing. Have you been in hospital before? No. Do you smoke? No. Drink? No. Have you asthma, arthritis, diabetes? No. Had a heart attack? No. Then, do you wear dentures and glasses and at last I could say, Yes!

I do not even remember signing permission for the operation and I have no recollection of where or when I came out of the anaesthetic. There was but one thought in my mind. I must get home to my very overworked sister as quickly as possible and thank goodness this is me, not her. She's the farmer. I'd never have coped with all those calves. I'm only the farm hand. Of course she would say that she would never have had such a silly, stupid accident. She managed to come and see me only once.

'Have you removed that rug?' was my first question. She had. I think, in hospital, I really began to worry about the safety of our premises for guests. The cottages were fine but the larger accommodation was a different matter. Previously any risk had been mine. Carrying hot food from kitchen to dining room meant a journey across the sitting room, through a very low doorway and down a ramp. Being small the doorway posed me no trouble and should I fall down the slope it was my problem. But it was also mine if some taller, self-catering guest cracked a skull whilst concentrating on a laden tray, or went flying down the slope carrying soup or a brimming tea-pot.

My mind was busy with this problem whilst alone but with Margaret at the bedside we talked about how she was coping at home. The Lloyds were being helpful. Margaret had asked Milford to go to Gisburn and buy fifteen more calves. 'We've got to keep going, haven't we?' she said. Aunty Mary, she told me with amusement, didn't seem to notice my absence, never asked after me or showed concern when Margaret told her every time I phoned, which I did every morning and evening. I knew full well what sort of a predicament Margaret was in.

'Don't come again,' I said. 'I'm not ill!'

I was walking again remarkably quickly. Things have accelerated recently. I felt embarrassed by the fact that my break had been an emergency. Others in the ward had had to wait months in pain and I'd been rushed into theatre, jumping the queue and maybe cancelling the operation of some poor soul who had waited ages.

Twenty years earlier and my leg would have been on traction and I'd have been in hospital for months like my mentor, Dorothy Clough, of Steeton Hall. After a night of severe frost she had broken her leg, foolishly crossing her yard to the Laundry and the Guide Rooms above the Stables.

I was walking immediately and had no pain but the doctor would not let me go for eight days. I was called the 'bed and breakfast lady' and they thought I would have to be back in harness at once. Friends came to see me and, on the day before their departure, the Lloyds came. Cousin Freda's daughter collected a trolley I was being loaned and I was taken home, next day, by the ambulance bus. I had a circular tour of Airedale as I was last to be dropped off. Aunty Mary and Meg ignored me. I think they were peeved that I had deserted them.

The trolley was so light it bounced all over the place and a full cup lost half its contents on route but it was more useful than my crutches. I found I could sweep the floor and wash it with a mop and bucket, whilst sitting in the wheelchair. I could relieve Margaret of most of the household duties but it was into the new year before I could jostle with calves. Most of our guests were self-catering and I had no problem making beds. Even so, I knew my impulsiveness had put an unacceptable burden on Margaret and I was ashamed. Six weeks after the accident I took a taxi and my crutches back to the hospital. The un-named consultant was satisfied and asked if I'd like to see the X-ray. I had never seen the first one. I think I must have been the least inquisitive patient ever. What you don't know causes you no anxiety. However he insisted and showed me the metal infra-structure inside my thigh. It was quite impressive. If I walk with a slight irregularity now I am sure it isn't the break. It is just continuous hard work. There is still plenty of that about.

Another memory which eludes me is of any activity over Christmas 2003 except that there was no Christmas Outing enjoying the tranquillity of December 25th, in the Yorkshire Dales and that I bought a Christmas pudding. My mother's daughter bought one from the super-market! For seventy-three years I had seen the festive, homemade clouties hanging from the beams. The bought one was horrible. I don't think we ate all of it. Harry would have been disgusted. Home cooking tastes so much better than the ready made, fast food presented to children these days. Mother called that 'muckment'. I think 'fast food' is a misnomer any way. I can make a traditional meal in quick time. You just need practise, or a queue!

We have never eaten a pizza or a curry. When we feed our guests our kitchen smells of traditional, Yorkshire ingredients. When guests are cooking their own meals strange, foreign smells creep under the doorway, alien to our nostrils. Mother would have been horrified. One group celebrated an anniversary by bringing in a Chinese Takeaway. She would turn in her grave, I'm sure!

I don't particularly worry about what holidaymakers eat though I am shocked by the amount some waste. As a headteacher for twenty one years I am concerned by what children eat at school. Is it so very long since I sat at the head of a dinner table and we all ate and enjoyed a traditional, nutritious menu? Once again I am tempted to warn of the acceleration on a downward slope. Sometimes deterioration is unstoppable.

I refused to worry about what guests cook but I began to worry about the safety of the route from kitchen to dining room. For nearly a quarter of a century I had carried steaming bowls of soup, 20lb turkeys, plates of meat, tureens of vegetables and trays of dessert. I had carried full pots of tea and coffee, often feeding over twenty people. I knew how careful one must be. I knew how dangerous it was. We did not wish to stop the pendulum from swinging towards self-catering. It was a blessing. But I wasn't even thinking about that when, on New Year's Eve, Margaret said, 'The trouble with families is, that when they've got their children to bed, the sitting room is too far away from the bedrooms. The children could be crying and parents can't, hear.'

I said, 'The real trouble with our accommodation is that the dining room is too far away from the kitchen.' I hesitated and said that again slowly. 'The ...dining room ...is ...too ...far ...from ...the ...kitchen!' Could we solve both problems by swapping one with the other? I wish you could see Margaret and me when a penny drops. We latch onto an idea immediately. We were desperate for a 2004 project. A revitalizer!

There would possibly be no holiday. Since 1970 we had been taking Aunty Mary. She had been with us near on sixty times, culminating in the somewhat difficult five days in Witherslack, in May. We had known then that we would never manage it again. Cousins had released us twice, to go to the Hebrides alone. We had been extremely grateful but, as things were now, we could not possibly ask them again, however much we were in need of respite. Aunty Mary was right, we were used to it and others were not. Leaving the islands the previous summer, after such a wonderful holiday, we had, fairly confidently, re-booked caravans for the following June. It had always been our practice to do so. Deciding we would not be able to go we did not cancel as we had done, in 1990, when mother was dying and we could not go. In the year of the Foot and Mouth disease, when to go on holiday was impossible, we had not cancelled either. We had just sent friends on holiday instead. We could do that again, we said. I remembered the joy it had given me to ring one of my helpful Guides saying, like a tour operator, 'You've just won a holiday on Harris!' We could do that again.

Without a holiday to look forward to, the next best thing was a project. I was house bound because Margaret would not let me handle calves or struggle with bales. We had occupants in the two cottages but those in the B&B, self-catering over the New Year, would leave the next day. I could not wait for them to do so and climbed our staircase and paced the passage above The Snug, even though I knew exactly how big it was having laid two carpets in the last twenty years.

The moment the festive-happy guests left, Margaret and I went into the room which had, in the 1500s been the only living accommodation. We did not run. Neither of us can. Since Margaret's fall, speed has not been a prerogative. Since mine I have found it impossible to get both feet off the ground at once. I fear that, when the surgeon stitched me up, he forgot to put back the spring. Silently we stood beneath the massive beams, smiled with pleasure in front of its inglenook fireplace and, turning towards the mullioned windows, looked out onto the garden, glistening with frost. The project, we decided, was possible.

In 1958, when we moved from the village to this sixteenth century ruin, this room, in which we now stood, had housed cattle and pigs. We had immediately divided it into two and transformed one half into a wash kitchen. This proved only a temporary measure for it was too big and up four steps. In the early sixties, we had built a utility kitchen and turned the beamed and mullioned room into the spacious sitting room we had always called the Snug. When we ventured into bed and breakfast we took down the dividing wall so that once again the room was very big. It was just right, we agreed. A dining room it should be! We were ablaze with enthusiasm.

Margaret went out to the cattle and I began the mammoth, exciting task of moving furniture. Very slowly, scared my impulsiveness would result in another injury, I pushed all the snug chairs down the ramp and, one by one dragged the dining room chairs into their new abode. With a gammy leg it was comedy, but there we go. With glee I discovered we could seat more than twenty. Why hadn't we thought of this long ago? Had we done so I would have been deprived of this unique January activity to aid convales-cence. It must be true that all things work together for good. We are adept at turning bad luck into good.

When Margaret came in for coffee we could not stop talking about it. Being Mother's daughters what we can afford we want instantly. We agreed immediately that the large room, entered through the barn door, was more suitable for reclining than for dining. For better or worse, for us, there is never any long drawn out thinking. We are doers. Like five year old Gillian. We get on with it.

We decided right from the start, that we would buy some new tables. We had used a medley of second-hand ones for twenty years. We could afford new; throw away a wobbly one, re-locate others. Removing one solid table to the Mistal cottage I was reminded of the givers, parents of a pupil who had stayed with us at The Currer until her March 11+ exam had been taken. Her family had had to remove to Leeds at the beginning of a very wintry February. Ciona had remained with us rather than enter a new school at a crucial time. Pupil and headmistress had walked to the bus through a blanket of snow and, returning, had sledged down the first intake. Those were memorable days. No longer could one do that. It would be inappropriate behaviour!

The January project, forty years later, proved once and for ever that Margaret and I do not belong to a throw away society. I just rearranged everything. I removed some of the furniture cluttering Aunty Mary's room. Her new ensuite had displaced some and the second bed even more. The enormous hoist needed to get her into bed twice a day had meant the television had to find a new home. Her arm chair had been replaced with

The dining room.

the wheel chair. Her room was very spacious but there is a limit. I brought things from the loft and played tiddley winks with the colour scheme. I took down all the curtains and put them with chair covers into the washing machine and denuded the walls of all the pictures. Whilst Margaret struggled on alone outside, I had a ball in the B&B.

Jean Collier, our weekly Social Services sitter, was due on Monday January 5th. This gave us two hours freedom. It was a bitterly cold day. Too frequently we were not ready when Jean came, but on that occasion we could not be late. We were going to buy three pine, extending tables and our errand must be completed within the two hours. I pocketed the cheque book.

It was so cold we were well padded with winter clothes. We looked older, probably, without the tan of summer, the sparkle of June. We looked what we are. Two elderly ladies, not very fashion conscious, both heavily shod as befits winter, both wearing shabby wool hats to keep ears warm. Entering a cattle market we would not have looked out of place but I admit we did not look like guest house owners, young enough to be entertaining a new project.

Our destination was an enormous pine warehouse on the hill above Haworth. There are shops everywhere, selling pine furniture but this was the biggest we knew and we wanted three identical tables. It is a wonderful warm place to explore, full of old world charm. Because it was January and very cold, open fires welcomed prospective buyers of which there seemed to be none. We limped around, conscious of the beautiful furniture but seemingly unable to find what we wanted, upstairs or down. We wandered clumsily and hesitated frequently in front of a fire, spreading our fingers before the glowing coals. There were sale notices everywhere and cards, (which possibly should have been removed for the new year), advising us that we could, 'Buy now and pay next year!'

The sales man eyed us suspiciously, maybe mistaking us for two old bag-ladies seeking a spell in the warmth, not intending to buy at all. Eventually he approached us and looked surprised when his offer of help was accepted.

'We are looking at the tables,' we said. 'Have you anything in darker pine?' We had decided that, beneath our heavy dark beams the tables must not be too light.

'Everything we have in stock is on display,' the man said. Anything else is to order.' He said that the furniture came from France and it was a three month delivery. Anything ordered now would not come before April. I had moved everything. I had taken down pictures from the walls. Margaret had brought emulsion white matt from the cellar, meaning to paint the walls next day and guests were arriving on Friday. Crikey!

We couldn't dally. Our eyes wandered frantically over the scores of beautiful pieces of furniture. Margaret said to the man, 'We need three identical tables at once.'

The man was obviously unbelieving but tolerated her because he had the perfect answer. 'Well,' he said, 'we only keep one of each design. Any more would have to be ordered.' I'm sure he expected us to go. Instead we remained grounded in front of the fire. I felt like one of my guests at the other end of the phone, having been told we had no accommodation, but refusing to hang up, believing I might, given time, come up with a solution. Frequently I did.

I am sure the man thought we were just delaying our departure, enjoying the warmth. He'll turn us out any minute now, I feared. And then I saw it, occupying a remote corner, laid with beautiful china.

'Margaret, 'I whispered. 'What about that one?' One table, seating eight comfortably and ten at a pinch, was better than nothing, in winter. When we did have larger groups we would have to use a table that didn't match. So what!

We walked over to this beautiful table and the increasingly worried man followed us. 'That's just what we want!' we told him.

He had nothing to lose. He said, 'Funnily enough that is the only table I have in stock, of which I do happen to have three. I have two more upstairs!'

Aren't we lucky? 'Can you deliver?' we asked.

'We deliver on Thursdays,' he replied. Our next guests were not coming until Friday. I pulled out my cheque book. I am used to making cheques out for thousands, for cattle and fodder, electricity and whatever. These tables were five hundred pounds each.

'We can't accept a cheque and deliver before it has been cleared by the bank.' I was told. 'Delivery would be next week.' You see he still did not believe us. What was all that jargon about Buy now, pay later?

'You'd accept cash presumably and deliver this week?' I said. Of course he would! So I took five £20 notes from my purse so that he would hold them whilst we hurried to the bank. We returned with cash. The amazed man gave us two candlesticks as a gift and our tables were delivered to a newly painted, once-was Snug and they transformed it into a dining room.

It is amazing what you can do in two days if you have created chaos and have guests arriving on Friday. Because it was necessary I had completely neglected everything else and Margaret had used what little sit-down time she had to re-emulsion. The two delivery men made no comment as they squeezed the three heavy tables through the narrow, low doorway and stood them in front of the mullions. The room with its beams and inglenook fireplace accepted them as to the manna born.

I could not resist saying to the men, 'When you see your boss tell him they look just right in their new home!' but, to be honest, we forgave him his mistrust. He could hardly be blamed.

It was we who were the un-believers the next day. Our two guests arrived, ladies coming to celebrate the 90th birthday of an aunt who lived in town. It was bitterly cold and a white tablecloth covered Ingleborough, forty miles away on the western horizon.

Serving breakfast I enquired, 'How are you celebrating her birthday?'

'We're climbing Penyghent,' they told me.

'You are,' I said, 'but what is your aunt doing?'

'She's climbing Penyghent!' they laughed. Why had I been so critical of the salesman's disbelief?

'Really?' I felt like Victor Meldrew and said, 'I don't believe it!'

'It's true. She greets every birthday with a challenge!'

I must confess to being worried for there was January snow on the Pennine hills but the old lady achieved her dream. By gaw, us Yorkshire tykes are tough! Unlike Aunty Mary, for one old lady, two legs were better than four wheels. A few weeks later the ladies phoned for another overnight accommodation, this time to come to a funeral. 'Oh! Don't tell me,' I feared the worst.

'No, no. It's not Aunty. It's a much younger member of the family,' and that, too, was sad.

Our winter project had done us a world of good. We showed each of the twelve members of the caring team, our new arrangement. Isolated as we are in winter it was nice to have some appreciative people to show the fruits of our labours. In December we had ordered two trolleys which we deemed would make safer, the carrying of food down the ramp. One was out of stock but the one delivered proved useful. When the second delivery came, at the end of January, our changeover meant it was redundant. We didn't unpack it but sent it back in exchange for a credit note and eventually had fun replenishing crockery and glassware, and buying three dozen place mats at a catering warehouse. No more washing of tablecloths!

There came the moment, one day in January, when Margaret said she was sorry but she needed me. A calf required an injection and it was too strong for her to hold. So I re-entered the farming arena and things gradually got back to normal apart from the 'spring'. That is still missing.

The new year burst of energy and enthusiasm had re-introduced the element of fun, so very necessary on our daily menu. It was difficult to sustain. Our own premises were badly in need of a face-lift but there was nothing we could do about it. Whilst the wheelchair and the hoist continued to tear the carpet into shreds and hay and straw made relentless wintry entry into the house, all we could do was sweep it up and not look too closely at the need to re-decorate.

When the beckoning year ahead apparently offered little respite and no holiday, it is not sufficient that the lifestyle is bearable and controlled. There must be excitement. There must be something to brighten the monotony. When times were hard Aunty Mary said, 'Well, you're used to it!' So we were but we were also used to fun. As each member of our family was lost so went a percentage of it. Harry was the most recent loss and he had generated such a lot, his absence left us almost handicapped.

We might have expected that being interrupted four times a day by the carers, would be annoying. Not at all. Their entry was always cheerful. They loved their job, found satisfaction and pleasure in their work and we reflected it. For fifteen minutes, four times a day, we were all laughing together. Amazing! They loved Aunty Mary and she lapped up their undivided attention greedily. It was such a blessing. The very nature of our work meant that we had to ignore her fairly frequently. She loved being the centre of attention and the carers gave her that. It made life easier than it might have been. A quiet life is something you pray for and don't exactly like when it arrives. With self-catering groups we were no longer servants in the dining room. They did their own cooking, made their own beds and found their own entertainment. After well over two decades it suited us fine but ...! Are we never to be satisfied?

If fun is not the energiser, sometimes one must resort to aggression, which is pathetic. We had an electricity problem. A main fuse had had to be repaired one Christmas Day, possibly two years ago. The electrician had told us what our own had, that we were overloading. Since then things had escalated. A new shower, an electric mattress, a hoist, the lift, guests bringing gadgets galore. In the autumn we had asked our suppliers to bring us more.

'Before Christmas,' we said. They replied that it was impossible. They sent someone with a contract for us to sign reducing our unit charge for loyalty but they could not bring us more electricity as soon as that.

There began a dialogue which threatened to send me round the bend. It lasted a year and stole hours of my time. There is nothing, absolutely nothing more infuriating than hanging endlessly onto a phone, waiting for an answer, listening to music which does not calm, being passed to someone else and never getting any answer.

At long last the supplier decided what was needed and sent us an upfront invoice for over £8000 pounds. They sent me an end of the first week reminder that I had not paid. I had been advised that I must pay a month before work commenced but I had not been given a start date. They could not give me one, I was told but, every week, demand notices came for their invoice to be paid. We were told we must arrange for a trench to be dug from the pole to the house alongside the existing supply cable and for a pipe to be laid through which they could pull the new wire. They said a small enclosure must be built along the wall to house the necessary equipment and that we should have our electrician there to connect us, immediately a new meter had been installed. They then said they could do the work in the middle of May so I paid the £8000 plus. Our electrician was horrified and consulted a colleague who said a far too elaborate system was being planned, sufficient for a hospital in fact! They stopped the proposed activity and, though they kept our money, everything was postponed until the autumn.

Memories of the spring of 2004 would be bleak indeed without the four times a day visit of the carers. Their cheerful entry brought sunshine into the house and news from the outside world, a part of which we had ceased to be. They were just as adoring as we were, of Diana's newest baby, sired by a Blond Aquitaine AI bull. It had been born with difficulty, as usual. Fortunately two strong boys from the Sugden family were unloading big bales of haylage. Their combined strength had not been enough and we had eventually sent for the vet. The golden baby, which had needed three strong men to calve, was beautiful. The vet said it looked three months old already! Diana had leapt to her feet at once, to lick the almost fluorescent baby. She is the world's best mother but useless in the labour ward.

The carers joined the 99% of the public who do not know that a cow must have a calf, every year to produce milk. The most senior member of the Home Help Team did not know. 'Is that true?' she said in amazement.

'How else do you think they give milk?' I said.

'I thought it was because they ate grass!' was the naive answer.

'You had children. Did you breast feed?' I queried.

'Of course,' replied the elderly lady.

'Did you have to eat grass?' I asked and everyone laughed. We were always laughing. How else could we have coped with the year of Aunty

Mary's severe immobility? It was so much worse for her. To be handled by even such nice people was humiliating for such a private person as she.

'I'll never forgive you for this, Jean Brown!' she frequently voiced.

Margaret had assumed the last-call duties following my leg brake and never handed back the 9 p.m. responsibility. She received as much criticism as I did. One night the carers protested when Aunty Mary, hanging in the hoist, being lowered onto the bed, shouted, 'I'll never forgive you for this, Margaret Brown.'

'Margaret looks after you better than anyone,' one of them said. 'You are the luckiest of all our clients.'

'Well, she's not very good at it!' said our frustrated old lady.

Shortly afterwards Tim had to do some drastic work on Diana's over-grown hooves. Margaret had assumed the role of chiropodist for Aunty Mary's toes but someone with equine equipment was needed for Diana. Tim brought a portable crush from his stables and Diana was persuaded, against her will, to go in. Well and truly trapped, each foot in turn was lifted with a rope and trimmed to perfection.

She glowered angrily at Margaret who says she distinctly heard her moo, 'I'll never forgive you for this, Margaret Brown!'

I am sure we are not the only carers or farmers who are so under-valued. Fortunately Aunty Mary behaved impeccably for the carers and they loved her. The very nature of our demanding work-load meant that we could not always be at her beck and call. Even so, the carers thought the Queen Mother could not be receiving more attention. She certainly wasn't neglected but, as is the way of it, more wants more. The carers gave her that extra and, boy, did she like it.

They would have done anything for us. Had it been possible, any one of them would have stayed on site and allowed us to go on holiday. As that could not be, they made life not only possible but they deluded us into thinking we could go on *ad infinitum* and that was maybe only an illusion. I do not want a reader to think we were unique. We just did not know that we, too, can hover on breaking point.

Spring brought new life into us, as it did to the trees around the house and in Jimmy's wood and to the meadow flowers in every pasture. We began to look forward to hiring the Dial-a-ride and pushing Aunty Mary round Coppice Pond, in St. Ives. We believed, as we always have, that we had the stamina to go on and on. Each challenge has not beaten us until we have reached the end of the road. We have needed the help of others and each other, but so far we have got there. Though she, like Hilda, might reach her century and receive her card from the Queen, we were game. I will wrinkle with age but Aunty Mary never did. Her weight prevented that. She never looked old.

We became expert at using the shower chair and wheeling her into the extra large cubicle. Being winched high out of her chair and lowered on to her bed was the most traumatic act of the day.

The carers would say, 'Your poem Aunty.' and she would obey.

> A chap i' Oworth t'other day
> Met Rebecca on her way.
> She turned and to him said,
> 'Wot yer follerin, me fer Ned.'
> 'Ah luv yer lass an' fain
> Would 'ave thi fer mi wife.'
> She answered 'im, 'Yer silly cawf,
> Ah Nell's a nicer lass be 'awf.
> See, she's cuming up fri mill.
> Go an' see 'er fer ye sel.'
> Off 'e went at a 'andsome pace
> 'An up she came wi' ugly face.
> 'E turned an' follerred Becky then.
> She turned 'er 'ead an' answered 'im.
> 'Yer sed yer luved me an' no other
> An' after that tha needn't bother.'

By which time the awesome operation was over.

After the Easter holiday, The Loft cottage became occupied by a lady from New Zealand. She was employed as a supply teacher at Greenhead Comprehensive. It used to be the Girls' Grammar School but its status had changed. Her presence was a balm. It meant we had a long-stay willing resident. Kathleen Lynch was a smallholder from South Island, used to handling cattle, strong and fearless. She brought a ray of sunshine to The Currer during the spring of 2004, being cheerful when we were low. She was a colourful character.

I turned my attention to the garden which could be seen, constantly, from the dining room tables. Because it was uncontrollable, I decided to turf it and, on one of our two-hour respites, we went to a local garden centre and bought a ready made lawn, some plastic tubs and colourful flowers. The wall needed rebuilding but that was a summer job for our wallers.

Unfortunately things began to happen towards the end of April. We do not frequently get coughs and colds but the outside world was not only visiting our holiday accommodation but social workers, doctors, friends and relatives were coming to see our old lady and a cough and cold virus penetrated our fortress. Both Aunty Mary and Margaret caught it. We thought it wise to send for the doctor and she prescribed nothing for Margaret and antibiotics for Aunty Mary, who generally found a cough hard to throw off.

We had arranged for the annual visit of the residents from White Windows

Cheshire Home to come on Thursday May 13th, but when a second dose of the treatment did not rid Aunty Mary of her dreadful cough, we decided the visit must be postponed. The doctor came frequently but the chest infection just would not leave the old lady. Margaret, too, was fighting it only slowly and Aunty Mary's was turning into pneumonia.

On Monday the 10th we decided a bed must come into the sitting room, though up during the day, Aunty Mary would not be taken back upstairs until she was well again. Her breathing had been noisy for some time. Now it became irregular. She appeared to hold her breath. She held it for so long she seemed to have stopped altogether, then the noisy intake would begin again. The doctor said it was a common condition but we began to be worried and neither of us went upstairs to bed. I slept on the divan in the alcove and Margaret on the floor.

On the 13th the carers decided not to get her out of bed. Ours is such a pleasant sitting room with mullions on the east and again on the south. The May sunshine floods the room from dawn to evening. Although the setting sun can only be viewed from the mullions in the dining room, or any of the west facing bedroom windows, the knowledge of its daily activity is no secret for a strange ethereal light floods the dyke and footpath fields and colours them crimson. It reflects scarlet from every leaf on the silver birches in the yard, the oak tree in the fold and the increasing woodland growth on the rough. The windscreens of cars coming over Baildon Moor, four miles away, suggest that dusk is already here and headlights are in use.

When Father lay in bed in the sitting room, in 1979, his eyes were perpetually trained on the horizon watching Margaret feed cattle on the snow. Even when watching television, the eyes of both Margaret and myself wander from the screen to the fields, where the movement of contented cattle arouses more interest. It was pleasant for us to sit beside the bed enjoying the view of the valley recently dressed for spring.

I reflected on how lucky Aunty Mary had been. Since Aunty Janie died in 1975 she had been a three day a week resident at The Currer, for fourteen years, before coming permanently in 1989. And now she was 97 and she had never had one day in bed in all that time. Not many ladies can say that!

Outside there was only the noise of birds and, sadly, the population of our winged neighbours has decreased recently. When the fans are turned off in the calf shed, you can almost feel the silence. Inside there was the intermittent coughing of Margaret and Aunty, her noisy intake of breath and the peculiar silences when she stopped breathing altogether.

Margaret does not normally have such an uncomfortable cold. In retrospect we acknowledge it was also that we were both much nearer the precipice than we thought.

On Thursday oxygen was brought and we were instructed how to use it should it become necessary, but our old lady was never in any distress.

She realised that her breathing was odd. 'I'm breathing funny!' she said. Her manner of conversation had never changed during all the seventy odd years I had known her. Like her father before her, she said silly things. Once she said, 'I am a comedienne' and so she was. Unlike Mother, she never talked about serious matters. Never about religion, or politics, never about philosophy, never about a joint activity and never mentioned death. That morning, for the first time, she did and it amused me that it was a comment in Aunty Mary's unique language.

She said, 'Am I going to die, tiddley iti?'

'Aren't we all, some day,' I answered. Nothing is more true.

When the evening shift came at 9 p.m., they decided not to disturb her. As she was peaceful, I persuaded Margaret to go to bed. She went insisting that I only stayed half the night and she would come down mid-way. I pulled the recliner near the bed and kept nodding off. All seemed well. I had grown used to the noisy intake. It was almost a tranquilliser.

Suddenly, at about 1 a.m., there was silence. There is nothing more awakening than sudden silence. In the calf shed, should the electric fans be turned off, sleeping calves jump up, and have even been known to jump out of the pen. Should I fall asleep in front of the television and someone switch off, I am immediately roused.

Perhaps I had dosed for a moment, in the recliner, before the dying embers of the wood fire. Maybe, but the sudden silence alerted me at once. I rushed to the other side of the bed but she had already gone, peacefully, at home in the comfort of her warm bed, eyes closed, asleep. To make sure, I watched quietly for she had stopped breathing so many times in the last few days. This time she did not restart, so I climbed the stairs to waken Margaret.

'Aunty Mary had just died,' I said. Death is very final.

Margaret had not expected to be wakened other than to begin her half of the overnight vigil. Had we done so, she would not have gone to bed at all. She pulled on trousers and came downstairs. We left Aunty Mary comfortably cushioned against her pillows and phoned the duty doctor at the hospital. She was a busy lady, on call for emergencies and ours didn't fit that category.

'Are you alright till morning?' she asked.

'We're alright,' I said.

'Go to bed,' she advised. 'I'll ring before I come.'

We turned off the light in the sitting room but the undrawn curtains let in enough light from outside to dispel total darkness. We called the dogs from the room and huddled for a while over the Aga, drinking a half cup of coffee. Then we placed the baby minder by the telephone and took the loud speaker into our bedroom lest we sleep too heavily. We need not have troubled for we were up before the phone rang. We put a message on the tape in the carers' office telling them of our loss.

The lady doctor was lovely. She came muffled in clothes for the morning was chill and she had spent much of the night driving to emergencies. She was cold, tired and kind. One trouser leg had escaped her boot.

It was the 14th of May. All the thirty years of her spending holidays with us, the spring ones had been in May. Had Aunty Mary persevered and kept active, I doubt but that she would have been looking forward to a 2004 one. But she hadn't and what you stop doing at ninety, or before, you don't do again. We had coped with six of the seven years since she stopped moving and openly declared that four wheels were better than two legs. Had she been the kind of ninety year old who had climbed Penyghent, we might all have been heading for Harris. Let it be a lesson to all to keep moving. Better to die at the helm. She might have been the first member of our family to reach a century and Margaret and I might not have been the wrecks we suddenly were.

The growing number of years, working and caring for people and animals had caught up on us. We had been so sure that we were unbreakable. Convinced of our tenacity, we had not considered that the summer ahead and another winter to follow, might pose a problem. However, this is an autobiography essentially honest so it would be wrong not to admit that, when Aunty Mary died, we became critically aware of exhaustion. Those who do not keep hens may not have experience of a wind egg, a perfectly formed egg without a shell. The inner skin encloses the yolk and white but gives it no rigidity. It is a floppy ovoid comparable to a plastic bag full of water. Margaret said she felt just like a wind egg!

Our undertaker is a cousin of a cousin which makes things easier and I managed to cope with the aftermath and the funeral arrangements without any visible signs of collapse. We returned the sitting room to normal and I managed to bake a variety of biscuits, enough to fill two big cake tins. When Mother wanted to say a special thank you, she often did so by baking. I remember Father wanted to thank the nurses when he had had his first cancer operation and had asked his eighty year old wife to bake them biscuits, to eat at coffee time.

Wishing to say a special thank you to our twelve carers, I followed her lead. I did not fill any cake tins for us. The holiday guests must have bought biscuits for a spell and the cakes and pastries Mother used to make were no longer necessary. They were not required for evening meals and there was now only Margaret and me.

On the day of the funeral we asked our holidaying guests to eat elsewhere and we, as always, had not arranged to bring anyone home. Rightly or wrongly we feel that the trauma of death and burial does not require a post funeral get-together. Attending funerals we never stay for refreshments, though invariably invited and we have never arranged anything after family funerals. For Father's there was deep snow, for Mother's a house full of Easter holidaymakers and for Harry's the Foot and Mouth disease!

The funeral service was taken sensitively by Billy Clayton, a local lay-preacher, because there was currently no vicar at our village church. Like so many, he had only known her as Aunty Mary. To hundreds she had no surname. We could feel exhaustion taking hold. All I wanted to do was to go back home alone and deal with this unfamiliar feeling, take off sombre clothes, sit down and breathe gently. I remembered feeling so after the final fortnight of camping with sixty children in the Hebrides, in 1980. Suddenly I had been inexplicably weak. It had been the completion of a thity-year job, successfully, without accident. I remembered sitting down, tears running down my cheeks. Tears not of distress but of gratitude that there had been no mishap, no memory of any guilt, no if only ..., no hard words, nothing left unfinished but being strangely weak at the knees. That's how I felt after the funeral.

There was something I hadn't bargained for or been prepared for. Previously the family had belonged to us only. Though she had lived with us and been our responsibility, Aunty Mary had belonged equally to nephews and nieces. At the graveside they decided they were coming back to The Currer. I was horrified because my cupboard was bare!

'You must not go back to an empty house alone,' they said, kindly. Ours ... an empty house! If only it were sometimes.

'We're fine,' we said, but they insisted and ushered us into one of their cars. I whispered to one, 'Bring me some whipping cream.' I had one half of a sponge cake, a handful of strawberries and two full cake tins of biscuits earmarked for carers.

'Oh Lord, do help me,' Mother would have cried. It was her prayer every time we were in a bonnie pickle. There was only double cream at the village shop. Though it thickened it would not achieve the consistency of whipping cream. My contribution to the refreshments was to layer-cut the cake, pour on the semi-liquid cream and top it with a handful of strawberries. Then, for what I believe to be only the second time in my life, I sat down and could not get my bottom off the chair. Others put on the kettle and lifted cups out of the cupboard. Others handed out plates and spoons, for the cream was too runny and others put out the biscuits, throwing away the packaging, meant for the twelve carers who had all been at the funeral. Seeing them sitting together, in uniform, had brought the only tears of the day to my eyes. Fortunately I had made many biscuits and the depletion was not too noticeable.

I had completely lost my ability to lead, to be in control. 'You must have a holiday,' everyone said. 'Take a break,' as if that were the easiest thing in the world to do. The thought of preparing this place to leave in other people's care, whilst we had a holiday, was enough to trigger a nervous breakdown.

We just can't up sticks and go. There has to be meticulous planning and enthusiasm for the task and Margaret was a wind egg and, to quote Aunty Mary, my 'get up and go had got up and gone.'

'It'll pass!' Mike had said two decades ago. Perhaps we just had to hang on until it did.

Next day callers came in plenty. The carers, suddenly axed of their twelve month job, came in penny numbers to say how sad to lose Aunty and how they would miss us. Others came with their condolences, friends and guests rang. Life became an ending and a beginning, the old order had changed for the new. We had closed one door and another was opening onto a life with only two in the family, a life without any member of the previous generation. We stood at a crossroads, about to explore unknown territory. Should we, or should we not go on holiday? Did we even want to? Should we offer the two caravans, booked in 2003 for the middle of June, to friends or go ourselves? If we could just pull ourselves together, perhaps we should go. In all truth we had not expected to feel like we did. You just never can tell how tight the elastic is until it snaps.

'Should we manage to go,' I remember saying, 'I'll cry all the way to Settle!'

Several things were in our favour. One was Kathleen, our New Zealander. She was wonderful. Every time she went into town she brought back strawberries and melons, cakes and delicacies and spoiled us outrageously. Another thing which pushed us towards a holiday was that, should we stay at home, we would deprive Dorothy of the summer income she had been able to rely on for sixteen years or more. She had been expecting us to stay at home because we had not been free to go. Now we were but had no enthusiasm whatsoever.

And the third thing which urged us to go was that Tim and Graham would be working on the premises, not over in the meadows. Leaving The Currer never seemed safer. The two men were to re-open the door into the stable alcove of the Mistal cottage and close the indoor entry made at the conversion of the barn in 1980. Noise had always filtered through the door. It had been minimal when everyone was having B/B and being reasonably quiet. Now self-catering groups were coming to re-unite and celebrate and there was laughter and sometimes singing. All premises must have two exits so Tim was closing one door and re-opening another and would be on hand for Dorothy should she have an emergency.

We must try to go, but first we must re-invite the residents of White Windows. We had cancelled their visit less than a fortnight ago. I phoned the day after the funeral and was told they could come on Thursday, a few days hence, so we had to emerge from our stupor very quickly. We passed that milestone before we had even time to think about it. One thing I remember to my shame is that, though feeding them and entertaining them was no problem, I found myself standing back from pushing wheelchairs or assuming a carer's role. It shocked me. I have since learned that Health and Safety rules now forbid me to do so. No-one without qualifications must attend to the handicapped who are cared for by the Authority. To do so I would have to go on a course and get a certificate. We have been told, too, that dairy farmers who have been using their pasteurising machines for decades, are required to take training before continuing!

That I stood back from tasks I had being doing almost all my life, shocked me quite a lot. Had I really done enough? I know I stand back from entertaining children and would make a poor grandparent. I had obviously had an overdose of them, teaching and Guiding. Will we one day stand back from rearing calves? Margaret won't!

People were right. We really did need a holiday, but first we needed to get borrowed equipment back to the hospital. The conglomeration was enormous. Our own wheelchair and commode had to be hoisted into the loft. The lift was turned off. The kitchen table, pushed clear of the lift entrance years ago, was brought back into the centre of the room.

Close on the heels of Aunty Mary's funeral there came another. Though thirty years her junior, Bill Marsden, our corn traveller, shared a birthday with her. That she had had so much longer than he, makes one consider every moment to be precious. The news of his death stunned us when we were most vulnerable and put all thoughts of a holiday out of our minds. We drove over to Earby to attend his funeral. The church was packed with men, farmers from the area he had served who, like us, had such a lot to thank him for. He had introduced us to Wilson's our well respected suppliers of hay and straw, to our contractors, John Sugden and his family who have virtually planned and built all our sheds and done our tractor work since 1980 and he had been the man to ask advice when we needed to switch to automatic milk feeders, several years ago. The almost total male congregation was a testimony to the fact that he had been universally respected.

I found it extremely moving, so many weather-beaten faces, so many working men, leaving their wives at home to bear tribute to a colleague who had served them far beyond the call of duty. His coffin was carried shoulder high which seemed to portray the esteem in which he had been held locally. He was buried in the village church yard, at Earby.

We really must go away for a little while, we told each other as we drove home through the pastoral countryside of Lothersdale, along a favourite route, a hidden hillside, empty of traffic on its narrow roads. 'Lo there's a dale' of great beauty. Bill loved his native countryside and the wildlife ever present, particularly the birds.

We phoned Oban and booked overnight accommodation at the dog friendly hotel. We tried to secure a room at the Castlebay Youth Hostel but it was full. The proprietor said he had booked us in at the home of a lovely lady, a few doors away. We phoned the 'lovely lady'. He was right in his description and we made an unenthusiastic attempt to spring clean the holiday accommodation and partially sort out the disorder in our own quarters, caused by twelve months of neglect. We came to the conclusion that to 'bottom it' we must decorate and that must wait until our return. It would be a major activity. A lick and a promise was all we could achieve.

Fatigue is not always recognisable. We do know that there must be thousands in the country who, having completed a job, thinking they were fine, suddenly found they were not!

We left our car in Sainsbury's car park and crawled up to the station to buy tickets to Oban; two, old, done-for farmers with sticks, almost at the end of their tether. I repeated to Margaret and to everyone I talked to, that if we finally got off, I would cry all the way to Settle!

We packed our small rucksacks with the bare minimum. An extra jumper, another pair of trousers. We did not go to the super-market to replenish household stores. There were breakfast things in the freezer and Dorothy prefers to buy when she needs. The cake tins we leave empty. We now buy when we get there. On this particular departure there was even less than usual in our larder.

On the morning prior to leaving we still had the land to inspect and the cattle to check. I could write a book solely about, 'The day before leaving.' I envisage that the day before I leave the planet earth, there will be an emergency. I cannot predict what it will be because we are slowly, but surely, going through every conceivable variation. The panic is never duplicated. We could place bets on there being something but never on what and never on a replay!

Just before mid-day the phone rang and a voice from the past said she was down from Scotland, attending a course in Bradford. The caller was Rona, a cousin twice removed. We had last seen her forty years ago when she, not even a teenager, had stayed a few nights at The Currer, with her parents. Not having a car she was bravely walking up the very steep lane locals call Ben Hill, trying to find where we lived. Her errand was two-fold. She wanted to see us and she wanted to put some flowers on Aunty Mary's grave.

'Margaret will come for you in the Land Rover,' I said. Silently I wondered what on earth I was going to feed her with.

I had bread and butter and tomatoes and there was one tin of corned beef hiding in the cupboard. Everything else was frozen solid. Our number one pet hatred is a tin of corned beef with a key to twist for opening! This one broke immediately, as it always does, leaving a square tin with which no tin opener in my drawer, can cope. Margaret tried, Rona tried and we became hysterical. We poked with a knife and extracted the meat bit by bit in the most unprofessional manner. It was the second time in a fortnight that, though there be room at the inn there was no banquet. I cannot ever remember Mother being in that predicament.

There was a secondary problem. We could not send a distant relative to a cemetery, three miles away, on foot. Equally impossible was it to send her by bus for it is half a mile to the village and two buses would be necessary. We must take her ourselves but we could not rudely hurry her departure. We must pretend we had plenty of time and that was certainly not the case. Rona was interested in our joint family history so we must unearth the family-tree, someone else researched and newspaper cuttings of two generations ago, whilst the enemy on the mantelpiece ticked away in an agitated manner.

At last we climbed into the Land Rover and drove to the Harden garage where there are always cut flowers. Rona hopped out with far more agility than we currently possessed and bought a bunch for the grave. We wondered whether the headstone would have been replaced after the necessary cleaning and engraving but it had. We'd already removed the family wreaths and all was tidy. The Keighley/Bradford bus stops outside the cemetery so we hastily said, 'Goodbye, browse as long as you like.' She'd look for other family graves, she said and then return to the city.

We sped back up the hill, opened the gate onto the pastures and carefully checked and counted cattle and the safety of our boundaries. Life is a kaleidoscope, the pattern of the next moment ever unpredictable. Other people have experience of this, too. I know because those who read about The Currer tell me they can relate so well. The unexpected can be fun. Why was it that I repeated, over and over again, 'I am going to cry all the way to Settle!'?

Perhaps because we never have time to mourn any of our loved ones, so embroiled are we in inescapable activity. Father died during the deep, deep snow of the long, long winter of 1979, when survival was our priority. Mother left us surrounded by Easter holiday makers coming home each evening for a four course meal. Harry died when the end of the Foot and Mouth was in sight but was more tormenting than it had ever been. If we could just get away, get onto that train, cry all the way to Settle, perhaps it would help.

Almost everyone reminded us that, now we had our 'freedom' we should use it. Friends and relatives have never understood that we have always been free. They consider we have been imprisoned by work and ageing family. Rubbish. Our parents allowed us total freedom. Aunty Mary hit the nail on the head by accident. She didn't understand either but whenever we were over-busy with life she would say, 'Well, it's what you want!'

What we call freedom has been our joy and what they insisted we now had, we interpreted as loneliness. We were totally bereft. No-one to share our holiday with, to plan for, pack up for, make way for. Carefree my foot! We thrive on sharing and had some major adapting to do.

Tim took us early to the station. He was in a hurry and we walked onto the platform half an hour before the train was due. That was surely a first and maybe a last. The Late Browns were early, cold and silent, sitting uncomfortably on the hard seat of the empty platform, each attached to the lead of a well-behaved dog. Mother would have had the perfect description for her two daughters. She would have said we looked, 'as if dead lice were dropping from us!' As if we were too lifeless to feed even a parasite!

We were waiting for the north bound train. Across the double railway lines, waiting for one south bound to Bradford, there was a very alert lady. She waved and shouted for our attention and in a pronounced American voice asked if she could photograph our dogs.

'Go ahead,' we said. We were used to Americans filming Danny and Meg.

'We have dogs in the States,' she shouted. 'I come from Wisconsin. I'm on a course in Bradford. What are your dogs called?' We told her.

'Are they sheep dogs?'

'Yes, but we only have cattle.'

'Are you farmers?' We nodded an affirmative.

'Where?'

'Up there,' I pointed to our hill overshadowing the station. A crowd was gathering on the platform and clustering round to watch and listen to this unexpected conversation. It was a good waiting-game entertainment. We were chuckling too.

'I'd love to visit you. We are farmers, too'.

'We'd be delighted to have you but we are going on holiday.'

'Where to?' We were suddenly telling all and sundry, honest or crooked where we were going. Every time a Leeds train stopped, then passed, she was still on the platform renewing the conversation and every time a local Skipton train paused on our platform, when it left she was still there. She found out we provided accommodation and told us she'd come and stay next time she was on this side of the Atlantic. She waved madly when the Carlisle train came and we boarded it.

I must tell you this. Margaret and I laughed all the way to Settle!

Chapter Nine

And after showers the smell of flowers
And the good brown earth.

Van Dyke

I F YOU HAVE NEVER BEEN to those far-flung islands which haunt us and beckon us with their beauty and spiritual rewards, you will now be weary of my songs of praise. We are always tired when we go and soul restored on our return. The railway lines northbound must be sprinkled with the dust of our fatigue as, little by little, it falls out of us. It is replaced by the stardust sparkle we collect as soon as we board the Caledonian MacBrayne steamer taking us to whichever island we are heading for. Every journey provides a memory. The June 2004 train one, was of Joy Sherriff who suddenly appeared at our side as we approached Oban. She and a friend were heading for Barra. Joy is the daughter of Barbara Sherriff, taught to love islands as one of my camping Guides and thereafter passing on that wanderlust to all her children, one of whom already lives on Eigg. All of them find wonderful, the wild, wet, windy islands not always bathed in sunshine, as her mother had once indicated by a postcard from South Uist. More and more there is evidence that the pebble Margaret, Hazel and I threw into the water, has sent ripples still affecting future generations, not only in the way they spend their holidays but in the way they view life and treat each other. All of them know the meaning of joy and the healing of laughter

Laughter is a clinically tested medicine. The boisterous landlord greeted us noisily at our overnight hotel but the chambermaid was more subdued. She was apologising all the way to our bedroom. The recent occupants had broken one of the twin beds. Maybe the previous user had been an overweight giant and had seated himself at the foot. Whatever the reason the base had collapsed. The hotel was chock-a-block and, though they had searched for a replacement, they had been unsuccessful and didn't know what to do. I have an affinity with chambermaids for that is one of my roles and bedroom predicaments have a special variety. I remembered a friend saying she had once hired a holiday cottage and found that one bed had been sitting with one leg on a biscuit tin!!

Believe me, a collapsed end of a divan was no problem to my pint sized sister. Neither would it have troubled me. We've slept too often on the floor to be worried about such a minor imperfection. Margaret is only five feet

Tiree.

tall and never uses the last eighteen inches of any bed. She demonstrated that she would sleep in comfort by lying on the bed. All we needed was uninterrupted sleep, where it did not matter in the slightest.

Finally the maid understood that it would not worry us but she would take no payment for Margaret's accommodation and we left for the early, Tiree boat, twenty five pounds better off than we'd expected.

Coalas, on the northern tip of Tiree is one of the most beautiful places to seat a caravan. Ours, for one week, was too perfect for comfort. A new, off-white carpet had been laid. On an island of white sand and machair, dirt is unknown, but wet dogs can be a problem and we were so near the sea Meg did not have time to dry. We could not close the caravan door on her, for the machair is dotted with sheep who believe, quite unnecessarily, that Meg and Danny chase. They do not but anticipation means they scatter. So we laid towels on the new carpet and not a mark was made.

We learned to walk again. We had neither car nor cycles. We would have received offers of a lift had we walked on the road but on Tiree you walk on the beach, on Caolis, or Gott, or Baugh, or Sorobay, or Balephetrish, Balevullin or Sandaig, Salum, Vaul or Balephuil. Wherever you are there is an extensive white beach on which to saunter, whilst Meg plays with the waves. Gradually, with no need to hurry, our tired injuries began to heal. The stresses of the last four years were given a chance to recover and our steps and spirits became more buoyant by the hour.

We went to inspect the shining new cattle market, used but few times a year. There were no animals and the concrete was spotless but the market cafe was open and we sampled beautiful soup and homemade cheesecake.

We visited each of our friends in turn. Most of them we have known for half a century. Ellen and Donny were watching their new house being built. We had brought Ellen home with us, in 1961, for a holiday at The Currer. Sylvia, a Guide I took there to camp in the early sixties, lives at Barrapol, happily enjoying life as a crofter. I have been responsible for the road so many have taken. 'It's all your fault,' they say. 'If you hadn't sent me to help at the Suffolk Diabetic Camp, I would never have married Peter!' says Dorothy, now a grandmother in Halton St Peter. 'If it hadn't been for you, Jean Brown,' wrote Kathryn from North Uist, 'I might have been in Benidorm!'

On one less sunny day we walked from Caoles to Salum via the beach and called for coffee with Effie to whom I can say, truthfully, 'It is all your fault not mine,' for it was she and John Lachie, her husband, whose welcome allowed us to camp there for so many years. It's passing the buck, I know but their part, surely came earlier than mine. They already lived there. Only God, who made Tiree, precedes their part in the series of events, that write the story of so many.

Our week was passing too quickly and we hadn't yet seen Margaret and Duncan MacInnes at Sackhill, only half a mile away from Salum. We had barely walked half way when the heavens opened. There is absolutely no shelter on Tiree. Margaret, fortunately, was wearing shorts but my trousers received the soaking of a lifetime. Reaching Sackhill I could not enter without taking them off. They were heavy with water and I wrang out more than a bowlful. When we eventually returned to the caravan I was wearing borrowed trousers and I was flying mine like a kite behind me, willing them to dry on the journey. I was nervous of the possible reaction of

Alistair's three, huge Belgian Blue bulls, eyeing us with suspicion from the other side of an unsafe looking fence. I am only half a farmer where bulls are concerned. I'm pretty sure they could have crashed through that sagging barbed wire had they chosen.

We caught the Thursday ferry to Barra and watched with amusement as others got wet in Castlebay. We did not need a bus to take us to the house of the 'lovely lady', but we were waiting in the bus shelter intending to speak to the driver and say we would need to be picked up outside our B&B next morning. It was not raining heavily but we soon realised that water collected on the shelter roof and, every so often, emptied a bucketful over whoever should be standing in the entrance. It amused us, waiting for the moment when the waterfall cascaded, knowing that the refill continued to fall gently from above. Some imperfection on the roof reacted as a tippler. We were as fascinated as school children, standing well back, in anticipation of the next deluge.

Two elderly gentlemen came to the entrance of the shelter. I have stopped saying 'old' for Margaret comments that those I describe as such are no older than I am, which I won't accept. These two well-dressed tourists halted below the collecting area of the roof and we thought it advisable to warn them to come inside. They were posh, loud spoken, obviously enjoying a first experience of the wild. We guessed they were staying at the multiple star hotel in Tangasdale. They were not dressed for the weather but shrugged their shoulders when we told them they would get wet. It wasn't raining heavily. They were unafraid of a spot or two. These were the Outer Hebrides, for goodness sake! They were toughies enjoying the weather! They completely ignored our warning, continuing their quite loud conversation and, of course, the inevitable happened. The moment of delivery came and each got the soaking of a life time. I am ashamed to say our ability to laugh had definitely returned.

The Youth Hostel, proprietor was right. The 'lovely lady', Mrs MacRury, was just that and our overnight stay at The Bungalow was a joy. Her husband was a man after our own mould. Late at night he was still struggling to finish concreting his yard, determined, as we so often are, to finish before bed-time, the hour of which was already gone.

Our bus driver, the following morning, was the daughter of a Tiree friend. She was complaining, too, that Health and Safety rules had gone too far having been recently summoned to drive five miles to the island school to give her fifteen year old daughter a paracetamol. No teacher had been allowed. Health and Safety once again. We remembered the First Aid box we used to take to camp with every remedy and dressing imaginable. How impossibly vulnerable we would have felt without it!

On the bus from the Eriskay Ferry we learned that the one on which we had returned, the previous year, and intended to use again in a week's time, now would arrive too late to board the ferry necessary to catch the one day a week boat direct to Oban. There would be no alternative but for us to return home via Skye and Mallaig. It meant cancelling the Oban booking and searching for a dog friendly B&B in Mallaig. However, to return via Skye and Fort William brought an unexpected pleasure to look forward to.

We had a pleasant journey up the Long Island with two bag-packing students from America, currently at Edinburgh University. It is necessary to travel without personal transport to have the enriching experience of meeting people from all corners of the world. We recommend it.

Harris gave us the tonic we needed, the peace, the solitude, the empty beaches, the eternal hills and the orchids at our feet. Entering our caravan we had nothing to do. Our minimal luggage hardly needed unpacking. We had eaten at John and Mamie's at Horgabost. The small box of necessary food, bought by Catrina, could be unpacked at leisure. We took off our shoes and walked across the flower strewn machair onto the beach, remembering the hundreds of footprints the overnight waves used to erase. It was high tide, filling Luskentyre's incredible beach with a swirling, turbulent green. It was an arctic evening with a white twilight over the bare mountains. It was almost fearsome in it's grandeur and remoteness. Again we wondered how we dared to bring so many children so far from home, to live for two weeks under canvas. One of their parents recently visited Harris for the first time. He told me they had had good weather and had found the island very beautiful but that he had said to his wife, 'If I had known where Jean Brown was bringing my children, I would have had a nightmare!' How did we dare? Because we were young and rode the sun and because we were among island friends. In today's Nanny State we would not have been allowed. We wouldn't have got beyond Keighley station with fifty children all dangling a penknife and carrying a sheath knife on their belts!!

Rachel's house had been sensitively modernised and was already being used by self-catering holidaymakers. It had once been a shooting lodge owned by a Lord. When he had left, it had been considerably reduced but the rooms are extremely spacious and eight people, or more, can use it. The old wooden schoolhouse, adjacent to it, had been pulled down and a new chalet, resembling it, was being built. This would give extra self-catering space and, we realised, would happily provide us with an ideal reunion base. Having lost so many of our family we had wondered if the road ahead would prove unexciting and lacking in fun. Well, now we had the answer. We were planning a Harris Reunion.

A friend was rejoicing on a much larger scale and we happened to be there at just the right time to share that moment of celebration with him. We had known Donald John MacKay for over forty years. He was only a boy when we first went to Luskentyre. He was frequently at Number 6, the home of his aunt and uncle and, year after year, we had watched him grow from child to skilled craftsman. He weaves the traditional Harris Tweed, in a shed outside the house he inherited, on a loom made by Hattersley and Son, of Keighley. Aunty Mary had worked in the office there, for forty years as a wages clerk. He had spent all his adult life there, as a shepherd and a weaver of the unique, orb bearing cloth. Coats I made from Donald John's tweed hang in our wardrobe. Though thirty years old they will never wear out.

He and other weavers had currently been experiencing a depression in their trade. Heated homes and cars, and man-made cheaper imports, had put tweed out of fashion and an island craft was being lost forever. We were as guilty as the rest. A Harris Tweed skirt was the 'uniform' in which I taught when classroom temperatures were lower than they are today.

The need was in decline for such beautiful material, woven with such skill from the wool of the Black Face sheep, native to the islands. With determination and sheer hard work, Donald John and his wife have hung on to their craft at Luskentyre. Their one-loom shed stands on a hillock, outside their house, overlooking beauty, unequalled anywhere.

In October 2003, an E-mail had popped up on their computer, requesting that a few of their best samples be sent to a factory, in Asia, at once. It had come from Niki, the world famous American company. After weeks of negotiation 12,000 metres had been ordered for the decoration of footwear and other weavers had become involved. They had hit the jackpot, but the amount of work ahead must have seemed awesome.

This unique story was just about to hit the headlines on the very day we were to cross Skye, sleep-over in Mallaig and head for home. As was our custom, we were visiting friends, to say, 'au revoir', on the late evening of the day Donald John had been interviewed and filmed by the media and television. His exhausted wife had gone to bed when we knocked on his door and obeyed his call to enter. We had no idea what had happened that day and our ignorance was a wonderful opportunity for him to relate the extraordinary story about to become nationwide news. We were two, wide-eyed friends who could fuel his enthusiasm. It was like entering an Aladdin's Cave. It was magic!

We responded far more convincingly than neighbours would have done, for success is never totally appreciated locally. We, too, were to experience this when our brief, lesser 'fierce hour and sweet' needed strangers. The next day the island story would hit the headlines of National Newspapers and be on every television news channel but we had had the remarkable good fortune to have received the news first hand, sitting on the crofter's hearth. We responded eagerly to his vocal amazement and applauded his achievement, allowing him to exhaust his pent up emotions. It was a night we will remember with joy, all our lives. When age makes me forgetful I will surely remember that!

Next day, travelling across The Minch on the MV *Hebrides*, from Tarbert to Uig, we watched television in the passenger lounge, a thing we never do. On it we saw Donald John and listened to his interview. We were so grateful to the conglomerate who had found our Gaelic speaking friend and rescued his craft.

We had phoned in advance to book accommodation at 'Spring Bank', a guest house in Mallaig run by people who love dogs as much as we do. They and we, are needed for dogs love a holiday, too and their owners enjoy having their company. If, for us, a beach is empty without children, it is essential that we have our dogs. We had no problem getting a bus from Uig to Portee and another to Armadale for the Sound of Sleat ferry to Mallaig. The welcoming couple were so concerned, that we would miss breakfast, in our haste to catch the 6 a.m. train to Glasgow, that they packed us a breakfast sufficient to last the whole eleven hour journey home.

I believe there is no route more isolated, more beautiful a wilderness than that traversed by the West Highland Line, through Fort William, over the Moor of Rannoch to join the Oban train at Crianlarich. This unplanned route was packed tight with memories, of being among my children, all going home contented, tired and happy. I would have preferred the 2004 silence to be broken only by the sound of the wheels, slowing putting the miles behind them. My thoughts were too private and my eyes too hungry for the view. It was not to be for a nice lady boarded the train at Roy Bridge, sat beside me and talked all the way. I could not, nor did I wish to be rude and present my back to her all the time. She was going all the way to Glasgow and crossing as we were, to Central Station. Her kindness was never ending. She would not leave us until she had shepherded us onto a Carlisle train. It pulled out of the platform three minutes before our tickets suggested and we were well beyond Glasgow before realising we were on a slow train, going a long way round and calling at Dumfries and Annan. Our tickets had been accurate. Reaching Carlisle the Leeds train was already leaving the station and we had a two hour wait. Train travelling teaches tolerance but we will not make that mistake again.

Chapter Ten

I am I and you are you
And we will work together.

MARGARET AND I HAVE EACH had a different role to play in our long, busy relationship, which is why we get on so well together. We do not tread on each other's toes and are seldom in the same vicinity. We have to tolerate each other's funny ways, of which there are many. We have no option for we are not quitting. No way and life as we know it needs two.

We have differing ideas about how to solve problems. Usually a little of both brings a joint success. We laugh at the same things, our basic principles are identical. We agree on what really matters. The Williams, from Anglesea, bought us a definition to hang on the wall. It said, 'Sister is another name for best friend.' Of us that is true.

She is the farmer, the driver, the painter and the toilet lady. I'm the chamber maid, the secretary, the farmer's man and occasional writer. I do not call myself an author because I don't make things up. What you read is what happens. We are both Jacks-of-all-trades, proficient in some, ham-fisted in others. What she can't do, I maybe can and visa versa. We are both philosophers, both content with our lot, both eager to take the biggest share of every load. So we get on fine. For a fortnight we had lived on the crest of a wave but now we had to come home to a new reality. We had no family to care for. Others of our kind would be just birds of passage, here today and gone tomorrow. We would still have status quo outside but now there would just be the two of us and the next family loss would reduce us to one and that did not bear thinking about.

When Dorothy had handed over all the post and phone calls and introduced us to any present guests, she left and we inspected our premises. The new door in The Mistal cottage was a perfect replica of the seventeenth century one we had taken out at the conversion. The garden wall had been demolished and the re-building had barely been begun. The flimsy, definitely inadequate fence, meant to keep out calves, attracted our attention and sarcasm but, as there were no animals in sight and being tired and two hours late home, we ridiculed the men but, unwisely walked away from the wobbly post and slack wire. It was a mistake. Next morning there was nothing left of our garden but the beautiful view. The newly laid turf had been uprooted with 280 hooves. Bedding plants had been trodden in,

The garden.

flower pots upturned and shrubs de-leafed. I was blazing mad. The wallers blamed the calves. I didn't! I insisted they made a proper job of the fence and Margaret and I went to the Garden Centre and bought more turf and plants. One benefit was that the garden had been well and truly manured.

The first unusual event on our full calendar was an Afternoon Tea we had been asked to organise for the Trefoil Guild, the Association of past members of the Guide Movement. One of their members had been enrolled as a Brownie seventy five years ago. 'Can I invite all my friends to a Strawberry Tea?' she had asked.

As a general rule we do not provide meals for non-residents. We make an exception for the annual visit of the Cheshire Home but that is by invitation. However my debt to the Guide Association is enormous so we said we would and I dashed into town for punnets of English strawberries and our milk lady supplied the cream. I taught her at primary school and she was one of my Guides. I am my mother's daughter when it comes to cake baking and cheer any opportunity to spend a whole day proving that I am still competent. One tragedy is, however, that I just cannot make scones. As these had been requested I had to resort to asking Dorothy. She makes beautiful ones.

How quickly a holiday is left behind but our enthusiasm for a whole upstairs makeover was still alive. It had taken such a battering over the last decade. To re-decorate and re-carpet had just been impossible. We went to a cousin's DIY shop and bought anaglypta paper and emulsion paint. Guests have knowledge of our network of rooms in the barn conversion, but relatives seem to think we only have our own front room and kitchen and that our lifestyle, away from the town, must mirror that of a recluse! 'You are hermits,' our DIY cousin said. I did what I seldom do. It doesn't matter if other people think we have no social life and that we must be lonely but on this occasion I waltzed him into the guest accommodation and took him round all the rabbit warren of rooms. 'Good Heavens,' he said. 'No wonder you want so much paint.'

We do not question the fact that we love decorating. Had we gone down a different road we might well have been property developers. Margaret can paint for hours and be happy. I am the paperhanger. We really went to town that August. We couldn't stop. It was the best medicine we could have. It is, however, impossible to be perfectionists in a house as old as this. Walls are not even and doors have wear and tear. Old beams are scarred with nails, used by previous generations to hang up cured hams and sides of bacon. Nor have we time to strip painted surfaces and sandpaper them. We cannot have a room out of use for longer than necessary so speed is vital. We cannot do the famous 60 minute make-over but I was not named Hell Fire Jack for nothing and Margaret can work past midnight if necessary.

We tore up the shredded carpets and took them to the household tip. Some of the old floor boards needed renewing round the area of the lift. They were of the nine inch wide variety of very old houses. We went from room to room until all four bedrooms and bathroom shone. Margaret's choice is always Almond White. It was dazzling. When our New Zealander returned, for her final week after a holiday in Scotland, there was no accommodation for her. She had to be satisfied with a bed on the bare boards in Aunty Mary's room. We had always, previously, bought sale price carpets and I had laid them. In 2004 we bought an expensive one which was laid, to cover the whole floor, by a professional. Ever since we have had leftover pieces on each step, to protect it, for it must outlive us.

On the 16th August we left our work to sit glued to the television watching the horrific flooding of Boscastle, in Cornwall. We were abruptly reminded of the predictions of environmental scientists that global warming will mean more violent weather. We were appalled by the sudden torrent of water and grateful, with the rest of the country, that there was no loss of life.

Things returned to an even keel and we began to get used to there being only two of us round the fire. The chairs of others had previously prevented us getting a fair share of the blaze. Suddenly we could share the rug and put all four feet on the hearth. The room seemed to have grown.

With this major job behind us we were ready to welcome The Gang, the group returning every year since 1985. We were over-full and Veronica was taken to Aunty Mary's room. Now we cannot persuade her to go elsewhere though she comes in February or with The Gang in August.

All farmers found the Autumn Sales less lucrative. Two years earlier, we had been forced to buy some heifer calves not eligible for subsidy. Since the war, cattle farmers had been receiving aid, first to encourage production, then to keep down prices to the customer. For several years the subsidy had been given only on steers and we, who buy at market, had only bought bull calves.

Farmers had become so proficient that cattle numbers had become an embarrassment and the Government sought every which way to reduce the national herd and enable them to buy cheaply from abroad. Farmers suspected food scares as ploys to achieve this. Some even believed the Foot and Mouth outbreak, if not exactly introduced, had been prolonged on purpose. Now, in the pipeline, was another innovation. Subsidies on cattle were about to cease and a Single Payment be made on acreage. Paperwork littered everyone's kitchen table. Would this really encourage people to keep less? I doubt it. I can never persuade Margaret to buy fewer calves!

Until the awful outbreak, we had rewarded ourselves with an autumn holiday, fortifying ourselves for the ravages of winter. We had believed it essential for the well being of our dependants and the physical health of the work force. It would have been sensible, after the traumas of the previous twelve months, to organise something for Saint Luke's Little Summer. We didn't even attempt it and it was not until the following spring that we accepted that all work and no play is not a good menu, even if you enjoy the meal. We are happy working.!

Perhaps we had mistakenly believed our friends who repeatedly said, 'You will have so much less to do now.' Maybe, but when the generation ahead live almost to the hundred mark, the one following has left the three score years and ten far behind. We were slower. I've got to admit that and, until the millennium, the other members of the family had been workers rather than dependants. Each of them had been more of an asset than a liability. Harry had dried dishes until the week before he died. Now everything fell on the two of us and we were still working a sixteen hour day.

I guess it was at this stage that I fully began to recognise the value of quality and reliability in the work force. I had taken the importance of the team for granted. I looked back and I saw my life only ever as a member of a team. First and foremost was the family, then a patrol, then a member of staff. The foundation stone of successful team spirit begins in the family and, sadly, that is becoming dysfunctional. From birth there is less sharing of space, responsibility and possessions and loneliness is becoming contagious.

Important members of our family team have always been our dogs. It was about this time that we began to worry about Danny. Not unduly for he was a tough old man but, following a minor collision with the Land Rover, one back leg troubled him. It was not enough to stop him being Margaret's

Diana.

constant companion nor deter him from cattle-control duties. This role also posed him problems because he, being totally unafraid, was frequently getting kicked. Unlike Meg, who only drives from the rear, Danny moved the front line forward, urging the foremost of the queue through the door or gateway and we often heard a veritable CRACK as hoof hit head. Fortunately the skull of a collie is unbreakable. Or so it seems. Meg had become a little impatient with all three of us following my broken leg, Margaret's 2001 injury and Danny's unfortunate wrong turn into the Land Rover wheel. Margaret had been driving whilst he was running alongside. He'd realised I was behind the vehicle, doing something more exciting. Instead of turning away from the slow moving vehicle, he'd turned into it, jolting and bruising a bone or a muscle, or both so that it now took him longer to rise from a sitting position and he was less speedy to respond. Especially so, when Meg demanded that he join her to warn off walkers, human or canine, using the footpath at the rear of the house. It also slowed his journey as a sniffer dog when out walking with us. More than most dogs he was interested in smells and, as his hearing deteriorated, we sometimes had to retrace our steps lest we leave him behind altogether. His coat, had he allowed Margaret to groom it, would have been beautiful. It was almost golden and as fine as silk. A farm is not an ideal place to live. Mud and manure, brambles and dead hawthorn twigs adhered to it frequently. To remove the latter, it required two of us, one to hold and one to extract. Because he would not entertain being combed, the rear of him was inclined to become matted. Before going on holiday I always held him firmly whilst Margaret, the inexperienced barber, cut off solid lumps of hair leaving him looking worse than ever. We had a guest who had a mass of unruly auburn hair and we were trying to identify her, by name, to another guest. Suddenly a six year old child said, 'She's the lady with hair like Danny!' I am so glad she did not hear!

Danny's obsession with Margaret was permanent. It was useful to me for wherever he was, I knew she would be. Meg could be in the yard and Margaret still in the Eight Acre, counting her cattle but if Danny was home she would be. If he was outside the calf shed, she would be in it. He would be agitated if he did not know her whereabouts and the biggest worry for him was when she was cleaning, or decorating in the holiday accommodation. This definitely flummoxed him and he would drive me mad wanting, first to go out and look for her then bark to come in and re-search the front room and kitchen. He never accepted the fact that she was only on the other side of the door and he went through the same performance when she had a bath. There was no problem when she went to bed. He just lay at the foot of the steps and stayed there until morning. It is sad that dogs age so quickly. Most of ours have lived to their mid-teens. Bess was twenty. People were beginning to ask how old Danny was. We didn't quite know. Only that he was fully grown when we brought him home from Harris in 1995.

In spite of the fact that Danny behaved impeccably with people he managed to bring a policeman twice. Once because he ran out to greet an unfriendly Rottweiler. The owner waited until she got home before phoning. There were more swear words in her short conversation than I have ever heard before or since. Nor had the policeman she phoned. He came to see Danny, as a matter of course, gave him a reprimand and a warning. The second time was more serious.

A lady came walking down the road with a friend's dog on a lead and, when Danny went out to greet her, she did what many people do which is ill-advised. She shortened the lead of her dog and when Danny came there was a tangle of legs. Ten in fact. Ten legs and a lead all became entwined and one of the human ones got bitten. The lady told the policeman it was Danny and it could have been. Collie cow dogs nip once and back off quickly to dodge the inevitable back-kick. Their nip must not injure, just encourage the animal to move forward if it is objecting. The nip on the lady's leg, whichever dog had misbehaved, was minimal but, unfortunately, the lady had a blood disorder and she had a massive bruise.

We were in shock. We had a too friendly dog and a footpath through the back paddock and scores of dog walkers. So Margaret bought a very expensive invisible electric fence and collar which would, when installed, deter Danny from approaching other dogs but not, unless they had a collar, prevent other dogs crossing it to greet him. We arranged with our electrician to fix it but he didn't come immediately, then presumably forgot and, as Danny was never in that sort of trouble again, the box containing that expensive equipment remains unopened in the loft.

There was one other incident when Danny's poor head got another severe crack. This time from a jogger's trainer. It is inexcusable for big, bare-legged, panting, sweating, swearing men to continue running on any footpath through a farm yard, whether it be concrete or grass. We have yelled, 'Walk!!' until we have been hoarse, but to no avail. This jogger kicked out at our approaching dog and caught him fair and square on the head.

'He bit me!' shouted the man.

'Before or after?' we enquired but there were no teeth marks. The man said he would kick harder next time and that he had every right to run on a footpath. He looked as if he meant it, so we employed our wallers and a fence was erected to enclose the footpath. All other dog walkers complained that it prevented their daily, friendly encounter with our dogs, especially with Danny whom every other person loved.

Anyone running, breathing heavily and perspiring profusely can stampede cattle in the stockyard. Should we be handling them an accident is just waiting to happen. We have frequently shouted after the disappearing man, 'You could at least say you are sorry!' Late in life we have finally come to the conclusion that men do not say they are sorry!

Danny had another admirer. A stray ginger cat had taken up residence in our barn, some time ago. We now have three farm cats. Two we rescued from a cat protection society, when all cats were removed from Bradford Market. They are Blackie and Smokey because of their colour and have never been near the house. They quickly rid the premises of pigeons proving beyond doubt that a cat among pigeons is an item not to be taken lightly. Never being house cats, they have seldom come within thirty yards of our front door. When our last feline inmate died we chose not to welcome another, for we had two disabled members and a cat on the hearth rug can cause an accident.

The ginger one, called Ginger of course, had a long standing love affair with Danny. They were the same colour and it waited by the front door for Danny to come out and then proceeded to walk beside him, so closely that one fur coat merged with the other. No matter what time of day, or night, Ginger was there waiting for Danny. We have spent some time watching colour preference in animals. It is not prejudice as it can be in humans, but many of our animals, over decades, have shown this trait. Black cattle seem to collect in groups of black, red ones stick together. Similarly the mostly-white sit close.

This preference for colour, we notice particularly in the goats. These cannot be classed as pets, for we ignore them. Of all our animals they are allowed freedom of spirit, but they are undoubtedly our nearest neighbours. Since we have had goats, we have had brown and white in equal numbers and the brown ones have preferred each other and the white ones separated when browsing. The ginger cat was the only Moggy who wanted to be with Danny.

He was not the only one showing signs of age. Both nanny goats, Rosy and Snowy, were ancient. Female goats out-live the males by a decade, or so it seems, but the latter are Good Luck bringers and this must never be ignored.

Meg is a younger and more agile family member but, though she never failed to alert Danny to the approach of walkers and their dogs, she always left him to do the friendly formalities. She will never get near enough to frighten anyone, except the postman. She, I am sure, is aware when the red van passes through the village long before it enters the gate, a quarter of a mile from the house. Entering the yard he will not get out of the car but waits until one of us appears and, at a word, Meg leaves her prey and eyes him only from the doorway. She does not like him, nor what he brings. Her eyes and agitation tell me, on no account, to open the letters he has brought. If I wish to do so, I must first give her leave to chase him up the hill and tear open the envelopes whilst she is so doing. If we are not about and she is on self-appointed guard, the postman does not deliver. He writes DOG LOOSE on the top envelope and takes the letters away to bring next day. Whoever else comes she greets them with pleasure, her tail wagging like anything.

Meg is a modern miss who likes to bathe frequently and it is convenient that we have so many baths inside and outside the farm buildings as well as the stream running parallel to the road. In summer she goes for her ablutions several times a day. If she chooses an inside water trough she comes home clean. If she has used the stream she will have churned up the mud and gravel from the bed and she will be dirtier than before but if she has taken her bath in the trough which collects the spring water, which has a definite, orange sediment, she will come home a glamorous gold where she should be white. Being a girl she changes her appearance at will and does not hesitate to run sopping into the house, dripping water all over the parquet tiles and leaving wet patches on the carpet.

Like all dogs she knows what is coming by the signs we are making. She knows when it is fun to come with us because she will be needed. When Margaret is only going to count cattle, no way is she going to mingle among them. They know she is scared, unless she is in control from the rear, just as the geese know I am terrified. In both cases she and I are likely to have to run. It is sometimes necessary for me and my stick to protect her, for I do not fear cattle, and for her to protect me for I am scared and she can cope with geese no matter how they hiss.

She knows that clean clothes mean a visit to town and she precedes the car nearly all the way up the road, far too slowly for comfort. We follow at 4mph as drivers did when cars were first introduced onto the streets and we have to wait until her need to spend a penny means she momentarily steps onto the verge and we can pass her and quicken our pace. She knows to follow and that, on the top road, we will pick her up.

How quickly the nights begin to pull in and the artificial light must be switched on sooner every night. At the beginning of October our dialogue with the electricity board began again. We were given a middle of the month date when the new transformer could be fixed onto the existing pole, not ten metres from the house. Again we were told we must employ someone to dig a trench and lay a pipe through which they could draw the wire. The wallers did this and in the space of four hours four men fixed the trans-former to the pole. They drew the wire to the base of the dining room wall, up it parallel with the existing supply and through the sixteenth century thickness of Yorkshire millstone grit. We were given an EN number to send to our supplier and told a new meter would be installed. Our own electrician must be alerted for he would have to do the connection. It suddenly seemed a whole waste of money for the loss of Aunty Mary had grossly reduced the amount of energy we were using. No lift, hoist or electric bed. No almost continual television beside an all the year electric fire. It had proved impossible to accelerate action but now there was no means of stopping it.

For a few years we had begun to put off calf buying until the very end of October and the beginning of November. In theory this extended autumn and shortened winter but it never felt that way. In spite of the experts saying spring is earlier due to global warming, those of us waiting for grass to grow disagree. Our opportunity to turn out cattle comes later and later. I amuse guests by saying I think extracting millions of tons of oil have unbalanced the planet and moved the seasons so that they do not sit on the calendar as they used to!

We had expected a meter to be installed immediately but nothing happened on that front and we went to Gisburn Cattle Mart on the last Thursday in October and again one week later and we had sixty eight calves. It seemed to me that it had been weeks not 12 months since we had last re-stocked, yet so much had happened since I had deserted Margaret by breaking my leg.

We bought good calves and all of them lived. In fact they caused us no trouble at all, Neighbours were complaining that there was a lot of pneumonia that winter and farmers' press reported it nationwide, but we escaped. Perhaps it was Margaret's increasing use of homeopathic preventatives. Buying, in our profession, is always a gamble. Because our turnover is every two years, we cannot anticipate the return of our outlay, so long in advance. Those who buy from us and finish animals in a few short weeks, can buy fewer or more according to market trend. We are at the mercy of two winters and goodness only knows how many government changes and mistakes which can affect the measure of profit or loss in two years' time. We are always at the mercy of the wind and must blow with it.

The coming winter promised to have two workers in the calf shed and no one to care for in the house. That we struggled through the coming months emphasised how much damage had been done by the last twelve. We would admit it to no-one. To all of the many who queried, we answered, 'We're fine,' but it was a tale, a white lie we glibly toted out to everyone. We overcame obstacles by scrambling rather than leaping but, of course, we are survivors. We just needed time. The spark was there. It just needed kindling and a few puffs to produce a flame .

Funnily enough it was the electricity board that inflamed me. There was no word from them, no meter, no refund. When, in desperation, I phoned I was told that, of course they had done nothing because I had never signed a contract. 'A WHAT?' I shouted over the phone. 'You have never sent me one! I must have my extra supply before Christmas!'

'That's impossible,' they said but I wouldn't accept that as an answer. It had to be.

We had another problem. It had not gone unnoticed, in the summer, that water was coming up in the stockyard. We should have done something about it then but it was inconveniencing no one and our contractors were busy with harvest and summer workloads of every kind. The stockyard is only in view when we climb the road. This we usually do in a vehicle and, as the sun dries up any leakage it is only when it became a stream that we got alarmed. We believed it was coming from the pipe taking water from the spring. This constant supply was being wasted. The trough beneath, collecting the water, was perpetually full and the overflow was piped under the stockyard to the stream. We asked the wallers to pipe the water into a drinking trough so that the overflow could enter the stream by an alternative route. This also meant that the cattle could have access to spring water and that our water bill would be considerably reduced. It was a success story only in that respect but it made no difference whatsoever to the appearance of water in the stockyard.

It was not until mid-December that the cattle came to take up residence in the sheds and yard. We had sent for John Sugden to sort out the water problem and these two events came at the same time. John sent his youngest son to dig a massive crater whilst surrounded by inquisitive cattle and we expected our problems to escalate. We had little faith in the teenage boy at the wheel of the tractor and none in the behaviour of cattle, just recently restricted of freedom. Miraculously Oliver solved our problem in just two days and, though they teetered over the brink of the crater, not one of the eighty animals fell in. Their entertainment was over quicker than we'd expected. Oliver had proved himself to be equal to the rest of his competent family. When the job was finished Margaret viewed the surrounding fence with trepidation. It looked extremely insecure. 'We'll have that re-fenced in the summer, John,' she said.

'We'll do it with motorway barriers,' he replied.

We reinforced the dodgy fence with a couple of iron gates where it was most vulnerable and crossed our fingers. There was other work to do. Somehow or other I had to accelerate the electricity board. I seemed to be constantly on the phone and our pre-Christmas activity was increased by the publication of *We'll buy another on Monday*. The arrival of three hundred copies, many to send to those who had ordered and wanted their copy for Christmas, stretched me to the limit. We were inundated with local people wanting to buy for presents.

My sanity was only saved by the arrival of a new meter, just days before the arrival of our first guests and pacified, shortly afterwards, by the receipt of a £2000 refund. The epic dialogue was over.

Water continued to rank high on our agenda during the festive season, completely stealing any opportunity to relax. It is essential and occasional lack of it over the past half century, has caused our premature greying. It was the first commodity we brought to The Currer. A polythene pipe was attached to a mains supply before our removal in 1958. It came long before electricity, before a road and four wheels to traverse it. Since then it has failed us on many occasions for many different reasons. One year, 1963, frost and snow deprived us of it for seven weeks. Then the only water we had to drink came from the spring which, coming from the earth and flowing perpetually, never freezes. For a while our insides must have been tinted with the colourful sediment. Several times it has been turned off at the mains, because of work being done in the area and once by mistake but, on average, our supply to the house is constant. Not so was it to the cattle sheds.

When water was taken there, it came from a ten gallon tank in the attic, above the Loft Cottage and originally served only one trough. However our bovine city began to grow to house our herd and problems began at least twenty years ago. This disgusts me because, in the spring of 2005, we solved the problem in less than half an hour. It stemmed from the fact that we had potentially one hundred and fifty cattle drinking gallons of water. They were not all able to do so at once but it was possible for enough to be drinking for the overhead tank to empty more quickly than fill. Then air got into the pipe and the whole system choked. In the nineties we installed a five hundred gallon tank which saved us from running out of water immediately, if the water board unexpectedly switched off, but it didn't solve the problem of the air-lock. Of course we had discovered how to deal with it but not the cause of it. It fascinates me how the pressure from the reservoir can supply so many, how our 2" diameter pipe can feed sixteen cold taps in the house, five water troughs and seven drinking bowls in the sheds, simultaneously, or near enough. The mind boggles when a city must be catered for. No-one should be critical of the water board and its maze of pipes and pumping stations.

The way we had solved our problem was to attach a hose pipe to the cold water tap in the Mistal cottage, then to a tap in the donkey-hole and let the pressure from the mains force out the air-lock. How stupid can you get. We knew that to by-pass the tank was necessary but we dare not make it a permanent feature, for then any leak would flood a shed remarkably quickly. We believed that to do so in an emergency, we would have to bring a pipe all the way behind the house and across the road. Forty years earlier I, in my role as an amateur plumber, had brought a pipe from the mains to a tap in the Mistal, to fill the bath in which we mixed calf milk. The barn conversion had destroyed all my plumbing. To bring another pipe meant a long trench so we had settled for the hosepipe attached to the cottage tap. It was a poor substitute for to get enough pressure to force out the air, there was constant risk of the pipe blowing off the tap and the cottage kitchen flooding. There was a similar risk of the pipe blowing off the tap in the donkey domain and there were only two of us and one was needed down in the calf shed awaiting the moment of success. If this evaded us we took the hose from the cottage to the calf shed and attempted to blow out the air that way. This meant we had to put an extension on the pipe and frequently the two bits would part and water go down the drain. One way or another we got soaking wet. Our tolerance is on a higher level than most. The whole process was so long all our animals were thirsty and because they all wanted to drink at once another air-lock was inevitable.

Having directed spring water into a trough, it took away some of this bovine demand during Christmas when the system played games with us. On the morning of the 25th we had no water in the sheds but we had Mrs Bullock in the Mistal cottage and an extra pair of hands to monitor the safety of the tap under pressure. I held the pipe onto the shed tap and she held one in the cottage whilst Margaret coped with the end of the line, where the supply came into the calf shed. We had an airlock so many times, and interrupted the festivities in the Bullock house so frequently, we were embarrassed and ashamed. But all our troubles dissolved into insignificance on the morning of Boxing Day, when the horrific Tsunami devastated Indonesia. With disasters possible, on such a scale, on our volatile planet, how dare anyone complain. We and all our self-catering Christmas guests watched the television with awe and horror.

Certainly no-one complained when the electricity in the area failed on the first weekend after the New Year. We had a wedding party group from Cornwall occupying all our bed spaces. The various cars began to arrive, as darkness was falling, on the late afternoon of the Friday. I love showing a new party round our house, especially at the festive season when a log fire is burning and there are lighted Christmas trees. As I took the leading lady round from room to room, every light was aglow. There was a buzz of excitement everywhere, a murmur of delighted approval, a shuffle of feet on the parquet tiles, a resting of cases in the sitting room whilst bedrooms were allocated and masses of food carried into the kitchen.

Suddenly the lights went out everywhere. If the fault lies here a flick of a switch in the box puts everything back to normal but a peep outside the front door showed us that every light in the valley had gone out. My opinion of the Board in question was already low. A phone call to their Helpline produced a taped message saying power had been lost in the area and hopefully it would be returned shortly after 9 p.m.

We should have felt anger but maybe it was that all of us had been unconsciously affected by the Tsunami and tolerance everywhere was at a high. There was not one complaint from the newly arrived party. I was a little flummoxed for I could not immediately think where on earth I stored my candles. There were Christmas ones still available and I ran for them and matches and re-entered the sitting room. The leading lady had beaten me to it. She had run out to her car for five candles she had brought in case of emergency. I couldn't believe it. We have taken a torch on holiday but never candles and we have been educated with the motto 'Be Prepared'

They were truly amazing, that family group from Cornwall, here to attend a wedding. Our emergency lighting provided stairway dimness and a similar twilight in the sitting and dining rooms. Our central heating and Aga are coke fired. More logs were brought in and the log fire was stoked. The cooks were given permission to use the Aga. I found enough candles, the adults played I Spy with the children and the episode turned into an adventure.

The calf shed was in total darkness. Once when this had happened, we had driven the Land Rover to the doorway and turned on the headlights. This time the yard was full of parked cars. Our group had problems enough, without emptying it and allowing us to drive out of the garage. So we took a big torch with us. If our guests could cope, we would do so also.

There was one great blessing. The water system was not air-locked all weekend. When the penny dropped that all we needed was for our plumber to connect an emergency pipe to the mains before they entered the loft tank, it took him less than half an hour. It had taken us many years, many struggles, many soakings and some less ladylike language to solve such a simple problem.

Bad news travels quickly when you have a telephone. They say it does so even quicker by E-mail but that is not available in our house. Shortly after the New Year placed a new calendar on the wall, a friend rang to say her husband had just been diagnosed with inoperable cancer. To each friend one owes a debt of gratitude in varying proportions. Mine to Hazel is immense and to Ray, her husband. For ten wonderful years she had made it possible for me to continue taking children to camp in the Hebrides, an opportunity I rank very highly on my quite extensive list. Cancer haunts us as no other illness does. We are surrounded by parents bringing children with cerebral palsy, to the David Hart clinic. Our life with Harry, until he was seventy four, gives hope of a future for them. Though medical science has improved by leaps and bounds, and many cancer suffers survive and regain excellent health, there are still far too many for whom the diagnosis is serious and we get far too many phone calls alerting us to rather frightening news. Margaret insists that the dreaded word 'terminal' be deleted from the medical dictionary. Life is terminal and when, and how, is not predictable. The premature use of it is unkind and many have proved it wrong. The news about Ray was unexpected and devastating.

My dislike of a New Year has bordered on paranoia. I annually celebrate it with relief only when it is behind me. I do not fear the future and given a few days forget the trembling start when, no matter how silly it is to antici-pate the unknown, I confess that I stand at the gate of the year wondering what on earth life is about to throw at us. The last year had reduced me in size quite considerably.

Time, as one gets older, seems to accelerate. No sooner had January come than it was gone and February arrived. The Fill Dyke month is no more. There is neither black nor white, scarcely no snow at all and far too little rain. Men searching for life on another planet look first for water. It is the very first on the list of the ingredients for survival. Though spring appears to get off to an early start, in these days of global warming, all advantage is lost because the earth is too dry and consequently impervious to water, even though it comes as a torrent. Though bulbs may waken, the grass does not and turning-out time gets later.

February brought the imminent arrival of Diana's seventh calf. She had not once performed well in the labour ward. We had needed strong men to help us help her, every time and we had had to send for the vet twice. We only have one birth annually on the farm and it threatens to give us a nervous breakdown. We remember having a suckling herd and cattle calving unaided in the field and, before that, a milking herd and babies dropping easily into the group behind the stalls. Our experience with Diana is never anything like that. Her part of motherhood, she thinks, will come after the birth. That bit is our responsibility, not hers. She will be an immediate, excel-lent mother after the event, but not during it. We had been lucky, so far, that each birth had been in the day-time. It was, therefore a disaster waiting to happen, we thought, when very late at night Margaret came to tell me Diana was calving. So she was and, as per usual, she was getting no where slowly. As always, she could manage two front feet without help, but that was all.

She is very precious to us and visions of dead cows on the apron of concrete at the knacker's yard, a half born calf protruding, are stored indelibly in my memory.

As the mid-night hour came and went, Margaret said, 'I can't risk it. I'm sending for the vet.' Too much work, for too many years, has weakened our grip. We both had perpetual pins and needles in our fingers, suggestive of carpel tunnel. There was no slot in our work schedule which would allow surgical, time-out if that could possibly be avoided. 'You go and ring for him,' she said.

So I did but it was a lady vet on duty. Now I have every respect for a female professional, in what ever field, but this news was alarming. We needed strength with a capital S. The only guests we had were old and in bed. We are ashamed of our labour-ward panic, especially when we remember that Anna, a student mid-wife who stays with us frequently, is engaged in that sort of thing with humans every day.

'Crikey!' I exploded over the phone. 'Do you think you can manage? For six previous births we've needed at least two strong men.'

'I'll come,' she said. 'I'll try. I'll be half an hour, at least!'

This news was not good enough for Margaret. 'You stay,' she ordered. 'I'm going to ring for Tim.'

So I was left to haul alone and she called Tim from his bed. He could get here in half that time but when Margaret returned we freed the head which was scary for we would now lose the calf if we could not get the shoulders. Suddenly our gorgeous Diana gave us that one bit of help we needed and, regardless of what damage it was doing to us, we freed the shoulders.

'God help us if we can't get the hips,' gasped Margaret. 'Twist a bit.' We did and a baby heifer lay at our feet.

'Ring and cancel the vet!' ordered sister. Elation gave me strength to run to the phone. In this day and age, anyone else would have had a mobile phone in her pocket. Why are we so old-fashioned?

I couldn't stop Tim. His head-lights showed at the top of our road but the lady vet could go back to bed. Tim wasn't critical at all. He joined us to watch the miracle of mother-baby bonding. The magic of it never dims.

A few days later a cousin's son's wife came with her toddler grand-daughter. That makes me sound very old and I'm not! Margaret and I calved Diana alone! Surely I'm not old!

The child, Amy, was so entertaining we were captivated and called our baby, Amy, too. We rarely name animals for there are far too many roaming our pastures. We had previously given Diana three adopted babies for her milk supply was incredible and her foster-parenting unbelievable. Margaret phoned a farmer friend, from whom we had bought calves after the Foot and Mouth, to see if he had a calf, maybe two. 'Sorry,' he said. 'I've just lost two with pneumonia.'

'What have I nearly just done?' Margaret exclaimed in horror. We knew farmers were experiencing this disease. She had nearly exposed us to buying-in an epidemic we didn't have. 'That's it,' she announced. 'No more calves for Diana this year!' There was no way we dare jeopardise the safety of our herd. Our animals were indeed healthy and they were beginning to get a February wanderlust. They were viewing with interest, the rather dodgy fence, which enclosed the stockyard, and wondering how to escape. When darkness began to come later and later, they began to get more and more frisky. Every wet night they re-entered their night accommodation obediently. On milder evenings they played us up outrageously.

I was reminded of children deprived of the 'Rec', pretending they had not heard the bell recalling them to lessons and snatching another circuit of the playground before responding. These yearlings, having chosen to come in out of the cold of December, were getting itchy for freedom. My job of driving them into the sheds became more and more that of a circus ringmaster. One of us was needed at the entrance to count the right number in and prevent any coming out. Margaret can count more accurately than I can. A task, so easy in December, can be a fiasco in February, when they have discovered the game of Dodge. Their weaving in and out between the free standing mangers, drives a drover to stick-flourishing and verbal abuse and we, like they, count the days to when the yard gate can be opened and freedom allowed. Human amusement at their antics, soon becomes frustration and then intolerance.

Amusement lasted longer than usual, on one remembered Saturday. Funnily enough I had recently received a letter from a guest who had stayed a few years previously. She had sent me a newspaper cutting, from Leicester, reporting the promotion of one of my pupils who had entered the Church of England after a brief period of teaching. All news of my children, though they have passed the half century milestone, interests me and I was delighted when, on the Saturday week, he appeared in person, on a motor bike, to tell me himself.

We were still chatting away when the time came for us to return the cattle indoors. If we are too soon they won't go in. Too late and dusk makes them spooky. There is a right time and it must be selected.

'I'll manage alone,' Margaret insisted.

'No you won't,' I said. 'Christopher will just wait here and we won't be long and then I'll make a cup of tea.'

'I'll come and help,' said the well dressed gentleman of the cloth.

'You can watch,' I said. 'That's all.'

So he did and the yearlings whispered to each other, 'I say, we've got an audience. Let's have fun!' They began at once to head-butt each other. They climbed the solid heap of bedding manure and galloped down it with glee. Seventy and more, they played cat and mouse, teasing me on purpose whilst my pupil stared open mouthed from behind the safety of the gate. Suddenly the performance ended as abruptly as if the curtain had come down on the end of a show. They looked at each other nodding, 'I do believe she wants us to go in,' and like naughty school children, finally acknowledging the end-of-playtime bell, they tip-toed inside. I am not sure which had amazed Christopher most, the obstreperous animals or their headteacher drover!

Margaret puts off letting them out onto the land for as long as possible. Waiting for grass to grow makes her impatient as well as they and the drier winters don't help. When the snows of yore melted there was always grass below and lush growth was imminent. Not so now. If cattle have nothing to eat they just romp about making a mess of gateways and causing irate ramblers to shower abuse. We apologise. Ladies say they are sorry many times a day! Local people never grumble. They park their cars on the space our side of the cattle grid and walk their dogs, without a lead. They do no damage and our cattle never even look sideways. The villagers are polite, gather mushrooms and bilberries gratefully. Only walkers from the town complain. They never think of picking up litter or replacing a topstone. Urban Litter-louts frequently throw cigarette packets, take-away trays and beer cans from their vehicles. They are not locals. Just youths who possess cars but no good manners. Their throw-outs are easily picked up and disposed of. Not so plastic bags containing dog droppings. Whoever told anyone to clean up after their pet and leave the bag by the wayside?

The stockyard fence actually survived the winter. It was the gatepost that didn't. It was a stout 8' by 8' beam and it looked fine but its root was rotten below the layer of surface muck. The cattle discovered this on the Saturday of the last week in February. It was not the hinge bearing one, so had not been weakened with weight but it was standing against the shed wall and must have received a considerable amount of roof water.

A family group from Oban and Mull had just arrived to spend a self-catering week in our six-bedroom accommodation, now so frequently used for that purpose. It was their first visit but they had previously lived in the locality and were long standing friends of Dorothy and her family. Indeed she had come to welcome them and had been the one to show them round and give them the key. She had barely done so before there was a thundering of two hundred and forty hooves past the front door and 60 hooves past their bedroom window. The animals escaping through the yard found instant access to the Five Acre, for the gate was permanently open to allow the donkeys to come and go as they pleased. Those galloping through the paddock found the gate closed and leapt the fence at the corner, dragging up the end post and leaving a tangle of barbed wire and sheep netting.

The sound of scores of cattle thundering through the yard is not one which we ever mis-interpret. We know immediately what is happening though it is by no means a daily, nor even a yearly event. It fills us with many diverse fears. First comes the possibility that there is someone in danger in the yard, unloading cases maybe, or just admiring the view. Secondly there is the fear that one or several of the parked cars will be minus a side mirror or a radio aerial. Thirdly comes the knowledge that muck, loose because excited cattle suddenly have diarrhoea, will be splattered all over polished vehicles and will mottle the yard artistically and colourfully. Last of all there is the uncertainty, the inevitable question, 'How will we get them back.?'

Margaret, who is a professional, knows the answer to that is, 'You can't. Not immediately.' Providing they are not over the boundary, in someone else's property, you let them have their fling. Dorothy and her friends came at once to offer help. 'Oh just leave them!' we said. 'Let them have their caper. They'll come back eventually.'

We all watched them careering round the field in joyous ecstasy making use of this sudden opportunity for much needed exercise. 'Which way will they come back?' our friends wanted to know. 'You'll have to ask them,' we laughed.

We shut the yard gate and all of us went to investigate the mutilated fence in the paddock. We dragged some sheep hurdles to repair it securely against their sudden return and we never noticed an old caravanette being driven down the road by an even older gentleman. He saw us and realised he had taken the wrong road and was about to enter somebody's farm yard. Embarrassed by this he pulled off onto the grass verge, intending to turn and reclimb the hill. He found it had been a mistake for the ground was wet and without help there was no way he was going to get back onto the tarmac. It was when he began to rev up his engine that we saw him and it took six of us to push him off the grass.

By this time we were all filthy. We had to improvise a temporary way of securing the injured gate from the stockyard. The post was flat on the ground and would never stand again. There was no better solution, overnight, than another metal sheep hurdle. What would we, who have no sheep, do without them? It was whilst we were doing this the man from Oban said, 'We haven't been here two minutes and there's been enough cartoon material for Warner Brothers!'

The escapees chose to return via the eastern doors. This is the logical re-entry from the Five Acre but was inconvenient for the thirty, to count into the bottom shed, had to climb over an unopened straw bale, eight feet by four. It was a moment of final fun at the end of their afternoon adventure. We decided that the wooden gate of the stockyard must be exchanged for a metal one. A new fence must follow at a later date.

Most things that are really laughable are not basically funny at all or is it that we have a warped sense of humour. Given that I laugh so heartily when it is inappropriate, how odd that I do not find slapstick at all amusing and turn it off television. Our daily life is a pantomime but I would never choose one for entertainment. Real life can never be improved upon.

It is nice to know, after what Mother would have called,' A right Carry On,' that one's guests are self-catering and no evening meal is necessary, that having regained our status quo, only the calves are to feed and ducks and geese returned to their respective overnight quarters.

If Ian, from Oban, described life at The Currer as suitable material for Warner Brothers, his family was to contribute to the script next day and it was his face which reddened with embarrassment. Perhaps it was because Dorothy, their long standing friend, had welcomed them in, or maybe it was that the Saturday afternoon fiasco had taken precedence over everything else. In the melee of excitement the message I try to instil on all our guests, was either not given or not heard. It is terribly important that no-one smokes in a bedroom. To do so sets off our very sensitive fire alarm. Fortunately smoking is now illegal indoors.

The decibel peak required by authority is so loud as to deafen but not loud enough to penetrate the calf shed with its closed doors and the constant whirr of the fans. Immediately Smart Test is alerted and we are phoned and queried as to whether the call is accident or genuine. We deliver our password, ask the caller to hold on whilst we check that it is a false alarm and that we are not going up in flames and nothing further happens. Should we not be there to answer the phone many wheels are set in motion. Fire engines are sent for and Dorothy called to drive quickly to the site, with her key for our front door.

On the Sunday evening, whilst we were feeding calves, a member of the family lit a cigarette in one of the bedrooms. Smart Test phoned and when we did not answer the Fire Station was alerted.

Dorothy, in her Bingley home, was expecting to spend the evening here with her friends, but had several chores to do first. She had returned from an afternoon Dog Show and was desperate for a cup of tea. She lit the gas and dropped the used match into her waste paper bin, hidden under the sink. She put on the kettle and, whilst it came to the boil, she vacuumed her lovely new kitchen carpet. Then, needing to put something else into the bin, she opened the door and a wall of flames sprang out. The used match had not been dead. It had ignited the paper but, short of oxygen, had only become an item when the door was opened. Bits of still burning paper were dropping on her new kitchen carpet and she was in a panic. She turned on the tap and poured water over the flames and stamped out the burning bits of paper. She heard the telephone ringing. Her small fire was mercifully out and safe to leave so she picked up the phone and a voice said, 'I'm the Fire Prevention Officer …' and a good deal more but Dorothy was in shock. How did he know? How could someone have seen her predicament and alerted the Fire Station. It just wasn't possible.

'What did you say?' she stammered.

'I said could you bring the key for Currer Laithe Farm. There is a fire alert!'

She was just recovering from one fire hazard and was now confronted with another. 'I'll come,' she promised, but first she must make quite sure all was safe in her kitchen. She was trembling when she got into the car.

Meanwhile I had finished my part in the calf-rearing activity. Leaving the shed I noticed there were flashing blue lights in the yard. I called behind me, to Margaret, 'I think we've got the police,' but it was two fire engines and two dozen, helmeted men. A very embarrassed group of holiday makers was explaining that it was a false alarm, that someone had been smoking in a bedroom. A thorough search was made but their smoke alone had caused all the fuss. Into this drama came a thoroughly mentally and physically exhausted Dorothy. It took everyone some time before we could all see the funny side and laugh. I think it was next day before Dorothy did. Fire is frightening to say the least and then laughter is most inappropriate but it really had been cartoon quality.

There can be nothing funny about floods and storms either. A dreadful one off the north west coast, a short time later, put Carlisle under water and gave the Hebridean islands their worst experience in living memory. Phoning Angus and Katie, at Luskentyre the following morning, to check all was well, we found them all in shock.

'In seventy years, I've never seen anything like that,' Angus said. They had been really afraid. The road into the minute township had collapsed and a caravan had unbelievably been blown across the estuary from Seilebost. It had landed on the beach below Morag MacKinnon's croft at No 1. Kathleen, their daughter, and her husband Bobby had thought the roof of their beautiful house would blow off but all the people were safe. There was damage to property but our friends had survived. Not so a family on Benbecula. They had tried to drive to safety across one of the causeways, had been swept into the sea and all were lost. Those who refuse to believe the climate is getting angrier, must think again.

Certainly, in the spring of 2005, we recognised that, even in Britain where the climate is noted for being fickle, it was definitely altering. Winter was beginning later by two months, there was little or no snow, far less rain in April and a colder spring was bringing May flowers out in June. We began to query whether the planet was warming-up and seriously wondered if it was actually drying up. Our land was parched and we were feeding big bales a month longer than usual.

The cattle thought it was time to stay out at night, tried it once and wished they hadn't and continued to come for shelter for some time longer. We were the ones who had to take the initiative and shut the gates to prevent them doing so. Our October calves, too, were to come home well into May.

We distinctly remember we used to turn out in March. During that month the grass would begin to grow and be nurtured by the expected showers of April but that had not happened recently. Leigh Sugden was able to take out the muck and to spread last year's from the heap, on ground starved of winter rain. The tractor wheels made no impression whatsoever. Adam Sugden was able to clean out the ditches down which there was no running water. Some places received a heavy shower, now and again and townies stared at us when we complained of drought.

'We've had rain,' they said having occasionally had to switch on their windscreen wipers but never having had to cut their lawn. There would sometimes be a heavy shower at Skipton, or Harrogate and even we experienced a downpour now and again, but all were localised. It might rain for five minutes in Keighley but we would not see a drop and visa versa. The ground was so dry, heavy rain ran off as if it had fallen on concrete or tarmac. What had happened to the acres of mud our Wellingtons used to plough through eight months of every year? Change is coming faster than predicted. Of that we are sure!

In April we accommodated three people who were to stay with us a long time. They had a three month contract to work at the Bradford and Bingley Building Society and it became extended. This booking meant we never had an empty slot to do any major work, let alone spring clean, so they had to suffer disruptions and temporary no-go areas. We snatched an opportunity to convert the wheelchair ramp into three, well spaced, flagstone steps. For some time we had worried about the slippiness of that steep slope. It had become much harder to push wheelchairs up it. Non-slip lino and guaranteed non-slip carpets, never lived up to expectations. Children turned it into a ski slope and we had known that, sooner or later, there would be an accident.

This had actually happened in February, when Mrs Hodges slipped and broke her elbow. We had, for years, laid three stepping stone mats on the fitted carpet, up the incline. This proved almost 100% successful but her children had removed these mats to enjoy sliding. It was accident number three for the Hodges family. They had arrived in a recovery vehicle having broken down just outside London. Their car had been lowered into the yard and then taken to a local garage for repairs. Their second misfortune had concerned Mr Hodges. He'd discovered a painful rash and went to the doctor's to be told he had shingles. Mrs Hodges' broken elbow had completed the threesome.

Sometimes I query my compulsion to write for our encounters on this, our journey through life, are seldom mind blowing or breath catching but there appears to be order, an inevitability which fascinates me. Which way the wind is blowing, that is generally the way to go. Easter was yet another illustration of what was happening to our holiday accommodation business.

The Hill family, with us in 2004, had re-booked, to self-cater, for 2005, so our premises were full. Until the Foot and Mouth tragedy we were full every Easter, but all wanted bed and breakfast and evening meals. That year we hardly had an enquiry for serviced accommodation. The wheel of change was rotating faster than expected but in favour of us.

There was no change, however in the amount of cleaning and laundering to be done. We went to bed every night, after draping the kitchen ceiling with innumerable sheets and pillowcases. The first half hour of each day was spent folding them and pressing them on the silver hotplate lids of the Aga. I do this with amazing gratitude when I remember seeing, through a door ajar, an hotel employee, in Oban, actually ironing sheets. It was an hotel with multiple bedrooms, where guests would not necessarily be long-stay, for it was on the quayside. I remember this every time I thread my way through the dry, hanging bed linen and give the Aga a fond smile of thanks, with each folded sheet I place upon it.

Margaret tackled the annual job of spring cleaning. She visited the DIY shop and purchased gallons of emulsion. I noticed an increased need to dust. It was blowing in, every time the door was opened and on a farm that is often. Every day the sweeping brush, on the parquet tiles, collected a dust pan of grit and the sideboard and welsh dressers needed daily attention. Large cracks appeared in the near-concrete surface of the bare gateways. We disgusted our guests, praying constantly for rain they did not want.

'I'm not opening the meadow gates!' Margaret said. 'I'll give it time to grow!' but some inconsiderate walkers did so and we found the herd demolishing what poor growth there was. Someone, too, had pushed over a boundary wall. Normally it would not have been enough to excite cattle to jump but, with a shortage of grass, they could have been tempted.

Into the newly emulsioned cottages, came a camera team from the BBC programme, Little Angels. A theatre group, performing MacBeth in various venues in the area, were self-catering in the B/B area. Weekend groups came one after the other; family reunions and celebrations, friends wanting to get-together, cyclists with muscular legs and crash helmets and walkers with rucksacks and maps.

We began to yearn for our holiday. What's new about that?

But there came a problem with Joe, our old donkey. We had recently had to apply for donkey identification passports and had been asked his age. When you acquire cattle, each has a positive record of date of birth. In future, donkey and foal births will be known but we had no date of birth for Joe. When we had bought him in 1991, he had come only with the vendor's guess. He did not look a very young animal as had both Jasper and Bobby when they had first come to The Currer. We reckoned he might well be now over twenty. We loved him and so did all our guests. They fondled him and fed him carrots which we never did. Our donkeys are not our pets. They are friendly neighbours, we see occasionally and search for if they are missing but they do not pester us, thank goodness, as they do our holiday-makers.

They enjoy a freedom to come and go as they please but any irregularity in their health is never missed by Margaret. When Joe began to get scabs on his skin and to lose his hair, she noticed it immediately. She had recently begun to use an homeopathic cream containing ragwort, a flowering plant we will not allow to grow on our land. Not only is it poisonous, it also grows rampant and will take over neglected areas and roadsides, within a very short space of time. On one memorable occasion, Margaret had been very badly nettled and there had been no docks nearby. In desperation she had used ragwort leaves and the itching had gone. They had also taken away neck pain whilst in Wales, which had encouraged her to ask the veterinary homeopath if there was an ointment made from this plant. The answer was yes and when tested on Joe it worked. The rash and scabs went and a new coat grew. A strange skin infection we sometimes get when using calf milk, disappeared and tested on eczema, our friends found that in some cases it worked. It took away one lady's leg pain and she has used it ever since. We were particularly pleased about Joe. Donkeys stay with us longer even than dogs and we were not ready to part with him.

Chapter Eleven

I am a link in the chain, a bond of connection between
persons.

> From a meditation by Cardinal Newman.

OUR HOLIDAY was not coming quickly enough. Half the fun of any
adventure is always in the preparation and anticipation. We had been
deprived of that for some time but we had begun to plan this coming one
twelve months ago, when we had realised that Rachel Macleod's house and its
adjacent chalet, plus a couple of caravans, could be the ideal venue for a May
Harris Reunion. We had shared the idea almost on our return and, as others
fancied the idea, too, we had booked everything in the autumn. To re-unite
on the Outer Isles had been a dream we had feared would remain so, but
plans had developed throughout the long winter and everyone wishing to be
involved had met to plan and voice memories of their teenage, annual joy.

Perhaps because we see them so rarely, we talk about them more often
and maybe I write about them too much. We have long regretted the fact
that we are only friends in need. Work, which we love, has always prevented
us from socialising and friends have had to come to us rather than we to
them. Nevertheless we love them dearly and have reason to respect them
unconditionally, for we remain a vital link in the chain.

So we made plans for a second holiday in 2005. We knew the spring
one was bound to be energetic and demanding. In appreciation of this we
decided that we would return to normality and take an autumn holiday
between the sale of cattle and the buying of calves. We had done this
annually since the early seventies.

Most farmers do not take a holiday, let alone two, but Mother's family,
cab proprietors in the early days of the last century, had adopted the modern
trend of a Feast Week jaunt, first at Morecambe and later at Blackpool. With
the exception of the war years, we'd been taken to the sea-side, to digs down
St Chad's Road. As adults we appreciated that Father and Mother needed a
break and that Harry deserved a holiday. We would have moved hell and
high water to make sure this happened. For all of us, who work harder than
average and have too many irons in the fire, a break in routine is necessary
if we are to continue stress-free. We were never looking for the accepted
kind of holiday and ours had to be inexpensive. We always knew what we
wanted and where to find it, and every holiday has been well nigh perfect.

Though we learned in a coastal resort to love the shore, such has not been our choice since the beginning of the fifties. We have rural peace at home and we want it when away.

Aware that the coming holiday would hold a different kind of peace, we were prepared for it to excite rather than cool. We had therefore booked an autumn holiday near to the North Yorkshire Moors, in a one-bedroom, converted cattle byre. With this opportunity to relax in October, we prepared to enjoy a spring reunion, no matter how tired we were at the end of it.

But there was a hitch. Danny had an attack of diarrhoea which necessitated a visit to the vet who shaved off some of his fur and scanned his interior. The prognosis given to us was not good but Danny was put on a diet and given medication. The problem was put in perspective and coped with. Margaret is expert at that. With Danny once more in control of his bowels, we planned to go north before the main party and return a few days after their departure.

Helen Tobin, one of the returning Guides, herself a Guider, bought some tins of catering size food which we sent up in advance, with Linda Akrigg, another Guide going to Luskentyre for the Spring Bank holiday. There was ample room in their family caravan to do so. She, too, had also been one of my pupils at Kildwick and had become one of our Queen's Guides. She had married and raised a caring family. Their summer holidays had been spent annually in The Hebrides. With her husband, she still works tirelessly for handicapped children. They adopted one and, every summer, have entertained children from Chernobyl.

We bought our train tickets and were to leave on the Monday previous to the Harris invasion of our excited adults. They, whose ages ranged from the late forties to the mid-sixties, would arrive on the Saturday. Only one, Dot, had had to give backward. Her newly retired, headmaster husband had been taken ill.

The news of this had come in January, soon after Ray had started chemotherapy but a different treatment for Peter had been advised and this seemed to be working admirably. Nevertheless a good wife does not leave her husband at a time of crisis.

We could not leave for Harris without a last minute visit to see Hazel and Ray, both of whom had accompanied our ever-growing party to Harris, in 1976. The heat, that year, had been phenomenal. We noticed that Ray was poorlier than we'd expected. I never cease to admire the courage of all who fight this so common disease. Whether they win or lose they remain calm and their humour never leaves them.

'How 're you doing?' I had recently asked Ray over the phone.

'I've just got to the Kojak stage,' had been his amusing comment. Sitting comfortably in his chair, in their beautiful sitting room, we sensed a resigned dignity, an acceptance of the unavoidable and were proud to know him.

What we did not suspect was that we would get the news of his death, just a few days later, before our intended journey north. We expected to be on Harris on the day of the funeral. When you rise each morning and turn over the page of life, sadness and happiness follow each other all the way.

A few days prior to our leaving, Danny's diarrhoea started again with a vengeance. This proved unsolvable. We began to realise we could not possibly take him, on a long train journey. We didn't accept defeat immediately. We phoned the dog friendly hotel, in Mallaig and made sure that the bedroom we had been allocated was the one downstairs, near the door. We visited the vet and Danny was prescribed extra medication. Never has any human illness stopped us going on holiday. The Foot and Mouth disease had and I had missed one holiday with the family due to the suckled herd calving at the wrong time, but people have always been fit to travel. It became increasingly clear that Danny was not and no matter what we did his journey north was just not possible.

Sometimes, in life, you have a choice. More often you have not. In this instance we had none. Both of us agreed that the only possible solution was for Margaret to stay at home with Danny and for me to postpone my journey north until the Thursday. Only my illness, or Margaret's would have prevented me from leading that Harris Reunion, as I had done all my thirty one camping years. Usually Margaret and I are needed together. In this instance she was needed at home and I was needed in Luskentyre. I can't tell you how disappointed we both were. Caring for animals, or people, has not been choice, just who we are. There is never any suggestion of dodging the issue. Choice is a fickle, selfish noun which has ruined society since Government and educationalists came up with it!

Cousin Freda's daughter, Kathleen, was one of the party intending to arrive on Saturday. She agreed to travel with me on the Thursday and we were able to alter the train tickets and the guesthouse booking. Things were not entirely against us. Dorothy was regretfully told she would not be needed. It turned out to be a blessing for her. News came a few days later, that her sister had died in Cornwall and she had to prepare and go south.

It is to be expected that problems will trouble our pre-holiday hours. Usually they differ but it is inevitable that, sooner or later one of them will get a second showing. It must be twenty years ago since a blocked drain almost defeated us on the day prior to leaving. Again, on the Sunday before the Monday we should have left, Margaret spent the whole afternoon, on her belly, trying to unblock a sewage pipe. I ran up and down stairs, flushing the toilet but to no avail. We couldn't imagine where all the water I released was going. We were on the point of accepting failure when, swoosh and everything disappeared.

We had a typical Currer Laithe day on the Monday we should have been travelling to Mallaig. It was a 'stunner an' no mistake!' It would have been awesome for any house-sitter on her first day and would have stretched Margaret to her limit had I not delayed travelling north.

These packed-to-bursting days are so common at our house few get recorded. Just here and there I include one, just for fun. At the end of the day, to be able to say, 'Phew!' with relief, is a form of success, maybe the only form we know. The reward is to flop into an armchair, as mid-night approaches and emit a prolonged sigh of exhaustion.

'It's a good job we were here,' we admitted. Had we been leaving on the mid-day train, our last minute scramble, to do all that was necessary and get to the station on time, would have been jeopardised by the unexpected, coffee-time arrival of Paul and Bunty, long-standing guests currently on their way to holiday further north. They came armed with the usual bouquet of flowers for our sideboard. Fortunately we were able to drop everything and drink coffee with them and listen to their chatter and update them on our predicament. They were concerned about Danny, he being everyone's favourite. We had brought him from The Hebrides in 1995, the year we bought a large contingent of pigs. Paul and Bunty had been here on holiday and the pig episode was of enormous interest to everyone. Every year thereafter, these two had bought us a pot pig to adorn the mantelpiece and hearth. That we have no pigs now, only pot ones, is sad.

Feeling we had plenty of time to enjoy our elevenses, we were unaware that our neighbouring farmer, having bought high-spirited cattle, maniacs they were, had decided to worm them in his yard. He had reinforced the field boundary wall but the yard one was, he thought, secure. He was mistaken. Two high jumpers leapt the wall onto the tarmac of the Top Road and headed for our cattle grid. This posed no problem for these two bullocks were long jumpers also. Unbeknown to us they had galloped down our road, joined our junior herd and there was bedlam. David and James, their owners, rushed into the melee but to separate them was impossible.

Utterly exhausted with trying, we all retreated to the house. A new tactic was discussed. A waiting game must be played. When a window of opportunity opened, that would be the moment to snatch. We were interrupted by a man on the phone wanting to graze his horses. Don't they all? 'Sorry,' I said, 'we do not do livery!'

There was someone at the door and I opened it to greet ex-neighbours who, having emigrated to Australia, were back here on holiday. It was already tea-time and we gave up all hope of having lunch. The kettle was put on for a snack and all other jobs abandoned. All this we would have missed had we been on the train heading for Mallaig. As our friends, the Davisons, were leaving an elderly man appeared wanting information about open coal mines on our land. It was almost dark when he left on foot. We trust he arrived home safely for he was not a young man and there are no street lights up our lane. It was almost too dark to put in the ducks. When dusk approaches darkness, they will not leave the pond. The encouragement of one person is not enough. Either the pond must be entered on foot or a second drover re-called from the house. Or both.

The ducks safely in their beach hut, the geese were returned to their summer quarters in the calf shed and we were free to put the kettle on the Aga once more. We realised, as so frequently happens, that brewing up to entertain others, meant we had supped but not eaten all day. We may be chronic stay-at-homes but we are visited more than most. It was comforting to know that Dorothy had been spared a first day as active as that one.

We wakened next morning believing we still had the problem of the two frisky bullocks which must be returned to their fellows, over the 'secure!' boundary wall. It had proved it was no such thing for the errant couple had managed to jump it and return to their herd. Maybe it was simpler for our neighbours to reinforce the long wall with a fence, than it would have been to separate unwilling animals from our herd. To drive them through a gateway without ours following would have been dodgy. Luck had not totally deserted us! Our patience had been rewarded.

Danny's problem persisted, leaving us with no qualms about whether we were doing the right thing. She must stay and I must go. It was tough but much sadder for Hazel. Margaret and I went with flowers and condolences to say that Margaret would be staying at home and that my departure had been postponed. Ray's funeral was on the Thursday. Margaret drove Kathleen and me to the railway station and dropped us at the entrance, then she and Barbara Sherriff went to the church in Oxenhope. Sadness overflows over happiness all the time, as clouds blot out sunshine and rain splashes on warm tarmac.

So much of life is unavoidable. I was leaving behind those who had made island camping possible. Without Margaret and Hazel's presence, over the twenty five years of annually going north, those experiences would never have been and the one ahead of me been not even a dream. I travelled north, not quite alone, but lonely, thinking of Joanna reading the Eulogy for her father. I knew how difficult it would be but how personally necessary she would feel it was. She had been a Saturday child at The Currer, devoted to animals. She had been a ten-year Hebridean camper, returning annually until going to Addenbrooks Hospital. Now she was a nurse teaching her profession to others, the mother, too, of a grown up daughter. I had so many memories of travelling to Mallaig, by train, with Hazel and Joanna and for many years with Jonathan, her brother. My gratitude to Ray, for loaning me his family, occupied my thoughts and blurred my vision of the beautiful countryside through which the Settle to Carlisle railway runs.

Poor Hazel! Poor Margaret! Without them the grown children, pensioners as they were now, would never have been able to have those annual Hebridean experiences on which they had built their lives. It had brought them to this moment in time when, together, they would re-live teenage wonder and joy.

There was always a journey-out wobble of my confidence. For so many years I had wondered if we could really pull it off again. Surrounded by other people's children, heading for remote shores on distant islands, was always awesome. Could I really feed them, keep them dry and entertained and return them all safely after over two weeks of freedom under canvas. I was never cocksure on the outward trek but we managed it. We never had an accident. We never had a camp which was not a success Now, twenty five years later would it really happen again?

We had known that there had always been THEM and US and this time there would be only ME on my fence. The age gap might not feel as big but amazingly, we admit the divide between leader and led cannot be crossed. Those who have followed have a unity, a wit, a related history Margaret, Hazel and I have never been able to fully share. The friendship between parent and child can be precious but never on the same level as the one between contemporaries. I was not surrounded by them on this journey, as I had always been. Alone with Kathleen I had too much time for thought. I was so sorry Margaret was going to miss the extraordinary experience ahead of me. She had sacrificed many years of camping with children, when Father had grown too old to be left with the summer haymaking and that, to farmers, was of survival importance. I was overwhelmingly sad for Hazel, on the threshold of a life alone, finding comfort in that beautiful garden she tends so diligently.

Perhaps I aught to write as things happen and not after so much water has run under the bridge. Unfortunately, but happily, I am not yet retired so there is, far too frequently no time to write and I must put off doing so, often for months. It is a while since a score of us returned to Luskentyre but the memory of it is still fresh. It occurs to me, this writing habit will be an advantage when I do retire for, when the material for my pen no longer occupies my life, I will still have the events of the previous year to record. Something to do, which I thoroughly enjoy if, God forbid, I ever become inactive. Should it be that I die before I retire, then the unrecorded will remain just that.

Lest my end comes suddenly the atmosphere of that unforgettable get-together, in the June of 2005 must, I feel, now take precedence over any opportunity which might come for me to lie later in bed, or switch on early morning breakfast television. August fills the house with self-catering holiday-makers and cattle feed themselves. The sun has risen before me and pours in through the eastern window so, to avoid it I must take my type-writer to the kitchen table, bare of the food and utensils which litter it when we are in full swing, making breakfasts.

I am aware that to perfectly capture the atmosphere of that momentous

Reunion, 2005.

week is impossible. My memories have matured, which always helps but, even as I start, excitement begins to throb and words begin to disappear from the vocabulary of a very grateful, grey-haired lady. It was not what we did, but how. Not whom we met, whom we conversed with, but how we so quickly related. It was not what we ate but how beautifully the team, that prepared each meal, worked as one. It was not what we said but how quickly we were understood, not what we felt but, more importantly how we expressed it, not what caused the fun but how quickly we laughed. We laughed, Pauline said, until we lost inches from our waist lines.

That they walked in shorts, barefoot on the shore and that most of them climbed Ben Luskentyre, pleased and amazed me. The latter I didn't do for I had promised Margaret to refrain. Way, way back in the seventies I had vowed that when I could not climb, I would stop taking children to Harris but we do not always do as we say!

When necessary they were prepared to walk the two mile shore road to catch the service bus and to retrace their steps at the end of their excursion. Jenny had once broken a pelvic bone and Heather had only recently had a knee operation. Joan had had a hip replacement but no-one was deterred. Though some had been at the first island camp in 1957, and others at the last one in 1980, we were a family to which each belonged equally and all had developed a love of flora and fauna and the sea, which we had tried to teach. This pleased me so.

They spotted seals and sea otters and they saw the corncrake. Yearly I have heard it but never seen it until then. Could it be that I have always been too busy organising, feeding, caring for others? When alone we have had dogs and seals have never ventured as close inshore as they did that May week of magic. Rabbits scatter quickly when they see our canine companions.

My 2005 companions' love of the sea encouraged us to sail to Taransay. We had previously only viewed it from a distance, mostly at sunset for then the sky behind it is scarlet. On family holidays, I had watched John MacKay's boat sail out from Horgabost beach to the island, many times, and longed to be in it. The island belongs to the MacKays who graze it with sheep and, during lambing the little boat would be on the island, where the shepherd would live for a while. Otherwise, it would be beached on the Persil white sand and we would drive the Range Rover onto the hard shore beside it and spend the afternoon with the oyster catchers and the kittiwakes.

John is now confined to the house but Angus sails back and forth to the island in an inflatable monster and will ferry anyone across the Sound, whenever they wish. My companions thoroughly enjoyed the crossing. Certainly it provided excitement for all. Did I see the island approaching? Did I look overboard into the turquoise depths, see the jelly fish, listen to the seagulls and think of Iain Og of Taransay? Did I trail my hand in the salty water and see the silver sand below?

I did not! I hung on for dear life, sitting legs astride a saddle, my small feet in stirrups made to fit the boots of lifeboat men. The bow of the orange monster rose above the waves and broke them into foam. What, I thought, would those see of the Grand Canyon, who rode the rapids in a boat like this? Nothing, I am sure! Nothing but tumult. What would they feel other than a rush of air laden with spray. I had waited thirty years to cross to Taransay believing that when I did, it would be across still waters and that the view, which is of Temple Hill and Chaipaval on the port and the North Harris hills on the starboard bow, would be breath-taking. I saw nothing but my hands clinging to the handle bars and the bulging life jacket I was wearing. Margaret would never have brought the dogs!! The speed of the joyride was terrific.

We landed safely within minutes. How could I have thought otherwise with Angus at the helm? On Taransay there is no jetty and the rocks on which we must land were slippy. The younger generation had enjoyed the thrill without any of my reservations. Light rain was falling but Angus put on the kettle in the steading and whilst we ate our sandwiches, the youngest member of our party suggested we update each other with our individual activities since leaving the unit.

All were modest but to a man they had been of benefit to the community in which they now lived, for the most part miles away from their origin.

They were all married, with children and grandchildren they took on holiday in remote and beautiful places. But that was not all. They were, or had been, nurses, teachers, social workers, farmers' wives. One was a pharmacist, one an undertaker, one a physiotherapist. Some were still active in Guiding. I am so proud of them all.

There was then time to partially explore the island. Beauty is not marred by a drop of rain and wind browns faces just as much as the sun does. One of our party had brought two of her children. It gave us all such joy. Me in particular. To see Sam and Charlotte, wide-eyed, barefooted children, watch, with wonder, the sun go down nearer to mid-night than they could believe possible, made me feel young again. Hopefully this present generation will pass on their love of islands to future ones and keep alive the flame of friendship we kindled and which was certainly burning strongly.

I am less happy about society in general as, daily, reports are broadcast of children being wrapped in cotton wool, imprisoned in their homes, no longer allowed outside their front gate. I hear of parents who deprive their children of school trips remembering that I took half my school, the eight to eleven year olds, for a week on Tiree in 1981. No parent prevented a son or daughter from having the experience. Trust was something we all shared.

On those empty beaches, all those remembered years ago, age was never a divider. Toddlers and juniors came from the crofts. Under-tens came with mothers and aunties. Teenagers visited crofters, students on vacation from college, Jonathan on leave from the army, all lived together on the machair. Children whose only experience is of loneliness or only with their own peers, do not know how to grow up.

Our final campfire was, as always, on the beach where the incoming tide washes the aged rocks and erases footprints so quickly that those made as we approached the fire were gone when we finally left the embers. It is always a poignant moment, a spiritual experience second to none. It was not far to John MacDonald's caravan. Mine for the moment. Morning had come and, so far north, night would soon be away but those in Rachel's house and chalet, walked back on the beach, the longer way home. How I longed for Margaret and for Hazel. It is not sufficient just to sow. The reward comes when you gather the harvest. They were deprived of the reaping.

In the present Health and Safety climate, what we experienced would not be allowed. There are too many prohibiting rules and regulations, too much paperwork. Thank God we were Guiding in the sixties and seventies and thank Him too that we had no accident. I do believe, however that we were more diligent, more caring and more aware of danger then, than society is today when laws come from the State and not from the family or the group. The Guide Laws were not to be just recited, they were to be obeyed and in doing so what wonderful fun we had!

Next day some left on the mid-day boat, some on the plane and went their different ways. Ann to Aviemore, Enid and Jenny to County Durham, Sandra and her children to Cumbria, Alison to Glossop, one Heather to Wales, another to Glusburn. Hazel and Helen to Birkenshaw, another Ann to Southport, Kathleen to join her daughter, a student on the east coast, and others to Keighley not having wandered away.

Barbara was pausing on her way home to stay for a week with her daughter, on the island of Eigg. From there she sent me this postcard.

> A way,
> R echarged by
> E ndless miles of soft white sand.
> N othing
> T roubles. In
> W onder we
> E xperienced one of
> L ife's richest gifts,
> U nimaginable joy in our
> C amp and,
> K indred spirit,
> Y ou made it possible.
> Thankyou!

Aren't we lucky!

There were friends I must see, friends I had neglected all week. There was Maggie to visit in Northton. The last time I had visited her, with children, was thirty years ago when her sister Angela had been alive and we had been planning our annual barn dance. Since then I had always had family. That was now down to two and the other half of it was at home, with Danny whose problem seemed in remission, thanks to some medication Margaret had acquired from the homeopathic clinic.

Maggie's fire was burning, as always and the tray she put before me was a banquet and I could feel my tiredness, hear it almost. It was a wave engulfing me. Maggie is shy and it was necessary that I should talk, a difficult thing to do after an active week, especially whilst relaxing in the comfort zone, in front of her blazing hearth. One of her daughters drove me to Borve where Margaret MacLeod lives. In the seventies she was Guider on the island and she is always full of news and I am an eager listener. Usually, but after the recent activity, I was weak and apt to drift away from her conversation. Suddenly I heard her say, 'Are you still with me?' I blushed with embarrassment for I had fallen asleep!

I stayed the night in Rachel's house. The last time I had done so I had been on the sitting room floor surrounded by children in sleeping bags.

I'm sure Rachel would have approved of our reunion in her house. Then I stayed two nights with Katie and Angus down on the shore. The last time I had done that was shortly after Father died. It was a lovely way to end a perfect week.

Rachel's nephew, Norman, took me to the boat and I sailed to Skye in a state of sleepy euphoria, in the observation lounge, at peace. I forced myself to get a bacon roll from the cafeteria. Margaret had made me promise to eat! At Uig the heavens were emptying a waterfall. The jetty is long but now there is a mini-bus to take foot passengers to the Caledonian MacBrayne's offices and waiting room. Skye needed rain. Travelling out, ten days ago, I had been concerned about the dry state of the Misty Isle. Only farmers and growers appreciate rain. I had noticed that the mountains of Skye, the Cuillin, Blaven, Ben na callaich, seemed bereft of the white water cascades for which they are famous. Was drought affecting this wettest of all islands, too? I wondered if, when Spain and the south of France get too hot, will the northern shores of Britain become the Riviera. I hope not. Unfortunately, just as one swallow does not make a summer, one heavy downpour would not submerge the pebbles on the dry stream beds. A week of rain was necessary.

A lady, who had crossed on the ferry from Tarbert, scurried with me into the waiting room and we chatted until the service bus drew up to the kerb. There were so few passengers we all had a double seat and the journey was in silence. In any case my mind had slipped into neutral. I could think neither forward nor backward. At Portree, however, where there was a wait for the bus to Armadale, I suggested the lady and I went into the little cafe, on the square, and have a cup of coffee together.

We had both been on Harris and it transpired that we were both heading for the same guesthouse so we had something in common. She was a few years younger, wore a skirt, carried an umbrella and pulled a case on wheels whilst I was a grey-haired, trousered farmer's man, with a rucksack. Different as we were, we had both found what we were looking for on Harris. I admired her courage in travelling alone. Reaching Armadale she suggested I go on ahead. I guessed she must think I would walk faster than she which was not so. I had to make a determined effort to keep well ahead and only when I reached the guesthouse did I learn the real reason. On the door was a large greeting. WELCOME MARY, it announced. I had barely been ushered into my adjacent-to-the-door bedroom when my travelling companion arrived. There was something special about her, I'm sure, but I never found out what.

I lay barefoot on the bed for some time, then walked into the village, bought a snack and found somewhere to sit and watch the constant activity in the harbour. I had an urge to find the path, the short cut leading to the school hall where we had slept so many times. Failing to do so, I asked the way of a passing native and learned that it was no more. Things change in twenty six years. I phoned Margaret. Danny was greatly improved. All was well.

I went back to my room and slept.

I was awake and dressing at 5 a.m. It was raining and when I reached the railway station I was wet. The train had arrived, as it always does, late the previous night. I could board immediately and had individual choice of seat in the empty compartment. I took off my wet outer clothes and settled for the long journey home. I can't think of anything nicer than handing over all responsibility to the engine driver. Every mile south there was an improvement in the weather. I was coming home, bronzed with Hebridean sun, to a veritable Mainland heatwave. This we could ill afford at The Currer where the ground was already dry.

From Mallaig to Keighley the countryside is beautiful thanks to the farmers who, from their isolated steadings, are custodians of its grandeur. Only occasionally does a village appear nestling in a valley. Much of the journey follows rivers and lochs, only occasionally is there a view of the coast. There is so much to enjoy that, even though the slow train is almost a lullaby, sleep is never attractive. A long journey through a wilderness is my idea of bliss.

There is an abrupt entry into civilisation when the Clyde coastline ends in busy, populated Glasgow. It was teaming with people and noisy with congested traffic. I could not live in a city any more than could the animals we tend. I could not breathe the polluted air, unavoidable in built up areas or continually jostle with others of my species.

Fortunately there is a mini-bus to transport passengers from Queens Street station to Central and a minimum wait for the southbound Carlisle train and after that my homeland. I love every bit of it, over the Fells and into the Dales. Scotland is for holidays but Yorkshire is the place to live.

Before the heat of summer withers the flowers of May, the countryside is garlanded and either side of the track is festooned with foxgloves pointing skyward. Drifts of oxeye daisies, red campion and meadow cranesbill quiver in the wind of the passing train. Eventually we were hesitating briefly in Settle, pausing in Skipton and then we were home. Margaret, my best friend, was waiting on the platform and the dogs greeted me in the rear of the Land Rover. My mission completed. Another success to welcome with grateful relief!

Chapter Twelve

Love, laughter and friends are always welcome here.
(A wall tile bought for us by The Gang.)

A PART FROM the damp day on Taransay and the showers on the journey home, I had had almost dawn to dusk sunshine. I came home to heatwave but to learn that a freak storm and torrential rain had caused a sudden flood in North Yorkshire. A friend, dating back to post-war Guiding, lived at Thirlby, near Thirsk and she had experienced water running rapidly through her house. Many had been temporarily homeless and debris and garden furniture had hurtled down the stream which runs through her garden. Doris she is called, but for more than sixty years I have called her Squirrel, an affectionate label she earned training for the Guide International Service, sent as aid workers in the displaced persons' camps dotted all over Europe. Though in her eighties, no doubt she had tackled this 2005 emergency with equal be-preparedness as always.

Naturally Margaret had had guests. We are seldom without. A Mr and Mrs Crook were visiting their daughter, resident and working in the locality. Three, who had often been before, we had put off until the day after our expected return. They had wanted an evening meal and Dorothy, sensibly, no longer wants to do that.

Having already done twenty five years of our holiday diversification, it follows that we will, occasionally have someone ill during their stay. No-one has yet died but we have occasionally had a nasty scare. These three well known guests were two days away from their return to Scotland when one lady wakened early, with a terrible pain. By breakfast time she was in agony and, when we were alerted, we called the surgery which now stands on the site of the demolished village school. An appointment was made for her to see the doctor but, should the trouble increase, we were told, we must ring for an ambulance. The lady was needing support for there were no arms on the chair she had chosen and every few seconds she lost consciousness. I thought she was going to die in my arms whilst we waited for the ambulance we had not hesitated to call. When it came, and it did so quickly, the paramedics tended her an alarmingly long time before pulling out of the yard and taking her to hospital. It was originally thought she had had a heart attack but that was not so and, a few days later she was taken to a hospital near her home. There is seldom any time between holiday and restart, between calm and alarm! This roller coaster on which we live does not pause.

Since the twin towers had been demolished in 2001, in New York, the British government had put out repeated warnings that a terrorist attack was likely in this country. As a teacher I acknowledge that to warn is essential but to do so does put ideas into excitable heads. There was so much talk of potential danger it was inevitable some extremists would get to work. The shocking news of the treble suicide bombs on the London Underground, broke whilst our guests were finishing breakfast and they, and we, remained glued to the television all morning. Contrary to normal definition we name as terrorists all individuals or nations who have weapons, small or monstrous, and use them to frighten, or kill civilians.

Extremism, human or weatherwise is alarming. Cottage guests from Birmingham had just witnessed a tornado causing havoc not many streets away from where they lived. On a much larger scale came the destruction of New Orleans by hurricanes and, before the year was out, Pakistan suffered devastating earthquakes. These alarming news headlines were brought into our everyday routine of summer by daily television. Disaster seemed to reap disaster.

On the lighter side we welcomed, with amusement, two new members of our four legged family. Kids had been abandoned close to Tim's farmhouse and he is a gentle giant and Margaret a soft touch so they were rescued and brought to our goat sanctuary, raising our herd to five. They were snow white and not very old but they made themselves at home immediately and did not appear to need milk. They were adored by guests but, as happens to our goat herd, they were practically ignored by the busy workforce. They were extremely agile and frequently pranced up and down The Loft cottage wall, to the amazement of wide-eyed guests. They amused Richard, from the Bradford and Bingley Building Society, because they frequently danced on his colleague's car bonnet. He took a photo of them doing just that for our archives. Not quite so amusing was their highland fling on the Kramer braking the windscreen wipers.

So now we had Three Billy Goats Gruff and our luck was under control. The cattle dealer who advised us to keep our first castrated one, for luck, over forty years ago, would rest in his grave, knowing The Currer was in safe, treble hands! These white kids formed a bond with the white goat, Snowy. Since the 2001 arrival of brown Charlie II she had been ignored by the brown nanny, Rosy. There is certainly colour selection in animals. Not in us to whom the creed and the colour and the name don't matter.

The most striking evidence of this being Ginger's adoration of Danny. Only black and white Diana, a Friesian lady from the upper class, does not seem to mind if her baby is a Blonde D' Aquitaine.

We had expected, and were getting, a calmer summer. We found far

One of the twins.

more opportunities to slip to the Leisure Centre swimming baths. With most people self-catering and little decorating to do, there were times we could walk round Coppice Pond in St Ives and once we joined some guests for a picnic at Bolton Abbey.

We sold our first twenty six bullocks on the last Friday of August before the arrival of the Bank Holiday crowd, who are special and get evening meals as well. We call them The Gang. Most of them met over twenty years ago, here on holiday. A few have already died but Joan and Patrick from Manchester, Veronica from Co Durham, Jacqui and Jose from Wanborough, Bill and Margaret from Kent, Cedric and Margaret from Surrey and John and Angela from Kettering, re-unite each year.

The first sale normally comes whilst they are here and some of them have been known to accompany us to the Mart, but that year it preceded their arrival by one day. We were seated in the auction ring waiting for our turn and behind us was a lady I did not know, nor do I still, but I will always remember her wit. Into the ring was urged a very over-fat bull. A Charolais, I think it was. It was obese. Great lobes of fat clung to its thighs and shoulders. I find obesity in cattle as unnecessary as in humans and I whispered, or thought I did, to Margaret, 'He needs to go on the Atkins' Diet!' The lady behind had heard and her wit exceeded mine. 'He is the Atkins' Diet!' she laughed. So did we which was unusual. We do not normally find the end product of our labours, even remotely funny. We enjoy the life of our animals too much. That sale brought us a moment of fame, for two of our bullocks brought the top price of the day and Margaret's name was in the local paper. We had bought the two calves, along with eight others from Tim, eighteen months ago and these two really were enormous. We have had top price, best pen, on other occasions, but this was the first time we saw it in print. We do not get a Yorkshire Post but a neighbour provided one. To be honest we don't buy any newspapers. Guests provide enough for fire lighting and potato peeling!

I get up early every day but I expect to see no-one until Margaret appears and we start the breakfast. I was therefore surprised to see an elderly man, in shirt sleeves, standing at the front door, before I had even put my kettle on. I saw him through the living room window. I could only see his back and presumed it was one of our guests. There are several grey-haired ones in that end-of-August group. I noticed however that the back of his shirt was mud stained. Thinking he must have fallen, I went to the door and opened it on a stranger who said, 'Can I come in and stay here for a few days?'

'Who are you?' I wanted to know. He gave me a name but did not know where he'd come from or where he lived. He was cold but reasonably cheerful. He didn't look like a robber so I felt it was safe to bring him into the kitchen. I did not expect Margaret for another hour but I called her to get up. It was obvious we had a problem.

I seated him in front of the Aga and he made himself as welcome as any old friend would have done. His shirt was mud stained, his arm was bleeding and one shoe was missing from a very muddy foot. Both socks were saturated.

Margaret questioned him as I had done. He continued to smile, told us his name but had no idea where he came from nor what he had been doing. We took off the remaining shoe and his wet socks but could find no replacements big enough. We provided him with a mug of tea and a bacon roll and broached the subject gently, that we ought to send for the police.

'I think you had better!' he agreed and laughed happily. It was difficult to believe he was in a mess.

We wrapped him in a cosy, crocheted blanket, Mother had made, and waited for the arrival of two policewomen. They told us that the old man had been reported missing, yesterday, from a residential home in the valley. There had been a helicopter search for the missing man. Indeed some of our guests had seen it hovering over the hillside. We see one so frequently we take little notice. There are often aircraft flying towards the airport at Yeadon but they are usually above the clouds and attract our attention only on clear nights when their twinkling lights can be seen, moving amongst the Great Bear and Orion.

We could not believe that the old man had been out all night. Surely he would have been suffering from exposure. Had he lain on the grass he would have been wet. It was September and there was dew and it was barely 7 a.m.

The recovery of his shoe, months later, by the wallers when working down the fold, led us to believe he had walked up from the hamlet of Marley. It is quite a steep climb but he had not appeared out of breath. The whole episode was a mystery. The old man's problem was dementia, not physical handicap. He was happy and strong but confused. The police-women sent for an ambulance and he got into it smiling and that was the very last we heard of him.

There was suddenly a panic to get breakfast ready for our paying guests. They were agog with gossip having seen a police car and an ambulance. What fun it is to be on holiday at The Currer where something new happens every day!

Aunty Mary would have said, 'You are used to it!' and so we are. We entertain happy people and never hear from them again. That is not true for all. Many return, some turn up after a decade, some after two decades, some just for coffee in the morning, some just in time for afternoon tea on the way elsewhere. All are confident that we will remember them or the unusual incident which happened and the guests who were here at the same time as they were! So often we do, for memory of yore is better than of yesterday. They are amazed and do not believe us when we say we now cannot remember who went out at the weekend. Of the old man we heard nothing more at all.

In the middle of September we had a phone call from the lady producer of an ITV programme, Dales Diary. A reader of my autobiographies, living in Wetherby, had alerted her to the fact that we had a busy life in Airedale and she said she would like to come and see us. This was unexpected and came at a difficult time for us, in the middle of our autumn sales and our end of summer holiday-makers. We had been appreciative viewers of that programme for many years and were always sorry when, on so many occasions, meal making had prevented our viewing. I didn't like to refuse and insult the reader, Mrs Meade, even though the moment was inopportune with winter and calf-buying approaching. A preliminary visit was just courtesy, I told myself. We didn't do anything spectacular enough. I've said so many times that we are just ordinary people, extraordinarily able to find fun in ordinary things.

Barbara Bugloss, the producer, came and had lunch with us. She was a kindred spirit, an ordinary lady, casually dressed in trousers and tee shirt, young and attractive, with a lovely dog that insisted on sitting on my knee all the time. Believe me, I do not normally nurse dogs. That is Margaret's job but this one adopted me. We were not being interviewed. She came just as a friend with whom we could relax. She'd like to bring the camera team, she said. They would not be intrusive but she was confident our life style was worthy of a ten minute slot in the 2006 series. Guests repeatedly say that coming here is home from home. I don't believe a word of it. There can't be all that many places just like this!! The camera team and Luke Casey, the programme presenter, would be in the area on Friday the 15th of October. May they come, she asked?

We would be on holiday, we told her. We were going for an autumn break to Wass, in North Yorkshire but Margaret, who had missed her spring holiday on Harris, because of Danny, insisted we could come home two days early. I was loathe to do so for the break was necessary for both of us but for Margaret in particular. 'We needn't come back until evening,' she insisted.

It was like buying calves. One nod of the head and you are committed. Unlike the calf buy, which ensures our work for the next two years, we really did believe that our nod of the head to Barbara Bugloss would mean just one day's inconvenience followed, months later, by a ten minute embarrassment on screen. It all seemed quite harmless. I was even quite amused and rang Mrs Meade, saying, 'What have you let us in for?'

We had other things to do. We eyed the shaky stockyard fence with trepidation and called on John to purchase the necessary motorway barriers and get the yard secure against the herd. Winter is not long in coming after the Autumn Sales have been completed. The last of the Movement cards had been posted, the junior herd had left behind their label, 'the calves' and become the 'bullocks', grazing the upland.

Farmers at the cattle market were calling for another book. Don't they know that material for one depends on a very full, hectic and often scary lifestyle. We prayed for a period when incidents suitable for my pen, were fewer and further between. We knew we needed the coming holiday. Whenever we turned on the television we fell asleep. For me that was not so unusual but for my sister to do so was a sign that the sooner we went to 'High Woods' the better.

There was, however, a problem. In the spring, thinking she would be caretaking whilst we were both on Harris, Dorothy had cancelled an operation on her wrist which would have handicapped her against farm and household jobs. It had been unnecessary, for Margaret had been at home. As is the way of things her next opportunity to have surgery fell around the time of our proposed week in North Yorkshire and we had no option but to say she must not cancel it again. She had too much wrist pain which the small operation was expected to alleviate. We were beginning to think there was a jinx on our 2005 holidays.

Danny, noticeably older, only occasionally had a relapse which Margaret cured with an anti-biotic and we intended to go by Land Rover in which both dogs would sleep. So Danny was not a problem. Neither was the supply staff, for Helen, who had sorted out the travel arrangements and the catering, in June on Harris, agreed to come with her husband and make possible our much needed five-day break. We live on a band wagon of problems we must solve one by one. Though I am convinced that the most important thing to teach children is how to do so, I am not over-confident that society realises its importance. The answer, too often now, is to press a button. To be able to find a way out of a difficulty, to be able to make things happen and to know where to go and whom to ask for advice is so important. That Margaret so successfully, manages so many cattle is because her ability to organise, to plan ahead, add up the pros and cons, comes from at least sixty years of experience. Handling animals well, doesn't just happen. A lot of time is spent and sleep lost, planning routine and ensuring safety.

Helen, with husband Chris, was the sixth Guide requisitioned to make it possible for us to have a break. There had been Janet and Joan and Barbara and Dot and Sandra and we are grateful to them all.

There were just eight days between the last sale and our departure. Tim had decided to take back the six heifers he had sold to us as calves eighteen months ago. They were beautiful animals and he was hell-bent on increasing his herd.

We had a weekend full of guests needing an evening meal but, to celebrate the success and completion of the sales, we escaped to Wycoller on the Sunday afternoon, our energy utterly spent. Having no longer any disabled passengers, we had to leave the Land Rover in the car park, well outside the village and walk down to the stream and the packhorse bridge. We dragged our weary feet increasingly slowly along the path leading to the clapper and the clam bridges and I, for one, wondered if I would make the short journey back. It was all in the mind, of course, but we did need a holiday.

However there was a very large booking to cope with first. Seventeen workers from Pedigree Chum, dog food manufacturers, were coming for a bonding experience. They were to provide their own evening meal. It was elaborate and extremely plentiful and a lot of corks were popped. We, who do not drink wine, are perpetually teased at the household tip when we drop scores of bottles into the re-cycling bank. On this rather unusual occasion, we were to provide the breakfast, for their day was to begin early and they were to do some DIY work in the headquarters of a Youth Club. There was an early morning panic for they had neglected to clear up the previous evening and we had to make breakfast, with difficulty, whilst they washed the dishes around us and attempted to dispose of masses of lovely, untouched food. We cannot say it was anything but a happy occasion but it was unusual! There followed a massive laundering of sheets and pillowcases and a stripping of all beds for the next guests were to be the thirty students from Holland, who come every year and all bring sleeping bags. They were to occupy all our premises throughout our absence.

Unlike our guests, we now take little luggage on holiday. We've been there and done that when taking children and family. Now we take hardly anything. We set off from home, shortly after mid-day, with few clothes and no food, so our first call was at Wilsden Co-op to fill our almost empty hamper. Not having eaten we bought hot Cornish pasties and we ate them in St Ives, only a quarter of a mile from our boundary wall. Danny thought we had just come on a picnic and indicated that he wanted to get out and walk round Coppice Pond. Meg was sure we had come to her favourite swimming baths and both were indignant when we set off for Otley. Then, I think they presumed we must be going to the cattle market.

We nearly did not go anywhere. A huge and beautiful stag leapt, gracefully in front of us and the Land Rover missed maiming it by a hair's breadth. What would have happened if we had, would have been easily predictable. There is no way that Margaret, or I for that matter, would harm and drive on. The near accident happened on the lane which slips, literally, on the slope of The Chevin. Someone on the media said it was continually sliding like a blancmange. We would only have had our own vet's telephone number. Margaret, not I, would have remembered that, but I'm pretty sure we would have got to our destination hours late. I suppose it was only because, as usual on that bumpy road, Margaret was driving slowly that we were, where we were, when we were and not already at the bottom of the incline like most people would have been. Even at our slow pace, brakes would not have stopped us in time. That deer escaped by a centimetre, I'm sure, and our brakes brought us to a standstill yards away from its crossing. A red deer once crossed our tracks somewhere on the West Highland road to Mallaig, but some way in front of us. I could well believe this one actually leapt the bonnet of the Land Rover.

When our guests say The Currer is home from home they must just mean they feel relaxed and comfortable there. We certainly do not want to go on holiday and find a replica of our seven-day, Open All Hours regime. We want to step out of the door and see something which does not spell work and we want accommodation which is as small as ours is big. A tent would still be preferable given the opportunity. Not a modern one with a sewn in groundsheet, lying on which you could not possibly smell the grass. I wonder if the little white tent I made from material bought in the market, from an Accrington man called Arthur, is still on the loft. The flysheet was taut enough to protect us from any downpour and in a gale it never blew down. We never pitched it anywhere that looked remotely like home. On holiday we do not want an identity. Now and again we need to be free spirits. Next to a tent, a caravan provides the mini-home we look for. The cottage we found among the woods, on the edge of the North Yorkshire Moors, occupied little more living space. It had a minute sitting room with a small open-plan kitchen, one bedroom with just enough space for twin beds and quite a large bathroom. We loved it. It was attached to the owners' house and, though it was surrounded by a well kept lawn, the terrain in front and behind was wild and wonderful. To approach the clearing, on which stood the house, our converted byre and a barn (which was also a holiday cottage),

almost two miles of woodland path had to be followed. The steadings had
been built on a plateau, above a small ravine and every which way we
looked there was woodland, alive with wild life.

Our arrival was greeted with a cream tea, homemade scones spread with
jam and cream and we were introduced to a new litter of golden retriever
puppies. From our wee cottage we could hear them yapping, every two
hours, day and night. The place could have been a retreat for members of a
monastic order. There was certainly a quietness, an out of this world atmosphere which was almost a medicine. No wonder the area was chosen for the
building of Rievaulx and Byland.

It is sheer joy to go away in the autumn and to dwell among trees. October
can be so beautiful. We do not really live above the tree line but the leaves
from our trees are snatched from the branches before they have reached full
glory. The fragile ones of the silver birch, round the sheds and yard, leave
the trees naked far too early. By sheer luck we had found a perfect place.
In several ways for we had one dog needing to run and another dog and
two tired ladies all needing to rest. The long approach to the clearing meant
Meg could run behind the Land Rover when we went out, and again when
we returned, without traffic danger. It was perfect! The track was carpeted
with fallen leaves, squirrels were busy hunting for nuts and pheasants were
everywhere. Meg will chase a pheasant when we are elsewhere but never
bothers the familiar ones, often just over the yard wall.

So near to Rievaulx Abbey, we could feel an affinity with whatever
monastic ghosts roamed the area, for monks from this order had farmed
our land centuries before us. We tried to visit and explore their headquarters
but the abbey was closed. Indeed there seemed a closedown everywhere, a
sure sign that winter was coming. We spent one morning wandering round
a yard, untidily filled with old farm machinery, remembering days of our
childhood with only horse power at our disposal. We were very happy at
'High Woods'.

On the last of our five days, we went to Thirlby to see Squirrel. Only
within the last few days had her house been returned to normal and her
carpets been re-laid after the June floods. She dined us royally and later
took us to see the woodcarver who signs all his furniture with a wooden
wren. Had our purse been fatter and our social class been upper, we would
have loved to furnish the house with such beauty. We are however, and
will remain, working class, for we fail to outgrow the habit. And, equally
interesting, she then took us a few metres down the lane and showed us the
home of the late Alf Whyte, the author whose pen-name was the immortal
James Herriot. His books we read again and again.

Too soon the brief holiday was over and we had to say goodbye to our
dwarf cottage and head home to face the cameras. Oh dear! To do so had
never been on our agenda. Wishing to extract every moment from our last

day we idled the afternoon away in Studley Royal park, obeying the warning notices telling visitors to beware of stags, for it was rutting season.

We were amazingly refreshed after such a short holiday, suggesting that we were in much better shape than we had believed. 'Are we going to buy calves?' we asked. Of course we were!! The first buy was still two weeks away and the shed had to receive its annual autumn clean, the milk machines had to be brought out of storage and Mr Lawson sent for to give them their pre-use overall. All these jobs were routine, things we had done so many times, year after year. What we had never done, nor expected to do, was to face the television cameras. That was a totally new experience, daunting when they were on us but really quite exciting when they focused on our animals and our premises. Just as we had found the lady producer to be easy company so did we find the presenter, Luke Casey, and the very competent team of camera, sound and production members so that, when they said they wished to come again in December, when the calves would fill the shed and the yearlings would be housed, we didn't panic. We had said yes, in September and now we just had to go with it, to be blown by the wind, for better or worse.

One fortunate discovery was made whilst we were all discussing their next visit. They asked Margaret to switch on the air system fan and in doing so we discovered that one half of the plastic tube had acquired a huge tear. Periodically this happens and we have to buy a new one. With two weeks to the calf-buy we had time to order one and for it to be installed before the shed was filled with babies. To do so then would have been well nigh impossible. Because the replacement one arrived with only one row of holes, a second line had to be cut in the plastic by hand. Then Margaret had to crawl up the tunnel, all ninety feet of it, emphasising the fact that we must, at all costs, retain agility. For some reason I cannot remember, I had to crawl just a few metres up that tube, so I know how difficult it must have been for Margaret!

There was one more hurdle before the calf buy. The Land Rover needed its MOT test. We were fairly confident that it would last us a few more seasons of minimal road use and all our necessary field work. Tim had reported that the engine was fine, just before we had driven to 'High Woods' and I had given it an inside hoover and an exterior car wash. However the test showed that the mud coated chassis needed extensive welding, too costly for an old vehicle. We had no alternative but to replace it. What with, we wondered?

We had to have a four-wheel drive. Whatever we bought must be a working member of our team. Since 1970 we had driven Land Rovers. In 1981 we had exchanged a long wheelbase Station Wagon for a two door Range Rover. Twenty years later we had reverted to the Station Wagon because it was too difficult, if not impossible, to get Harry into a newer, four door edition of a Range Rover. Now, six years on, our family reduced to two, we seriously thought we could manage with a small wheel based Land Rover. A second hand one, of course. We no longer needed passenger space but we still required room for equipment and dogs. It soon became obvious that a bigger vehicle was the only option. So, against all expectations, we decided on a twelve year old, but well preserved Range Rover waiting, presumably just for us, in the showroom. It looked monstrous and far two pretentious but the need for it spelled out the obvious fact that we were still a working team living in a place needing a four wheel drive, overland facility in the summer and a snow capability in winter. For twelve months of the year, we needed enough back space to house several bin bags and boxes of bottles to be taken to the household tip, sacks of poultry and dog food and bags of cement. As long as we were providing bread and breakfast and the occasional evening meal, our weekly shopping was an item and there had still to be room for two dogs. The Range Rover it had to be but we would keep the Station Wagon for as long as it moved, for land use only. We had to have a vehicle almost immediately for we must go to Gisburn Calf Sales on the following Thursday or disrupt our routine.

It was delivered at 9 p.m. on the Wednesday evening, complete with road tax disc and insurance but untried and looking too spanking new to go to a cattle market, early next day. It wasn't new by any means but the age of technology was catching up on us and driving us mad. All these safety buttons to press before the ignition worked or windows went up and down. The worst thing to get used to was the absence of a choke. When we set off to Gisburn, early next morning, Margaret petrified in the driving seat and me equally scared in the passenger one, you may have thought we were learner drivers. The bally thing kept stalling. Everything seemed opposite to the Land Rover we were used to and equally different from previous Range Rovers. We were confused with the dashboard and, when the vehicle stalled at the traffic lights, at a junction where a decision could be made, we did not hesitate to take the fields way even though we were short of time. Off the main road and in the absence of heavy traffic, Margaret began to get the hang of things and our pulse rate went down. Unfortunately, ahead of us there was a road closure and a diversion. It meant more miles added to our journey.

'Do you think we are being warned against buying calves?' we asked each other knowing that two more years ahead were committed immediately the auctioneer's hammer came down in favour of Margaret. 'We've always thought like this,' we remembered, 'and we've always headed for the hanging cliff, just like lemmings!'

As usual we were greeted by buyers who, good naturedly accepted that, today, they had extra competition. 'I'd better just go home,' one said. Sellers smile benevolently on Margaret. An extra bidder, out to buy many, would up the price. We took home thirty seven and returned the following week for another batch, taking our autumn intake to seventy four. Then we put the lovely Range Rover into the garage and hardly used it again until spring. I never drove it at all. It gathered a coating of dust, as everything did that dry winter of 2005/06 and looked uncared for when, every fortnight, we went into town for groceries.

The Crooks rang wishing to use The Loft. They told us they were looking for a new dog. We told her about the Golden Retriever pups at 'High Woods' and they drove up to Wass and bought one, the one with a pink collar. They had all looked the same and had been identified by colour. They called the pup Lily. Lilly the pink! We had every intention of returning to that very peaceful hide-away the next year but the proprietors decided to sell and the cottages were no longer to let.

The Sunday after this was a beautiful November day. Things were running smoothly in the calf shed and the late autumn sunshine, though it did not take away the morning chill, was greatly welcomed by our remaining self-catering guests. We, too, were on a high and, earlier than usual, the cattle came to drink at the trough nearest to the steadings. Margaret went up the hill to check and count them. She saw a Staffordshire Bull Terrier run into the herd and the cattle ran amock. Shouting angrily she hastened to call it to heel and, having caused chaos, she was surprised that it came to her rather than continue the chase. She grabbed its collar, a thing I'd never have dared to do, and she managed to slip a piece of binder twine under it and tie it to a fence. Knowing that it would soon eat through that she came into the yard, shouting for help, for a thicker piece of rope and her glasses. There might be a name or even a telephone number on the collar. There was neither so she told me to send for the police.

'We don't do dogs!' I was told. 'We can't help you at all. You'll have to take it to the dog pound!' I think he said it was in Wakefield. 'Don't forget it's Sunday,' he added.

'It may be,' I almost cried. I was distressed and angry. 'This dog has just chased over seventy yearlings across the pastures riddled with footpaths. Weekend walkers at risk. We are in danger of being bitten. It might be sunny but it's bitterly cold and my elderly, younger sister is standing shivering watching this bull terrier eat through the rope. We cannot release it, we don't know who it belongs to. We daren't put it in our car or drive with it to a dog pound. What have we to do with it?'

'Shoot it,' said the policeman. 'You are allowed!'

Need I say more? Margaret, monitoring a dog intent on biting its way free, was beginning to freeze. I took her a cup of coffee and an extra coat. An enormous, several sizes too big, pink thing she wears all winter and washes each spring. In it she looks like a homeless tramp but it has served her well for years. I went back to the phone and rang some neighbours, enquiring of them did they know anyone locally with a white Bull Terrier.

After several calls I had success. David Bailey said someone on the top road walked one daily and he'd call them and see if theirs was missing. The lady of the house said her husband, who had been very ill, went walking every morning, across our land and into St Ives, taking with him their normally well behaved dog. They were out now. The man carried a mobile phone so she could ring him. We, who do not carry mobile phones, are occasionally grateful to those who do.

Her husband was located walking round Coppice pond, as he did every morning It was a long walk for a man who had been ill but a reasonably flat one. Yes, he had lost his dog but it knew its route. When it had disappeared in the undergrowth, on the Druids' Altar path, he had expected it to catch up. It is hardly safe for anyone to go scrambling down that precipitous hillside so he had called but continued walking, fairly sure he would be followed. He was on the point of retracing his steps but he dare not hurry.

David came to tell us and we secured the prisoner more firmly and chatted for a while but David had long since gone and the clock had ticked away another hour before, in desperation, I got into the Land Rover. I drove it as far as our gate entry, it being no longer licensed for the road, and went to the lady's house. She called her husband again on the phone. He was coming along our track, he said and he and I reached the Land Rover simultaneously. I drove him the last quarter of a mile for him to collect his dog. I'm sure he had no idea what trouble it had caused. The cattle Margaret had gone to count had all dispersed and she was so stiff with cold it took her some time to warm up, wrapped round the Aga in the kitchen. I suppose it would have been worse had the sunny morning turned to rain. We had nothing but respect for a man whose heart had failed him once, who walked that distance every morning but we remain very wary of Staffordshires!

Work on the stockyard boundary barricade continued all November and more concrete was laid over the area where the broken drain had caused such havoc. We had feared that the heavy motorway barriers would look like a prison compound but they blended in beautifully and John called it The Corral. We still called it the stockyard but it did look posh and would restrain a herd of elephants should we ever go into that line of business!

Three weeks into calf-rearing, one beautiful Belgian Blue calf was found to be very blown when Margaret did her middle of the night round. She tried to let out air by the usual method of a syringe needle but had no success. I invariably waken when she goes out. The light from above the outside door shines on the ceiling above my bed. When she did not return I got up and joined her in the calf shed. 'I'll have to send for the vet,' she said, 'There's something seriously wrong.' We do not send for a vet unless there is and certainly not in the very early hours of the morning.

Charlotte, one of the lady vets now in the Practice, came and she really fought for that calf's life, with every ploy she could think of. She put in

Loading pen and stockyard.

a red devil to let out the gas and she put in a saline drip and darkness had turned into dawn before she left. We really thought she might have succeeded but there must have been something much more dreadful the matter with that calf for, barely an hour later, he died. We had had eighteen months without any death, human or animal. When that calf died we were shaking at the knees.

Winter, so loathe to depart and give way to spring, now tends to delay arrival until well into December. At the beginning of the month Sandy Lane Guides came for their 23rd annual weekend. We could hear them singing carols as they washed their dishes and round the campfire at night. Two decades ago they had had to get fathers to come to dig out the road, for snow had fallen during their stay. The change in the weather is unbelievable. It was so mild the yearlings, who had been given access to the stockyard gate, ignored it completely and we began to fear they would not seek shelter before the expected return of the ITV camera team on Thursday, December 8th. However Monday proved to be a messenger of winter and, as can always be predicted, the bullocks came home and filed into their sheltered accommodation. But seasonal temperature had not accompanied the rain and only half of them came home on the Tuesday and none at all on Wednesday. One of the film producers came to talk over the procedure for the next day and we had to tell him that, unless the herd returned that evening, there was no way we could encourage it to do so. The seventy three calves were all we could offer. It was nothing short of a miracle that they did. All of them. Just as if it was an established routine, they came home for their photo call. Next morning log fires were lit. Winter was planning residence.

On this visit the cameras were turned on animals and on the Robinsons, from Tyneside, in the Mistal cottage. We began to enjoy the company of the team for lunch at our kitchen table. They were from the north-east, too, and we find all Geordies really nice and easy to be with.

Then, suddenly it was Christmas and three hundred cards came through the letter box and more than that were posted. The trees were decorated and lit and The Bullocks and the Greens self-catered as they have done for years.

We had had the Range Rover for three months and I had never driven it!! Shame on me! So, on Christmas Day I got into the driver's seat. I had to take the plunge and the empty roads made it easy.

'I can drive it!' I said but I have no urge to do so if I can sneak into the passenger seat.

Chapter Thirteen

You my precious friend,
To the very end,
I'll be there.

PERHAPS the most interesting phenomenon of all time, is just that. Time! Surely it is not a fixed identity. It must be that the earth is now travelling round the sun faster so that days, though they begin with sunrise and end at dark, are shorter. I am sure that the heart beat of the planet is accelerating and the life of each season briefer and the year contracting. Once there was time to do everything. Now one Monday follows the last with incredible speed. Once we had time to do a much more demanding routine, time to care for our dependants, be obsessed with new projects, plan our holidays, follow every moonbeam.

Whenever did we find time to keep so many animals, heave so many bales of hay and straw, do our own walling and fencing, shop for and feed so many people, make so many beds, sew so many sheets and pillowcases, launder and dry them yet still drive occasionally round The Dales? Before all that we harvested our own hay, built our sheds and, every winter dug out the road when snow drifted down the one we had excavated and surfaced ourselves, so that I could get to the village school, in which I taught and to evening Guide Company meetings. Then there was plenty of time.

An era has come when we have no family to care for, no bales or sacks of fodder to carry on our backs and fewer guests to feed, for the wind of change has brought big bale silage, a Kramer and self-catering people in numbers we never envisaged. How come is it, that time is shorter than ever it was and every twelve hour, working day is now filled with a routine minus all those historic ploys?

Even the weather is not as demanding as it used to be. Or is it? It is certainly a topic of our conversation. The meteorological office insisted that 2006 would begin with a severe winter. Surely all its employees must be under forty and unable to remember what a severe winter is like. Three inches of snow which disappears over night does not make a winter any more than one swallow makes a summer. Our generation knows the meaning of severity, but then there was time to gather and chop logs, to walk two miles to school, to tend the tilly oil lamps and do home baking and preserving. There is only one explanation. The planet is spinning more quickly than it used to.

Time, however, is increasing the number of our friends. Statistics show that teenagers are the ones with the highest count and that, the older one gets the fewer friends one has. That is absolute nonsense! Ours are repro-ducing at the same rate as wire coathangers in our guest room wardrobes! For people, like us, who live on the edge of civilisation, this is amazing. People and animals find refuge here constantly. Animals bovine, equine, furred and feathered come and stay permanently and take precedence. New human friends, native, foreign, old and young are being added to our list, daily, often by the hour. Time is not erasing addresses from our overfull book. Only the Final Reaper takes away loved ones and He is not over active.

Though the days hurried by more quickly, that very dry spring, the grass did not keep apace. It just would not begin to grow until the year was a teenager. Time certainly seemed to be outstripping nature and this, we believed, was because the missing element was rain. The land was so dry it became a dust bowl. There was no mud to be brought into the house on paws or Wellingtons, but a layer of dust seemed continually to decorate the furniture, no matter how many times I cleared it and grit was swept from the parquet tiles, enough to partially fill a dustpan every day.

The first two months were surprisingly monotonous. We knew we could change all that by embarking on some hair-brained scheme but we just seemed to have enough to do coping with routine. It wasn't straight forward by any means. The previous year's January/February guests were returning for another two month stay. They had intended to occupy The Loft cottage but the lady had recently broken a leg so I prepared The Mistal. At the last moment they decided first to have a winter break in Malta. Initially this proved to be a blessing for we had unexpected travellers mid-week who wanted a two day cottage stay. It was not a problem because the pre-booked couple were on holiday in Malta. I thought! That same evening their daughter rang to say her parents had, unfortunately, booked 'an hotel from hell' and were on their way home and could we house them immediately. The Mistal now being occupied, I had to do so in the bed and breakfast accommodation whilst they secured a trip to the Canaries instead. Mid-winter shocks are debilitating to say the least.

We had so many guests, the central heating in their department was fuelled all winter and, I must confess, our own was never lit. It seemed the last straw intent on breaking our backs, to bring up three more hods of coke from the cellar for we who were seldom in the house. Margaret does most of this and even the five hods needed for the conversion heating and the Aga, seemed five too many. Fearing to light an open fire and leave it unattended, or even an electric one which Danny approached too closely, we spent winter sweating outside and shivering indoors. I did not suffer so much because I came in to work close to the Aga and flesh, which had become rigid outside, thawed as I made dinner. Margaret, who came straight from the sheds, found the electric fire I had switched on was insufficient and before she sat down she filled a hot water bottle. It is a fact that work outside can make you sweat but, on investigation, flesh feels as if it has been in the freezer. We were determined that we would solve this problem with a wood burning stove next winter.

Danny's condition seemed in remission but Margaret did need to let him out during the night. Whilst calves had to be revisited, the two jobs coincided but it was unfair that, having had interrupted sleep for many years of caring for family, that we now had an old dog. We could not bear the thought of losing him. We also had an old donkey and an old goat. Joe was looking very ancient. He was wearing an old horse blanket so that he could leave his shed during the day, as often as he wished. Joe loved human contact. His head was first to lean over the gate or push through the open window of a car. He had been with us since the death of Chocolate fifteen years ago and had not been a young donkey then. We did not really know his age but he was looking much older and finding it difficult to keep up with Bobby.

Rosie, the nanny we had thought too old to survive the winter of 2001, was still with us. Five years ago she had chosen to join our neighbour's out-wintering flock of sheep, in snow, which was not a sensible thing for the matriarch of the goat herd to do. She'd had to be brought home in Harry Raw's Land Rover. We'd expected, then, that we might lose her but, apart from chronic arthritis, she ailed little. She took to sitting astride a bale of straw so taking the weight from her problem legs. We were fascinated by her ability to solve her pain problem by shuffling onto this belly rest and dangling her feet. The wallers, unaware of this, removed the stranded bale and she was mortified. It was very quickly put back for her convenience. She also found the Land Rover a suitable leaning post, one we had to walk round before getting into the driving seat, lest she should be leaning on the near side.

The first, sad death of a winter which dragged its cold, dry feet even into May, was a mouse. We do not have mice often in our house. I could not count five times in fifty years. Nor do we see many in the cattle sheds due to our cats, Blackie, Smokey and Ginger who must be the most competent hunters on our hillside. I heard a fairly near neighbour, at the vets' reception desk, say he thought his horse had been bitten by a rat. 'There are hundreds of the beggars!' he said and he didn't believe me when I said, truthfully, that I hadn't, then, seen a rat in a dozen years or even the evidence of one. Not since we pulled down the old dutch barn. We used to, in the sixties and seventies when, after harvest, we sometimes heard them in the underdrawing of the house. That ended when the hay was housed elsewhere and the barn converted. Nevertheless we know the signs and, touch wood, there had been no recent evidence due to our extraordinary cats, that is until someone deposited pet, white rats, under the duck hole, eighteen months later! We used to have pigeons too, remember. Now we have none.

However, one cold Sunday evening I saw a mouse crouched beside the Aga, leaning on it for warmth. It could have been drawn with a Beatrix Potter pen. I tried to catch it but it moved too quickly and disappeared under the central heating stove which, due to our winter weariness, was not lit. Margaret got out her live trap, fuelled it with a piece of cheese and placed it beside the Aga and we went back to our armchairs. When I re-entered the kitchen, to make a goodnight cuppa, the little fellow was again curled up against the warm enamel, the cheese untouched in the empty trap. He shuffled under the stove and we decided he must be ill and we returned to the sitting room. Every time one of us passed, he was crouched in the heaven he had found and each time he went more slowly to the sanctuary beneath the stove. Next morning he was there again, snuggling against the Aga, but this time he was dead. His demise affected us strangely. We were glad that he had found an animal hospice and died in comfort.

We were beginning to be very worried about the twin billy goats Tim had brought the previous summer. We are never particularly aware of their presence for they find their own food and come and go wherever and when they please. But it was impossible not to notice that these yearling goats were no longer agile. They were walking with their front legs bent at the elbow. Both of them. Thinking their hooves must need a manicure, one was given but it soon was evident that we had two severely disabled goats.

The Ministry informed us that one of our November calves had come from a southern herd troubled with TB and our vet must come to test it. The disease had not accompanied it but the Vet's visit gave Margaret an opportunity to ask for an explanation re the goats. It must be a genetic abnormality, was the verdict. It was certainly becoming a huge problem for their spines were bending and their knees were sore. She gave some steroids to the one most affected. After a while there appeared to be a slight improvement so Margaret gave more of the medication and treated the other twin. It was awful watching them struggle across the concrete, trying to get upright but continually reverting to a half crawl. Occasionally we saw them standing nearly upright but they were not properly on their hooves. When eating they were kneeling and when not they were sitting, so they were reasonably content and no guests seemed to notice. Margaret was sure they were improving so we let time be the doctor.

At the beginning of February, a ninety six year old sculptor came with his family, some from France and some from America, to attend a Leeds exhibition of his artistry. We entertain such interesting people. Equally so were an editorial team visiting the publishers of their magazine. I nearly made an enormous blunder with their booking. I must stop assuming that weekend guests will come on a Friday. This was for a long weekend and I had correctly shaded in the Thursday to Sunday area on my chart and had equally so entered a one night bed and breakfast for a couple bringing a child, to the David Hart Clinic, on the Wednesday night. Looking at the calendar, at the beginning of the week in question, I said, 'Whoops, I've got this wrong. Groups come on Fridays!' so I altered it and was surprised when the family for the clinic arrived on Wednesday, when I expected them to come on Thursday and I wasn't intelligent enough to realise I had altered a correct chart. Consequently the editorial team came on Thursday when no log fire was lit to welcome them.

'This is serious,' I told Margaret. 'I'm starting to make grave mistakes.' I have always narrowly got out of a wrong booking, throughout the many years of serviced accommodation, by vacating our own bedroom. To make two self-catering bookings, overlapping, would be a disaster. I know people who have done so and have heard the havoc it has caused. Each time, living in a village where there have been other holiday cottages, they have found a way out. Mine would be for us to vacate the farmhouse and relocate to the barn!!

Margaret's late night prowl of the calf sheds continues almost until turning out time. She signals that she is out by putting on the outside light so that I am aware. If she is gone longer than usual I follow, more often than not to be greeted with, 'Oh go back to bed, I'm coming.' It was a cold February night. I awakened, shortly after midnight, hearing an odd noise. The light was on so I remained alert and I tried to identify this unusual sound. I didn't connect it with air sometimes trapped in the water pipe. I didn't think it was distant shooting. It might be somebody in the valley partying and setting off fire works. Maybe, I thought, I should get up and investigate but it was cold and I decided to give Margaret time to return to the house and we'd investigate the noise together.

So I lay listening to the tapping which was intermittent and had no pattern. Eventually I heard Margaret's steps approaching the house. I know she often leaves the door wide open but I heard her close it and the light went out and a loud exclamation followed. 'Oh my goodness, gracious me!!'

Standing with heads over the Aga, enjoying luxurious warmth, were the two donkeys. It had been their foot-tapping on wooden tiles which had so puzzled me. During winter, Joe's condition had deteriorated and it was only a matter of time. Margaret said it was one of the hardest things she had ever done, to turn the donkeys away from the heat, even though she knew they had luxury accommodation in the deep straw of the Donkey Hole.

A few days later, Joe lay down and died peacefully. Had a donkey era passed? This seemed likely. Bobby was distraught. All donkeys fret terribly when they lose a friend. He could not be kept alone but he was young and could well out-live me at any rate. Donkeys must be occasionally caught and tethered for the blacksmith and ours are free spirits, wild if restrained. Tim knew of a pony in need of a friend, whose owner had asked him if he knew of anyone with a donkey he could buy. Knowing Joe was not expected to last the winter he had said, 'Maybe!'

So when Joe died it was suggested that Bobby might fill that role. Margaret came to me and said, 'I think I've made a wise decision. Bobby must have a friend. He'd have one if we let him go. What do you think?'

'I think it is the wisest decision you've ever made,' I said. Perhaps we needed to down-size but I had not thought she was capable of an agreement such as that. Through hell and high water, what is hers is hers! Joe was removed. Funerals for animals do not cost as much as human ones but £96 is necessary to have a large animal taken away. None, now, can be buried on the farm.

Almost immediately Bobby was taken across the valley and a non-payment was arranged until a fortnight's trial period had elapsed. We accepted the inevitable. The Currer without donkeys! For over a quarter of a century two had roamed our acres with total freedom. Their shed had had an ever open door. In winter they barely left the yard. They were synonymous with The Currer. Guests had returned because we had donkeys. They were more photographed than any other animal, human or otherwise. They were featured in all the advertisements and had a slot on our website. Disappointment would show on the faces of all returning holiday-makers when they were told the news. The villagers would miss them immediately. Local children would come in vain to see them. It was unbelievably sad.

We remained confident we had done the right thing. Donkeys are not easy to locate and very expensive to buy. We rarely admit it but we did, on this occasion say, 'We are growing old and have far too many animals!' Tim passed the field daily, in which Bobby had been re-housed and he reported that our four year old was settling happily and that is all that mattered. Animal contentment. We were sad, our guests would point accusing fingers in our direction but we would all eventually forget.

The fortnight trial period was over and I took Bobby's passport from the desk drawer, wherein lie a hundred and fifty cattle passports and we were about to collect the money. Margaret made one last enquiry. 'Are you sure Bobby is alright? He is happy? You're quite sure?'

'I'm quite sure,' Tim said and then put a spoke in the wheel by saying, 'He's on his own at the moment because the pony has gone for two weeks schooling. They are going to show it this summer but Bobby is fine.'

It was a bomb shell exploding in our kitchen! We had let Bobby go to find him constant company, rather than search once more for one to befriend him here. Now he would not only be twice bereft, but mourning in a strange land. What's more he, who brayed every time Joe had been out of sight, though only yards away, would be left alone every time the pony left the field to attend a horse show or take its mistress riding. What had we done?

Tim was adamant that the donkey was fine. He suggested he took us there to see for ourselves. So we took Bobby's passport and a bill of sale and we went to see him. Our donkeys have never been family pets. They are just friendly neighbours. Others feed them carrots and apples. They didn't expect us to do so. They did not ever respond to our recall. Our relationship with them was to chase them out of the corn store, if someone had accidentally left the door open, or to occasionally put on halters, restraining them whilst the blacksmith trimmed and filed their hooves.

We saw Bobby in the field as we approached and half wondered if he would acknowledge our presence. He was just a small dot on a very sloping field. He looked so lonely. Donkeys are inseparable, seldom can you even photograph one alone. There are always two for the camera. We felt awful. Bobby had been so sad when Joe had died, only two weeks ago, and now he was abandoned in a strange place. I'm not sure what we would have done if his sharp ears had not heard Margaret's voice. He pricked them immediately, though she had not spoken his name and had merely been talking to his new owner. Without hesitation he brayed and came bounding towards her and that settled any argument.

'Oh Bobby,' she said. Just that. 'Oh Bobby.'

'If you want to take him home, do.' I said. I knew she would never forgive herself if she didn't. Of course we looked rather foolish in front of two broad-shouldered men. It had been Tim who suggested we insist on a trial period but for the buyer's sake, not Bobby's. Fortunately, we had possession of his passport. We had exchanged no money. He was legally still our donkey. We paid the man keep for the fortnight's food and brought Bobby home. He was a very distressed donkey, searching for Joe all the time, but he was at home.

Margaret phoned the blacksmith's father, Jack Pack, from whom we had bought Joe. He does not keep donkeys but had found someone willing to part with Joe, when Chocolate had died. Once again, he immediately found someone with donkeys, willing to sell us Ben, a two year old. He will certainly out-live me!

He was transferred from one trailer to another in the car park adjacent to Otley Cattle Market. There was no trial period. We paid the bill and pocketed his passport and Tim drove home. Ben settled immediately but Bobby was quite traumatised. It took several days for him to regain his confidence. I could hear Margaret constantly saying, 'I'll never do that to you again, Bobby. Never! You are here for always. I promise.' Before long we had the two happiest donkeys in Airedale.

Bobby and Ben.

A similar situation presented itself shortly afterwards. For some unknown reason the three remaining geese started to wander further and further afield. We frequently had to collect them and drive them home at dusk. That was not a problem if they were in the vicinity, but they started to venture to the top of the Footpath Field and it was tiresome to have to climb the hill and bring them back. Then they wandered even further and one night were so far away Margaret left things to chance hoping they would come of their own accord. They didn't but they were all still alive next morning and thereafter, for a few nights, they came home.

Suddenly we had rain. It fell on earth as hard as concrete and could not be absorbed. The dyke field retained pools of standing water and the geese just loved it and, one night, did not come home. Next morning only one returned. Scattered down the field were enough white feathers to testify to the fate of his comrades. The fox had found them and only one had escaped.

'It was your own fault,' Margaret said, time and time again to a miserable gander who feared to leave the forecourt. For a week he mourned, seated alone in the safety of the yard. Eventually Margaret could stand it no longer and she rang Paulette, who had first come here from Essex, on holiday, liked the area and bought a small holding in Hainworth. She had a spare goose we could have. The arranged marriage was an instant success and the gander appeared to have learned his lesson.

The goose began to lay eggs and it was necessary to replenish the cake tins and the freezer with cakes. If you wish to make a perfect sponge cake you must have a goose egg. No other egg is lighter. Some large gathering was necessary to reduce the number of cakes and one was looming on the horizon.

But first we had a major job to do in the dining room. The carpet must be replaced. The existing one had been tortured since the millennium. Originally few guests drank wine. We have never taken to the habit, having no taste for it, or for smoking, dining out and all normal human pursuits. This has been a blessing for our purse is ever light and there is always a greater need than ours.

Guests increasingly drink wine and occasionally they spill it and we could not remove stains on the carpet, however hard we tried. It had also had two major soakings from burst pipes and, although we had been able to dry it, we knew it was rotted in some places. In 2006 we said it would have to go. We debated whether or not it would be better to put stone flags down instead. It had been flagged originally but, until we came to the windowless ruin in 1958, it had been converted from human dwelling to cattle shed and often pigs had farrowed in the far corner. The inglenook fireplace had been discovered but restoration, sixteenth century style, was not only too expensive but had not then caught our imagination. So the cracked flags, stained as they were with cow dung, had been covered with a layer of concrete.

Should we re-flag it, we wondered and went down to The National Trust property at East Riddlesden Hall, to walk on flags in front of their inglenook and decided it would be the right thing to do if we could find the right hearth rug. We possessed nothing remotely suitable to lay on flags. We are impulsive and let no water flow under the bridge when an idea becomes an obsession. We went straight to a carpet warehouse in town, where we have often found cheaply, just what we wanted. We said we needed a heavy carpet mat about six foot by nine foot and the good man took us to see an array of hanging carpets of very modern design.

'No, no!' we said. 'We will want it to lay on stone flags under massive oak beams and to sit it before a very old inglenook fireplace, complete with beehive oven. Those are not what we want at all!'

I knew exactly what I wanted and I have found, so frequently, that you can have what you want if you stick there long enough, look around corners and lift eyes upwards. Hanging from the ceiling, to display it to advantage, was a heavy mat, fractionally smaller than we'd envisaged, with an antique design, deep blue and red and green. 'That is a very expensive rug,' the sales manager said but he was willing to lower it on the pulley so that we could feel the quality.

'The problem is, 'I said, 'we would need two exactly alike.' It would be highly improbable, I knew, but you get nothing if you do not ask.

'Well, I do have two mats,' he replied, 'but they are not quite alike. They are both exactly the same pattern and colour but, if you look very carefully you will see that red has been used for the background in one and blue in the other.' You had indeed to look very carefully to notice the difference, the quality of the wool and the depth of the colour and the intricacy of the ancient design, hid the fact that they were not really identical twins.

We did not hesitate. We bought both. They were very expensive. How fortunate that we do not personally indulge! When rolled for transport in the Range Rover they were nearly too heavy to handle. We were triumphant.

Having paid so much for the carpets we had no alternative but to have stone flags laid. Our wallers were professionally capable of that. Only two things were needed. Flags and opportunity. The latter had to be in the last week of February. That was the only gap on the chart with no guests using the dining room. Being able to buy enough old flags at the last minute was one of those miracles which punctuate our lives. Had a source not been found in time, the old carpet may have been replaced and the new mats may have lain, rolled, in Harry's room for an indefinite period.

Luck being our lady we were able to empty the room of all furniture and the laying went smoothly for the weather was dry and the garden door could be used to pile up the flags, sort them and to mix the concrete outside. My poor lawn suffered seriously but grass is a survivor second to none. The men had a deadline, for the dining room was to be used for a celebration on the 4th March. They were unable to point the flags in time for them to be exposed for the gathering, so the old carpet was hastily relaid and the furniture re-instated to wait for another opportunity after the Big Do!

We were planning to celebrate the twenty fifth annual Guide Reunion on the first Saturday in March and to do so we had told everyone to come for lunch rather than for the usual evening buffet. We expected over fifty. Some would have been in the company in the early fifties and every year would be represented until closure in 1981.

What would make it more exciting was the fact that The Dales Diary camera team would be there to record it on film for posterity. The producer of this programme was interested in filming as many facets of life at The Currer as possible and had asked to see our dining room occupied with feasting guests.

'You can't do that,' I had said. We can't intrude on self-catering groups and we have so few main meal serviced occasions, now, I could not possibly manufacture an opportunity, just to suit them. 'You could come to the Reunion,' I'd suggested and they'd been immediately interested.

'We'll do just that!' they'd said.

Six volunteers were enlisted to carry extra tables into the dining room and to cope with the menu and decide who would provide what. It was all tremendous fun. They agreed to come on the Friday afternoon to set the tables. We had managed to seat forty six diners. Those serving would have to stand and any children would have to be in the kitchen.

'We'll all come at two,' they promised.

The Currer in the snow.

At mid-day on Friday it began to snow heavily. Oh! we had had snow on Reunion Day many times over the twenty five years, but not recently. Not since snow had become a rarity. On one occasion we had had to cancel it completely. On others we had told drivers to leave cars at the summit and walk. We had often laughed and predicted snow for this annual event but it had been some time, long before the millennium, since we had had a white entry into March.

On this occasion I phoned my volunteers and said it was foolish to come at 2 p.m. I would set the tables and we'd have to do whatever was necessary if this blizzard persisted. It certainly looked set to produce a heavy fall. Had it not been so serious we would have been hysterical.

One of my volunteers did come. Barbara Sherriff left her car at the cattle grid and walked down the hill, enjoying the experience of snow, of which we are so deprived. Children of today miss so much of the simple fun of waking to silence and snow curtaining a frosted window pane. They go ski–ing, which I'm sure is good, but to watch snow falling on bare trees in a winter garden, from the front door of home, waiting for there to be enough to get out your sledge and polish the runners, glancing through the class-room window onto the white playground, willing the playtime bell to ring, surely, that is children's idea of heaven.

Old as we are Margaret and I cannot lose the thrill of falling snow. We knew it would cause problems, that it may deter the television team. We did not think it would deter many of our clan! Margaret was left with all outside chores whilst Barbara and I set the tables for the forty six we had managed to seat. It was a mammoth task, taking thrice the time we had planned. The sky looked absolutely full of snow but the 'geese from Scotland, dropping feathers here, took their feathers back again' and left a depth of little more than four inches. Next morning, with the camera team arriving at 9 a.m., we had no alternative but to phone for Tim to come with his tractor and clear the still pristine whiteness from the road. The bonus was that now we have snow on film and we couldn't have ordered that, not for any price!

We could not have wished for a happier day, a day full of unforgotten, spontaneous, traditional joy. All had remembered every detail of the easy discipline, the instant silence provoked merely by the raising of my hand. The hubbub, when seated round the table was awe inspiring. They were as noisy as starlings gathering for their nightly performance. It would have been believed by those with no history of Guiding, that silence was unachievable between those who had not seen each other for decades. Yet when I raised my arm, one after the other did so and you could have heard a pin drop. A lump rose in my throat so that I could barely attempt the Johnny Appleseed grace. We took the camera team by surprise. 'Sing it again' they said.

The meal had been prepared in seven different homes by a team thrown together at the last minute, yet it was a banquet fit for royalty. Margaret, Hazel and I sat among those, who as children, we had guided along the road to happiness and it was obvious that each, and every one of them had continued along that route. They had blossomed and were reaping their harvest, comfortable and content with the way their lives had progressed, proud of their children and grandchildren but, for one remarkable afternoon,

The 25th Guide Reunion.

they were careering down memory lane with healthy appetites, lots of laughter and, later, round the fire in song.

Make good friends and keep the old,
One is silver and the other gold.
Each campfire lights anew, the flame of friendship true,
The joy we've had in knowing you will last our whole life though.

Aren't we Lucky? We have indeed been singularly blessed. We had been able to give them the freedom and the fun, now deprived to children by a society which fears so unnecessarily, that they may be harmed. In so doing they have created a situation rather than erased it. We are in danger of having a generation of inactive, overweight children who do not know how to be as happy as their forebears were, nor as creative. So much has been lost since the advent of the television and the computer, incomparable to any gain. Giving children choice has resulted in taking away their freedom.

Just before the television team left I had an inspired idea. I don't know where it came from. They had been so unobtrusive, so wide-eyed seeing all these lovely, attractive ladies and these huge masculine men who had run barefoot, as children, in the Western Isles. I desperately wanted the camera team, and the viewing public, to see them as they were. Yesterday's children!

I said to Barbara Bugloss, 'I have some videos of the sixties and seventies, taken from 8mm film, of them as children in the Hebrides. Would they be of any use to you?'

'Maybe,' she said and suddenly I was immensely grateful to Mrs Meade, of Wetherby and to Keith Whalley who had taken the films.

Capable to the extreme, my team washed the dishes and tidied the kitchen. Helen stayed until late to finish the clearing whilst Margaret went out to the calves and I, the Teacher and Guider no more, resumed my role as farmer's man. It was late when cattle were all fed and bedded down and all was done. When is it ever not?

The celebration over we could take up the dining room carpet for the last time and the men could point the flags and seal them as they were meant to be. Little by little history returns to The Currer. We have a more posi- tive urge to return to the past than to embrace the technological future. We brought the two new carpet mats from Harry's room and, when laid, we thought the room looked beautiful.

Diana was due to calve again, any day and, as usual, we were on tender hooks. However the incident passed without drama. We thought it might be because Margaret had ordered semen from a native Aberdeen Angus bull and not from the heavier, Canadian breed recently introduced to the UK. We have since been informed that there is only one Aberdeen Angus bull there. Take it or leave it! The three of us, Margaret, Diana and I managed without male help and all three of us were cock-a-hoop and able to display the baby bull calf to the camera team when they came again towards the end of March. We were used, by now, to their visits. They interviewed and filmed the mother of one of the children currently visiting the David Hart Clinic. We had recently had a summer cancellation from a Maltese family due to the fact that, 'He is walking!!' Those alterations to our chart raise our applause. A relative showed amazement that the team decided there was enough material here to fill the whole half-hour programme. It caused Margaret and me amusement for days!

It seemed as if the winter would never end. Everything was late. We had hoped the daffodils would be out before the fourth visit of the camera team but they were tardy in showing their annual, golden splendour. The tits and finches found no other food than that provided by our resident St Francis and some of the seeds and nuts, put out in the hanging holders, were stolen by hungry squirrels having exhausted their hidden, autumn harvest. A couple of pheasants found treasure on the grass below and a family of mice found the bag of sunflower seeds and played havoc.

Everyone complained that there was no food in the dale. Pauline, my pupil, Guide, friend and milk lady, complained that they had let out a thousand sheep and lambs and there was no grass! We bought more and more bales of haylage and straw and kept the meadows gated. The lack of rain dried up the pastures until they were cracked and the muck was spread without tractor wheels making any indentations. Footprints made by cattle in December were preserved, rock hard so that my ankles were at risk when walking and it was wise to take a stick.

I was weary of Margaret saying she was cold, that there was no grass, that she was fed up of feeding animals and that the winter would never end. It was strange how, having experienced snow into March until the 1980s, we found the dryness so exasperating. Snow had been a fertilizer. Growth followed immediately. Lack of rain was a killer.

We ordered another load of logs to keep the open fires burning for the almost perpetual mid-week and weekend bookings. Everyone was celebrating and re-uniting. I was perpetually re-making beds and washing hung from the ceiling every night, like some Chinese Laundry.

At last the cattle were able to be deprived of their overnight accommodation and, shortly afterwards Margaret and I opened the gates and checked the boundaries of the fields we still call the meadows. There was by no means a luscious growth but it was beginning to smell and we knew the cattle would not be long in finding it. To our horror, early the next morning, our Altar Farm neighbours phoned to say the wall was down where our eastern boundary meets the green lane to Bingley and the gate into St Ives.

Knowing that the cattle had free access into all eight fields we leapt into the

Land Rover in a panic. Our seventy head herd may already be promenading down Bingley Main Street! The locked twelve foot wooden gate onto our pastures had been lifted off its gudgeons, to allow a vehicle to pass through and onto the village road. Tyre marks indicated that a trailer was towed and that it was being pulled by a quad bike. We drove to the boundary and found that the wall had been systematically pulled down, stone by stone removed out of the way to allow a vehicle to pass through. Just one field away the cattle were grazing. We hurried into the woodland, in St Ives and brought out some timber. Dead wood littered the ground and we were able to temporarily fence the enormous gap. We immediately sent for our wallers and for the police. The latter phoned, two days later to say the quad and trailer had been stolen from the estate. The men lifted the hinges back onto their gudgeons and we fixed it so as to prevent that ever happening again, which is a nuisance for now, if we forget the key, we cannot do likewise. On occasions like this we have to accept that the world is not full of law-abiding people. If it were not for television we, in our capsule, might believe that our country is peopled with happy, caring, family orientated human beings. Only rarely do we experience that it is not.

We particularly want to say something positive about today's young people. Let me tell of a phone call I received from a lady who had been a member of a family celebrating an eighteenth birthday. She immediately insisted that I may say an instant, 'No!' to her request. 'I won't be offended,' she assured me.

'Let's hear it,' I said.

'It's my son. He is nearly 18 and in the sixth form and would like to come with 12 more boys from school, before they all split up and go to university. You may not want to take them. I'll understand. But I can vouch for them. My son won't invite any one who would cause trouble but do say at once if you'd rather not.'

Thirty years of my life I spent with teenagers I could trust to behave wherever they were, whether I was there or not. Have things really changed? Are the young people out of control or is it just hearsay and media exaggeration?

'If you can trust them, then they can come,' I said and so they did and they were normal teenagers, laughing a lot, eating a lot, going to bed late and getting up when the sun was high. And they went out. They went down to the Leisure Centre, hired the football pitch and had a game. When they went they left the house tidy. 'Can we come again,' they asked.

'Of course,' we said. Their temporary stay had boosted our theory that most teenagers are responsible citizens worthy of trust and we love telling this story.

Chapter Fourteen

O Danny Boy, O Danny Boy,
I love you so.

W E HAVE LONG KNOWN that animals, weakened with winter, are apt
to worsen with spring. It is unwise to expect turning-out to aid every
recovery. We glibly say, 'Dr Green is all we need,' but so often a calf which
has not done as well as the rest, begins to go downhill when it leaves the
shed. When the baby herd come home at night, one is found to be panting
and in need of an anti-biotic and a further spell indoors. This very late
spring caused Margaret to say she was fed up of animals. Two calves needed
to be brought back in. The others, hale and hearty, immediately thrived on
their new found salad but one of the two brought back into the shed just
could not make it. One recovered slowly with the aid of sugar, honey and
warm water and lots of TLC.

Rosie, our ancient nanny, made a temporary recovery, staggered round
the yard and ate a little from the paddock, alongside Poorly-getting-better.
The twin billies continued to eat in a kneeling position and only rarely stood
upright. We knew they could, but feared they had formed a dreadful habit
and were incapable of breaking it.

Danny was slowly deteriorating. Accepting the fact that he would never
again be a train-traveller, we had decided to make Tiree our summer destination. In the event of him being still alive we, who had declared we would
never drive so far again, would have to, and so chose the nearer of our two
island venues. Old and wobbly though he be, he never failed to accompany
Margaret wherever she went. If she got up to go out so did he. The ramp I
had made was carried to the Range Rover, if we were going by road and to
the Land Rover if we were going overland. His name could have been Harry,
for wherever we went so did he. Margaret got up once, sometimes twice,
every night to let him out. Very occasionally his diarrhoea returned and
disappeared almost immediately. He was kept on a strict diet and became
ravenous for tit-bits. He searched for them perpetually and, in the end we
relaxed and his condition did not worsen. We loved him to bits. Meg had
lost her companion but true to his nickname, Danny clung to Margaret like
Super Glue.

We were still desperate for rain. We wakened to a shroud of mist and
gently falling, persistent rain on the morning of the television crew's final

visit. They had wanted sunshine to film the wild flowers which carpet our pastures in spring and the trees so newly in leaf. They had wanted to film Airedale in colour and capture Ingleborough on the western sky-line and, whilst we welcomed the rain, we had wanted everything to look beautiful, too. Mist can be so. When it lies in the valley, deceiving guests that The Currer is in The Lake District, it foretells a hot and glorious day. It was not so on the crew's final, May visit. It was almost autumnal, damp and void of distance. Some things you can change but the weather is not one of them.

The cattle had not quite got used to being separated from us and we knew they might gather round the Land Rover, as we drove the men up to the high ground with their tripod and filming gear. Eventually they ignore us but in May they still behave with curiosity and, on this occasion, they emerged out of the mist like benevolent monsters of the prairie. They surrounded the vehicle, licking the windows and disturbing the side mirrors but allowing our fearless friends to step out into the rain and push through them with their awkward equipment. We could only shake our heads in amazement at the situation comedy we had created. Whatever would the film editor make of all the footage the camera had amassed? The team had come in October, expecting to produce a ten minute slot, about a lady recommended because she had had a go at writing. They had, unexpectedly, found she didn't have a separate identity, that she was highly dependant on a sister and that both were only cogs in a wheel that was far more interesting than they. Whatever others might think, there were a heck of a lot of spokes in our wheel!

The Senior Herd.

There followed, immediately, the re-visit after a few years' lapse, of the Smith family. Once again we had the pleasure of Richard, now fifty, who has coped so admirably with Down Syndrome. They had first come in the early eighties and been annual visitors until the Foot and Mouth epidemic changed everything. As he had always done, Richard stayed to help us on the farm whilst his parents toured the locality. He and I were on the hillside, closing gates against the eighteen month old cattle, when the first heavy shower of the year threatened to drown us. Richard, running far more quickly than I, leapt every gate with a sudden agility I had not expected. The downpour was a life saver. After it the grass shot up and the paddock offered such succulent fodder that the twins abandoned the hay available in their shed and, in their haste to get to the tastier table, they rose from their knees and their bent legs began to straighten. They were akin to toddlers. They tottered a few steps and then sank back on their knees. Their condition had mystified us, and the vet, but the signs of progress were encouraging.

As our day of departure for Tiree drew nearer I began to worry about driving north. I was out of practice. I had avoided driving as much as possible ever since I'd broken my leg. I do not belong to a generation for whom driving is the be all and end all. My driving licence was forty years old, but the faster traffic and the busier roads did not turn me on. If Danny had died, relief would have accompanied the sadness of parting and we would have scurried to the railway station to buy tickets. But he deteriorated without succumbing to what is inevitable in all life.

So we decided to take three days for the journey to Oban and I booked our Travel Lodge accommodation. Until we made the railway our mode of transport, we had always used such, whether our journey be north or south. They were havens of rest before the excitement of Highlands and Islands. I had an unusual, modern experience booking by phone, for I found that the receptionist was just a voice. It said I must state the place, date and type of accommodation I required and the answering machine would tell me if there was a vacancy and make my booking. Where did I wish to stay?

I said, 'Ayr.'

'I do not understand,' said the voice. Repeat the name of the town.'

I said, 'Ayr.' The voice repeated its misunderstanding. Spelling the word did no good. Fortunately, after several repeats, the voice said, 'I will put you through to a live operator.' He understood me immediately and laughed. He was witty enough to explain, 'She is having a poor Ayr day!'

The immediate run-up to any of our holidays is interesting, different, unpredictable and fearful. The only safe gamble to make is that some incident will make a lasting imprint on the memory. The first spanner in our wheel was the news that our holiday and Dorothy's overlapped. We would not be returning before she would embark on her almost annual trip to Mull. However Helen and Chris were free to release her, to prepare and leave. After that small hitch, there seemed no other obstacle so, with bated breath, we concentrated on the mammoth task of leaving house and businesses in order. Then, with only three days to go, the FABBL inspector rang to say he was in the area and would come the next day to make his full annual inspection. It meant several, precious hours would be stolen from our already full agenda. The language of farming used to be, NOWT WRONG. Now it is NIL NON-COMPLIANCE if you believe what is written before the signature of the good natured inspector! Bureaucracy is a forest of words. Small print almost unintelligible. Political speech meaningless. The days of calling a spade a spade have gone, totally.

On buying the Range Rover we had removed one of the back seats and the other had been permanently folded against the driving seat, to allow easy access for Danny and a four star spaciousness for both dogs. We cut five squares from the redundant dining room carpet and put one on top of the other in the back of the Range Rover. Under the top layer we put a waterproof and, at the last minute, we put a serrated carving knife there, too. We realised that, on the long journey north, our old dog might have the occasional accident. If so we would be able to cut away affected squares of the carpet. Danny watched our preparations with a holiday sparkle in his eyes. He knew we were going island hopping, I'm sure. Meg had a medley of holidays preventing her learning a car routine. She had only been nine weeks old when we had last driven all the way to Tiree. Then had come the Foot and Mouth disaster followed by the dormobile fiasco and subsequent journeys by train. Danny hung about the Range Rover, eager to get in lest he be left behind. As if we would ever do that to Danny! All our dogs have hovered as we have loaded the vehicle. We had taken Lusky when he could not walk and had to be lifted in and out but he had not been ill, just disabled. Danny was ill. We knew that. We knew that if he died before we left we would put the car back into the garage and go by train. Our first night was booked at the Travel Lodge in Penrith. Had he died during that first night, I know we would have returned home, buried him and proceeded by rail.

We had been too busy to fill up with petrol. It is always the same! Our immediate need of it caused us to draw into the first petrol station en route. We both got out, Margaret to fill up the tank at the pump and I walked towards the pay desk. Perhaps the most handsome Afro-caribbean man I have ever seen was staring open mouthed at my minute sister. Both of us are getting smaller, I am sure. His cheeks had a powdery bloom like a grape, the whites of his eyes stood out and the pupils sparkled. His mouth dropped open, revealing not only Persil white teeth but also that the upper incisors were totally covered in silver. He was asking me a question but I couldn't hear what it was, so I went towards him. 'Is she driving that?' He was shaking his head in wonder.

'Yes,' I said. 'Why?'

'How old is she?' We have always encountered people who think Margaret is younger than she is.

'She's sixty seven,' I answered.

'Good God!' he spluttered and I suddenly realised, in horror, that he judged her to be far too old to drive a Range Rover!

I was really reluctant to take the wheel, grossly out of practise and unused to the Range Rover. We had almost all the time in the world. Although it had been 2 p.m. before we left home, our Penrith destination was near at hand, allowing us to follow empty B roads all the way. At Hawes I took the bull by the horns and got into the driving seat and, throughout the ten days we were away, I did an acceptable, if not a half share of the driving. I think, perhaps, that three day journey along memory lane, was the most beautiful driving experience we have ever had. For one thing the weather was glorious. For another the route was unbeatable. We were under no pressure at all. Every bit of the way we knew so well, we were re-living the past, the sixties and seventies when our vehicle was full, when there were Father and Mother, Harry and the Aunties, Janie and Mary, all of them loving holidaying in Scotland. Then the Land Rover was so full, the driver not doing her bit, rode on top of the luggage in the back. In those days, when we paused to eat, we lifted a calor gas ring from the rear and cooked a meal. On this journey we just opened a flask and ate sandwiches, thoroughly enjoying the pleasure of remembering. As always Appleby Horse Fair was imminent and gypsy caravans conveniently slowed traffic on the short journey along the A66 to Penrith.

In the so small car park at the Travel Lodge, we had difficulty fixing the ramp but Danny got out without aid. He had known so many overnight stops like this one, his tail wagged with pleasure. We returned both dogs to the vehicle and went indoors. We like Travel Lodges. We had a bath and got into bed. Never needing to lock our car doors, in the forty years we have been driving, we had not mastered the act with modern technology. The press button thing remains a partial mystery to this day. On the verge of sleep I suddenly said to Margaret, 'Did you manage to lock the car doors?'

'No,' she said. 'Does it matter?'

'My cheque book, plastic card (which I never use!), driving licences, insurance and MOT papers are in the glove compartment!'

'Oh, go to sleep,' she said so we did. We slept like logs.

Next day Margaret fancied she detected Danny was experiencing some pain, so we sought veterinary advice at the Brampton surgery. The service was excellent. The lady vet phoned our home practice to determine Danny's current medication, afraid to give him something unsuitable. She gave us three pills, each cut into four pieces, most of which we took home for, throughout our holiday, though his condition worsened, he was never in distress. The thick layer of carpet and the gentle movement of the journey suited him. I will remember that visit to the vet mostly because another patient, a collie, was brought into the waiting room and the lady vet spoke to it, saying, 'Hello, Delilah!' Whoever would give a sheepdog a name like that?

We bought fish and chips, as always, in Longtown though the price of them has rocketed since the seventies. In the thirties we bought a fish and a pen'orth of chips for less than a shilling. The coast road from Gretna to Dumfries has not changed at all. The journey to Ayr via Monaive is a path through wonderland, utterly beautiful.

In the United Kingdom there was currently an amnesty on knives. It again amused us to remember we had taken more than fifty children through Glasgow, every year, all with a penknife and a sheath knife. That could be no more. What followed our arrival at the Ayr Travel Lodge, very nearly put me in a police station cell.

We introduced ourselves to the receptionist and were given the room key. We put out the ramp and gently encouraged Danny down it and onto the grass verge. A small square of his carpet was wet, so I took the large carving knife from beneath it and Margaret put the severed piece into the bin. We returned the dogs to their accommodation and I picked up a plastic bag containing food and the contents of the glove cabinet. I was about to leave and go inside when Margaret said, 'Take the knife in. It could do with a hot wash!'

I picked it up and, unaware of what I was doing, walked boldly into the foyer brandishing a huge carving knife. Margaret, hot on my heels, gasped, 'Jean! The knife!' The foyer was empty. There was no one behind the desk. In a panic I hid the knife in the plastic bag, regardless of the fact that it contained food. Where was the receptionist? Where was the CCTV camera? My guardian angel was there alright. He had conveniently removed the one. I would most certainly be on the camera.

'You stupid thing!' Margaret said. 'You could have been in jail!'

So I could. Passengers are no longer allowed on aeroplanes with a sharp instrument in their luggage, let alone a carving knife, held menacingly. Phew!

Do you get the impression that these two ladies, the older one in particular, do not belong to today's world?

We rose very early for we wanted to catch the first boat from Ardrossan to Arran. The road was busy but wide enough for those behind to pass. Nevertheless it is always a relief to leave the Mainland. We left Danny in the car but took Meg on deck. Already the sun was really hot, enshrouding the island in the brand of mist which foretells heat.

It was one song of a morning!

We were relaxed. We had travelled with an unopened map on the passenger's knee. Now we put it away altogether. We crossed Arran with the confidence of experience. At the Lochranza jetty, we let the dogs out and Meg suddenly saw the sea. She ran the few yards to the water's edge, then hurried back to tell first me, then Margaret who was sorting out Danny. If we ever go to the sea without Meg it will be because she is dead. She loves it and expresses that adoration dramatically and aquatically. I sat on the grass verge watching her and the approaching ferry and was at peace.

We had intended to picnic at Skipness, just east of Cloanaig on the Mull of Kintyre, but Meg's obsession with the sea made us stop immediately after the crossing and eat close to the mini-terminal. We talked only of our holidays at Skipness. The last had been during the Spring Bank holiday of 1975. I had accompanied the family for the weekend only and returned home early to hold the fort with suckler cows calving and Guiding activities prominent on my agenda. I had accompanied the family to start things off at Skipness, knowing the holiday might be difficult for Margaret to be alone. Aunty Janie's recent death had left Aunty Mary traumatised. We had not known that trouble was looming in Father's anatomy. A prostate cancer was about to cause a painful blockage on their journey home and the result was immediate hospitalization and an operation which was to give him four more years of life. Sitting, eating on the floral carpet, we talked of Father hoping that, if there really is an afterlife, he will be able to know and maybe see what has progressed at The Currer. He would be so pleased. We will leave no descendants behind. Perhaps when the last Brown leaves The Currer, we will all be able to leave the planet earth behind and head off into eternity together. We have secured the preservation of our home and land and have recorded more than a century of our family history. It hasn't been our roll in life to pass on our family genes and contribute to the human population. To all those ancestors who make up our family tree, I can only apologise. Maybe, in other ways, they will not judge us as having let them down.

The holiday that followed will be remembered mostly because of Danny. We half expected him to die on Tiree, where it would have been so easy to dig a grave for him in Hebridean sand. It seemed, however, that his responsibility to Margaret was not yet over. He drifted into a contentment which allowed us to have a quiet, almost spiritual holiday, walking the length of every one of the beautiful Tiree bays with Meg. It was as if Danny regretted having prevented Margaret from accompanying the Guides for the Harris Re-union and was determined to make amends. Mid-holiday she stopped struggling to get him out of the car but nursed him with the loving care she gives all animals. We allowed Meg to be in the caravan with us rather than sleep with Danny, for she was getting visibly worried about his immobility. In her canine way she was aware that he was dying and we were concerned lest he did. It would have confused her had we had to remove his body from the car, anywhere other than at home. Each night Margaret went to assure herself that he was comfortable. Each time she said, 'Goodnight and God Bless,' she thought it could be her last time, but when she made her frequent checks during the night he was always sleeping peacefully.

I am an early riser, even on holiday. My first job was to peep into the Range Rover. I always found him breathing easily. Neither he, nor we suffered any distress. We did what we never do, however. We bought skimmed milk. He had stopped eating but enjoyed milk. Fearing full cream would be too rich we bought the watery liquid so many people buy today. It cannot have any goodness in it at all. A guest was complaining of modern food.

'Even milk tastes different these days!' she grumbled. The milk we buy from a local farmer is delicious.

'What kind do you buy?' Margaret asked.

'I always get skimmed,' she replied. Say no more.

There were others from our locality on holiday on the island. My fault, of course. I remarked on the fact to Ellen, of Salum, who, with her Skye husband, has built a house at Ruaig. One of our Guides was on holiday at Scarinish and two local people were visiting Sylvia, another of my Guides who has been living on Tiree for almost a decade.

Ellen said, 'I met a holidaymaker, the other day, who said her mother had come here with the Guides.'

'Was she enjoying herself?' I needed to know.

'She was having a wonderful time,' Ellen answered.

We called on Sylvia, as always, and we asked if she knew anyone with a collie pup. We were soon going to lose Danny and a Tiree pup would have been a choice worth considering, but she knew of none. All our friends were concerned about our dog but, peering into the Range Rover, all could see that he was at peace. When fondled, his tail wagged with pleasure. Not for one moment did we regret bringing him but we dismissed the idea that we'd had, that we would take three days to get home gently. There was an urgency, if he was still alive, to get home before he died.

Seldom do we re-visit an island without there being an empty chair, and a friend whose relatives we must visit to convey our sympathy and our regret that their loved one is no longer there. This is the penalty of ageing. We had, a few months ago, been alerted to the fact that Mary Davis, our friend for over forty years, was seriously ill with cancer. We had hoped to see her again but she had died quite recently. We located her daughter, who manages the Hynish Centre providing group accommodation on the south western waterfront of the island. It was a simply beautiful morning. The fact that now you can buy flowers at the Co-op in Scarinish, is a welcome innovation, emphasising the fact that we have now seen fifty years of change on Tiree, from pumping our water to buying flowers! Armed with a bunch we could have purchased in any supermarket in the land, we paid our respects to Mary's daughter, Monica, and shared with her a moment of remembrance beneficial to all of us.

It is impossible to have a journey home which is uneventful. Ours almost qualified but not quite. We left the Ayr Travel Lodge at six-o'clock, aware that we had had to leave Meg all night alone in the company of her almost comatose friend. It was beginning to distress her. We left without breakfast and drove at Brown speed, down the Fields' Way to Dumfries and along the coast road to Gretna. At Longtown we paused and sought a mid-morning snack at a small, empty cafe owned by a very hospitable lady.

'I could murder a cup of tea and a bacon roll,' I said. Other than the occasional snack in the Caledonian MacBrayne cafeteria, we had not been in a cafe for decades. How un-modern can we be?

'No problem,' the good lady said and brought each of us a dinner plate with a sandwich the size of which I had never seen before. It was triangular, very thick and dry, certainly not the breakfast bap I had expected. We often wonder if the anatomy of today's youth is different from ours, in the jaw area. Ours are not hinged to accommodate double-decker beef burgers and we were reared on bacon oozing with fat. There was no butter on this 2' thick wedge, sitting amongst a veritable garden of salad, beetroot and crisps. MacBrayne's bacon butty had cost us £1.50, a quarter of what this feast cost. We are totally out of touch with eating-out, wide-eyed at the price and pastoral in our ways.

We are equally out of our element on busy roads and were dreading the sixteen miles we must drive on the A66. For us that cross-country highway, linking Carlisle with Newcastle, is nothing less than a nightmare, no less so on a Sunday. On such brief, unavoidable stretches of any journey, Margaret drives silently and I sit tense beside her. It began to rain and where there was dual carriageway, huge lorries belted past us, tail on tail, belching spray. We needed to enter the fast lane in order to take a right hand entry, into the B road leading to Kirby Stephen. The thought of doing so paralysed us.

'Don't risk it!' I warned. 'Drive forward to the roundabout near Brough, if you have to!'

Then an amazing co-incidence interrupted the fast flow of traffic. We relaxed and we laughed. A few vehicles in front of us, a huge tractor and trailer pulled out into the road. The speed of all of us dropped to 20mph and overtaking was prevented. Margaret switched on her indicator and we turned right, away from the bedlam, into rural calm which is our natural habitat. 'Hooray!' we said and laughed again. We do not need big miracles when little ones are happening all the time.

We arrived home safely. The holiday had been perfect. We did not mind how much rain fell on Yorkshire but worried about Dorothy, on Mull, a notoriously wet island. She loves The Hebrides and has a sense of humour second to none but unlike we, is invariably unlucky with holiday weather.

Helen and Chris helped us unload Danny, carrying a corner each of his rug and placing him carefully in the sitting room. For three days we switched on the television, when we were out so that he had sound. He loved Margaret to groom him, a pre-holiday-only activity he had always objected to. For three days he loved it and wagged his tail for more so that the dog we buried close, to his predecessor, Lusky, among the daffodil bulbs, on the bank of the stream, looked to have come straight from the salon. The era, the wonderful life with Danny, was over. Digging a grave deep enough was almost impossible, so dry was the earth.

Our life goes on. There is always the upside. Returning after ten days we saw a remarkable improvement in the lungs of Poorly-Getting-Better. The pneumonia had been already sorted when we left. The sugar, honey and water convalescence treatment had been continued by our stand-in patrol and all was well. Also the steroids Margaret had given the twin goats must have been what was needed for they were standing almost straight and, by August, walked perfectly normally.

We had an amusing phone call from the Ministry. At least we found it rather funny. It concerned the goats, two of whom were very ancient nannies. Rosie, we reckoned, would be approaching twenty if not leaving that milestone behind. Snowy had joined the herd from the wild, years ago. There had been bad times during the winter when Rosie could not lie down, due to arthritis but she was now summering quite well. Then there was the billy we had brought to The Currer, with his twin on the very day Foot and Mouth was discovered in Queensbury and all movement had been halted for over six months. Both had been ridiculously small and the nanny had had a fatal accident, eating leaves in our bottom pasture. A branch over the hollow had caught in her collar. It had swung, failed to take her weight and broken but not before breaking her neck. We had called her twin Billy and she Nanny but Margaret, taking off his collar immediately, re-named him Charlie. Since 2001 he had grown into stag-like proportions, proudly balancing enormous horns on his somewhat arrogant head. When his authority was questioned he rose on his hind legs like an aggressive red deer but he followed Rosie, his adoptive Mum, like a soppy poodle. Then there were the two lame billy kids, definitely on the mend.

The man making the phone call said he was from the Ministry Veterinary Office and would be in the area the next day and could he come to do a brucellosis test on our goats. I must admit I thought it was a joke. This disease manifests itself by causing abortions. Aware that we had the most unlikely herd of castrated males and geriatric females, I dared to argue it was unnecessary but apparently it is law.

Several times lately, I have wondered if a call from Defra was really just a joker. To interrupt my story momentarily, a call came to say I no longer was forced to send in movement cards. There are several of these cards in

Charlie.

each passport and every time an animal is moved from the holding, this has to be reported to The British Cattle Movement Centre in Workington. Each card is perforated and has the animal's fourteen digit ear tag number on it, the bar codes of its origin, previous habitats, market experiences and a final one of its current abode.

All I needed to do now, I was told, was to phone a new number and read out the identification. As we invariably buy upwards of forty calves at a time, twice within seven days and sell them in batches of twenty six, my mind boggled at the thought of dictating UK 126643 500232 or whatever, for every moved animal, over the phone. It seemed to me the most dodgy arrangement, surely a joke. I opted to continue sending the cards! No wonder so many mistakes are made.

We were more than a little embarrassed to entertain the veterinary tester of brucellosis and display our non-breeding herd. However he proved to be a friendly man who reckoned Margaret was right when she said that to catch and take a blood sample from Charlie, a Zoo Vet would be required.

Eventually, after a wait of many months, a message was sent from Defra to say Britain was free from this particular disease in goats. Margaret has always said that to film us straight there would be no need to introduce the imaginary. After every episode, the next follows on its heels.

A walker alerted us to the fact that we had a sick animal, alone in what we call the Far Footpath Field. Investigation proved we had an animal which could not stand, semi-conscious only. It had to be brought down to the shed on the tractor shovel and when a vet was called he identified some dreadful brain disorder, possibly meningitis. It proved fatal. There we go. We can't win 'em all. A young one dies and the old goats live on. Life goes up and down just as do the Pennine ridges of our native Dales.

We had hoped that the summer would provide us with some time to indulge ourselves and not be always totally at the beck and call of others. Just possibly, we believed, we might go regularly to the swimming baths. Exercise would do us good and the summer promised to be hot. We went only once for we needed to replace Danny. Meg was mourning so. She no longer hammered on the window for entry and she would not come into the sitting room in which he had died. We could bear it no longer and, as Helen and Chris were going on holiday in the Outer Hebrides, we phoned Angus to see if there was any hope of a Harris pup. He was sorry. He could not find one which could be brought home with our friends. They sent us a card from Barra with but one word of message. 'Wow!' It made our day.

With no island puppy success we had to look nearer to home and Barbara Sykes, the very competent shepherdess so many of our guests come to visit, gave us the phone number of Ian Ibbotson, at Oldfield and he had two pups, born in April. At twelve weeks they were a little older than we would have wished. One was spoken for but we could come and look at the other. Both were dogs and that was what we wanted. We went immediately and as we were the first to arrive we had the chance to choose but he recommended the one he thought was the least energetic of the two. We pity the eventual owner of the other, if ours was the passive one. When his daughter put down both pups they streaked off, up the hill and did not turn until they had traversed two fields and encountered the boundary wall. Help!! There seemed no difference whatsoever in the energy levels of the twins. Released from their shed, nothing would have stopped them other than that boundary wall and soon they would be capable of leaping that.

We were suddenly interrupted by a call from the road, several yards away. A lady, passing on horseback was calling, 'It's Miss Brown. Isn't it?'

The rider proved to be a child I had taught prior to my retirement, twenty-six years ago, one I had taken to Tiree on a school holiday in 1981. However had she recognised me after so long and at such a distance? I must have looked old to her then or, better still, maybe I hadn't grown significantly aged. It was such fun to talk to an adult Tamsin Hinchcliffe. I love all my children.

The era of Danny became the summer of Sam! We adore all our animals and had an instant love affair with him, though we quaked when we thought of the environment we were bringing him home to. We had daily discussions on how to handle him. Our situation and occupation were problematic. Joan Armstrong, my successful infant teacher, in the village school where we had both taught so long, always advised, 'Have 'em and love 'm and leave 'em alone.' Nothing is worse for a child or an animal than to be constantly disciplined.

Of necessity we have always brought up our animals in this way. Guests bring dogs who are constantly told to sit and stay and come here. They tear on the lead and scatter all in front of them when released. Our most recent pup had been Meg, brought from the Lake District at seven weeks old and taken, within days, to holiday on Tiree. There she had learned that she belonged to us. She was a bitch, given to Danny for hours on the beach. Returning to The Currer she had been loved and left alone. From that day onward she had posed no problem at all. She knew her name and came when called. She has never known the words Sit or Stay for she has done so automatically. She ate the kitchen chair legs, demolished a lot of biros and a pair of my spectacles but that was all. Sam was older than she had been when we brought him the The Currer, and he had lived in a kennel. He was coming to a house, to freedom and to people in big numbers.

Initially we feared that this casual method would not do at all, for Sam. Allowed far more space than he had known previously and being capable of terrific speed, he seemed all set to cause us problems. He hadn't a clue to whom he belonged, what was his name and which was his home. Being a dog he was not so home orientated. Had we been alone at The Currer, learning would have been easier but we had holidaymakers and children galore, who wanted to play with him and you can't prevent them from doing so, or from calling his name. He was idyllically happy and totally confused as to whom he must obey. Walking alone with him and Meg, neither Margaret nor I had a problem and we soon realised he was intelligent and learned quickly. Back in society he was crazy and totally deaf. Margaret nearly resorted to tears but I was the first to come home in real distress having lost him completely.

He and Meg and I had walked down to the far eastern boundary and the two dogs were playing amongst the rushes in the Dyke Field. Meg had not previously taken to any dog but Danny. She kept a disgusted distance from any visiting dogs and it relieved us greatly that she was not only tolerating Sam but enjoying him. Suddenly I heard the thundering of nearly three hundred hooves and saw the seven month old calves hurtling towards us. Meg made a quick get-away and, for a few yards, Sam followed her. Then he turned back and stood challenging them, right in the gateway all seventy two were intending to use at speed. Braver than Meg he stood his ground until the stampeding herd was within feet. Then, and only then did he about-turn and flee. Seeing him the herd took up the chase and I lost him completely, quite a long way away from home. I followed the calves to the boundary where a gate enters the wilderness of bracken and bramble and the hillside plunges towards the valley bottom. I called and called but there was no Sam. Eventually I had to go home and tell my sister I had lost her pup.

We set out together, deeply depressed, knowing it would be well nigh impossible to find a baby who did not yet respond to our call or whistle, but we had hardly got through the gate from the yard before he came galloping home. If we had thought a hurdle had been leapt we'd have been mistaken.

Poor little man he did not know whom to obey. We seemed to be surrounded by children who interrupted our training with echoing calls of, 'Sam! Sam! Sam!' He ignored all of us. We trained the young not to shout but the adults took no notice of us and should they hear one of us calling, they added their voice to the fray. We are indisputably a country of dog lovers. Sam found welcoming arms everywhere. He loved every doggy guest, ignoring Meg's cautioning growl and he began to follow any dog walker passing through the paddock.

Inevitably, one evening, he was missing. Margaret set off across the fields to the village, the destination of most men after walking their dog. She did not pause to tell me. The children did. They came running to the door with the news that Sam had disappeared. I followed her but as there was no sign of our pup on the busy road, I hurried back to the house to beg a lift from a lady occupying The Mistal cottage. We informed everyone en route to the post office, that we had lost our pup and at the crossroads I intercepted a man who said a pup was playing football with boys in the pub car park. We hastened to look but it was empty. Children in one of the houses said a man had picked a pup up and put it in his car and driven away. Sadly we gave up our search and went home not knowing that Margaret, spreading the news around the village, had also spoken to a man, stepping into his car, preparing to drive away. Passing 'The Druids' he had seen boys playing football in the pub car park, had grabbed the pup, put it in his car and returned to Margaret still searching every which ways.

This incident, with a happy ending, prompted Margaret to stretch chicken netting on every gateway. She asked Tim to reinforce the fence which had been put to deter Danny but Sam occasionally found an escape route and one day accompanied a man walking his dog to the rocky outcrop called Druid's Altar. It wasn't long before he could leap the cattle grid. However the school holidays ended and child guests became few. Our hypo-active, but highly intelligent pup learned which door of our complex was home, who were his owners and, though extensive freedom was curtailed, the yard, paddock and sheds were a playground second to none. Other inhabitants of this kingdom, in which he found himself, were the goats, the geese, the cats, Poorly-now-quite-better and of course, Meg who patiently played with him hour after hour. When tired he sat staring at the calf or at Rosie the goat-not-getting-better. She could no longer get up alone but needed the assistance of both Margaret and me. Tim would pick her up on the mornings the wallers were working. There were now only metres left of the 4500 begun nine years ago.

We knew that Rosie, who had been old when we bought her, nigh on sixteen years ago, was seeing her last days. Is there a heaven for animals? If not then there certainly is not one for the less deserving one called Man. All day Rosie sat on the bale she had turned into an armchair, her belly resting on the hay taking the weight off her legs. Though she found difficulty in rising she could shuffle onto her bench. All day she chewed her cud happy as a sand boy. Margaret put sugar in her warm water and fed her the choicest vegetables from our larder. There is, however no cure for old age and we lost her in September, shortly after the cattle sales. The price of stores had risen and were on a par with 1994. Unbelievable!! No wonder farmers were diversifying or going out of business. It is a great temptation to sell up and put money in the bank instead of watching the account slither into the red.

All the cattle at market were beautiful. There are no bad rearers these days. Ours were beautiful too. It continues to be sad to see them move on but they had grown too big for diminutive ladies to bring indoors and finish themselves. The Autumn Sales mark the year-end for we who rear stores and gives us a short period of less activity. It is annually welcome. A guest, Kay, who has been coming for many years, accompanied us to the Cattle Market. Yorkshire is home ground to her and her September stay, every year, is a pleasure we look forward to.

The Autumn Sales were reversed by a minority buy of two Simmental heifers. Having let our seventy ten month old calves have access to the hill, it distressed Margaret to leave Poorly-now-quite-better behind with no over-the-paddock-fence companions. Although his health and progress seemed OK, she still brought him indoors at night, still gave him corn and he still demanded sugar in his water. He was doing so well she chose not to take any risks so, just before our last fortnightly detachment of bullocks entered the sale ring, she outbid another buyer for two Simmental, eight month old heifers and phoned for Tim to come take them back to The Currer. They brought joy to the recovered Limousin which is what most farmers want, happy animals. In anticipation of this October calm, we had booked a minute cottage in Wensleydale for a week of ignominy. When the news came that the Dales Diary Programme, featuring The Currer, would be screened on the Thursday before our week at Hardraw, we breathed relief. If the whole thing proved to be an embarrassment, where could we find a better hideaway?

Chapter Fifteen

If you have a laugh to spare, always let it go.
In this world of wear and tear, laughter's wanted so.
Troubles coming on your way, all divide in half,
If you lift your chin and say, 'It do make I laugh!'

I F Roal Dahl hadn't beaten me to it, this chapter could easily have been titled, 'Tales of the unexpected!' If I devote a short chapter to the events following the screening of the Dales Diary programme, I hasten to insist it was not a success story to be laid at our door. I'll take the credit for having offered the 8mm archive films, to the lady producer at the Twenty-fifth Reunion. From that moment on, the programme took on a new meaning. It was no longer about Us, but about Them, about all the animals and people that have populated our lives. It's success was totally due to the excellent camera team, who put together a kaleidoscope of 70 years of photographs of family, my teaching career, our Guiding era, our animals, our holiday guests and our acres of pasture.

Margaret and I took an equal share of the background music. We are a team, operating separately but inter-dependently. I barely recognised the old lady wearing my clothes. Her mannerisms, the sound of her voice and her unusual gait made me cringe but, watching it together, in the isolation of our sitting room, Margaret and I did not crawl under the settee as we had expected we might. We were just jubilant at the way our environment, the house and land, its animals, its people, its welcome had been captured. We could now go on holiday, leave it all behind and relax.

It was accidental that, having chosen to take a week's holiday in a very small cottage, at Hardraw in Wensleydale, it was preceded by the ITV programme by just one day. It was screened on Thursday evening and we were leaving for our autumn break on Saturday.

A week, they say, is a long time in politics and I guess that it will take a whole chapter, to tell of the fun which followed. That was totally unexpected and we will continue laughing into the next decade, if we are spared. We are always hungry for fun and were aware, in the years following the Foot and Mouth and Harry's death, that maybe we weren't really laughing as we once did. Not really laughing. Perhaps when I read what I have already written, that will become noticeable in the previous pages, and this millennium account may have sounded dour, so I must make amends. After Dales

Hardraw.

Diary we were really laughing again. How we wished Harry had been still here. He would have laughed so much his not very agile hand would have been fully occupied preventing his teeth from falling out. Mother would have held her head high, standing straighter than we do now. Father would have wiped away his tears but Margaret and I just laughed until we had bellyache and lost inches round the waist.

It wasn't the programme that made us laugh, nor even our amateur moment of questionable 'stardom'. It wasn't like that. That was just the stone thrown into the pond. The excitement was all on the ripples circling wider and wider, right back into the past. At first it was just shock and disbelief. Then it became amazing and finally it was just immensely laughable.

As it ended, we turned off the television to answer an insistent ringing of the phone. Farmers in the Ripon area had picked up theirs immediately. That was fine. If the farming fraternity approved we could safely go to the cattle mart and buy calves. Women in their domain could have been open to ridicule. Especially if the farmer's man is a retired headmistress!

I hardly had time to put the receiver down when it rang again. A ninety year old lady was ringing from Hebden Bridge. 'You won't remember me,' she said. 'I was on Harris in 1973. We went down to the beach at Luskentyre expecting to find it empty and it was full of your children. I bought, *A Song to Sing,* and acquired one of your brochures. I kept it and I remembered where it was and that it had your telephone number!' To say I was flabbergasted is not enough.

It was the beginning of a thirty six hour journey into the past, remembering old friends, old ways and values and our gratitude to the film crew remains immeasurable. We were supposed to be packing and preparing for a holiday in Wensleydale but the phone never stopped ringing all evening and all the next day. Unknown people were booking accommodation or ordering books. We had a pup to take on holiday, guests and animals to leave behind. We should be full time focusing on that, not talking to voices out of the past. We threw a change of clothes into a rucksack and a few items of food. Dorothy was waiting at the kitchen table eager to take over and the phone was still ringing and we were talking to folks we had not seen for years or never even met.

Escape was imminent. We were half grateful, half sorry to leave but Dorothy was ready and the owners of Cissy's Cottage, in Hardraw had promised to lay a fire to welcome us. Ahead lay a week of being unknown. That too was beckoning. Not even the lady who owned the cottage lived in Hardraw. In Cissy's Cottage we could sit and giggle for a while and then have a lovely peaceful holiday.

I must say the turmoil we were leaving behind had been agreeable. What is nicer than old friends and new, ringing to say they had happy memories, too. That's all they talked about. How we and they were, several decades ago.

Meg and Sam.

They related to so many of our experiences. Indeed they talked more of their lives than ours. We had ignited a desire, in them, to talk, to remember.

They said, 'We did that, we've been there, we have camped. We went to a village school, were teachers, are farmers.' They were all so pleased to declare their ability to understand, to tell us we were not alone, others thought like we did. It was lovely.

However, holidays are essential for us. We always thought they were for our aging parents, Harry and Aunty Mary, who were deprived of retirement because of us and the activity which surrounds us. We used them as an excuse for a second, autumn holiday but now we had to use our own advancing frailty to condone a week of respite, before the annual calf buy. So we walked away from the noisy phone and headed for the sanctuary of Cissy's Cottage. We were exhausted, comfortable, satisfied that we'd not looked ridiculous. What could we ask for more?

We made no attempt to talk, aired none of our usual compliments of the Dales' scenary. We did not remark on the very beautiful weather, either. Auntie Mary's St. Luke's little summer had arrived once again, exactly at the right time and was travelling with us. The sun shone, as it had on Harry's funeral exactly five years ago. Perhaps that was why we were so quiet. Maybe we missed him most in the Range Rover. It was too empty. The roads were empty, too, but we had no complaint about that as we headed towards Kettlewell.

We experienced a little inner emptiness. 2006 had not been without sorrow, Nanny and Joe and then Danny and the meningitis steer. Our vehicle seemed too big. We take so little with us nowadays. Loneliness is seldom a feeling we are allowed to experience. I don't know whether our silence, on the relatively short journey to Wensleydale, was an inner need or a weird form of bereavement, a jerk from intense activity to bland tranquillity. Whatever the reason, we felt it odd and were grateful of a brief interlude at Buckden.

Julia lives there. She was one of my pupils, became one of my Queens Guides and is now a farmer's wife and mother of two boys. Her parents, who have been our friends for half a century, live in Buckden, too and we had promised to call. They had all been present at the Twenty Fifth Reunion and conversation hovered momentarily over that, before turning to the subject of farming, as it is always wont to do. Julia takes Bed and Breakfast guests as we do, but it's farming we mostly talk about. John's dog had just littered eight collie pups and, had we not already got Sam, we would have been spoilt for choice, a thing I don't think we have ever had puppywise. We have been handed Hobson's and come away with a canine treasure.

Leaving Redmire Farm, the journey over the Pennine Ridge, from Wharfedale into Wensleydale, carries less traffic than the road crossing Harris but the scenery is that of home. The Dales are our land. Nine year old David, on a school trip to Tiree in 1981, said to me, 'This is not a bit like home, is it Miss Brown?' True. The islands are not like The Dales. The Dales are homeland and we felt comfortable in Cissy's Cottage.

The key was in the lock. A coal fire had been laid in the hearth. It was the first thing I noticed when I opened the door. The second was a large bowl of fruit left for us on the dresser. The cottage, in the centre of the minute village of Hardraw, was extremely small and the ceilings were low. In the two minute bedrooms they were only six feet high and many would have had to permanently bend. It did not hamper us in the least. I put a match to the fire and flames danced up the chimney. The kitchen was the feature of the cottage we will most remember. It was a perfectly round extension at the back of the house. It was as if the builders had imagined they were constructing a baby castle and had begun a tower, thought better of it and used the area as a larder. Jutting out of the perimeter there were stone slabs and a sink. Originally, I'm sure, the one, beamed and stone-flagged room would have been both kitchen and parlour but, incredibly, all modern conveniences had been squeezed into the circular space, giving it a charm and an individuality second to none.

We had brought no luggage and food to last only over Sunday. We found there was a door from the front garden, leading onto a large, secluded, very well cut lawn, ideal for our energetic pup. And beyond this enclosed area, a stile led to a pathway climbing the fell. It was just lovely. The early setting sun painted the green fields golden and the stone walls reflected their colour as they do in the field we call the Eight Acre at The Currer.

Here begineth a week of anonymity! 'There's only thee and me,' we said. It was a most unusual situation. In the Hebrides there is always someone. At 'High Woods' there had been the owners. This, we decided, was maybe what we needed. No phone, no-one to knock on the door. No guest or animal to feed.

However, we have long succumbed to the blowing of the wind, accepting that we cannot charter our own way. There is rarely just Thee and Me and the dogs. At home there is Them and seldom is there Us. In Cissy's Cottage there was only Us. Was it going to be challenging enough?

On that first beautiful morning in Hardraw, I got up with my usual enthusiasm for the day, released both dogs from the Range Rover and took them to scamper on the back lawn of the cottage. So much of any learning curve is to be left alone, child or pup. Few adults get the balance right. The dale looked beautiful. There was no colour anywhere which was not a natural one.

We are passionate about water, which seems a stupid thing to say as I type this, for a deluge is pouring down the window pane and the planet has had far too much rain lately!! But we do like lakes and rivers, waterfalls and peaty burns and the sea. We love the sea as much as Meg.

'Let's go to Semmer Water,' we said over breakfast. Do we eat bacon and egg and all that lark on holiday? Rarely. We see too much of it at home. We avoid the frying pan and the necessity to wash greasy dishes.

So Semmer Water it was and we drew up on the empty shingle, in front of it and opened the car windows to let in that breath of air peculiar to waterside vistas. It was beautiful!

A notice advised us that we were parking on private land and we owed the farmer a one pound fee. This we could pay at the farmhouse a quarter of a mile up the road.

No problem. We put the dogs on leads and walked to the farm yard. A young man, washing down the floor of the dairy, disappeared as we approached. Margaret held the dogs and I went to the house door. Its adjacent window displayed daily, weekly and season parking payments and fishing charges. I knocked and waited. There was someone behind the door. I heard approaching, then disappearing footsteps. Then silence so we returned to the dairy and called, 'Hello! Hello!'

The young man came. 'We need to pay our parking fee,' I said.

'My mother's in,' he answered.

She was. The door was opening and she was coming towards us dragging a somewhat embarrassed husband. She said, 'I had to fetch him. I said you've got to come. Come and see who we've got at the door!'

We must have looked bewildered. 'We saw you on television,' she said

I don't think we have ever been more open mouthed and amazed. Would I recognise someone I'd seen briefly on the screen? I doubt it. I would never be sure even if I saw a celebrity, let alone just an ordinary member of the public. Perhaps we are just too weary when watching TV and, shall I confess, falling quickly asleep, to really notice what people look like. This woman was absolutely sure and absolutely confident that we were approachable friends and of course she was right

Suddenly we were all shaking hands and laughing as we, Margaret and I, hadn't laughed this century. It was so totally unexpected. The husband was a little embarrassed but he and the son stayed throughout the half-hour we talked because, of course, we immediately began to talk about farming today. Don't we always? When we started the holiday accommodation diversification, Margaret always threatened to wear a tee shirt on which was written, 'I'm a farmer really!' We talked about Single Payment Subsidies, the state of market prices and the insanity of Government and we parted as friends.

When we returned to the almost empty car park, we stuck our parking ticket on the windscreen and opened our flask of coffee in unbelieving silence. We decided not to walk around the lake where the farmer's suckled herd and bull were grazing but, instead, to follow the river towards Bainbridge. The footpath was level and easy to walk. There were no sheep or cattle there so we were able to release Sam and to let Meg sample the water. As climbers tick off

Munros, I am sure Meg ticks off water courses. Sam went to the water's edge. No further for which we were grateful. We have never had, nor do we want, a dog that swims! Meg never gets out of her depth.

We eventually came to a stile she could not climb. Sam we could lift but Meg is a lady of large proportions. We sat on the stile, content and alone in the middle of the emptiness we were in need of. There was an almost summer growth of grass and insects and butterflies galore. No wind disturbed the leaves, still avoiding autumn colours. Even the seasons seemed to be standing still.

Eventually we began to retrace our steps, amazed at how short was the distance we had walked. It was the first day of a dawdling holiday.

Ramblers were coming towards us in a crocodile of more than twenty. They were the only walkers we had seen out enjoying that balmy October Sunday. Several yards away from us the leaders lifted hands in amazement and gasped, 'We saw you on television last week!' They were all strangers but they had been watching Dales Diary and so had a party of Skipton walkers we met soon afterwards who stopped us with the same confident exclamation. All were eager to tell us where they were rambling, how they spent their weekends, how much they loved Wensleydale. All stroked the dogs, even though Meg was wet. All assumed that we were fellow soul mates as indeed we were.

Back in the Range Rover, watching the sun drop slowly in the west, Margaret thought it an opportune moment to phone Dorothy and check that all was well at home. There was just one other car on the car park and the lady occupier must have been watching and, when Margaret failed to get a signal, she came over and told us she was local and that we would be unable to use a mobile in that area. We would have to go back to Hawes. We'd manage fine there, she said. Then recognition flooded her face and she said, 'I saw you on television!'

By this time we were, as was Alice, in Wonderland. How come we were so recognisable. Everyone we had met in an almost human free environment, had seen us before. They hadn't approached us as if we were apparitions, ghosts from the Box. They had come confident that we were who we were and we would all be friends.

I think perhaps the happiest realisation of my life is that there are people everywhere who think like we do, have our priorities, hold our philosophy on life and whenever I feel depressed about the present society I will step out of it and remember all the people we have met recently who understand our slant on finding happiness.

Of course we admitted, driving back to our cottage, it's Sunday and a beautiful one at that. It is normal for ramblers to be out and normal for those frequenting the Dales to watch any programme about the Yorkshire countryside. Tomorrow would be different. One comment which had been expressed by all was that the social environment had changed. All had been children of another time and all had expressed sympathy for today's youngsters imprisoned by the unreasonable fear of their parents, teachers, the community and the government, that harm and disease were hiding round every corner.

We had a great deal to talk about, sitting in front of that coal fire in Cissy's tiny cottage not far from the plunging waters of Hardraw Force. We analysed the dialogues we had had with these passing strangers, so eager to tell us all about their childhood, their worries for their grandchildren, their Scouting and Guiding days, their teenage camping, their freedom. We, in shock, had been listeners. We sat laughing for much of the evening. Whoever would have thought?

We went to bed and I fell asleep remembering the experience following the publication of each of my books. Hundreds of people, each time, have written of having had their memories of childhood reborn, of their village school experiences, Guide and Scout camps, holidays in Scotland, wanderings in Dales and on islands. Many have written of personal bereavement, of ups and downs in farming, of fear for the way education is heading ... *ad infinitum*. I felt privileged to be unlocking doors for everyone to remember the way things were. It is so true that often we must look back to go forward. Today's politicians, educationalists and social workers should take heed and weigh what we have gained against what we have lost.

The expertise of the camera men had highlighted the security which had come with freedom and all everyone could talk about was the fear generated by protectiveness.

If we had expected a return to the working day would deprive us of further encounters with the viewing public, we were mistaken. We just could not believe what was happening, wherever we went, each day during our week in Wensleydale and neighbouring Swaledale. It mattered not whether we went east or west, uphill or down, meeting locals or holidaymakers alike, they had seen us on television and wanted to talk, as friends do when they meet unexpectedly and find they have so much to say, so much in common. There were so few people but wherever we went we saw recognition light their faces and knew they were heading eagerly in our direction and we began to laugh. Always to laugh. It was an unforgettable experience. It is still happening, as I write this eighteen months later and we always laugh. How we wish Harry was with us!

A couple touring the Dales in a caravanette, had seen us in black and white on their portable. Two couples from Oxford crossed the cafe floor to introduce themselves having seen us on the television in their holiday accommodation and the cafe proprietor came from nowhere to say she had seen us. So had the girl at the pay desk and the lady at the cashout when we replenished our stores and the man at the petrol pump.

We were aching with the laughter, bewildered by the popularity, not of ourselves but of our lifestyle. What we do in our rather old-fashioned backwater, our simple, undemanding avoidance of the speed of technological advance, appears to be desirable! Everyone we met wanted to talk about the way things were and how lucky pre-television children had been. Before mobile phones and computers other children had played out all day. They had waved Goodbye to mother in the morning and not come back till dusk. It was everyone's topic of conversation.

We decided a more at home day was needed, a day when lunch could be eaten at Cissy's Cottage, tongues could rest and laughter lines have an ironing-out opportunity. It was a glorious day so we went no farther than the pub, only yards away from our garden gate, through which we must pass if we wished to walk up the cared for footpath to the noisy, leaping water of Hardraw Force.

The village was empty for the children, who had played ball and cycled safely on Sunday, were all back at school. We used to be able to play in the street before the war. Infrequent traffic crawled slowly by, in those days and we had learned to respect it and avoid danger. The Hardraw children had retained this opportunity of outdoor play learning road sense incidentally and, like the generation before them, still spoke courteously to strangers. They were unaware of the horrors which urban people think might happen, but so seldom do.

There was only one car outside the pub and the strangers, who owned it were just coming out after having visited the Force ahead of us. Their eyes opened wide and they came straight towards us. 'We saw you on television,' they said. They were on holiday. We met and parted sometime later as friends, then we and our dogs passed through the ancient premises of the bar, which boasted the biggest wood fire I have ever seen, other than a campfire. We paid our small entry fee and, from then on we never met a soul.

The track to the Force was, in its October emptiness, little less than wonderland. You go through the dark pub lounge, heavy with oak and smelling strongly of beer and burning wood and the daylight is suddenly blinding and the air, filled with the scent of fast flowing water and autumnal decay, is so intoxicating one feels to be in some magical, spiritual place, noisy only with birdsong and the heavy weight of falling water.

We went to the foot of the Force and then, rather recklessly, decided to climb the path winding up the sheer hillside, in order to view it from above. Not very long ago the scramble would have posed no problem, but years of hard work have shocked me into admitting that I'm not so young as I used to be! Comfortably on ground level once more we threaded our way back to eat at leisure in our tiny cottage. On holiday I want the minimum of indoor space, and little or no possessions. Guests at The Currer bring far too much, clothes galore, books, laptops, radios, goodness only knows what. We take only what will fit into a minute rucksack and we would still prefer a little white tent, secondly a caravan, failing that the smallest of holiday cottages. It is surely because we live within a multiplicity of rooms and space unlimited within the walls of home.

It had been a wise decision to lunch in Cissy's Cottage because Julia and her mother, who had not been there when we had passed through Buckden on our way out, knocked on our door and we enjoyed an afternoon not talking farming. Julia was planning to accompany her son on a yacht crossing the Atlantic. She, and so many of my children, continue to amaze me.

It would be incorrect to say we had a shower-free holiday. We only had one but it lasted two hours of heavy rain whilst we were in Muker. We had decided to sample Swaledale. Wherever we went we had to get out of the car and walk. We had a six month old pup of perhaps the most energetic breed there is. We drew up in the Muker car park and I searched its perimeter for any signpost signifying a footpath. Another car drew into the otherwise empty car park and the alighting couple immediately came towards us. We were beginning expect this repeat scenario but it was too funny for words when, two hours later we were hurrying back to the Range Rover to escape the only downpour of our week.

We desperately needed a loo. Margaret ran inside. I stood it for a few minutes, holding the dogs and feeling rain penetrating my neckline. There was not a soul in sight, so I led the dogs inside the ladies and leaned against the tiled wall. Suddenly an umbrella was being shaken in the doorway and a lady followed it. I quickly apologised for having brought the dogs inside to shelter. The rain had caught us all by surprise. Then the lady spluttered, 'I saw you ...!' and I could hear Margaret laughing in the cubicle and I was in danger of losing my dignity for I was desperate too. She was a lovely lady and I'll never forget chatting away to her, wet through, in the Ladies Toilet in Muker.

The rain did not follow us back into Wensleydale. Darkness comes too early in October but we had time to take a level path which follows the river at a distance and provided us with a pre-dusk walk most evenings. There were suitable stones to sit upon whilst we watched the dogs tiring themselves out at play, wrestling and rolling and chasing each other round a telegraph pole.

We were thoroughly enjoying our holiday in the most unexpected way. We walked through the Market Square in Reeth, the following day and the man selling walking sticks had also been on Dales Diary. Twice. Once as a woodcarver and once as a walking stick maker. He recognised us immediately and was amazed we did not remember him. Fortunately we did remember his hobby being screened.

All men with beards tend to look alike. 'I might have thought you were Bill Oddie!' I said.

'I've met him,' the friendly man said. A group of shoppers gathered round and the stallholders selling fruit and vegetables came and told us they had watched the programme too. We were embarrassed but not uncomfortably so and Margaret insisted on buying one of the beautiful walking sticks made by the skilled craftsman.

We avoided going to the same place twice, as you can imagine, so we drove over to Dent, that gorgeous village of cobbled streets and old world charm. The post office was closed and I needed stamps. A delightful lady ran into her house to supply me with some. We needed a snack for our lunch and were immediately recognised in the village shop, by the lady keeper and a farmer following us to the counter. It was such a beautiful day she was sitting on the seat outside the shop. There are such nice people in The Dales to whom we relate completely. Far from the city crowds we all can relax in each other's company immediately and we were having a ball.

The riverside walk was empty. The only other time I had viewed the river at Dent, was when, with my Sea Rangers we had stayed up all night making refreshments for Scouts doing The Dalesman Walk. Then, after heavy rain, the river had been so high we had monitored it constantly in case of overflow. I had had with me a German exchange teacher spending six weeks at my Kildwick School. Joan Armstrong, my infant teaching assistant, was about to return with her to Germany. I remember that Jimmy, Joan's husband, asked her to buy him a pipe at the Woolworth's store in isolated, minute Dent. Her face had been a picture when she realised her leg had been pulled.

Returning from the riverside walk we sat for a while on a convenient seat, near to the stile back onto the bridge and the road crossing it. It was there that we saw the first walkers of the day, three elderly men, sauntering along the footpath, unhurried, enjoying retirement to the full. One turned out to be the late Eddie Waring's nephew. Did we remember him, the television sports' commentator? Of course we did and his nephew immediately said he had seen us on Dales Diary, took a photo of us and later sent us a copy.

We returned from a magical holiday to the seclusion of our own territory having had an experience difficult to explain. Were we signing autographs, people here wanted to know? It wasn't like that at all. On Harris there was a very old lady the Guides loved because, Linda said, she had only one tooth. She told us we were not tourists, we were friends of the people. We had found that very comfortable. In Wensleydale we were comfortable, all friends together, all dalesmen, farmers or of farming stock, walkers, country lovers, full of fun, eager to laugh.

I think we owe those we met on our brief holiday, a mention in this autobiography of ordinary people getting the maximum of fun out of ordinary things. They proved once again that life isn't ordinary at all, but a miracle from first to last. We have found it so and continue to do so all the time.

Those people had believed in us much more than those living nearer and those of our kin. They don't know what is happening in the backwater in which they think we live. They do not drive into our yard when it is full of cars or sit at the table when it is alive with people, or watch food served from the oven to the many. They are not with us when we buy or sell cattle and rear calves. Some who walk their dogs, do not know that the land is ours.

They have never visited, with us, the Hebridean islands or taken hundreds of children on camping experiences they'll always remember. Those distant from us believe the magic. Those close to home think our life may look idyllic on screen or in the pages of a book, but in fact it is just a lot of hard, dirty work. They are wrong. One man from the village actually drove into the yard to question whether we still do Bed and Breakfast. We do not mind. We are a quarter of a mile from the end of a road and our yard and workplace, and our front door is completely hidden from the footpath.

Our return was to an avalanche of letters and book orders and strangers appearing in the yard and advance bookings being made for 2007. We were pleased these were interested in our lifestyle, our children, our animals. They understood our regret, that life had changed in the last two decades. They talked continually about their childhood, their Scouting and Guiding days, their early farming, their simple upbringing and the discipline which had been normal. A household tip attendant said to Margaret, 'I bet those kids had a bloody wonderful time!' and she answered, 'Yes, they had a bloody wonderful time. It's just no longer possible to do now what we did then.'

One close friend said we looked serene. Well, I suppose we are. We are happy with the life we lead. Our brief screen appearance escaped local criticism and that suited us fine.

Chapter Sixteen

There is no hearth like your ain hearth!

R ECENT EVENTS halted and reversed any tendency to disappear more
and more into retreat. It may be inevitable, someday that we really
do become hermits for we have no affinity with the town and, since our
removal to The Currer, fifty years ago, we ceased to become members
of the village. With the postal service in decline our weekly mingle with
neighbours is no longer. Having no Aunty Mary and Hilda to take to the
chapel, we miss even the briefest of local contact. We now have no corn
representative bringing us in end- of-month farming gossip and, with the
near completion of the re-building of the dry-stone walls, we will see less of
the wallers during summer. Large groups, self-catering, mean we visit the
super-markets infrequently and once annually, to the Cash and Carry has
become the norm instead of every week.

It should have followed that we had more time but the repercussions
following that brief interlude, prevented any such thing. We were grateful
for the slow down because it meant we could cope with the acceleration.

More frequently even than usual, we had to change gear. One minute
we were in reverse, talking to people we hadn't seen for decades. Then in
neutral greeting those we had never met before and, as we waved them
Goodbye, slipping into fast forward to tackle the immediate unforgiving
minute. Life had never been more hectic.

Thinking it was now or never, we plunged straight into a project we had
been planning for some time. It was so easy, with Aunty Mary and Harry no
longer needing the warmth of the sitting room, for us to switch on an electric
fire when we came in and turn it off when we went out. We became more
and more lazy about stoking the central heating in our part of the house. It
was coke fired and to replenish the Aga and both the stoves meant nine hods
of coke daily from the cellar. So we neglected our central heating and in 2005
we had been cold. We have had experience of senile relatives who would
not turn up their gas fires and have been in danger of dying of hypothermia.
Determined not to join their ranks, we had promised ourselves that, immediately on our return from Hardraw, we would get a wood burning stove
in the sitting room and have it connected to the central heating radiators in
our domain. This project was very much in our own backyard. We knew it
would cause havoc in our kitchen, isolate us from creature comforts and our

only consolation was that Tim-the-Builder is a Hell-Fire-Jack, too. With him and his team mate, Graham, the turmoil would be short lasting.

Before leaving for Wensleydale we had ordered the woodburner of our choice and it had been delivered in our absence. We all went to the stone yard and ordered a lovely surround. I remember that it was during that annual week of peace, when the Dutch students take over the whole house and release us to do our own thing. They were followed by an October half-term, self-catering group. Having installed them satisfactorily we just had to prepare for a visit from a Glossop Guide Company led by one of my Queen's Guides. Then we could blow the starter whistle for Operation Soot. It could not be labelled any other.

The visit of the Guides delighted us. For a few hours we were transported back in time. They could have been our own children for Alyson, a caring undertaker by profession, quietly controlled all forty of them, as I had done. They were courteous, happy and friendly, just as Guides of the sixties and seventies had been. They were lovely to be with and they sang all the songs we had sung. It was great. Margaret and I may have little doubt that today's children are born little different from their predecessors. It's the way adults treat them which is lacking.

When they left we engaged low gear and immediately and painstakingly removed what furniture we could from the sitting room. We took down the curtains and rolled back the almost threadbare carpet ready for the men to come next day and the work to begin!

The plan was to expose the original seventeenth century fireplace. We disposed of the modern one by burying it in the extension we had had built thirty years ago. We had done this so that Father might view his land and the activity in his yard, from the comfort of the sitting room, without venturing into the cold. We had done so as cheaply as possible, for funds were ever low and, therefore, we had not flagged it with the Yorkshire stone with which the rest of the room was floored.

Fifty years earlier, when we had come to The Currer, Mother wanted an Aga and a wall to wall carpet. She got the Aga immediately for we had no gas or electricity. It cost the enormous sum of £200, exactly as much as Grandfather had paid for the family home in Bradford Street and seven times as much as Arthur Currer had paid for The Currer in 1571.

When I began writing this personal history I did not really expect there to be so much social and economic change in my lifetime. Recently climate change is equalling both at tremendous speed. This is another reason I have begun tapping away at this word processor after months of letting it gather dust. There is a change in weather and seasons but it is not quite as it was predicted and is taking many people by surprise.

Mother had got her Aga and she had made it work overtime using it for cooking and baking, drying and ironing clothes, preserving summer fruits, and drying herbs from the garden. She had found an hourly use for it daily and so do we fifty years on. The wall to wall carpet we could only afford later, much later when she had carpeted the rest of the house with tabbed rugs. Even the staircase boasted a carpet made from material cut from the discarded coats of family and friends. People do not wear cloth coats and tweed skirts any more and the material for Mother's rugs would be no longer available. We made no noise as we climbed the stone stairs to bed and it appals me to think that members of this modern generation are preferring uncovered, laminate flooring which echoes with every footstep.

After replacing the dining room floor with the original flags, so successfully, we now asked the men to take up the wooden flooring in the sitting room extension and match the ancient flags hidden by the wall to wall carpet. It was almost threadbare, having suffered nearly thirty years of foot traffic. It was our plan to repeat the dining room success story when and if we could afford it. Whilst there was chaos and dirt everywhere it seemed the right moment to rip up the floor boards and where was there a better place to put the broken, modern fireplace than in the exposed cavity. It would reduce the number of barrow loads of stone and quarry bottoms needed to fill it completely.

It was the dirtiest, sootiest job we had done for half a century. Floor boards were thrown out of the window and cement and stone wheeled through a kitchen piled high with front room furniture. We escaped, two days into the project, and drove to Gisburn to begin buying the autumn calves. It was a relief to get out of the filth and mingle again with the farmers of our locality. Even though Gisburn is in Lancashire there is no feud between us and them. Nor was there any criticism, only good humour, about our exposure on TV. Some asked permission to come and see Margaret's calf-rearing methods. We bought forty eight babies and twenty three the following week, glad to have outdoor work to do. The self-imposed discomfort within the house was gradually driving us insane.

Inquisitive guests came galore and the dirt and dust everywhere became increasingly embarrassing. Paying guests wandered in to see what the activity was. These we could give a conducted tour and return them to their clean premises, on the other side of a closed door. Not so the unexpected ones who just appeared in the yard. People we had not seen since childhood rang to say could they come? They were in the area and had but one opportunity. It became a nightmare. In the calf shed we had 71 baby calves. We had three families of self-catering holiday makers. Our sitting room was a building site, our kitchen a storage space. There was a succession of friends and long lost neighbours chatting round the kitchen table, drinking tea and eating scotch pancakes fresh from the oven. The secret of freshly made scotch pancakes is to make them periodically, double or treble quantity and store them in the freezer ready to be defrosted in a hot oven, if and when suddenly, unexpectedly needed.

Many wanted to see what the men were doing, steering wheelbarrows through the kitchen, whilst they were eating and peeped behind the door to see the threadbare carpet draped over the stacked furniture and the gaping hole in the chimney breast.

Finishing our evening chores Margaret and I sat uncomfortably by the Aga. The television, brought through the door and connected with an indoor aerial, kept refusing to work. Normally even interesting programmes will send us to sleep but slumber was not possible among the chaos which lasted far longer than we'd expected.

Most of those who phoned to come and re-unite with us, we managed to put off until we were relatively straight again, but there must always be a welcome for unexpected arrivals if we are to continue Mother's tradition. It was less than easy during November 2006. We were harassed further in a way we have never really succeeded in making our builders and plumbers understand, throughout all our projects. They will not accept that any hole in a five hundred year old wall, full of random stone, has the potential to hide a network of footpaths for one mouse or a multitude.

The men painstakingly cut into the wall behind the bookcase and passed the two central heating pipes from the new woodburner, into the kitchen to connect with the pipes servicing our radiators. It is impossible to cut a small hole in a two foot thick wall which has stood for centuries. Returning from some household chore I found the men had left, abandoning this enormous cavity until morning. I raised the roof with horror and scolded them next day as only a school ma'am can! I had tried to stuff up the hole myself but was no competitor against field wayfarers. They have a sixth sense where possible entries to the castle are concerned. Within hours we saw a mouse and Richard, who had been with us mid-week for over a year, saw one in the guests' domain. Margaret went on a witch hunt among our thirty and more rooms. And all the while we were rearing very young calves and the men were restoring order far more slowly than either they or we had expected. The installation refused to be easy but the weather remained dry and the big cattle kept their distance. An end to disruptions finally came but not until we had called in the makers of the stove and they had told us we needed to line the centuries old chimney. Even then it was not perfect until we abandoned the idea of burning wood from our unseasoned pile. Experienced guests advised us to use coke ovals. We bought a load and then it was perfect.

There came a weekend of re-laying the carpet. We had decided it would last over the winter at least. We had no heart for any more. Margaret emulsioned the walls of the sitting room and I hung the newly washed curtains and put back the chair covers. I bought the three hundred Christmas cards needing to be signed and addressed. We were tired out but still the weather remained only autumnal and the cattle found enough grass to cause us no trouble. Every cloud has a silver lining.

I found writing the envelopes quite difficult. My right hand fingers had been feeling nettled for years. Since Harry's death they had gradually deteriorated but not enough to deter me from doing anything other than drive a long distance, sew or wield a pen for any length of time. Buying calves, at the edge of the auction ring at Gisburn, we had been startled to hear the lady auctioneer describe us as two old ladies. There, of all places, we should appear to have enough youth in us to be buying seventy calves. A farmer, from whom we had just bought four, had wanted to hand 'luck' to his successful bidder. Pound coins are usually passed between seller and buyer. He had called out, 'Who bought those?' and the auctioneer had said, 'The two old ladies.' I had shaken my fist at her and everyone had laughed.

Margaret is not old, though as I write this she is entering her seventieth year and I don't believe I am until I look at my hands. Actually they are the only part of me I see. I really don't know how grey my hair is or whether I am wrinkled or stooped for, unless I look in the mirror, which I rarely do, I remain blissfully ignorant. But my hands I see constantly and they let me down. The veins are proud on the back and the fingers are so worn none of the prints, which would identify me, are left. The carpel tunnel, paralysing the nerve and eating away at the muscle belonging to the thumb, makes holding a needle a farce. I tend to look at my hands with reverence for they have served me well for many decades. In spite of the auctioneer's graphic description we had returned to a marathon project and Margaret had nurtured seventy calves. No small achievement but faced with three hundred addresses to write on Christmas card envelopes, I almost caffled.

I was extremely grateful to our postman, a heavily laden mid-day, Christmas delivery man. We are always too engaged with the job of calling in our dogs, (who would willingly eat him,) to have time to say more than, 'Hi!' and, 'Thanks!' when he comes all the way to the door. However, shortly before Christmas, we were returning, in the Land Rover, from a cattle count and check, over the acres which were once moorland. He and we met at the farm entrance simultaneously. I got out of the driving seat and, whilst Margaret re-locked the gate, I collected our mail. From the safety of his seat, the postman was able to say, somewhat belatedly, 'I saw you on television!'

'Did we do alright?' I ventured to ask but was quite unprepared for his reply.

'You were bloody stunning!' he said. Oh! The wonderful man! What a compliment! No way am I looking in a mirror when the village postman says we look bloody stunning! I'm just going to take his word for it. Harry would have so enjoyed it, Mother would have recognised the back-handed compliment, Father would have grinned. He liked working men. Aunty Mary, I fear, might have been disgusted!

The continuity of the fun generated by Luke Casey's camera team must surely be on record, in this account of a life which is ordinary but never mundane. It rejuvenated us and prepared us for the winter. Sadly there is now only Margaret and me still here to laugh at the comedy of everyday life. Fortunately we share the same ignition for laughter. We have always pursued different jobs, had different priorities, utilised different skills but, added together, rooted in the same basic philosophy, we make a very good team.

There were several reasons why the winter was less taxing. All our guests were self-catering. Our premises were always full but we had no breakfasts to make. Also the cattle looked as if they were going to out-winter altogether and did not come home to sleep permanently, until Christmas Eve. But the biggest item on our goodie list was the sitting room stove which never went out. Every morning I found our comfort zone, warm and inviting and re-fuelling it excited the central heating radiators to make sure that all was cosy on our return from the outdoors. Using coke ovals meant infrequent re-fuelling so we chose the easy option of which we have grown to be daily advocates.

'What's easiest,' Margaret says when I ask what she wants for dinner and that suits me, too.

Margaret's priorities are less selfish than mine. Our sighs of relief do not correspond. Her concern is that all her animals are well, housed and fed, however long it takes. Mine, I regret to say, is that this is all accomplished without accident. When the stockyard gates are closed on nearly eighty big steers, our safety other than theirs, is my first concern. Margaret thinks only of them! She is content only when calves and steers are checked and re-checked and, at midnight, it is alright to turn off the main lights, come indoors and go to bed herself. I can only rest peacefully when the lights go out and she is in. I repeat, my priorities are more selfish than hers and acknowledge that she is a far better farmer than I am. Left fully in charge I'd have to adopt her way of thinking. I am fully aware of that!

The herd actually sampled their winter accommodation one night prior to coming in for good on Christmas Eve. They came to the east door long after dark and we had the awesome task of letting them flood into the lighted sheds. To describe them as a river of heads and legs is my only way. I initially wondered what would be their reaction to a nine month old pup mingling amongst them. Their appearance out of the darkness had been too unexpected for one or other of us to remove Sam out of harm's way. Both of us were vulnerable in the pitch darkness for Margaret must open the first shed door and reveal the brilliance of electric light and, should there be a sudden stampede, my sheltering nearness to a barbed wire fence would not really protect me. But there was no danger other than that of over eager steers, trying to enter the door more than one at a time and getting wedged in the process. Sam proved to be no problem at all. He had formed his own special relationship with them in summer and autumn, accompanying Margaret on the daily counts and they simply ignored him. He was deceived into thinking they were obeying his command by going into the shed, little knowing they needed no encouragement. Having made sure the comfort of the shed was still available, they happily stayed out several more days.

Amazingly each cattle activity is less stressful than my anticipation of it. This, I am increasingly aware, is because Margaret also has a special relationship with her animals. The value of this was to be experienced in January.

Christmas proved to be a period of normal routine for us. Guests celebrated as one is supposed to do. They went to church. They put turkeys in the oven, switched on Christmas lights, pulled their crackers and drank their wine. We have been there, done that. They opened the presents they had piled under their Christmas trees and filled the dustbins with wrapping paper. I surreptitiously removed it all and put it in the incinerator. The redundant milk feeders had been brought into the kitchen and I spent the festive day washing them thoroughly, truly content, singing, 'Go well go safely, the Lord is ever with you,' which has a lower key than Christmas carols! 'Have a lovely Christmas!' everyone said and we did blissfully unaware of the stress and turmoil the coming year would bring to so many people.

Our one fear, at that time and during the first four months of 2007 was that people would actually welcome global warming. Why not? Frost and snow appear to have gone. The winter promised to be short and spring was already disturbing the bulbs and willows. Mother would have maybe said, 'Don't be tekken in!' and she would have been right.

Christmas passed without incident but on the morning of New Year's Day, our neighbour, already farming George's buildings and top land, rang to tell us he had just found that George had died peacefully, asleep in bed. It was not the news one wants to get, whatever the day, and it cast a shadow on our expectancy and we hung up a new calendar and stepped rather hesitatingly into the unknown. George was my generation. He had retired at sixty five and we had since rented eight of his fields west of our road.

Our confidence was not boosted either, by another immediate phone call from Dolores. She and her husband Raymond have lived at Cliff Farm, on Harden Moor, for nearly as long as we have lived at The Currer. It was an SOS call saying that Raymond had severed a blood vessel in his ankle and could we come?

'The ambulance will reach you more quickly. Ring 999!' I said. In a panic we all begin to flap and we had twice had the experience of a burst, leg blood vessel. Once Mother had had a similar accident and the paramedic, arriving to the bloody scene, had said with morbid humour, that he fainted at the sight of blood. Years later Aunty Mary had tripped over her brass jam pan and had rushed bleeding to her neighbour who had suggested she sit outside on the garden seat whilst the ambulance was called, to avoid irreparable damage to her carpet. A few weeks ago Tim had released a fountain of blood whilst dehorning a Simmentel heifer, evidence of which will stain the shed wall for ever. Real help reached Cliff Farm quicker than we could. When the calves were fed and we phoned, we found order and confidence restored.

Someone rang for spring accommodation and gave me a Ripon address. I can never let that happen without remarking that I received my teacher training there. 'At Ripon St John!' the lady said with confidence though the college no longer houses students.

'Ripon St Margaret!' I corrected her, for so it was before the amalgamation with York St John, years after my time. It highlighted the many decades and experiences which have passed since my two year training, shortly after the war, but the huge gap narrowed into insignificance following another call. This time from the north of Scotland.

A couple wanted a cottage for five days and were lucky for Mr and Mrs Bullock were preparing to leave after their annual Christmas and New Year stay. In the course of this conversation we found we had a joint past. I was the teacher who had taught the caller when she was a six-year-old in 1950. There are not many children, I do not remember and I knew a lot about the rather chubby little infant, Jennifer Smales. I could hardly wait for the almost immediate arrival of this couple now living well over the Border. I remembered Jennifer as a mature, sensible infant who had left Lees Primary as a competent eleven-year-old. She had been friendly then and though she was now a slim pensioner, she was the Jennifer I had known and taught. She had brought photographs and I dug up mine and we had a trip down memory lane which excited both of us.

Funnily enough, soon after this visit, another of her classmates halted me outside Wilsden Co-op. I hadn't seen her for fifty years or so. 'It's Miss Brown. Isn't it?' she said. 'You used to teach me.' Her auburn curls had turned to grey and I would not have recognised her as the skinny little Geraldine Thompson, firmly lodged in my memory. It was wonderful to be able to name her brother, Melvin and sister Ann and even know the balcony on which she had lived. I had a life before this holiday accommodation era and I haven't forgotten!

A retired Keighley teacher, living in Scotland had sent me a Christmas card following the Dales Diary programme and, having read *A Song to Sing*, questioned me about a Guide she had taught who was now in New Zealand. I took the opportunity of getting back in touch with Christine Calvert, living half way round the world away. Two thousand and six had its wonder moments. Busy as always, we continued to re-unite with a past of infinite value

A bed and breakfast guest recently voiced the opinion that it was fortunate that we had this opportunity to house guests. She feared we would be so lonely here without them. I think I may have shocked her by saying that, much as we love having visitors it is also quite lovely, occasionally, to be on our own. To take time-out, now and again, is necessary. We tend to live in an environment of extremes and love both ends of the spectrum, though one is much heavier than the other. Few know how much we occasionally welcome a yard empty of cars and, when darkness falls the only light comes from our own kitchen window.

The year 2007 began on a different key. The death of our good neighbour George, marked the end of an era. His family must have already been farming Moss Carr Hall Farm when Grandfather bought The Currer in 1929. George, the only child, was born there in the mid-twenties and had lived there ever since. He had retired from farming in 1990 and David Bailey had had cattle on the upper fields and in the buildings and, for all those seventeen years, we had rented the grazing rights of the eight small fields we will always call George's.

He was very well respected in the village and had been our contact with local and market gossip all the while, for David had taken him everywhere even as we had taken Harry. George had enjoyed a weekly visit to the abattoir and another to the mart. Every day he made at least one journey on foot to our entrance and, on our increasingly fewer trips into town, he was always somewhere on the road and always full of news. He would be sadly missed by everyone. George's health had been failing recently with spells in hospital and frequent visits of his doctor so, although all sudden death, however peaceful, is a shock, no-one could argue that it was totally unexpected.

He had made plans for his funeral, asking that the hearse would take his coffin to our cattle grid entrance, his daily walk for so many years of retirement and, out of respect, we planned to be safely out of the way so as not to interfere with this lap of honour. We have so often been labelled The Late Browns but, on this occasion, we left early for the church and all the way up our road and along Moss Carr, our Range Rover made an appalling noise. We stopped at the Post Office to put a letter in the box and investigate. We had rightly guessed the problem. We had a very flat tyre.

Fortunately the wallers were working on a boundary wall and could be contacted by mobile. We almost ran the last quarter of a mile to the church arriving somewhat red in the face and wind blown but mercifully before the cortege.

We are prone to incident. Whilst returning to a vehicle the men had restored to four wheel excellence, we and other walkers smelled gas outside a house with a caravan in the drive. For a brief spell on television, an advert had been repeatedly giving the emergency telephone number to ring if anyone smelled gas. Immediately we entered the house Margaret picked up the phone and rang this call centre. It was far from local. Valuable time was lost whilst the lady tried to read a map of an area she did not know. 'What is the post code?' she wanted to know. Margaret could not say. We live half a mile away.

'What is your code?' Margaret was asked. A fat lot of good that would be for we have a Marley code which sites us a quarter of a mile from the hamlet of Marley. We sit on top of a steep hillside boasting only a cart track accessible by foot or tractor. When this error was discovered, years ago, there were too many addresses in our book, too many business connections to notify that to change it was unthinkable.

'It's on Calton Road,' Margaret said and called to me, 'How is it spelled O or E.'

'O' I called back. It took the woman over twenty minutes to pin point the location during which time gas could have killed someone. Margaret was eager to put down the phone, she had work to do, but there was one more legal requirement even though we were half a mile away.

The lady detained her saying, 'Wait. Before you go I have to tell you not to light a match, a fire or smoke a cigarette!' Having done so she said someone would be there within the hour. So much for modern technology and emergency telephone numbers!

Three quarters of an hour later a man rang to say he was on Calton Road and was the house at the bottom or the top?

'At the top. By the caravan,' I replied.

'How many caravans are there?' he wanted to know.

'Only one, I think. I don't live there. We were just returning from a funeral.'

If there had been another fatality in the village we were never to know for sadly our only source of village information had been buried that morning.

George's Will gave us the first right of option to buy the rented land and we advised his solicitor of our willingness to do so and the long, slow process of transfer began.

January brought the worst gales for many a decade and the entry to our farmyard experienced a wind surely topping the 100mph mark. To cross was to risk imminent danger. Trees were blown down everywhere. We lost one of the Scots Pines we had brought from Spean Bridge, more than thirty years ago. Gales nationwide made the news headline and posed us an unexpected problem. We had put all our faith in the security of the motorway barrier surrounding the stockyard. When the gatepost had rotted and been pushed over by the inmates two years ago, it had not been replaced. A hole had been made in the concrete shed wall for the spring fastener to engage. This closure mechanism always proves difficult for feminine fingers but, should we not wish to struggle there was, we proved time and time again, no danger for the shed door hinges, three inches away from the hole, were a safety net.

One morning, battling with this unusually strong wind, Margaret by-passed the hole and trusted the hinges. What she did not bargain for was the strength of the wind. Apparently it was capable of blowing an outward opening door, two inches inward and releasing the twelve foot gate. I was working in the sitting room when I heard the thunder of hooves passing beneath the window. I rushed to peer through the glass and watched the whole sixteen-month-old herd hurtling, six at a time, through the open gate into the Five Acre. Their speed was being accelerated by the fright-eningly high wind. Had the gate not been open there would have been a catastrophic pile up. The gate is always ajar in winter for our donkeys are allowed free access. It is their Divine Right and, on that very windy day, it was a blessing.

There was nothing we could do but wait for the return of the escapees. It was not immediate for the gale from the west propelled them away from home and became a head wind for any return. It was after dark when they returned, over eager for the warmth of their bedding and once more we had the awesome task of opening doors on lighted accommodation when they, like naughty children, all tried to enter at once. First I must open the twelve foot gate from the Dyke field, a frightening task with eighty animals behind it. When the binder twine is untied I scarper quickly to the safety of the fence knowing that the weight of the herd will open the gate and up-skittle me in the process if I am slow to escape. Cattle are spooky in darkness and there is always a fear that they will suddenly turn and stampede which is why we prefer to handle them ourselves. They know us and they have learned to know Sam. Our only fear is that a car will draw into the yard and guests approach to see what we are doing.

Margaret made sure, next morning, that the gate fastener went into the hole. The wind blew for days and we became heartily sick of it. When it dropped the mild, dry climate, unusual in January, tempted out the walkers. Some must have taken a short cut through the western entry into the stock-yard which has a very secure fastener but, once again, the spring needs strength. The trespasser had struggled with it to open the gate but not to close it. The herd had managed to open it a few feet, enough to make their escape and, the day being gentle they did not come home. I am usually in bed long before mid-night but I waited, still dressed, until Margaret had made her last call. They still had not come so we went to bed.

Margaret always gets up at least once every night, to check the calves. She had left the stockyard gate open lest the herd returned. At four o'clock in the morning she roused me saying, 'Jean, can you come? They are all in the stock yard. We'll have to let them in!'

That, too, was a fearsome task but it was over in minutes, so keen were they to get inside. Margaret was unsure she had counted the right number into the first shed. It didn't really matter. She opened the second door and within seconds all were in and before the doors were properly secured all eighty were lying down.

The unique, January experience was not yet over. Several days later, just before dusk, we went to let the steers back into their overnight accommodation and found them all tearing up to the summit of the road and the too full cattle grid over which they could walk, if they so wished. Margaret hared up the hill knowing they may turn and return downhill more quickly than they had climbed it. They came hurtling back to the small gate they had somehow opened to escape but there was no way they were going to return through it. Seeing that I was not winning and aware that the naughty animals would turn again, she opened the gate onto the pasture and away they fled into the early darkness. Once again Margaret roused me, this time nearer 5 a.m., and once again we let them in and went back to bed. Next morning Margaret doubly secured every gate with several strands of binder twine and permanently closed the door on that chapter of our ridiculous history.

So many people will find their names recorded in this collection of anecdotes but they represent only a few of the thousands who have been a part of our busy life. Some I have included after the briefest encounter because of the novelty of the event. Not many have rubbed shoulders with a richer variety of human beings than we have and I apologise to the majority who may assume I have forgotten them and to reassure them I have an elephantine memory. Amongst the thousands some have an importance incalculable, placing them among the few who have changed the course of our lives.

I do not hesitate to say that foremost amongst these I rank John Lachie and Effie MacInnes, of Salum, Tiree. Why? Because upon them Margaret and I built the Hebridean connection which has nurtured so many children. We first met this crofters' family on our first trip to the island, when Margaret was only twelve and I a young teacher of twenty-one. We were attracted to them because of a common bond of husbandry. This young couple and their three little girls, living in a thatched island cottage, fascinated us. They had only hand-pumped water from a well and no electricity but I recognised the potential, of those three children and, of course we were captivated by the sun blessed island. So much so that, a few years later, we returned with one of our sixteen year old Guides and became obsessed with the idea of bringing Guides to camp on the island the following year. 2007 marked the fiftieth anniversary of that first of twenty five island camps.

What the Guides never understood, for they were only children, was that we could only do so if we were confident of the support of the islanders, John Lachie and Effie in particular, for it was on their land we would pitch our tents. The parents of the Guides, the Camp Advisors, the children and

Me, left back, Margaret, right front, with
Effie, John Lachie and the MacInnes family.

even the islanders themselves, believed the enormous success of our island camping depended on me. They were wrong. It depended on my confidence in the islanders themselves and on those who owned the site in particular.

John Lachie died in 1988 but his wife remained an active crofter until well into her eighties, helping her son, born after we first met the family. She was still working in the field and caring for him in the house he and his father had built, on the site of their thatched one, several years ago. Twice I had had the opportunity to tell her she had been the real star of our camping success. It had gone unnoticed by everyone, but Margaret and I were well aware of it and were, perhaps, more grateful to her than to anyone. We have been indebted to many because they have altered our lives, but Effie and John Lachie had altered the lives of hundreds of children. If you ask those children they will say it was my sister and I who did that, but we know differently. It was the security provided by the islanders which made it possible for us to do what we did.

For Christmas we had sent her a DVD of our camps in the sixties and seventies and one of the Dales Diary programme and she and her son and daughters had been able to see the transition from happy children to confident adults and, I think, they had all begun to understand the enormous roles their parents had played in our history. Then suddenly Effie became ill and all too quickly died and we were grieving for a friend we had known for fifty-five years.

At the 26th Annual Guide Reunion we collected money to send to Mary, her eldest daughter and told the family to buy something which would be a memorial to a lady to whom we were all so immeasurably indebted. They bought a marble flower holder for the grave and on it was,

Fondest memories of
Effie and John Lachie
The Keighley Guides.

We felt this a gesture of their love for us and were deeply moved. I cannot tell you how important it was, to us, that they should know how indebted we had felt to be. That they responded in the way they did was unexpected and so very, very precious.

Effie was not the only Hebridean we lost at the turn of the year. We had discovered Harris later than Tiree and had been capable campers by the time we took children to a shore belonging to John MacDonald at No 9, Luskentyre. We were no longer amateurs in the beautiful game of island camping but our need of security there, many miles further north than Tiree, was no less. We had already known Effie for ten years before we met John and extended our camping experiences to Harris. When we first knew him it was his mother who had been in a wheel chair and when we last saw John, at the 2005 Reunion on the island, it was he who had been the user. Though physically immobile, he had been mentally lively and we had not expected to lose him for several years. He had gone into respite care at the

Tarbert Residential Home, whilst his house had undergone some repairs and modernisation. He had been taken to view the improvements but had said it no longer looked like his home. He was never to experience a return for he died before completion. His house, almost on the shore, is now used by self-catering holidaymakers. We donated a memorial seat for the lawn so that the beautiful vista can be viewed to advantage.

The third sad loss of 2007 was that of Patrick Entwistle. He and his wife, their daughter, son-in-law and grandchildren had been part of our lives for twenty one of the twenty -six we had been bed, breakfast and evening meal landladies. Pat was born with cerebral palsy but had conquered it well enough to marry, rear a family and deserve an MBE from the Queen. His wife, Joan had had two, below the knee, leg amputations in her teens and their joint history was a story of courage and achievement second to none. But most of all we will remember them for the fun they generated with their presence. There was more laughter coming from the dining room, during their annual week at The Currer, than during any of the other fifty-one.

For two years Pat's health had been deteriorating but not his sense of humour and our respect for him had grown and grown. It had grown, too, for Joan, now permanently in a wheelchair, whose independence made her a legend. Pat's last few months were increasingly difficult so that we began to pray for his release from suffering. We were constantly in touch and when the end came we went to bed at peace. I am not a poet but, just occasionally the right words come without my intervention. I wakened next morning and before even my cup of coffee, I wrote on an empty card,

> Pat
> Smaller than most but taller,
> Dafter than most but wiser,
> Weaker than most but stronger,
> Sadder than most but happier,
> Wittier than most but kinder,
> Poorer than most but richer.
> A man we'll remember more than most,
> A better husband and father than most,
> More worthy of his MBE than most,
> A finer role model to follow than most,
> A rogue with a twinkle
> And a heart of gold!
>
> Pat!

It is inevitable that as the circle of our friends expands, and many become more, that our losses will increase. The fewer cattle one has the less stressful the responsibility of care. Many friends means there will be more phone calls alerting us to a bereavement. It is, I think, particularly sad to lose loved ones at the onset of spring when all forms of life should have summer to look forward to.

The sad fact is that winter weakens and spring takes its toll. In our domain, within our walls and boundary, things were looking well. The calves and yearlings were doing well. Weather wise the winter had not been at all bad. We had had just one day of snow. One foolish guest tried to use the road out, which is steep. He failed and blocked the track so that even we, in the Land Rover, could not get up. Next day the white carpet was gone.

All children brought to the David Hart Clinic have quite severe physical abnormalities but most of them are determined to stand tall and move alone. One of the most memorable was a little girl from Belarus. A British charity, Belarusian Ray of Hope, was responsible for bringing Valentina and her mother and a Russian interpreter. The little girl was absolutely dedicated to a walking future. She was such a happy little girl.

There was continual talk about an early spring. March looked ready to go out like a lamb. We had one problem calf. It was not growing. Eating heartily, it remained like a dwarf and a vet on a routine visit, confirmed Margaret's suspicion that the calf had contracted BVD, in the womb and, though it would be cheerful for a while it would probably not live to see next winter. This little Hereford was a real little codger and that became his nickname. We accepted the inevitable and recognised him as a little toughie. There is always a place for such at The Currer. There was one other member of our ruminants causing concern. Snowy, our ancient goat sat down behind the corn bin and was to lift onto her legs every day. There was time for that chore, too.

Two magpies were engaged in a building project on the roof of the top bullock shed. Margaret christened it The Grand Design, the title of a current television series. It had to be a build of mega proportions and we had no faith, whatsoever in its success. The nest was being built across the ventilation gap and, of necessity had to be a bridge spanning nine inches, or more, twenty feet above ground level. Eighteen inch sticks were needed, stout ones at that and we were terribly worried that all their extreme effort would be wasted and their house collapse. It did not and, when they had reared their second family, they were able to take away the key ready to return next year. The severe gales of the following New Year did not dislodge it. It was indeed a Grand Design.

Chapter Seventeen

Mother.
She stands proven master of her craft,
Relaxed and floury in her gaudy pinafore,
Wedded to the ingredients with which
She creates the cakes and pastries
That proclaim her skill.
Plenty has never been enough.
Her Yorkshire hospitality decrees
Her tins must be well filled, the variety
Such that she can set a splendid table
For unexpected guests who casually call.
Her success can be predicted.
From the warm depths of the Aga
She lifts each perfect sponge,
Each apple pasty, oozing the juice of autumn,
Puff pastry, crisp and ready to receive
Whipped cream from the dairy; light scones
Eaten warm with butter freshly churned
And Bramble Jelly she made last September.
Her octogenarian energy astounds
The young and old who come and adore her!

WE HAD the Pearce family group for the weekend of the March Mothers' Day. They come bi-annually at least. We never celebrated Mother's Day any more than we ever did birthdays and anniversaries. There was no need because we always lived together. We were never separated by phone or post or miles. Every day we appreciated our mother and she knew without our telling her so. Just once, shortly before her death, I had told her I loved her and she had not returned the sentiment. 'Don't you love me?' I had said and her reply had been, 'What d'ye think?'

I remember no Mother's Days, so I salute her in questionable poetry, the verses written in the seventies, before Father died and I'll remember both of them with love. None of us have been demonstrative but we have revered each other and cared for each other more than most families.

The annual event of 2007 I will remember also, but for quite a different reason. Margaret had decided to de-louse the calves. This can be a simple operation whilst the calves are in a row eating at the manger. All that is necessary is to walk down the rear of them, scattering a little powder on their backs, as one goes. Not a dangerous job compared with many that we do.

I was busy in the kitchen when I heard Margaret come in and say. 'Are you there?' These three words freeze me. She's got a calf out in the passage was my first thought, or one with a head stuck in a manger or gate, or maybe one needs a jab of anti-biotic and I must catch and hold it. Or something quite awful has happened. I was unprepared for it to be my sister who was personally in trouble. I could see at once that she was in pain. A second glance and I knew she was in real agony, holding her right arm awkwardly.

'I was de-lousing,' she said, 'and one stepped back and knocked me over!'

Behind the row of eating calves there grows a ridge of muck we do not cover with straw. Calves would never lay on it but it is a Wellington trap at the best of times and in the best of mobility and Margaret is nowhere near as agile as she was. She was far too tortured by pain to explain even if I had needed such. She must have had difficulty in getting back on her feet. She would have known that when she had not appeared for breakfast, I would have searched for her as I so frequently do though it annoys her. I would not have come immediately and the calves would eat up and begin childish frolic, so she had gritted her teeth and struggled through the muck to the dividing gate which had enabled her to rise. Then she had had a left handed battle with several gates and doors, catching her breath with every inevitable jerk. Entering the house she did not even know how to sit, so excruciating was the pain.

It was obviously a hospital job and it was equally obvious she could not get into the Range Rover. 'Send for an ambulance!' she gasped. I did and then I went into the guests' sitting room to tell them what had happened, where we were going and that they would have to leave before our return. Luckily no group was following them.

The ambulance took only minutes but remained in the yard whilst Margaret was thoroughly tested. She knew she had not fallen because of stroke or heart attack but the paramedics did not, nor did they seem to mind that she was liberally coated with cow muck! They gave her pain killing inhalation but it scarcely had any effect and, when A and E was reached, not even morphine took away the pain. X-rays revealed a dislocated shoulder which had been our amateur diagnosis from the start. Hours later, she was anaesthetised and the ball of her humorous was jerked back into its socket and her right arm strapped securely over her mucky jumper. A filthy hand protruded but no attempt was made to clean her up. The paper covering of the stretcher, on which she had lain, was covered in stains from the calf-shed, for she had not been divested of the trousers she had worn all winter or her shoes. With my help she managed to discard both to get into bed at night but the mucky jumper remained imprisoned beneath the strapping. Would you believe it in this day of fanatical hygiene!?

Only when Margaret talked to muscular rugby-playing men, who had also dislocated a shoulder, and heard them describe their pain, did she convince herself that she was not a wimp after all. The pain in her shoulder had gone but she remains convinced that she had also cracked a bone lower down for all pain was centred in her hand and it took months to recover.

The harness, she was told, she must wear for a month and it was obvious that the weight of work would have to come my way. I do not think Margaret ever stopped looking for what she could do, but there was such a lot she could not. What she did, she did awkwardly which put strain on every muscle. Returning from the hospital, late afternoon, we knew we had to get evening help. Always whilst Margaret feeds corn, I spread straw simultaneously. I could not do two jobs at once. Had I been seventeen, maybe, but my seventy-seventh birthday was only weeks away. It was imperative that we seek help for at least two hours every evening and, as is expected of us, we sought Guide help. It was Mothers' Day and we fully expected Helen to be with her parents. Actually, when I rang, she and Chris were just returning. They did a U turn, got back in the car and came. With Margaret giving orders and our friends having health and speed we coped fine. One or both came every evening, seven days a week, for a fortnight. Mornings were not a problem for, should help be needed, Tim was still coming every three days to fill mangers and he and Graham were rebuilding a boundary wall not very far away.

We found there is a way to do most absolutely necessary things and a way of avoiding those unessential ones. Margaret found a lopsided way of giving even an injection. That was the most difficult problem to solve but, amazingly she injected the struggling calf and neither of us by mistake. I found I was fitter than I expected but we were both grateful that the end of winter was nigh.

At the end of a fortnight, when Easter came and Helen and Chris had booked a holiday, we were able to shut the seniors out of the shed for good and separate a third of the calves into the adult shed, giving them a manger of big baled hay. They were let out during the day giving me access to their quarters and an opportunity to bed them down during the afternoon.

There was no pause in the flow of self-catering guests and the inevitable mountain of washing. The premises never being empty, was the excuse we gave for doing no decorating there. It was the first time in twenty-six years that Margaret had not wielded a paint brush.

We had learned, the hard way, that to run this business needs two of us and a tractor man. We had learned that thirty years ago when John Sugden was first needed at muck-spreading time. There appears to be no way either of us could carry on alone, so I'd better remain healthy for a good while yet! However we had also learned that help was really only a phone call away and that remains a great comfort!

The weather puzzled everyone. It was only early April and it was summer. We had had a particularly dry winter and spring was truly beautiful. There was an abundance of bluebells. Many metres away, in the wood we call Jimmy's but Defra calls Elm Close, there was such a rich blue carpet the scent of it reached the house. The fields never showed their pre-growth grey but became greener than usual and the bursting tree buds excelled in their display. The earth was so dry the tractor could spread the manure early and leave no wheel trail and the duck pond began to dry. April was the warmest it had ever been and temperatures nationwide made headlines.

But May proved the age old saying, 'Don't cast a clout, 'til May is out.' From beginning to end it was remarkably cold. Cold but dry and Margaret had to fix a hose into the duck pond lest it dry up altogether. I had assumed the duck caring job for it entails climbing over the fence and, though Margaret no longer wore a sling, she hadn't taken back the climbing jobs. One morning I saw a drip white rat drinking at the pond. It nonchalantly walked back under the duck house. Had someone just presented us with a pet, we wondered? If so it had found a rare home, indeed. Food, water and hideaway.

The dry weather brought out the walkers and encouraged our guests to do likewise and as we were unusually busy, or maybe increasingly slower, we didn't give Sam the long distance walking he needed. Every other day we drove across the land with him and Meg galloping alongside and if the opportunity arose, Sam would tag along with a dog walker, a rambler, children and joggers. If Tim could be heard talking on the boundary, he would hare off to join him. All this was very bad for our beautiful collie but, since Margaret's accident, life for us had been taxing. The telephone number, dangling from his collar wore thin and became hidden in his lengthening coat, so I slightly reduced a cattle ear tag and put the digits in bold, indelible black. And I put a notice on the footpath,

IF OUR DOG FOLLOWS YOU SAY GO HOME FIRMLY!

Some good that was for when spoken to Sam promptly rolled over begging for his belly to be tickled. He was rapidly acquiring a fan club and we wanted the holiday to come when we would be his only companions for two weeks.

Walkers here for a week at Spring Bank, set off for Haworth the fields way via Fairfax Coppy and John Brown's Lane. They had walked a mile before realising they had a follower. Two had to bring him home and join their party by car. We had never before had a dog which attached itself to all and sundry. Meg never did. Meg has never done anything wrong except eat the kitchen chair legs when she was a puppy and chase the postman. She is, however, a control freak. Never reprimanded herself she reprimands me continually, barking chastisement if I go into either of the cottages. If some enthusiastic guest thinks fit to hug me on arrival it is I, she says, who am at fault and she growls disapproval if I open letter post. She understands every word of English. She is adorable!

However she cannot stand any cross word from us and hearing our frequent, 'No Sam,' she sits down and will not follow until she gets the invitation,' Oh! Come on Meg.'

Sam loves everyone, anywhere. Meg loves anyone who will sit on the settee and stroke her perpetually. She never pesters us when we flop exhausted into a chair, except when she wants a Bonio. Then her demanding bark can be interpreted as, 'I want a biscuit. Now. Have you heard? Well … where is it?'

Children finding Sam at play, in the paddock at the rear of the house, saw his telephone number and, being children with a mobile, rang to ask if we had lost our dog. I answered it with fear which changed to relief and then amusement. All too often such a call meant a leap into the Range Rover to collect him from the village.

May is the month during which we have our annual visit from White Windows, Cheshire Home. The previous year they had objected to our three, well spaced steps into the dining room. All other wheelchair users had found no difficulty but carers, these days, are besieged by health and safety rules. We were asked to return the tables to the sitting room, something we could not do. They are heavy pine. We'd have needed to remove the hand rail and employ some strong men to carry them. The White Windows carers then said they would, in that case, bring their own trestle tables. We were mortified and fully expected chaos and the visit to be their last. They had been coming for more than forty years. To cease to do so would be sad but we never thought the operation would go so smoothly. It was a piece of cake! Rarely should you panic until you have tried! 'See you next year,' they called when leaving.

When I was head at Kildwick C of E School, a PE advisor, Yvonne Easto, lived nearby and she was very well respected in the profession and in the village. We who taught in the school, knew her as a very caring person with a family history of cancer. She was responsible for one sister in particular, who was dying of lung cancer and she admitted to us that she was scared, not of the death but of how the end would come. Her husband's excellent advice had been not to anticipate. It had been wise for sudden pneumonia is a friend which often takes away quickly and quietly. When Joan Armstrong and I visited her, shortly before cancer claimed her, too, she was fully in control, sitting up in bed having just been visited by her hairdresser. She looked beautiful.

I have many times remembered that advice not to anticipate even though it seems to contradict my BE PREPARED upbringing. Things seldom turn out as you might expect. To be prepared for all contingencies is necessary but to fear what might be is foolish.

We could not anticipate the behaviour of our yearling pup on the train journey north, but we did think we ought to introduce him to the railway station at least. The cold May was relenting and on one very hot Monday we took Meg and Sam to sit for half an hour on the platform, to watch the trains come and go. Keighley is a very small station with only two platforms and Meg recognised it at once. Sam was interested but showed no fear.

'We could take him on the Worth Valley Steam Railway,' Margaret said and on the following Sunday, a week before Spring Bank Holiday, she came in for morning coffee and announced that this might be our only chance and that we should take it.

It too, was a very hot day. We would have taken the bus had there been a convenient one from the village. As there was not we decided to walk through the wood into town, a journey I believe we had not done for more than thirty years. Before we bought our first Austin Gypsy, I used it to hurry down into town to catch my bus up the Aire valley. This retracing of our youthful steps would have been interesting had Sam not been somewhat eager on his new lead. Meg was disgusted with the narrow steeply cobbled path under the dark canopy of trees. How tall they had grown in the last thirty years. Meg kept sitting down every time I chastised Sam. We weren't at all comfortable but we did, by a hair's breadth, manage to catch our train and Meg was overjoyed. She jumped on with an eagerness missing on our woodland route and Sam followed her without hesitation. We will not forget Meg's look of sheer joy as the steam train slowly pulled out of the station. 'Hurray,' she said. 'We are going on holiday!'

At the end of the line, I got out onto the Oxenhope platform and bought two tumblers of coffee and a muffin, with a real holiday feeling. We take too few days out these days. Margaret had remained with the dogs who were perfectly relaxed. The train eventually began its return journey and a disgusted Meg found we had come home without any beach experience. Alighting from the train it suddenly let off steam and frightened the dogs. They were terrified and we had to hold on to the leads. When the noise stopped and peace was restored, the dogs walked calmly up the ramp. If they could stand that deafening noise, we deemed all would be well.

Fifteen minutes later we caught the village bus home and Sam had had his introduction to the coming holiday.

I have said so many times that before we go we must prepare for leaving but what to expect is unknown. We try, Margaret on the outside and I do my best on the inside, to reach perfection. Is there ever a time when we have not one old and decrepit animal? I think not. Our present one in May 2007, was Snowy, the white nanny goat we had adopted years and years ago. We had thought she might not survive the winter but it had been mild. The goats are free-range, can do what and go where they like. Snowy preferred the garage.

Years and years ago she had preferred the wild. We had seen her grazing with the deer, half a mile away, for all of eighteen months before some children of holidaymakers made her acquaintance and led her to our hospice, where she stayed ever after.

A Mr and Mrs Robinson, whose small children had achieved this Saint Francis feat, were here at the beginning of June. Their children are now adults in their twenties and they were delighted to see Snowy was still with us. She was receiving palliative care in a cosy square, behind the corn bin in the garage. Each day she was helped to rise. The other goats talked to her over the gate. Margaret bought carrots galore and apples and pulled a bucketful of grass for her every day.

In the adjacent shed were four calves, three were recuperating, two from sudden pneumonia, one from New Forest eye infection. The other was The Codger, still not growing but eating well and cheerful. Every morning they were let out into the paddock and he was first out and last in. His life expectancy was still brief. He looked barely a month old but he was happy and for us, that is all that matters. Margaret decided to transfer these to a bullock shed and to bring Snowy back into the larger accommodation she had always been used to. Dorothy, on holiday supply, would cope better with her there.

Margaret was sure Snowy could not walk but her dislocated shoulder was still weak so we employed Graham and he and I put a blanket beneath her belly and carried her to a better hotel. Five minutes later Margaret came into the kitchen. 'Guess what,' she said. 'Snowy has just walked back into the garage!' Obviously she knew best. Obviously she wasn't as decrepit as she made us believe.

We had given up all hope of decorating. Margaret's hand and forearm were still painful and she must avoid any danger of dislocating the shoulder once again. So the white walls were not given their annual refreshment and, I'm afraid, some cobwebs remained. Guests followed guests so quickly we had no time to take a breath.

Suddenly it was warm enough to shut the calves out at night. This was much later than previous years. We had been forced to pay rent once again for the grazing on the fields which George's Will had promised we could buy. Probate takes so unbelievably long.

The two weeks before our departure on holiday the weather was beautiful from one end of the United Kingdom to the other. The Hebrides were basking in sunshine. We feared we had chosen wrongly. We lifted out our minute rucksacks and put in just one change of clothing. Our camping days had taught us all we needed to know about lightweight travelling.

We had a busy bed and breakfast week and, on the Friday before our Monday departure, the weekend self-catering group booking arrived. They left later than we usually allow on Sunday, but presented me with their dirty sheets early so that the washing machine could work all day. When they eventually left we had the marathon task of remaking all the fifteen beds and polishing the parquet tiles. I blame this for nearly causing me to scupper our holiday by missing the train.

With our two minute rucksacks and our two dogs, we were half way down the Brow when I realised I'd forgotten my money bag, which should have been strapped round my waist. Tim, taking us to the station in his Shogun, did a U-turn in the village bus terminal and raced back to the house and averted disaster.

I am, and have been for thirty years, sole holder of the family purse. Margaret will tell you she never has any money and she is right. The money, tickets and cheque book are all in my possession and all were in my belly-bag on the kitchen table. I had forgotten in error but remembered in time. The next train is too late if you are going to Mallaig!

Safely on board, I pondered on the incident, now barely worth comment. It proved several things. Most people would say, 'Poor old lady, she's getting forgetful, as they do!' Rubbish! I've been guilty before. Many times. Frequently when I was young. It did, however, prove my reflexes are in good working order, respond quickly and accurately and in time.

Others would say, 'She has too much to do at the last minute!' They'd be right but there's nothing new about that? When have we ever gone on holiday, camping, driving or by rail when our work has not increased dramatically at the last minute? That we had managed to wash those twenty-four sheets and twenty-four pillowcases and re-made those fifteen beds, between the large group leaving and our departure, cancels all belief that we've had it!

The real reason that I made that error, and the many that have come before it, was also that we are, what we have been named, The Late Browns. We are always ten minutes from finishing when Dorothy comes and Tim urges us to get in the van! If we were already coated and bagged before she drove into the yard to take over responsibility, all would be well. But we are not. Our bags are ready, our walking sticks, my waist bag is on the table, complete with its all important contents but we are still filling a flask, taking a phone call, clearing dirty mugs to the sink.

That our train was not until 1 p.m. should have given us plenty of time but we had driven over the moor and round the boundary, dogs running alongside, to give them the only exercise they would get that day. We were taking the beautiful weather with us north.

It was one song of a morning! Perhaps we had dallied too long, enjoying our 'ain countree'. Whatever the reason, we had been short of a few minutes more before Dorothy and Tim, came firing questions about animals and people to be left in their charge. Personally I think they are either brave or mad to agree to be left in charge of our crazy, unpredictable environment.

Which? When? Who? What? They are full of questions. 'It's all written down!' we tell them but they continue to fire questions and we lose control of our departure and that, I insist, is why I make last minute mistakes. I blame no-one. The two we are leaving are among our best friends. Without them we would have no train journey to the Land of Make Believe.

The two little hiccups on our journey were not caused by the behaviour of our dogs. They were polite, as always. The Settle to Carlisle line gave us a freight train ahead making our arrival late and we made the connection to Glasgow by the skin of our teeth. Taking dogs on the railway is a doddle. We saw one man with three, all beautifully behaved.

There is a free connection, by mini-bus, between Central and Queen's Street stations on which you now cannot take two dogs! That had never been the case before. It was fortunate we had time for Margaret had to stay behind and catch the next one with Sam. Hurriedly I gave her money in case she had to resort to a taxi but I forgot to give her a rail ticket so she was not allowed a free ride. Every time we brush shoulders with society, Health and Safety rules put a spoke in the wheel. We did catch the Mallaig train on which we had over five hours to become empty of urban stress.

The sun shone all the way and we watched, with alarm, the empty corries down the mountains, which usually spouted cascades of glittering spray. Then, suddenly, as we were approaching Loch Shiel, the heavens opened and a party of back packers, boarding the train at Glenfinnan, were saturated. It had been raining an hour they told us but the cloud must have been coming east for our experience of it was only momentary. Nevertheless, down each crack in the hills, water was pouring at speed. The evolution from dry wilderness and no movement as far as the eye could see, to living, glittering, functioning, breathing Highlands was inspirational.

Considering we have seldom left our native soil, devoting our lives to the area in which we were born and returning again and again to the holiday places we love, our journeying never lacks adventure. Each day bears little similarity to the last. There is always something new heralded by every dawn and no holiday mirrors the last. We had given ourselves plenty of time to cross Skye and board the Harris boat at Uig. We had breakfasted at Spring Bank early after sleeping lightly, Margaret still holding Sam's lead. Unlike a human baby, he generally slept all the night through but we had been on the train eleven hours and he was unused to sleeping in a bedroom and still had puppy ways. He was toilet house-trained, always had been, but he still loved to tear up paper, shake mats and devour wood. Thankfully he did none of those things on holiday.

Spring Bank is a haven for those travelling with dogs, or cycles, or rucksacks. The proprietors are the friendliest of people creating an atmosphere of calm. It is not silent as is The Currer, when the calf-shed air system is turned off in March. Our goats, unlike those at Spring Bank, are not in our backyard clattering about even in darkness. We have no cockerel as do our hosts, nor seagulls of which Mallaig is full. We have no noisy harbour, no flashing lights from the water but, just as our guests appreciate our silence so do we love the busy activity of the West Highland terminal and the sea road to the Isles.

We found the same 'one dog only' rule on Skye. We were flabbergasted. There were only two other people, waiting for the empty bus and we were told we could not get on with our two dogs in case they might fight! A new ruling from on high. As so often happens to us, the driver closed his eyes, told us to tell no one and Meg crawled under the seat and only Sam was visible. We had to change buses at Portree and the lovely man said, 'Hurry, the bus about to pull out is for Uig. That man will let you on!' He pointed to Meg and explained to the driver, 'That one is a horse!'

He did not tell us that the bus was not going direct to Uig and that it would take nearer two hours as opposed to the 30mins of the direct one. On it we went all round the Staffin peninsula, and the Quirang, the driver stopped frequently to point out landmarks, the Old man of Storr, the Kilt Rock and many more. We loved it, having not travelled that route for more than thirty years. It was fortunate we had heaps of time, otherwise we would have missed our boat. At Uig Margaret saw a taxi driver and asked for his telephone number and if he would pick us up on our return and ferry us and two dogs, to the Armadale boat. We could not have kind bus drivers risk losing their jobs by allowing us to break the rules.

If phone calls home had not been quite so alarming our Luskentyre holiday would have been another peaceful moment in time for the weather was perfect. We had dawn to dusk sunshine without the blistering heat which would never be my choice. Bare legged and bare armed we spent long soul-restoring hours on the beach, or communing with our island friends, whilst those we had left behind were drowning under storm clouds, unprecedented in the UK. Could this flooding from above really be due to global warming? We had been promised extreme heat but during June and July it was confined to the continent where forest fires were raging. Rain came to England and the islands thought they were in the Caribbean.

We could not believe the television news of severe flooding in Yorkshire or Dorothy when she told us a man had had to be rescued from his Land Rover, in Harden, scarcely a mile away. The storms which accompanied the deluge were momentous and Margaret's concern for her animals escalated. She phoned more frequently with orders for Dorothy to leave shed doors open so that the calves, not long deprived of overnight shelter, could come in at will.

The duck pond over flowed and both cattle grids filled with water. Gateways became mud baths and the fields resembled the swamps following a rapid February thaw. We had left John with instructions to fence the two sides of the locked gate, leading onto the land at the top of our road and to do something positive about the cattle grid he had installed nearly thirty years ago. It had gradually filled with grit from the road leading to the village and our four convalescing calves could cross it and find grass, which always appears greener, on the other side.

The repair of the fence had been urgent since youths with a motorbike had driven it through the ramblers gate, creating an exit for the seventy-seven heavy bullocks who, should they have had time to discover it, would have danced across the grid and waltzed into the village. But we had heard and seen the biker from the yard and we'd made a temporary repair, aided by Helen and Chris who have a habit of appearing at the right time.

To avoid any more wheeled trespassers, John made the fence with motorway barriers. It would now last our life-time, but the cattle grid, being full of water, had to be left. In our absence the four calves ventured over it too often so Tim took up a gate and swung it across. Drivers had to alight as they had for the first twenty-five years of our residence at The Currer.

All this was happening whilst we sauntered on the beaches of an island in the sun getting browner by the minute. The human race has not, yet found the paradise which is Luskentyre. If global warming ever does tempt people north, they might find it and that wonderful God-filled emptiness may be invaded. It would be sad. We invaded it for twenty-five years in the sixties and seventies, with children, and many of them and their parents and friends have been excited to find it and have become addicted but they are but a drop in an ocean.

Sandra took her family and friends and her parents-in-law caught the fever. One morning, whilst we were preparing to leave the ideal chalet we had rented, they appeared on our doorstep. 'We could not keep away,' they said.

We were walking on the empty beach but noticed it wasn't quite deserted. Two ladies, younger than we, but only by a year or two, were strolling along wide-eyed in wonder. We gravitated towards them. This, they said, was their second visit but it would definitely not be their last. It was out of this world, they said. Unbelievable! Amazing!

'Shall I tell you something else unbelievable, something equally wonderful?' I replied. 'For twenty-five years we brought hundreds of children for long, glorious weeks, under canvas, just among those dunes and many of them come back, again and again!'

When I continued to say we had been Guides from Yorkshire, one lady began to sing a camp-fire song, 'Swinging along the open road, swinging along under a sky that's blue.'

There followed an out-pouring of memories, she of her Guiding days, we of ours and when we parted company she and her friend were walking backwards to prolong our encounter and she was singing, ' Go well and safely, the Lord be ever with you!' Ours is a truly wonderful Movement!

Our sojourn in the chalet, which now replaces the school house and snuggles closely to Rachel's lodge, would have been perfect if news of incredibly bad weather was not daily reported by television and phone. Every morning the early rising sun had warmed our bedroom already. Every evening, if we were not hobnobbing with friends, we watched it go down from the window of the chalet wishing, above all things, that we still had Harry. How he would have loved that window overlooking the activity of Luskentyre.

The first to leave the township was Angus MacLennan in the heavy lorry parked overnight on the road side. He had been a heart-throb of our senior girls. Then Harry would have monitored the time it took for the school bus to pick up the few children attending the senior school in Tarbert. He would have seen Bobby bring five-year-old Kate to the road end to catch the later one going only to Seilebost. He would have awaited the appearance of the council graveyard attendants who seem to find daily work in the well kept cemetery and he would have remarked on the arrival of those still laying the garage forecourt of the new house of Morag Ann MacLeod, built on the site of the one in which she and thirteen brothers and sisters were born. Her parents, Dolly and Lexy, had provided us with milk and crowdie and made us oatcakes in the halcyon camping days now gone.

He would have seen the postman come early to collect the minimal letters from the red box and his later arrival to distribute post, of which there is hardly any these days. Junk arrives on the island even as it does on the Mainland. This activity was new to me, sitting in front of the picture window of the chalet, waiting for Margaret to make her appearance. Meg and Sam waited patiently too, for all three of us had already had our morning stroll.

To actually be in Luskentyre township was a new experience. Initially we had stayed at Angus and Katie's, only yards away but hidden from the road. Their morning activity I could not watch, for I could only see the roof of their house and from it the sea and the hills are the only vista. From the early sixties onwards, when staying at Luskentyre, our home had been in tents on the machair and, more recently, in the caravan hidden behind the dunes. This new location offered sea and mountains and activity on foot or wheels. Every evening a colony of starlings did a spectacular air display in front of the chalet. It would have suited Harry enormously but we would have to have been there on car wheels. The beach was easily accessible but not with a wheelchair.

The School House Chalet, Luskentyre.

Our footprints were made on the sandy route to the shore twice or thrice or more every day, barefoot, sleeveless and with a joy which, even at it's height could not compete with that of our ecstatic dogs. They raced ahead of us to wait eagerly at the closed gate to the track, squeezing through when it was only inches open and, gaining access to a playground of dune and marram grass, rabbit and gull, gushing stream and silver shore, they were in heaven. We knew, though we could not see, that Meg would first rush to the burn tumbling into the sea below Angus's. She is a lady who requires a shower every morning and several times a day. Then, dripping water from her long, shiny coat, she could be seen stalking the higher dunes, a black puma against the brilliant white. Sam was all Billy Elliot, hidden when grounded but soaring continually over the green spikes of the foothills.

There was nothing ageing about Meg's behaviour. We had feared she was getting too fat but her agility did not seem impaired. She had a simply wonderful holiday and came home a different dog. Her year of worrying about Danny, her last holiday on Tiree, frightened because he was so ill, had taken away that freedom of spirit which had personified her. Then had come this past year of schooling Sam. She, not we, had been his mentor. Her role as responsible foster parent had matured her. On Harris she became young again, threw caution to the wind, climbed dizzy heights and braved deeper waters. We became totally in love with Meg and, though eager to get home and sort out whatever deluge disaster awaited us, to take Meg away from her paradise was unforgettably sad.

We left Luskentyre telling her and all our island friends, that we would return next year, God willing, to a place glorious in sunshine but be it wild, wet and windy is always wonderful.

We sped across Skye in a rather expensive taxi driven by a pleasant, talkative man, knowing this would have to be our way in future. So be it. Health and Safety Rules OK. We refuse to be intimidated.

That evening we had a new experience on the hillside above Mallaig. A narrow, steep path leads from the shore road skywards. Suddenly coming towards us was the first otter we have ever seen on land. All previous ones have been off shore. It came towards us, nose to the ground and we nearly met before it scuttled into the undergrowth.

Boarding the Glasgow train, next day in Mallaig, we watched a bearded, French camera crew taking footage, for use in France Their aim was to promote tourism in the Highlands and among the Islands. They were noisy and dramatic and fun to watch. They were mixing French and English and amusing the few passengers.

Their attention was predominantly with a couple of middle-aged cyclists, from Sweden, whom they had followed from Skye. Their cameras were focused on the storage space for the bicycles on the train. Had anyone been filming the cameramen it would have been pure comedy. Sam was interested in their activity.

One of the French team sent for the tea trolley and asked us to buy refreshments for which he would pay but he forgot. The amusing thing was the tea lady had not been ready for the quick sale and our beverage was only luke warm. However all was in a good cause and amid healthy laughter. Viewers in France will see a happy shot of Margaret and Sam, she bronzed with the sunshine and he cleansed with the sea!

The team alighted at Glenfinnan possibly to re-board the steam train we saw in Fort William, carrying the Harry Potter enthusiasts. Books became a topic between ourselves and the couple from Sweden who became interested in the fact that we came from Bronte Country. I told them we had recently had a bed and breakfast visitor intent on filming in Haworth and preparing a website about Wuthering Heights. He had thought our farmhouse might look like the home of the Earnshaw family. People have strange ideas but to tolerate all eccentricities is necessary in our profession. The Swedish lady asked if we had read this book and that and we ashamedly told her we were farmers and landladies with days so full of work we would have to wait until retirement for the privilege of reading. Our excuse appeared pathetic so I told her we were fans, of course, of James Herriot, the Scottish vet practising in Yorkshire, that we had read and re-read The Robe and The Big Fisherman by Lloyd Douglas and recently a modern author, Ben Sherwood, whose book, The Death and Life of Charlie St Cloud. I had read it in Luskentyre, over the weekend, after the 2005 Reunion. Occasionally you have to say something which infers that you are a normal, educated lady, not just a slave to your environment. But, I concluded, our favourite novelist is still Nevil Shute. I never mentioned that I was an amateur writer myself.

Then the grey haired, sunburned cyclist said, 'Nevil Shute was my Godfather!'

I cannot tell you how much pleasure that gave both of us for Margaret, too, is a Nevil Shute fan. She has read his books more often than I have. He was one celebrity we would have loved to meet and his Godson was as good a representative as we could wish to get. It was an encounter we will never forget.

The heat, the bustle, the smell of a Glasgow teaming with people, we avoided by hiring a taxi to Central Station and escaping the embarrassment of mini-bus regulations. I hate city railway stations and it was a relief to get on the south bound train, though it was full and went faster than we prefer. We are told that shortly after we left a cloud-burst saturated the city. We could well believe it for, whenever our train followed the motorway we saw the traffic slowly moving and sending up a spray the like of which I had not seen before, but not a drop of rain fell on the window of our carriage.

We changed trains at Lancaster. The Leeds one was almost empty. The only passengers we met were travelling to a house boat on the Leeds Liverpool canal. We were to think of them often, in the days that followed, for the weather became appalling.

Chapter Eighteen

River stay way from my door.

Dorothy had left early to attend a weekend Dog Show in Blackpool and Chris and Helen had relieved her, but such had been the horror of storm and local flooding, she had waited until Sunday and had experienced blown down tents and an abandoned Show Field. The wet weather had been an ordeal for almost everyone except for we, who so often fall on our feet, and had had weather to die for. We were somewhat embarrassed. That we do fall on our feet and drop our toast, marmalade side up is testament that we do fall and that we do drop things like everyone else. We are never ungrateful or forgetful that one day we may fall face downwards and one day we will pick up our slice all covered in dust.

Throughout our holiday and in the days that followed, rain had fallen on South Yorkshire as never before. Thousands of homes had been flooded in the Hull and Sheffield areas. It was unbelievable. June and July are haymaking months but no fields could be cut and many on the flood plains were under several feet of water. We, on the hill, had suffered least but the ground was like a sponge and the gateways deep in mud. There was a pool in every hollow and grass looked grey and unappetising. Cattle could find no dry land on which to sit and didn't need to come to the trough to drink.

Our Little Codger, bravely came out every day and climbed the road to eat himself full then sit on the gravel at the summit and view the sodden landscape. The grit and mud of nearly thirty years, which had accumulated to almost fill the cattle grids, was now so soft it could be scooped out with a peat shovel and professional tractor help was not required. It was the only good thing to come out of the deluge. It saved us a whopping big bill during a season when farmers and holiday caterers seemed to lose money every which way. Holiday makers were avoiding the Dales and coasts and who could blame them. Fortunately we were almost fully booked except for a month in the cottages. Three weeks in The Mistal and one week in the loft we simply could not fill. A workman, who had been with us already for two months and was expecting to remain over the summer, would have to be rehoused, either in Auntie Mary's room or in a cottage and the latter seemed most likely. Suddenly he was moved by his agency to Sheffield and, the summer weather being the way it was, the cottage accommodation was more than likely to stand empty. Never in twenty-seven years, had this happened. No-one was in a holiday mood. Bookings made in spring were kept but new ones failed to come in.

Then, unexpectedly, we received a phone call from Mr and Mrs Crook, the couple who had used our Loft cottage previously. When they had wanted a Golden Retriever we had pointed them to 'High Woods', where we had stayed shortly after the birth of eight puppies. They had bought the one with a pink collar and had called it Lily-the-pink.

Poor Jenny Crook was in absolute distress. Their house had been flooded, twenty miles north of Hull. They had put up with dire conditions for three weeks whilst all their downstairs furniture had been thrown out and whilst plaster had been stripped from the walls. They had stayed in spite of the atrocious smell, but now the humidifiers had been switched on the fumes had become unbearable. They had been told to vacate the house for maybe four months. Had we a cottage free, she wanted to know? To have one was as extraordinary as was her need

Life isn't ordinary at all. It is a miracle from first to last. I've proved it and said so time and time again. At least we find it so. The Crooks found it so when hearing we had a vacancy for a month. It would give them plenty of time to find a caravan and excavate a plot in their ruined garden, on which to place it. Time, too, to recover from shock and regain health, close to their daughter who lives at Queensbury. They, like the many others, had a story to tell of sudden disaster, the devastation of their home and property and the slowness of a grossly overstretched insurance facility. They were with us for four weeks before buying a small touring caravan. They were to return again on the run up to Christmas and again the following Easter for they, and hundreds more, were still unable to occupy their houses.

For three weeks after our return, England suffered the worst flooding ever experienced in Yorkshire. In the south of England it was even worse. Snatching the headlines, for a brief moment, was the shocking news that terrorists had tried to ignite car bombs in London and at the entrance to Glasgow Airport and all this came at the very moment when we had a change of Prime Minister. All who aspire for that job must be mad.

The attention of the nation was immediately returned to two flood fatalities, to property loss, interruption of water and electricity supplies, fear that a dam would burst and widespread social upheaval.

The farmers and growers of the nation's food took a lonely back seat, watching with horror their uninsured profits disappear under the filthy, polluted water. Vegetables, fields and fields of potatoes, soft fruits, corn and grass ready for harvesting, were all lost. Farmers struggling to retain normality, after the wipe-out caused by the 2001 Foot and Mouth epidemic, sank once more onto their arthritic knees. The countryside was empty of tourists. There were vacancies in all guest houses. Britain was on the brink of an economic recession. Few recognised it and many went deeper and deeper into debt, borrowing far and above their means.

Margaret had planned a summer to thoroughly enjoy. All August we had self-catering groups already booked. We'd assured ourselves that they would provide the opportunity for us to wander our neighbourhood, visit our friends, drive up the valley and cross into another dale. As it was we, like thousands more, stayed at home and watched the rain splashing on the window-pane. The media began to refer to Climate Change rather than Global Warming!

There was no movement whatsoever toward the transfer of George's eleven acres onto the Deeds of The Currer. We had been asked for three months rent and told it might be much later in the year before completion. However it was insisted that we must remove our cattle on the 13th July, when our three month rent ran out. The only reason I am recording this is because we got an urgent message to say we must not do so, after all. We must pay a peppercorn rent and leave the cattle there. I was told the selling solicitor feared that ungrazed land might be a fire risk. A Fire Risk? In the summer of 2007? Nothing could have been lit even with paraffin. It was akin to issuing a hosepipe ban, there being 'water, water everywhere'.

Then, amazingly, there came a fortnight of weather suitable for farmers to cut their sodden, overgrown grass and bale their hay and haylage and tractors were busy as never before. The speed at which they harvested must have been unprecedented but damage to the wet land, with their heavy machines, was unavoidable. Tim managed to secure three hundred bales for us and we could safely anticipate winter and buy calves. Not until the bales were opened in winter did almost every farmer find the contents well below standard. New grass had grown near the roots, mature grass had partially died and tractor wheels had churned up soil. Only because there was plenty, and cattle could pick and choose, did the animals do well in the winter.

During that brief respite, Janet Hillary came with dog Tony. She has been an annual guest for many years but had never been in St Ives. So we all went together, walked round Coppice Pond and had coffee in the tea shop, just as if we were here on holiday, too.

Showery weather returned and we longed for a project. The way we are, who we are, our inactivity could not go on indefinitely. Motivation was triggered by my sister finding a bullock with foul-of-foot. He was limping rather badly and we knew he must be brought to the crush and given an anti-biotic. Our cattle roam freely within our boundary and we must always wait for an opportunity when the herd congregates near a gateway onto the road and, whatever the hour, we must snatch it if we wish to separate one from the herd.

Margaret wakened at 5 a.m. and saw all our senior bullocks encamped at the summit, close to the locked gate. She roused me. 'Do you feel fit to get this bullock?' she said. We went to the top of the road in the Land Rover and, as luck would have it, the lame bullock was nearest to the gate and, as he was handicapped with foul, we had no difficulty in guiding him towards the gate or in taking him home. Foul is easy to treat. One dose of anti-biotic returns a very swollen foot to normality in no time at all. Having behaved well and received the necessary treatment, we were able to return the animal the quarter of a mile back to the herd and to the Land Rover we had left behind.

'Let's do our morning survey,' Margaret said and we drove through the gate and crossed the soggy land to check the boundaries and make sure no animal had been left behind. The dogs enjoyed their early leap across the pastures and, when we returned home it was only 8 a.m. All the day was at our disposal.

We could go into town and buy paint and wallpaper for the kitchen. We'd have to redecorate it and the wet weather was an opportunity we ought not to miss. I'd decided to paper with anaglypta so that all future activity would only need a paint brush. We are motivated, due to age, to make things easier saying frequently that whatever we do now must have the quality to last our lifetime. We went into town with a long list which we did not complete because I suggested that it might just be an idea, to call at our carpet warehouse and investigate a carpet square for our front room. We had re-laid the twenty-one year old one after the stove installation. Calves are a priority in November and we had frequently wondered when to tackle the carpet's removal and with what should we replace it.

I feared we would have a problem and fought shy of changing the colour scheme and the many new curtains and covers that it would require. The wrong colour would maybe mean a new suite. Ours was old but comfortable. The last thing we wanted was one of the huge, modern ones always advertised half price, on the screen. We were perfectly happy with everything except the carpet and feared that to buy the right one for the job, would be difficult. However we were determined to expose the long hidden flags beneath it. Any rug had to be in keeping with the beamed and mullioned room and sit comfortably on a stone flagged floor.

'We could just go and look!' I said. 'We don't need to buy but we could see what choice is available.' There was no choice. With the advent of imitation wooden floors there was an assortment of big rugs with modern geometric shapes and unattractive colours. The proprietor of the warehouse knows us well and told us of a friend up the dale who had a stock of large mats.

He picked up the phone and called his colleague. 'I've two young ladies here wanting a busy rug.' He couldn't have described it better. A multi-coloured, patterned, antique looking, heavy carpet square, was what we needed. The man answered that he might be able to satisfy us and, having so much unexpected time on our hands, we decided to drive up the valley and investigate.

This firm certainly had scores of rugs, most of them were of modern design but amongst them Margaret uncovered one, discontinued and with a SALE tag because of it's old fashioned design and colour. It was absolutely the right carpet for our five hundred year old sitting room. It was busy enough to camouflage the ravages of a farming winter, heavy enough to sit without movement. I had neither enough money in my purse nor my cheque book and we certainly were not ready to have it delivered. We could not let it go, so I put all I had in my purse, as a deposit and secured it.

The colleague of our carpet man was an extremely handsome, courteous man. He looked at us with interest. Then, 'You've been here before,' he said.

'No,' we assured him but we might come again when you seem to have just what we need!'

He persisted in saying he had seen us before and suddenly his eyes were shining. 'I saw you on television,' he said. That was ten months ago. Are we so odd as to be unforgettable? Our laughter was infectious. He and we and the lady assistant were all laughing. It was good for the soul when Noah's Ark was the only safe refuge.

Then, revitalised, we went to the wallpaper shop and bought what we required on our account. Then we went home with an empty purse preventing us from buying anything more.

We could not begin until the friend of a friend, who was occupying Auntie Mary's room, went home on the Monday morning. Then we lost no time and began the moment she left. We knew that in six days a college colleague was bringing a friend and our kitchen must be finished at speed.

We have been known for this for a lifetime, but we are not so agile at climbing ladders as we were. We have the advantage of large rooms so that furniture can take centre stage and we can work round it The eight foot table meant I could paste the paper without kneeling. Margaret was a slave driver, insisting that with a beautifully clean kitchen/dining room, we could not possibly have a less immaculate utility room so she painted that. She continued into the downstairs toilet and sent me into the front porch. We were crazy. The Crooks thought we were demented and that we would eventually drop. We told everyone that to get a job done quickly you must have guests expected at the weekend. Then you have to make the dust fly. You have no alternative but to rise early, go to bed late and eat little!

On Friday the six o'clock news sent us into panic. With the depressed tourist trade sliding further and further into the Slough of Despond, a new alarm caused the Government to get off its backside as never before. Foot and Mouth disease was spotted and confirmed at a farm in Surrey, near to Pirbright. The Government controlled experimental laboratory is there and Foot and Mouth viruses and vaccines were being experimented upon! From that very moment, the finger of suspicion was pointed at Pirbright. Memories of 2001 scared the living daylights out of every farmer in the country. Instantly all animal movement was stopped and all markets closed. The year was proving to be a total disaster. The hot summer forecast was miserably wet and cold. Thousands were living rough, in caravans and whatever alternative could be found. Fields and crops had been ruined. Tourists either braved airport security and went abroad or stayed at home. And to crown it all there was a Foot and Mouth outbreak, and then another adjacent to the first. Six hundred beautiful animals were killed and their owners were shedding tears of pain and anger. There was little doubt, this time, as to whose fault it was! The virus was identified as a Pirbright strain. Almost within the hour, restrictions were put in place and every avenue of control accessed. Many farmers had thought blame lay with the Government last time. In 2007 they were sure. Farming had barely made a come back and could not afford a second disaster.

Margaret found a bullock with what appeared to be Lumpy Jaw and we cleverly managed to tempt him to the gate and administer medication but when she later found one slobbering from some mouth wound we brought it home and reported it to the lady vet.

'I'm sure it's not Foot and Mouth,' Margaret told her, 'but a man was walking by and saw me. Goodness knows what rumour he might be spreading in the village!'

'Come down to the surgery. I'll give you something. It won't be Foot and Mouth,' said the expert and it wasn't but the man walking our pastures had to be appeased.

Our mega-decorating stunt over, the arrival of Barbara and Lillian meant we could legitimately sit and talk at length and stroll again, leisurely round the lake in St Ives, We could sit outside the newly opened cafe, eating cream cake destined to increase weight alarmingly. Fortunately activity keeps us slim. We are masters of role change, wearing a different 'hat' frequently. Because we try not to work whilst callers come, perhaps our friends think we do nothing but laze about.

Margaret had become increasingly worried about the twenty foot hand-rail on the wheelchair ramp. Many years ago Fell Lane Chapel had closed and we had been given the Communion Rail. No-one had wanted it. It had looked rather splendid for a long time. Sadly it had been made of softwood for indoor use and the seasons' elements had weakened it over the years. To lean on it, Margaret declared, would result in an accident. The rotted wood was all sodden. Everything was wet in the summer of 2007!

Our friends left, taking with them the brief spell of good weather which had given the farmers their much needed opportunity to harvest some of their meadows. Suddenly the mowing and reaping was halted and Tim and

Graham came and took down the rotten rail. They built up the wall and cemented in it, a stout metal rail which will last longer than we will. Another job done for life!

There was a family group in the B&B area we now refer to as The Barn, for such it was for four and a half centuries. They were concerned, as we were, about our little Codger who never grew. We used to lie about his age. He was approaching twelve months old and was the size of a month old. All summer he had eaten enough, and chewed his cud enough, to be a normal size but he didn't grow. The vet had said those with BVD never live but Codger had tried hard to do so. With the advent of August he began to go down hill and walkers and guests noticed this. He climbed his last visit to the summit of the road, sat there all afternoon and came home to the sanctuary of the shed. His breathing became audible and Margaret had to tell our guests that he was ill and later that he had died. We hide sudden death from those on holiday, if we can at all, but in this case to do so was unavoidable.

'The little calf died,' Margaret told the Grandmother of the group.

'Oh dear,' said the old lady. 'Have you had one die before?'

'Yes,' said my grieving sister. No more. To me she complained, 'They haven't a clue. No-one knows anything about real life these days!'

The blessing, during this strange summer, was that all our premises housed self-catering guests, albeit naive ones. Aunty Mary's room kept being used in an emergency B&B but, all in all, we felt a freedom which was necessary if we were to get a few major jobs behind us. Whilst the men were walling in the yard, Margaret and I took up the sitting room carpet and exposed the long hidden flags, scrubbing them with ammonia and caustic soda before sealing them. On the Friday afternoon the carpet was delivered shortly before three bed-and-breakfast guests arrived. They were regular visitors, for whom we had promised accommodation for one night, up our family stairs. Next morning, before they appeared for breakfast at the kitchen table, the new carpet had been laid and the newly washed curtains hung. Phew! I repeat, if you really want to get a big job done quickly you arrange for weekend guests for whom you MUST be ready!

Miraculously the dreaded Foot and Mouth was being controlled but markets were not being opened and the Friday of the first day we had hoped to sell, came and went putting our autumn holiday in jeopardy.

We had booked our Aberporth Dolphin Cottage for a week in October. If we hadn't sold all our eighteen month old stores we would have to cancel. To return to Wales had been Margaret's idea. To do so after a seven year gap would suit me also. We began to look forward to this autumn break with increasing anticipation and the Foot and Mouth incident cast an unwelcome doubt. This disease had been the reason we had had to cancel a planned one in Aberporth in 2001.

Dolphin Cottage Aberporth.

The end of August brought the annual arrival of the group we identify as, The Gang and our yearly opportunity to prove that we can still do large group evening meals for friends. We no longer have one to prove that we can cope with seven days of massive dishwashing, for the lady guests roll up their sleeves and help.

One founder member of the group was missing. It would have been his twenty-second year, his wife Joan wrote in the Visitors' Book. Sadly Patrick had died in the Spring. His whole family came and his ashes were scattered on the wind, in The Five Acre, below the house. A circle of inquisitive calves joined the mourners. Their presence was quite moving. We had feared that, without Patrick's unique humour, the house party would be rather sombre but his spirit, always vibrant, was still alive amongst us and will remain so.

Having identified the source of the Foot and Mouth outbreak and controlled it, bans on movement were suddenly lifted so we were able to round up our lovely animals, sort out the first twenty-six for sale and show them at the first autumn market, in Otley, on the 7th of September. We did it easily, without incident and were happy with the price which we had feared might drop out of control. We had expected the market might be bulging with animals but there were fewer than normal. We had an early draw and left the ring with plenty of time to visit Olga, our eighty-five year old friend, who used to spend the summer in a caravan on Horgabost beach. She makes delicious meals and will never agree when we suggest a cup of tea will be ample.

But the window of opportunity to sell lasted a few days only. On the 12th September, we were enjoying a relaxing cup of tea, at Dorothy's in Bingley, viewing her newly decorated kitchen, and were unaware that news was being circulated of another Foot and Mouth outbreak, near Pirbright. Our phone was ringing madly as we re-entered the house. Lifting it I heard a recorded voice from Defra telling us the ban had been imposed again, immediately.

Sheep already in the market could not be sold and were being sent home. What a mess we were all in. The very future of the markets hung in the balance. All, however was not lost for us. Towards the end of the fortnight which separates sales, the government decided that farm to farm sales could be allowed, in the north of the country. We had booked twenty six animals in for sale. The auctioneer rang to offer us the possibility of by-passing the market and, on the 20th September, came to see all fifty we still had for sale. He was satisfied he had a buyer and promised to come at the beginning of the following week and on the 21st we had an experience we dare not, ever again, repeat. Asked to do so our answer would be a definite, 'No. Sorry but no!' even though no harm came of it other than severely frayed nerves. This for a multitude of reasons, not least the anxiety over the Foot and Mouth scare and the imminent, unusual way we were about to attempt to complete our autumn sales.

Preferably we wish to be in control and in this case we were not even remotely so. This is too often the case nowadays when so much of our trade is in self-catering and success is in the hands of others. So too, are electrical appliances, Christmas tree lights, open fires, children and dogs. Having given away the key of our property, we have to cross our fingers that all is well and hope that the weekly tested Fire Alarm still works.

Possibly we could be labelled control freaks, Margaret as a farmer and me as a headteacher/Guider. Margaret can hang on to her stockman role but I have to relinquish mine and it is scary. I have to stand by and allow others to choose how they celebrate, (even if it means Chinese Takeaways). I have to tolerate an accumulation of empty wine bottles and take them shyly to the household tip, though we do not drink. I often yearn for the era slipping away, when I could impose tidiness, daily re-make beds, choose the menu and serve it my way, like a proper traditional B&B landlady. I must be grateful that I do not have to and admit that, having added years onto my shoulders, worked too hard and too long, to do so would not be possible. But it was safe.

Margaret yearns for the days of small bales and no dependence on the Kramer, which is equally unavoidable. Not all to do with age and injury. With modern mechanisation has come increased dependence on energy from outside. When you can't mend the car, or the roof because it is too high, or service the milk feeders or re-fill the mangers in the bullock sheds, there is inevitably, a modern day stress.

We must just welcome the benefits, and go the direction our controlling wind blows. Nothing comes without a price. We could return to independency by down-sizing but, as Grandmother Smith used to say, 'You are what you are and you can't be any are-er,' and that is not an option.

Chapter Nineteen

A little while, a little while,
The weary task is put away,
And I can sing and I can smile,
Alike, while I have holiday.

Emily Bronte

O UR MEMORY OF THE WEEKEND of the 21st 22nd and 23rd of
September will remain alive not just because it warrants a mention in
this now over full collection of anecdotes and jeopardised, even more, our
holiday just a fortnight away. Mostly it is because it was definitely one of
those 'tales of the unexpected' which pepper our calendar. We had phoned
Jan, in Aberporth, saying Foot and Mouth may put a spoke in our wheel
again, never suspecting that there might be a different potential calamity
on the horizon. This one was spectacular and will remain unique because,
hereafter we will say, 'No!'

It began with a normal, August enquiry from a husband wishing to
celebrate his wife's fiftieth birthday. There was nothing unusual about that
or the fact that the weekend he wanted was the only vacancy in September.
That happens often. Coincidence, miracle, magic, you can call it what
you like. Could he book all the accommodation, all three units? Could he
erect a marquee? That is when things began to cross over the boundary of
normality.

They were a local couple living less than ten miles away. It being Sunday I
suggested they would have to make a visit and they quickly appeared on our
doorstep. They were happy about the indoor space. They would arrive on
the Friday and celebrate on the Saturday. Being local they would have more
guests than usual, hence the wish to erect a marquee. The man measured
the paddock behind the house but his eyes drifted to the sheds and barn.
That is when we first began to fear things were getting out of hand. We felt
reasonably safe for two sheds still had manure and bedding had been laid in
anticipation of the expected cattle sales. The barn housed the Kramer and free-
standing mangers and the feeding bay was the summer residence of BERTIE
the miniature bus, owned by the Rotary Club. It attends all local Galas, giving
children rides and earning money for charities in the area.

It would have to be the marquee, we said but the man had smelled
opportunity and wanted to look and when he did we could see delight and

anticipation ignite a flame we were not going to be able to put out. There was no holding him back. They were such a nice couple and we learned that staging celebrations was the man's profession. His company, 'Raising the Roof', was responsible for grand occasions in the city. Machinery could be moved out, BERTIE taken to the calf shed, and the floor swept by his men. It was getting wildly out of hand and that was only the beginning.

We were, however, at a disadvantage in the argument. We had been there before and we had been the ones wearing the moccasins. How many times had we begged the use of Calum's barn? How many times had we converted his space into one suitable for a céilidh? How often have we said we would leave everything as we found it after a barn dance?

I think however, that if the party had been for today's teenagers we would have been beyond persuasion but this was for middle-aged professionals we could presume to be responsible They were local people, employed frequently by the Metropolitan Council so we said yes and at the end of the month wished we had said nay.

Within days of taking his deposit, the announcement of Foot and Mouth disease had petrified the nation. The fiftieth birthday party was temporarily forgotten and all was confusion.

Meanwhile organisation on a grand scale was being nurtured by those planning lighter entertainment. They had decided to bring false flooring for the barn and, during the week leading up to the finale, they successfully transformed the barn into a dance hall. They curtained all the high level Yorkshire boarding and hung fairy lights everywhere. The visit of the auctioneer on the Thursday went unnoticed by the Party workforce. A massive lorry and crane was installing a generator, in the very loading pen we needed for the shipment of cattle, to North Stainley, should Tuesday's buyer be satisfied.

Our load of small bale straw was being dismantled to provide seating and tables for a bar in the feeding bay. A stage was levelled on the straw for the expected musicians and we were helpless to do anything but panic. Only the collecting of the big animals for sale the following week, remained our responsibility. Everything else was in the hands of the auctioneer and the entertainment organisers.

If the buyer wanted our cattle he would not hesitate to remove them immediately, before DEFRA imposed any more restrictions. Conversion in the barn had taken a week and would take a similar amount of time to reinstate. So often have we repeated the catch phrase of Laurel and Hardy and this was a bonnie fine pickle we had got ourselves into. There was nothing we could do to prevent the incoming tide of events. Nothing at all!

An awning appeared outside the feeding bay. The manger separating it from the barn, had been dismantled and steps brought to assist those wishing to use the bar. Oh Golly, and we, at The Currer do not drink! What was the most spectacular of all was a blue, polystyrene Pegasus standing at least

BERTIE, Dennis and Lucie.

fourteen feet high, enormously winged and perched on the hill at the entrance to the farmyard. It began to attract villagers with children and cameras.

From our mullions we have a wide view of the land. Our cattle can occupy many acres and be within sight but we cannot see what is happening in our stockyard, unless we specifically go there, and that we did not do, it being the case of 'what the eye doesn't see'. And, regrettably, we did not take photographs so cannot now produce visual evidence. We rear cattle not Pegasus monsters, rearing on hind legs, wings lifted ready to fly! A herd count by Land Rover took us up the road so we did see the two enormous tigers, roaring a welcome to walkers, of which there appeared more than usual. To 'come an' look' was a day out for the villagers whilst we stayed indoors, trembling in front of a television we were not watching!

For this extraordinary weekend we were totally unprepared and our time schedule was as tight as it has ever been. A holiday seemed most improbable. 'You'll come and join the festivities,' the gracious, competent organiser said.

'Not on your life!' we replied. Are we really as unsociable as that? Not really. As the cars began to arrive and guests to flock round our door we greeted them as always and invited them into our kitchen. They were professionals from every field. Education, medicine, art. They were colourfully dressed, well spoken, happy. They had active well mannered children. They also had a whole village of tents in the paddock and cars and dormobiles lined the quarter of a mile of road.

Were we scared? We were petrified. One dropped match, one thrown away cigarette-end and straw would be ablaze. It only needed one careless person in what looked like being 150 people and all we have ever worked for would disappear in smoke and flames.

Barbara Sherriff rang for some forgotten reason and I alarmed her so much, with my fears that she rang early next morning to see if we had survived. What happened in that floodlit barn, what joy there was, what music, what song and dance I cannot share with you because we never went near.

All night long the festivities continued. Margaret came to bed well after midnight and I got up at 3 a.m., unable to sleep. A constant flow of merry-makers came up to the house where the only toilets were. They chattered happily and banged doors so much I crawled out of bed and took sanctuary in our sitting room, curled up in an armchair, tense and unable to sleep.

Dawn brought the awareness that all was well and morning the reassurance that all was about to be left intact. Those in tents were competent. It was a performance to equal the best. Everyone was tired, but happy. They left not one piece of litter and deserved applause. The organisation had been superb and we are ashamed of our doubts and fears and make our public apology in this paragraph as we greet their success with profound relief.

Would we do it again? No. We are farmers. Our barns are for housing cattle and storing fodder and life is stressful enough without taking unnecessary risks but, not for one moment do we regret that one experience of meeting those responsible, happy revellers.

All was well, one hurdle leapt. Now all that was needed was the successful sale of our remaining fifty stores. The auctioneer arrived on Tuesday bringing the prospective buyer and we walked, fairly confidently, among the herd. We had good animals and we were all in a predicament together, we the vendors, he the buyer. We had to agree amicably for farming practise to continue. Walking round the lovely cattle, we were unaware that there was suddenly another spoke in the wheel. Even as we all chatted together, a new disease was being identified. Blue Tongue, spread unbelievably by midges! What defence have we against them? A system of Zoning was introduced, restricting further movement of animals but which did not affect us yet.

Having come to an agreement, it was essential the cattle were transported to North Stainley as quickly as possible before anything else should happen. The buyer said he would organise two transporters to come on Thursday. Surely by then the party workforce would have finished dismantling the floor and stage, re-stacked the straw bales, removed the generator and the sculptured Pegasus and Tigers. They would have to complete the operation, though they worked overnight. The removal of the generator, in time, was the most scary. It was a tight fit in the loadening pen and it was, with bated breath, that we watched the enormous crane heave it cleanly up and over and onto the transporter.

One of the workmen asked that the crane would lift Pegasus onto his trailer. The huge, blue animal looked grotesque. Minus his wings, he reared 16 feet into the air and had to be securely guyed to the trailer sides. The driver, taking it back to the city, decided to take the short cut along the road to Harden. The trees in St Ives Estate overhang the road and, on reaching the Bingley junction, the man in the passenger seat turned to look through the rear window and saw a beheaded Pegasus. It was a sad ending to an otherwise extremely happy weekend.

It was now our turn to perform. At some point, during Wednesday, we had to gather everyone of those fifty stores and lock them up safely in the two awaiting bullock sheds. We prayed there would be no rain providing drinking pools. It was essential that the cattle came to the trough for water. Daily, if there is no rain, we see the migration of them trek across the pastures to their water hole. If we open the gate adjacent to the trough they, being interested in the novelty, file through it onto the road and career down to the stockyard and never object to entering winter quarters even though it be summer.

On this occasion it was a doddle. Mission completed I sorted out the passports and paperwork and Margaret alerted Tim to be here early to help with the loading. We were on a roller coaster but things were going without a hitch. How dare we ever say that?

Mark, our straw haulier from the Vale of York, rang to say he would be delivering a load around noon. Margaret told him we had cattle being moved, two loads early, the final load after lunch.

'That's OK,' he said. 'If I'm there at the same time, I'll help.'

The next morning, early, the two cattle wagons came and one was an articulated monster. Our stockyard is big and turning space more than adequate for corn tankers, massive straw and hay deliveries, giant tractors and plant but an articulated vehicle is in a class of its own.

Of the fifty cattle to move we had thirty three ready to load in the first shed and seventeen in the adjacent one. They had all spent a comfortable night and were eager for morning release. Fifteen went easily into the first lorry and twenty were needed for the monster. This meant it was necessary to transfer two from the sister shed leaving fifteen for the return of the smaller vehicle in the afternoon.

We had an audience. The seventy strong, yearling herd had gathered at the stockyard exit gate and were watching with interest, these unusual antics, from the gallery. Cattle are the most curious of all animals.

A transfer of two is a job which always should be left to Margaret. I have known her select and re-locate without any help at all. It is essential that you do this manoeuvre via the small eastern doors. The very last thing you do is open the twelve foot western gate on seventeen big bullocks wanting breakfast. Before we could prevent him, one man had done just that. There was a bovine tide, a tsunami towards the five foot high exit gate. Two animals cleared it immediately and mingled with their younger relatives, whilst we all scrambled up the slope to turn back the fifteen and chase all of them into the loading shed.

The watching audience was more than happy to file into the stockyard, when Margaret opened the gate, bringing with them the two high flyers and perfectly happy to flow into the empty shed, all seventy two of them. The shed door securely fastened and the men, embarrassed by the fiasco keeping well away, Margaret brought out the two bullocks for sale, from the eastern door and transferred them without stress.

It was then the turn of the ladies to keep out of the way whilst the men attempted to turn the articulated monster and get it's nose facing in the right direction for re-climbing the road out.

We could not leave so many animals in the shed but we snatched an opportunity to restrain one due for a veterinary TT test. Defra had, again, sent us instructions to have one stirk tested as tuberculosis had been discovered in the herd from which we had bought it, last November. The 6th of October was the deadline. Without any effort we suddenly found we had the required animal trapped. We restrained it with two or three companions and sent for the vet. Every cloud has a silver lining. The tiny group had to stay indoors for the return of the vet, three days later, to check that the animal was clear. They were not amused.

The men were not having a similar success. It took two hours, three men, a tractor and a hawser to turn that mechanical beast and most of the time Mark had to sit in his cab on the lay-by on the top road, unable to approach with his load of straw. At last there was success but, on reaching the summit the driver could not turn right, over the cattle grid and on to the road. Instead he had to reverse all the way down to the crossroads.

It was far too late for the smaller wagon to return that day and fifteen animals had to spend another night indoors. Next morning the collection went without stress and I phoned Jan, in Aberporth.

'We're coming,' I said, 'See you a week tomorrow.'

The next day was Saturday and we hurried to the railway station to buy tickets for Wales. The man in the ticket kiosk was having difficulty sorting out our route and the lady assistant came and took over.

Which one of you was the Guide Captain?' she asked. She had been too young, when I retired from Guiding but four of her older sisters had been with us to the Hebrides. The stress of the past weeks dropped willingly from our shoulders. She organised everything for us. We would have to go via Carmarthan because of work on the Aberystwyth line and no dogs were allowed on the shuttle bus ferrying passengers!

There was currently work on the Skipton line and the forecourt of our station was full of passenger carrying buses. Amid this confusion we were stopped by the handsome son of Julia, from Bucken and immediately

Barbara Sherriff's husband, Arnold came to put an arm round each of us. We are singularly blessed. Wherever we are, we are cared for.

Dorothy's daughter was going to Spain and leaving her in charge of her pedigree pack of show collies so Helen and Chris were taking her place.

Suddenly we had to move with speed to prepare for holiday and I began to be nervous, unnecessarily, about the journey to Carmarthan.

This coming holiday, we had fully expected to be cancelled and preparations for it had to be squeezed into seven short days. Our yearling herd had to be introduced to the upper pastures. Normally we did this after the second sale, Margaret believing that the remaining two year olds could teach them new tricks of where and when to find gateways and shelter. Having been deprived of a third sale, everything had to happen at once and the new, younger occupants had to teach themselves the way to the waterholes.

We were leaving behind an ailing animal. When you have many there is nearly always one causing concern. 'Little cattle, Little care,' has proved to be the case down the ages. This sick animal had been one of the two pneumonia cases of the spring turn-out. One was now a healthy, normal sized bullock but the other was a frail little fellow with badly damaged lungs. Margaret hates leaving ailing animals when we go on holiday but termination is rarely discussed and only used in extreme cases when pain and suffering cannot be prevented.

The stirk currently causing anxiety, grazed with two healthy companions, up the roadway. He must have heard us talking about our coming holiday and decided that heaven would be a better place if Margaret was not going to be here. He sat down on the tarmac determined to die. Margaret found it blocking the road and came running to me. It was a poorly grown animal but nearly one year old and to die on the road must be prevented if at all possible. We couldn't make it stand so I ran for an old square of carpet on which we intended to roll it and drag it onto the roadside. Nothing was possible. To struggle would have been to cause it stress and that we always avoid. The animal had to stay there and await a quick visit of the fallen stock removal van. So we were leaving no problems behind. We were grateful to the only sick member of our herd for choosing to die before we left rather than waiting until we were away.

There was an over-riding feeling that we were really meant to go on this particular holiday. There were too many disappearing stumbling blocks to believe otherwise. But first there was a change over of guests and all that that entails.

The down side of this job we got ourselves into, twenty eight years ago is the massive amount of cleaning and laundering we have to do. On the plus side is the opportunity, most elderly people welcome, to meet old acquaintances and talk about what has become history. I had one such during the middle of the week prior to leaving for Wales.

Simultaneously with the ending of World War Two, I was choosing my Fifth Form subjects for the School Certificate of the day. I chose Additional Maths and found myself in a group of only four. To be in such a small group can be beneficial but can also be embarrassing if the other three are very intelligent and you are only mediocre. The brightest girl in the year chose as I did. She was nicknamed Swot Maude, which was unfair because she was so clever she did not need to revise. After our entry into the Sixth Form, her parents emigrated to Salt Lake City, in America and I heard no more of her.

More than sixty years later she, with her brother and daughter, booked three days Bed and Breakfast at The Currer. It was wonderful. I stole too much time, talking time, remembering school days time. There was masses to do prior to our weekend departure.

She and her family were followed, on Friday, by the large group we were to leave in the care of Helen and Chris, next morning when we left for Wales.

Had this re-visit, to a place we had enjoyed for so many years with Harry, not been meant to be, an incident in Leeds Station would have put a final end to it! I accept all responsibility. I won't put blame on the current work being done on the track making us miss the train which would have given us more time for the Leeds changeover. Trains to Leeds are frequent and the next one meant we had to hurry, for the Manchester train necessitated crossing the line by bridge.

How stupid can you get? I tried to take Sam up the escalator. I should have known it would cause disaster. I went, he didn't and I fell flat on my face. The elevator tried to take me up feet first and Sam, on his lead, prevented any such thing. A man ran to stop the movement and two hoisted me onto my feet. It was cartoon quality. Margaret ran for a uniformed railway worker but all he wanted to do was to have me come and sign an accident form and there was no time. It was a helpful young lady who pushed us and dogs into a lift and pressed all the buttons and it was our Guardian Angel who held up the train.

It was crowded to standing room only. Somewhere there were our reserved seats but we were beyond looking for them. I sat on one vacated for me by a considerate youth. It was a pull down one right outside the loo for the disabled and Margaret perched on her too small rucksack, in the wheelchair space all the way to Manchester!

I began to conclude that I had not broken my arms, just given them a severe shock. We were apprehensive about our next changeover but found our Carmarthan train left from an adjacent platform and that there was a seat to sit on whilst we waited.

We are so out of our element in any city. We even look furtive. We feel as if we have stepped from a time machine. The clothes people are wearing seem different. As if they have put underwear over top wear like six year old Jill used to do, or visited the school rummage sale the evening before imitating Roddy all those long, lovely years ago. There was no longer evidence of class, none of the Designer clothes everyone seems to talk about. There seemed to be no average. Either you dressed like a Joker from a travelling circus or as if you were going to a funeral. We saw no lovely summer dresses, no-one dressed for Wimbledon.

Leaving Aberporth in 2000 we had even booked our return for the following year. Harry and Aunty Mary had loved it as much as we had. In 1999 we had been the last to occupy The Cedars before it was demolished and we had watched the foundations of Dolphin Cottage being dug on the other side of the driveway. This delightful bungalow had been our interpretation of near perfect. Only its elevation caused a problem and the difficulty of pushing the wheelchair up from the beach was easily forgotten when it provided such a wonderful vista of Cardigan Bay.

We have missed so few holidays, but the 2001 was one of them. If Foot and Mouth had not cancelled that, Harry's October death would have done so and this was our first re-visit and it was a joy. It had been Margaret's request and fulfilled all expectations. So close to the sandy beach and sea it is an ideal place for dogs and St Luke's Little Summer was all it could be expected. It is such a safe and friendly environment and this has been a prerequisite for most of our holidays. The safety of children, the suitability for the elderly and disabled had been our first concern yet no-one believed we had achieved that by taking children so far, to such remoteness or wheelchairs on boats and beaches. We had even been thought to be foolhardy when 'Cautious' is our middle name. It has been believed that in remoteness we have avoided people when the truth has always been that the local people have been our security.

Without children or family it still felt comfortably safe to be once more in Dolphin Cottage and on the beach, a haven for dogs with friendly owners. We had spent eight previous holidays in Aberporth, we had good friends, no traffic problem and a village shop on the other side of the miniature bay. We felt immediately at home.

We found that buses took two dogs, that The Rocket could take us to Poppit Sands and Newport beach in the morning and return us in the afternoon and the lovely weather allowed this so that rainwear was never needed. We enjoyed Jan and Tony, our hosts and Eveline and Geoffrey Gibbings our resident neighbours and the holiday-makers across the driveway. We were able to invite Sylvia and Henry Haywood to have afternoon tea with us as we so often had. Until their removal from Kent to Haverfordwest, they had been frequent holidaymakers in the Mistal Cottage.

News from home was without trauma for Helen and Chris.

'Let's stay here,' we said. The Currer, though we love it, can be a nightmare. Those who cannot be bothered with holidays don't lead the life we do. Would we return to Aberporth? God willing, of course we will.

Chapter Twenty

It is sometimes necessary to look back,
to move forward.

IF THERE HAD BEEN TIME, in mid-October, when we returned from Wales, I would have been writing this instead of just working with a head full of memories. Is it never to be that I have time to write at the appropriate moments? I have to wait for dawn to come late and morning chores be delayed by darkness. Last century I wrote whilst on holiday. Not now. Holiday must be a rest time.

Returning from Wales it was Merry Bells, or so I would have described it, sixty years ago, when we were in college and that was the jargon of the day. I am not acquainted with the present vocabulary. Only adults speak clearly. The children of this era should have elocution lessons, for their speech is little more than gibberish.

If there had been a suitable pause to wield my pen, it would have been taking me down memory lane to the year 1957, fifty years ago and to my father's dilemma. He had needed to come to a decision about the way ahead.

*Harry,
Father and Mother,
fifty years ago.*

Me, fifty years ago.

Margaret, fifty years ago.

His situation had been precarious for many reasons. On the death of his father, six years earlier, he had taken over the business. His brother had not wanted to farm but they had not inherited the property jointly until their mother died in 1956. Their inheritance had been two properties. The home farm, High Fold, with a liveable farmhouse, several buildings, and 10 acres of land, some of which were suitable for building. Then there was The Currer, 170 acres, half of which was moorland, and a ruined, 500 year old house and barn. There had also been a four figure overdraft which Father had shouldered and which was presently crippling progress.

Alone he had debated possible ways of survival which didn't involve selling and finding an income elsewhere. The only alternative was to sell his only asset, the family home and remove everyone to his mother's house, High Fold or to the ruin standing on the larger property. If he could persuade his brother to agree, perhaps the two properties could be divided, leaving him with the greater acreage but no buildings or habitable house. The two brothers had never worked amicably. Uncle, the elder, had re-married and lived in town but he was a partner in ownership and his consent was crucial.

There was too much of Grandfather Brown in Uncle Percy's character to expect him to want to sell property and to do so was the last thing my father would ever consider. He had two very important people to think about. Our handicapped brother Harry needed the farm for work and interest and Margaret did not even think of any other career. She was eighteen years old but already dedicated to Father's profession. A solution had to be found.

Without voicing his fears to his family, Father had toured both abandoned farmhouses. His mother's house had been empty since she had come to live with us in 1954. The house at The Currer was a window-less ruin without road, sanitation, water or electricity. There were no farm buildings other than a fairly useless barn, nowhere to house animals and the least likely place to bring a sixty one year old wife and a handicapped son.

It had crossed his mind that he might suggest, to his brother that the property be divided and each go his own way amicably. His wife must be consulted first. She was the more important and the house at The Currer was nothing more than a shell, a hovel through which the wind could blow continuously.

So, in a moment of privacy he had said to her, 'We can't go on. We'll hev t' sell t' 'ouse an' go int' mi mother's or go T' Currer.'

And she had replied, 'I'm noan goin' t' yer mother's. We'll go t' T' Currer!'

It had been what he wanted but had not expected. He had been confident of his daughters' interest but not his wife's. It was probably the first time he had ever asked her consent and she had said, 'Yes.' He was flabbergasted. I know he had never asked her to marry him. She told me so.

The Currer, 1957.

He had been confident then and had known the answer. The question had not ever been needed. This one had and her willing approval changed our lives completely. Uncle's equally unexpected agreement followed and here we have been ever since. An aunt on mother's side said no man would take her there, but mother defended her corner and became queen of a kingdom now covenanted in perpetuity. A friend said, 'It will take you five years to perfect that!!' We haven't reached that, even after fifty.

There now, it didn't take long but there wasn't even that length of time in October. I was greeted with a pile of post. A letter from the Ministry Vet said we hadn't complied with TB regulations and had our calf tested so we were not allowed any movement of cattle, so we phoned our vet who said he had posted the negative result. Aware that there had been a recent postal strike, we phoned the sender but it did not prevent his secretary sending another letter. Our vet's report had still not been received. Presumably the strike had disrupted things but had not lost another letter in the pile awaiting my return.

This was from the Rural Payments Agency. Word for word it was identical to a letter I had received from them twelve months ago. It, like its predecessor, said another farmer was also claiming Single Payment on fields for which I had made a claim. It had taken two months, many phone calls and the appointment of a personal consultant, to prove those six fields were on our land! I was not amused. Eventually two letters came, re the two discrepancies, one from the MV and one from the RPA, without apologies but admitting that I was right. Nobody ever says sorry these days. Margaret queries the possibility that men never did!

We had entertainment, however, in the arrival of six female members of the same family, from America, in search of their family history. They were the most boisterous party we have ever catered for, women re-uniting, on holiday, in the UK, searching for common ancestry, noisily vocal and as happy as Larry. They exhausted themselves and me. Fortunately they were out for the day when Diana came to the fence to tell us she was in labour with her ninth calf and to ask us to do something about it?

We did try but had to send for the vet who described her as, 'Too posh to push!' This amused two long time friends, staying a few days at Skipton Travel Lodge. Angie and Ian are both in wheelchairs after separate road accidents many years ago. They stayed at The Currer every year for two decades and hope to be able to do so again. They spent the whole day with us and it was like re-uniting with family. Indeed these twenty eight years of serviced accommodation have swollen our family to mega proportions. Sometimes it feels completely out of hand when I'm trying to find time to phone a Guide or pupil, friend or guest, bereft after losing a loved one, personally suffering from illness or recovering from an operation. Margaret is constantly saying, 'Have you written, have you sent, have you phoned?' and every week guests add themselves to our list! They all become special but Angie and Ian belong to the Most Special category.

We had to do some urgent shopping. Something I needed necessitated a visit to The Cavendish Market and I accidentally walked swiftly into a solid pane of glass I mistook for an open door. I thought my bleeding forehead was the only damage. Someone who knew me, though I could not return the compliment, stopped me on the kerb and mopped up the flow of red with a tissue with which I had not come prepared.

I seemed to be walking very badly, my shoe appeared to be too tight. My first job on entering the house is to slip off my shoes but on this occasion a car was following us into the yard. A couple from Rotherham, on a day out, had been determined to find us. They'd read my books and wanted to meet us. So the hurting foot was never investigated and the kettle put on the Aga without shedding footwear. The grimace and the hobble went unnoticed by the excited couple to whom we fed coffee and biscuits and who would have stayed longer had we not booked the Range Rover's MOT test at Simmonites in Thornton.

I was limping badly as we both went into Reception. The owner, David Simmonite had recently been tragically killed in an off road accident. We were, perhaps, his longest known customers. He had serviced our vehicles for forty years and we had enormous respect for him and his team. We leaned on the office desk for quite some time, talking about him and the awful thing that had happened.

We spent the necessary half-hour wait, walking the dogs round a nearby graveyard. There was a convenient seat. I felt incredibly old and it was not until we returned home and I finally took of my shoe, that I discovered why. My big toe had swollen enormously and my foot was a deep purple. I am recording this because, a few days later I made history by going to the calf market, on a buying expedition, wearing Harry's leather slippers! I must have banged head and toe into the glass panel simultaneously.

That we were able to buy calves at Gisburn was sheer luck. Blue Tongue was disrupting markets. Areas were classified as Clean and Dirty and it depended where you were and where you wished to buy. We didn't really understand more than that we could buy at Gisburn

We bought forty three calves and went home in a hurry for we had to settle them in and introduce as many as possible to the milk teats before the expected 8 p.m. arrival of Denis and his wife and toddler from Rumilly, in France. It was to be his first visit since Harry died. In the years which had followed he had qualified as an engineer, had married another Emilie and their baby, Lucie, had been born. His sister, Emilie and her husband to be, Benois, were to join our House Party a few days later. And we had just bought over forty calves and must top up to seventy in less than a week!

Twenty years had elapsed since first we met the Barbault family, Bernard and Yveline and their children, Denis little more than ten and Emilie seven years younger. When Denis was fourteen he came for the whole of July and August, alone. It was one of the happiest of Harry's summers. Denis related to him better than anyone we have known. His visit was repeated for many years. When Emilie was old enough she too, came alone. They became part of our family.

To have them and their partners could not possibly be difficult even though we were at the very beginning of the season of calf-rearing. Nor was it. Denis and his Emilie were awaiting a second baby in May and our Emilie was also on the threshold of a February wedding. We were all so happy, we for them and they for us.

The biggest delight of all was Lucie, not yet two but as bright as a golden button. It had been so long since we had had the experience of so young a child. Most of the time we were not all in the calf shed, we were sitting mesmerised by her intelligence, the capability of fingers so small and the strength dormant in such little legs allowing her to walk all the way to Druids Altar. We were spellbound. We are not educated regarding two year old little girls. She embraced the calves, goats, donkeys, cats, dogs and fed the ducks. She was as well behaved as her aunty had been a generation earlier.

A week later we went back to the cattle market to top up our calf population with another thirty calves. The Barbaults came with us and I was remembering 1991 when Denis came with us to the Store Market and wanted a calf so much, Margaret bought two and he bottle fed them all summer.

Returning home we found the postman had brought Margaret a letter saying she must go for Jury Service later in the month.

'Not on your life!' she said and wrote a letter we were sure would not be believed. She would soon be in her seventieth year, had just bought seventy three babies, she expected last year's seventy bullocks to need overnight housing any day and she ran a busy holiday accommodation business, without staff other than her seventy seven year old sister. She pleaded that it would be impossible to leave me each day, for as long as it took. Posting it we thought the recipient would say, 'Well that's a new tall story and right!'

Apparently it is we who have an exaggerated opinion of our potential because a reply came back, saying our situation warranted exemption, as if such letters as Margaret's were all in a day's work.

Fifty years ago Mother had answered, 'We'll go t' T' Currer!' when two thirds of her life story had been written. Ours is now well into the final chapters and we are eternally grateful for all the opportunities it has afforded for us, living on the outer rim of society, to meet so many from within. Perhaps what we value most was to meet the Barbault family. When they had grown from children to adults we had thought, perhaps we would not see them again. When they left ten days later, there was a new confidence in the knowledge that we would.

Margaret prepared herself to spend the next five months in the calf shed unaware that the Spring of 2008 would come so late more than six months was nearer the mark. Fortunately the yearlings made no attempt to come home. December was mild and there was still grass. As always the Ministry sent the 210 fourteen digit eartag numbers for us to check. We buy seventy, sell seventy and keep seventy for a second year making a total of over two hundred. Having recently checked those sold in October and those bought in November, to have to do it all again in December, at Christmas time, is infuriating. There was, however, a less awesome task, than previously, concerning the sending of some three hundred Christmas cards. Helen had put all my addresses into her computer and all I had to do was tear off sticky labels. My scorn of the computer is less violent than it was.

In the middle of December, a railway track repair team, working nights, booked four twin bedrooms and the Loft Cottage. They parked huge lorries in the yard with JCBs on trailers. Whatever next? Whilst they were all asleep, one day, the man came to check the fire extinguishers and I sent him away saying, 'For Goodness Sake come in the new year. I can't go and wake up these hard working men!!'

Rather than 'climate change' I lean towards 'season slide'. The 21st of December is no longer the beginning of winter and, though bulbs have begun to grow and buds considered bursting early, all seem to hesitate as winter, when it finally comes, staggers on into late April and May. It is as if the planet has readjusted its balance. Thirty years ago we were bringing cattle indoors in October for grass had ceased to grow. Hay, harvested in our own meadows, had been eaten by Christmas and more supplies had to be bought in. In those days snow may have carpeted our hillside for twelve weeks of the year, but when it melted in March there was grass underneath and Turn Out could be early. We may be getting floods in summer but there is now not enough wetness in winter to suckle roots and nurture grass in spring.

The summer of 2007 had been appalling and harvests ruined, so farmers were glad of December grass. Our cattle spent only one night in before Christmas and thereafter stayed out frequently and only came home when the fancy took them. Eventually we had to shut the gate and enforce a curfew.

One guest said she had heard cattle were getting more dangerous, even as today's teenagers acquire this reputation. For over seventy years I see no change. Ours are as docile as ever. Neighbours who walk dogs among them will agree. I saw no change in my primary school children, my teenage Guides. We experience little change in the friendliness of our guests or the behaviour of their children and their dogs. We hear no swearing. Where there is no change in attitude, or method, you get what you expect. Constant change is harmful. To mend what is not broken is wrong. Certainly the behaviour of our senior herd was beyond reproach and the quality of the August harvest was so poor their objection would have been justified. They ate the overgrown haylage without a grumble and thrived.

If I had been a gambler, I would have put money on there being no white Christmas but that the climax of legal proceedings, appertaining to the purchase of George's land, would come within a few days of it. Does the rest of the world not know that, for us, festivities have to take a back seat whilst Margaret weans calves and houses her yearlings, whilst I thoroughly clean the milk feeders, dry them out in the kitchen and prepare for four groups of those who can celebrate even if it is not possible for us to do so? Oh no! Defra bombards us with extra work and, at the last minute, we are called to sign and pay for the fields we have been renting since 1990 and agreed to buy twelve months ago.

In desperation I asked our Skipton solicitor to come to The Currer and save us half a day when we were at our busiest. The newly bought fields had fancy descriptive names, according to the legal papers, but to us they will always be simply 'George's'. He'd like that. He had only a small farm but, to him, land was important.

Having brought up the male holly for the calf sheds, to deter ringworm, I brought more to 'deck the hall' with its shiny, green boughs. Next year I am going to put conkers on the window ledges, see if they work against spiders as it has been suggested. This old wives' tale may be just as accurate.

We went to the nearby Garden Centre and bought a live tree and brought the artificial ones from the loft above The Loft cottage. Edgar and his wife and disabled daughter, Maria, from Malta, were here to visit the David Hart Clinic. They decorated them with lights and baubles. We had four different groups over the festive period, all frequent occupants. The only decoration in our part of the house was the continuous evening festooning of the kitchen with laundered sheets.

At the last minute, before the first eighteen strong group left, on the day before Christmas Eve, a child was sick all over the bedspread. It was possible to do the panic washing necessary to restore order but we were nervous all Christmas. A nasty bug was prevalent throughout the country and people were asked not to take children as visitors into hospitals. We seem to escape urban diseases of sickness or flu. We don't want either, for our guests or ourselves but whatever had caused the child's sickness was not infectious. Everyone had a lovely Christmas. The Bullocks came for their fifteenth time. Holly, their granddaughter was with them. She had been the only baby to be born here in my living memory. Beulah had not expected a birth until mid-January. Instead we had experienced a Nativity. The Green family were here for their sixth time and the Hodges for New Year were frequent visitors, too.

It is inevitable that I am about to be obsessed with the Fifty Year Mile Stone of 2008. On January 1st I turned the pages of *We'll see the Cuckoo* and read.

* * * * * * * * * * * *

The last day of the year 1957 closed with torrential rain which turned to snow over night and next morning it lay twelve inches deep and persil white. Margaret and Father had shut some yearling heifers in The Currer barn and it was a daily job to go and water them. I decided to accompany Margaret and we planned to spend the day making a start on the house. The first day of 1958 seemed the right moment to begin in earnest. The surface of the snow remained unbroken all the way from the village except for bird and rabbit tracks and the lonely trail, with its brushing of top snow, left by a hunting fox. We had food with us and yard brushes and shovels intending, at least, to sweep out the snow and to clear the debris of broken glass and plaster littering the floor.

Snow lay deep in the parlour. The east wind is a snow bringer and a good depth had been hurled through the gaping windows. We gathered up a pile of splintered, paint flaking wood and put a match to it in the fireplace. The reflection of the flames danced round the room in friendliness. Outside the east window, the sycamore stood almost white against the blue of the sky for the snow clouds had passed and a weak January sun flooded the yard and threw a pattern of mullions against the west wall of the kitchen.

We shovelled out great drifts from below the empty windows and, with stiff yard brushes began to sweep up the mass of shattered glass. The icy, cleansing wind filled the house, ridding it of any smell of human occupation. We blessed the open windows. They did for us what no amount of soap and water could.

With crowbar and sledge hammer we tore out the rotted window frames and doors and stoked up the fire until we could feel the heat. With broad scrapers we began hacking off the layers of whitewash down to the smoothness of the cow hair plaster. Lime is clean and sweet smelling and there was a freshness in the clean white dust.

Neither Margaret nor I can sing very tunefully but on that first day of January we filled our ruin with song, experiencing a new-found freedom. The sun, shining on the snow and decorating the valley with icing sugar, quite literally turned us on. 'Oh what a beautiful morning,' we sang. 'Oh what a beautiful day.' Our repertoire of campfire songs carolled out into the morning followed by all the joyful hymns we knew. 'Glad that I live am I, that the sky is blue.'

We had brought a large tin of soup. Puncturing the lid we set it among the ashes and then sat, drinking it in turns from the can. We sat toasting ourselves on the hearth imagining the new life beginning at The Currer. Looking through the mullions we visualised the many visitors who would come. They would appear round the corner of the stable and take us unawares because the road, which was then just an overgrown cart track, cannot be seen from the house. They would surprise us into action and one of us would greet them at the door and the other try to bring order to whatever chaos reigned at the moment, just like any normal family. We imagined ourselves standing at the door waving farewell and Mother inevitably calling, 'Come again.' It was optimistic imagery, for who would come to this out of the way spot with no road to it and no street lights to guide the way?

We'll see the Cuckoo

* * * * * * * * * * *

Come they did. In their multitudes. Never could we have imagined what has happened between then and now. I asked Canadians, recently, why they enjoyed reading about our goings on.

'Because it is life,' one lady said. 'Your life, our life. Life is more interesting than fiction.' Ours has occupied every hour of every day so that, as yet we have had little time to read fiction.

Perhaps because we were looking back so frequently and so nostalgically, I think we yearned for snow more than ever. To do so was foolish for, advanced in years, it would be more than ever a struggle to cope. But snow is so beautiful and inspires sunshine. The artistry of crystal flakes cannot be surpassed. Colour drains from the hillside in winter and that of 2008 was grey and drab. There seemed to be a perpetual cloud cover. The sun appeared to neither rise nor set. Though February was not a fill dyke one and tractors did not mar the land, even the daffodils were less glamorous than usual. We'd have given anything for a clean, white snowfall and dazzling sunshine.

We had signed documents and written our cheque for George's acres but finalisation did not come until we were four days into the New Year. The solicitor phoned that evening with the awaited word, 'It's yours!' Margaret told her housed cattle that they would graze OUR land in spring but the new fields would, in our life-time, be George's just as Elm Close Wood is Jimmy's. The buying process had taken a year and four days. We contacted The National Trust and set things in motion to have the land added to our Covenancy.

It occurred to me, early in January, that it is impossible to know how lucky you are unless you need it. Near disasters have to be happening all the time or you just don't know. I am sure most people think that it is a negative attitude, requiring an upset apple cart and the arrival of help to pick up the apples. A current television advertisement warns viewers that their luck will run out and that they should take out an insurance. So it may but luck was on our side in January.

Someone from The British Cattle Movement Service phoned Margaret to say Ear Tag Inspectors would call, in two days time, to check all our 140 identification tags. Surely this is an intrusion in January when Epiphany is only hours into history. Margaret put her foot firmly down and said she would not agree to 140 animals being stressed by being individually trapped in the crush. Our babies were too small and our yearlings only just brought from the hill. A calmness reigned and we, old ladies as we brag to be, when the situation warrants and age is a defensive mechanism, were unprepared to create chaos for the sake of yet another ear tag check. I reckon that at least twelve checks of our tag numbers are necessary to satisfy the EU.

The young lady inspector who phoned said, with a confidence which was risky, 'That's alright. We'll just walk among them and do it that way.' I have to admit neither she, nor her assistant, hesitated when confronted with a stockyard of seventy, fifteen month old animals. Had it been my job, with other people's cattle, I would have run a mile. I watched them from a distance, not daring to show my face for the bullocks would have pestered me, eaten my jacket, licked my face. They took no notice of the strangers at all. They stood still whilst they uncovered ear tags lost in hair. I was flabbergasted. We have lovely, lovely animals and the girls were professionals. They said every number was checked correctly and I have no reason to doubt them or think they avoided any monster or over-lively calf.

'All correct.' They beamed and we, who had feared we might have to carry one out on a stretcher, exhaled our bated breath with relief and everyone had a cup of tea. Had there been an accident, we'd have been ill-equipped to deal with it! Had we had to force each animal individually into the crush there could well have been a fiasco. We were more than grateful to those able young women. I have frequently referred to the valley housing the stockyard, as the Vale of Tranquillity. Because of the capability of those female inspectors, peace was maintained there. Whilst I don't approve the system I respect those who have to administer it.

In spite of the poor quality of the overgrown haylage, nobody's fault but the weather at harvest time, the outdoor loving cattle, finally penned in the stockyard, continued to do well and the calves grew by the minute. Margaret decided they had outgrown their space and that some must be re-housed in the yard bullock shed. A delivery of big bale, rectangular straw made this easy. Tim, a professional with his tractor fork lift, barricaded a passage way and fourteen were transferred.

A few days later he was filling the manger in the Top Bullock Shed, with the Kramer and the unexpected noise frightened them so that one calf leapt skywards and landed trapped between the wall and the feed barrier. It was an accident waiting to happen. Had the noise been that of the dustbin collector, helicopter or whatever, we may have lost a calf for it was beyond our strength to lift it out the way it had fallen in. It needed two wallers whose job it is to heave heavy stones to shoulder height. It had been one of those imperfections in the shed which had gone unseen or neglected and it was a blessing the men were here and that the Kramer had caused the fright.

One other imperfection had not gone unnoticed by Margaret but had been unheeded by the builders who, understandably, did not believe her anxiety was justified. Water drains into the duck pond from a trickle appearing from underground, a few metres up an otherwise dry valley. The overflow from the pond travels under the cattle grid, into the drain which disappears under the stockyard to reappear and fall into the beck. During a deluge this trickle, feeding the pond, can suddenly become a cascade. It has to be seen to be believed.

We have long known that our hillside is riddled with water. Our own spring produces gallons every minute and others on the land, are continually weeping. When torrential rain falls it cannot be absorbed and finds the nearest tributary heading for the river. The trickle which feeds the pond can become a tidal wave in minutes. Margaret is so afraid of it, she forks muck to the doorways of the sheds and barn to divert it in a sudden emergency. Men taking out muck, or scraping the yard clean, never put this manure barrier back because they do not believe her prediction or her fear to be justified.

It is! The overflow from the pond can be many times greater than the pipe under the stockyard can take and a twelve foot wide river can cross the concrete. It looks impossible but it is a well proven fact. No man believed Margaret until the 19th of January 2008, when Tim was moving straw in the barn. There was suddenly the most impressive cloud burst I have ever seen. Fortunately, because Tim was working with the tractor, the bullocks had not yet been let into the yard. It was as if sluice gates had been opened. A cascade of water plunged down the supposedly dry valley, overflowed the pond, doubling its ground area, filling the cattle grid a foot above the iron work and spreading across the yard like a bore sweeping across the bay. Terminating in the triangle at the foot of the yard, it was deepening fast and entering the feeding bay.

Tim, already on the spot, already on the tractor, was jerked into immediate action. The south wall of the feeding bay is made of railway sleepers slotted loosely into metal upright posts and, without hesitation, he drove the tractor fork under the bottom sleeper. He lifted one whole ten foot section to allow a waterfall to plunge into the beck. We ran from the calf shed (I'm sure we did though I am normally convinced I no longer can!) We ran in fear knowing all sheds could be flooded but Tim's jerk reaction had averted disaster. The river subsided with the disappearing rain and we sought wedges to preserve the ten foot escape route should anything like that happen again. It will, in this funny climate of extremes. We were shaking our heads in wonder at the knowledge that Tim, tractor and knee jerk were all there, in the right place at the right time. The stockyard was as clean as it was when the concrete was first laid. How luckier can you possibly get than that?

We were on a roller coaster of snatched opportunity. Towards the end of January frustration with the haylage was beginning to give us a nervous breakdown. We had hay for the calves but our well behaved bullocks were struggling to break into the bales harvested for them. These were solid and the grass had been overgrown. Cattle have no top teeth. Their mouths are designed to crop grass not to tear open bales damaged by unseasonal weather.

Tim takes his son to the station where James catches the train to school in Bradford. On feeder filling days, he comes here for breakfast and we were all discussing this big bale problem.

'We're not coping,' Margaret said. 'Next year we'll have to have thought of some way of chopping up the haylage.'

'Perhaps you could do with a Bale Splitter, a guillotine,' Tim said.

We had thought we would have to sort out this difficulty in summer, before the haylage was baled, but this sounded to be an instrument which could be used now when the problem was frustrating us. A phone call straight to the supplier advised us he had none, now the season was well started. He'd try the manufacturer and ring back. He did but he'd had no success. In the summer there would be plenty, ready for next winter. He was reassuring, but we like things to happen at once and were anticipating that nervous breakdown always on the horizon. Margaret was frequently trying to break into the bales with torn hands and broken nails but it was unrewarding. Then, as happens too frequently not to merit comment, two days later Tim rang to say he had just returned from a trip to Blackpool having located what he said was, 'the only bale slicer in the country.' After making

Snowy.

a journey to North Yorkshire to buy a necessary fitting for the Kramer, he was able to chop each bale in two and the nervous breakdown was returned to the cupboard to await another opportunity.

I cannot explain luck. I refuse to believe that it is God looking after me for as I write this Burma has suffered a terrible tragedy, losing tens of thousands from the ravages of a cyclone and flooding and there has been an earthquake in China and thousands have been buried, whole towns having toppled in ruins. If He were to care for me and not them, He would not be worthy of the accolade He receives worldwide. Where, and to whom you are born, is not a divine selection process. Surely. Luck can't be the billy goat either. Or can it? A Guardian angel maybe. All I know is that luck has to follow dilemma. It catches you on a downward slope, generated only by a problem needing a solution, an accident needing recovery. It is necessary, also, not to be too ambitious of a result, to be satisfied with just a little miracle and to be consistently grateful, to eat the toast which falls butter side uppermost. Good Luck must never be wasted.

Snowy, our old white nanny goat was still thriving on her daily banquet of one banana, two carrots, one apple, some celery stalks and cabbage leaves. The colourful bowl looked equally tempting to my palate. Her luck had been to follow children from her home in the wild and arrive to the care of Margaret. We used to go to the supermarket to buy for the evening meals of numerous guests. Now our shopping basket seems to cater largely for dogs and cats and geriatric goats! We spend an enormous amount on wild bird food. It's meant for the tits and robins, the finches and sparrows but we have thieving squirrels and pheasants and once, after dark, Margaret found a young badger scratching below the hanging utensils. The dogs became alerted and were curious from afar, which made Margaret investigate. We have known there were badgers but this was the first time one was spotted. I have never seen a live one. A squirrel has occasionally been known to gnaw through the string dangling the feed net to steal all the peanuts in a take-away bag.

We had a winter without geese, the first since Ghandi was found by the RSPA, in a sack hanging from a lamp post, one Christmas nearly thirty years ago. When our current goose had died we had brought one in from Paulette and, when the cattle had to be housed at Christmas we had a problem where to put the geese. A few years ago I'd have thought nothing of making some accommodation. All summer they had occupied the calf shed and the previous winter they had slept in the barn but that had been ear-marked for Diana, her calf and two-year-olds who would not be separated from her. As a last resort Margaret asked Paulette if she would winter them for us and later she found a foster home for them and our experience of geese may well be over. Variety, they say, is the spice of life but it is very time consuming. When the 140 head herd has been sorted, and our meal is ready, I often investigate the possibility that Margaret will come and dine.

'How long will you be?' I ask.

'Not long. I've just Diana and the cats and the ducks and geese.'

Half an hour later she will come, collect Snowy's platter, or the milk for an ailing calf, or the sugar and water for one which was ailing and won't be weaned from sweet water. Then she will take a jug full of bird food and spend a while filling the hopper, absolutely inconsiderate of my frustration and the ruining of our joint meal. The Aga simmering oven is a godsend but it does nothing for the pangs of hunger. I was glad the foster family, taking the geese, reduced chores by one but it came only with a price. No more goose eggs for perfect sponge cakes!

The wind, our counsellor, was our tormentor all winter. It never seemed to stop blowing. Something heavy needed to be carried across the yard entry to anchor one safely. One day Margaret went empty handed and was blown flat on the concrete. I took to monitoring her activity, when darkness fell. When the garage door was closed and the light from within suddenly dimmed, I knew she would be facing the jet stream of air likely to upskittle her again. I watched her to safety and curtains were never drawn until she was in.

Wind is a distributor of urban litter. The nation is attempting to wage war on plastic bags and so it should. They gallivant up Moss Carr like nobody's business and festoon themselves, at inconvenient heights in the branches of the silver birches and, caught in the barbed wire of the roadside fence, they flap an accompaniment. In our youth we could negotiate the steep gradient of Jimmy's Wood to retrieve whatever was deposited among the brambles and the hawthorn. Now we cannot attempt it for, not only have we aged but so has the growth on the earthen walls of the dry valley. Since we fenced out cattle, thirty and more years ago, the undergrowth has become impenetrable. The one footpath, to the floor of the deep valley and up the northern face, is so overgrown by little usage, only the entry and exit gates indicate its whereabouts. It is sad that we cannot retrieve the plastic imprisoned there and are grateful to the spring coverage when grass and bluebells grow and leaves hide the alien, man made material. We poke the plastic waste from the branches wherever a broom handle will reach. We tear it from the fence and dump it in the enormous skip we have, in which, by law, we must put all the plastic waste from the haylage bags. I noticed, when admiring the daffodils below the feeding bay, that one of these bags had escaped the skip and been caught by a dog rose. I scrambled down the bank and crossed the beck but a hundred thorns secured it firmly. Only a freak wind will release it.

Wind is an ever present neighbour but it is seldom as strong as it was in the January of our fiftieth year at The Currer. It persisted from an easterly direction and delayed the spring, causing Margaret to moan constantly about the lack of grass and the late arrival of Turn Out and Doctor Green.

One week into February it became necessary to send for the artificial insemination of Diana. We had hoped this would never again be necessary, that she would become geld and could be retired from motherhood. She had done her share, and more, of raising a family to be proud of. We would have gratefully allowed her retirement into matriarchal status, allowing her a well earned old age but it became obvious her breeding days were not over so Margaret rang for the AI man. We waited all day for him to come, knowing that next day might be too late. It was Saturday and the message to come had to be put on an answer phone and when, by midday on the Sunday, he had not come, Margaret rang to ask why. This time the man himself answered and said he had never got the message. She was cross. To wait for the next opportunity, in three weeks time would result in a December birth when it was bringing-in time. I know that to dairy farmers with cows calving daily, our emphasis on the stress of our one birth, will sound pathetic. Nevertheless we do approach it with trepidation and Margaret was cross especially when the man assumed she, a lady herself, did not fully understand feminine cycles.

She was even more cross when, later in the afternoon an AI man rang to ask her address and said he had received the message and was on his way. Knowing it may be too late and that it would cost £60 regardless, she was reluctant to tell him her address. When he insisted she did, he exploded with disbelief for he was in Nottingham. So much for modern technology. Three weeks later there was no hitch but our problem will not be over when December comes and our expectant lady is too posh to push and the Labour Ward is full!

For years a carpel tunnel had been troubling me, restricting the distance I could drive without uncomfortable pain in my right hand. It had begun way back in the nineties but I'd decided I could live with it. I was doing less and less driving. In fact we were no longer doing long distances and using the car mainly for errands and seldom for pleasure. As I am the shopper, our role became more and more that of driver and hopper out. Margaret at the wheel pausing on location, whilst I hurried into the Post Office, the village shop, the bank, the supermarket and wherever was necessary.

Eventually I found letter writing, accounts, sewing and typing were becoming difficult so I decided to give it a go and applied for the very minor operation. I had to choose the right time for I'm needed for calf-rearing. Most of the indoor chores are mine and I prefer to do all the bed-making. I had to refuse the first appointment which came early in January but took the second one at the end of February believing Margaret was on the eve of Turn Out and that the holiday-making season would have not quite begun. We were wrong and Margaret was to struggle almost alone with the prolonged winter of 2008. The longer the calves stayed in, the bigger they grew, the hungrier they got and the more fodder had to be fed. I had an immobile right hand for ten days and a fairly useless one for six weeks or so. I carefully and slowly used it for the end of year accounts and balance sheet and for two-finger typing, wishing all the time that I hadn't bothered. The operation had only taken a quarter of an hour as an out-patient but the surgeon told me it might be eighteen months before the pins and needles in my fingers disappeared. The avoidance of driving had to continue.

Shortly after the annual Guide Reunion, always held on the first Saturday in March, Helen brought her Guide company for a weekend of activity and a fortnight later Guides from Sheffield, destined to camp in Russia in the summer, spent the weekend being genned up on the travelling and the kit they must take. They were all as eager for adventure as we, and our Guides, had been in the middle decades of the last century. It gave me hope that the present generation is little different, fundamentally.

The first warm day in March triggers the beginning of our calves' experience of the great out-doors. It did not come until the very last day of the month and was a 'one day only' activity, for the 1st of April was back to windy winter. Their first day experience was in the paddock only and it was towards the end of the month before they could be allowed out again and to greater freedom. Margaret remembered hearing March being identified as 'Colourless March' in some book she had read. March 2008 was totally drab. The earth was dry and grey, good for muck leading and spreading and Grasstrac scattering, but hopeless for spring growth. We went through the delayed ritual without enthusiasm. The dogs and I shut the three gates which forced the herd to stay on the hill and my sister groaned continually and feared there would be insufficient growth to sustain seventy big animals. There was some bovine erosion of the half dozen bales of debatably uneatable haylage and, just as the cattle appeared to have done well on last summer's unappetising harvest, they continued to do so on the retarded growth of April.

Park Rangers came to re-new the Rambler's Gate entry to the footpath. They returned it to its previous location on the north side of the wall to avoid mud caused annually by drinking cattle. However there was no mud. The season lacked April Showers and people blindly ignored the posh new gate and its ramblers arrow and found they had made a mistake only after walking a quarter of a mile. We could not believe it. The gate and fence were of shiny, new wood. Even as they walked through the old one, left because we needed access, they could not have done so without seeing it. We have so little trouble with people using our land we cannot possibly grumble. Nevertheless someone used a gate and left it open. All the bullocks came home. I took white paint and put large arrows and one No Entry sign.

People may walk anywhere on our 190 acres for those leaving the footpaths alert us to any animal in distress, a fallen wall or a left open gate and are invaluable when there is any such need. Their dogs seldom disturb the cattle any more than Sam does and it is an asset to have animals so used to dogs when almost all our paying guests bring one. A persistent dog walker, however caused us to put up a notice saying used dog waste bags must not be left on our land for cows to eat!

Health and Safety rules seem to be depriving people of common sense. I credit most of mine to my mother who was seldom deceived by words or actions, laws or advertisements, politicians or media. She would listen, then she would say, 'Well, Ah'm not tekken in!' or 'That's all me eye and Peggy Martin!' It can become frightening if people listen and don't evaluate what they hear, discount most and interpret sensibly. Too many believe the media, never putting two and two together and making four.

Suddenly we had to say Goodbye to Snowy. She, and we, had got used to her infirmity. She seemed to have an infinite ability to survive. When she died we viewed the fruit and vegetable harvest in the larder, with real regret that there would be no more preparation of her tempting meal. So now we only had The Three Billy Goats Gruff and someone who does not know us at all, asked, 'What are they for?'

'They just are,' Margaret replied. So many, whatever their religion, think God made animals just for the several needs of human beings. I assure you we are only one of many kinds and the planet would be in a far more stable condition without us.

I was tidying the house ready for the arrival of someone calling for coffee when Margaret came in speaking the three words which make my heart sink into my boots. 'Are you there?'

There is absolutely no mistaking the message. She is only dependent on me if there is dire emergency.

'What for?' Need I ask?

'I have a calf with its head stuck in a manger,' she said lifting the hacksaw from a hook in the front porch.

The baby herd had been removed from their quite spacious shed, to the even greater accommodation of the two bullock sheds. The feeding of them now could be done with big bale Kramer usage. It made things simpler but ease seldom comes without a price.

The manger barriers in the bullock sheds, had been purposefully made with slanting iron bars so that hay had to be eaten in the manger and not pulled out wastefully. At the end of each section was an upright necessary to join the rectangular units together but creating a triangle in which an animal head could get stuck. Margaret, ever expectant of calamity, always had that space blocked with a wooded stake. She had noticed that it had been broken but six month old calves do not have very big heads and a replacement had been neglected.

Some of this batch of calves were older than usual, their movement having been banned by the Foot and Mouth outbreak in September. Their turn out was six weeks later than usual, hence the dreaded call for help, 'Are you there?'

I scrambled, in Wellingtons, over the hay in the over full manger. All the other calves were standing at the shed door waiting to be let out. One black Limousin was trying to pull its head from the triangular space. We tried, first with bare hands, to give it our extra help but just like a child who puts its head through railings, its ears prevented any retraction. Struggling with a frantic, quite large calf with its head crashing on iron, is ill-advised. Fingers get bruised if not broken. We tried this method first, because there was hardly enough room to saw through the bar with a wriggling animal frantic to get out. However there was no other way but for me to hang on to the head for the twenty minutes it took to saw through that bar. We changed places once but Margaret was better with the saw than I was.

So often it is our lot to greet visitors covered in hay, to hesitate to hold out a hand in greeting, which is too dirty and to stand back if they prefer to hug, knowing we have been sweating profusely.

So rarely do we have repeats at The Currer. Emergencies tend to differ making this series of anecdotes never humdrum, but we did have an identical repeat of an incident which happened all of twenty years ago. It came within a few days of the calf experience and was, in itself a rare coincidence. Our huge skip, overflowing with plastic bale bags, was being removed and replaced by an empty one, ready for next November. I was guiding the heavy vehicle reversing when a villager, a retired farmer who walks his dogs on our land, came hurrying down the road to tell me we had a bullock with its head stuck in a triangular section of a pylon. Now this was really serious. There was no way it could get out, he said.

I dashed into the house calling to Margaret the dreaded words, 'Are you there?'

'What for?' she groaned and then, without hesitation, phoned 999 for the Fire Service. Within minutes there was an enormous appliance hurtling down the road. We and two male guests had only time to leap into the Land Rover before the Skip Remover, Fire Engine and we were all vying for road space.

The engine could not go overland so the four firemen, brandishing a tool kit, squeezed into the Land Rover. Our two dogs always bark when we drive up the hill. Maybe we should have taught them otherwise but their joy has always been allowed to exhibit itself. They stop when we reach the summit and behave perfectly thereafter. If we are going overland they are released at the gateway and streak across the pasture.

Again it was a Limousin. Margaret says members of this breed are born with nothing between the ears. Maybe nature provided cattle with horns so that they could not get into this predicament and it was all our fault for taking them off whilst they were still only buds. The big, black beauty had spent itself struggling. No doubt it had had a tickle between its ears and had needed a good scratch. The lower cross bar on the pylon leg, had tempted it into near suicide. These giant metal legs tend to stand in a hollow for the excavated land sinks several inches and our unfortunate animal had got himself into an impossible mess. His head was facing north and so was his mud encrusted tail. He had jack-knifed into the hollow. Had that retired farmer not discovered him he would have died before nightfall.

The previous accident, some twenty years earlier had been identical, same pylon, same south-westerly leg, same triangular space but then the firemen had been able to unscrew the bolts constructing the giant Meccano. Since then they had become unscrewable and the emergency team had to prove their skill with a hacksaw. Then, with a rope round its back legs all six men were needed to un-jack-knife the exhausted animal. Slowly, very slowly, he found his feet. Alone, bewildered, surrounded by people, coated with mud he started to walk towards home, half a mile away. I followed, accompanied by a guest and Margaret drove the triumphant firemen back to their engine. The bullock, shocked and mesmerised paused only once on his downward, unsteady trek to the place he called home. Almost immediately he stopped to empty his exceedingly over full bladder. Relief is expressed in many different ways. He didn't hesitate again until the safety of his shed was reached. Some would say our cattle are humanised. I contradict all those who say evil humans have become like animals. They respect each other

Pylon victim.

more. There are no paedophiles in their communities. They have quality family relationships and are role models to their offspring and to human kind, for that matter.

The firemen were so delighted by success they asked Margaret's permission for them to tell the local newspaper. 'People like reading about animal rescue,' they said. We don't disappoint happy, 'little boys' so she agreed. She kept the shocked animal indoors all night and, next morning, gave him into the motherly care of Diana who, with her own fast growing baby and her retinue of last year's two problems, had not yet joined the main herd. You have to look no further than Diana if you are looking for child care and family perfection. We give her all our extras and ask her to cope with all our problems and she never complains. She is the matriarch of the herd, the foster mother on whom we rely. Harassed but uncomplaining.

I am reminded of a poem my mother used to say which is applicable to the animal kingdom too.

> Aye what a life 'as a muther,
> At least if she's 'ampered like me.
> From morn t' neet Ah've sum bother
> An' Ah guess Ah s'all 'ah till Ah dee.

Margaret did not close the book on that chapter until she had convinced YEDL that the Fire Service had saved them a huge compensation bill and that, immediately, they must send someone out to bind the lower legs of the pylons with barbed wire. They did a satisfactory job ensuring that that will never happen again.

There had been a succession of funerals. We are at the centre of a web of relationships. The loss of Gladys Crossley, our school pianist and secretary and mother of two of my Queens Guides, was sadly unexpected. My two remaining assistant teachers and I attended the service together. We had not seen each other for some time

Lady Green had appeared as if by magic. Her carpet was littered with butter cup, daisy, milkmaid, bluebell, lady's slipper and dandelion. Everything came at once. Coltsfoot and Marsh marigold preceded the rest barely by an hour. Unfortunately May will be remembered again for a cool east wind which tore the new green sycamore leaves from the trees and scattered baby silver birch foliage all over the ever dry yard. We needed warm rain. The young calves didn't seem to mind at all. One small red Hereford, we suspected of having been stunted by BVD, joined the herd wherever it went, differing only in size. Margaret monitored it daily along with another quite normal calf, the only one of the batch she had named. His head was very slightly on one side. As a baby he had eaten corn too quickly and had been delegated to a fenced corner, every meal time so that he did not steal more than his fair share. So he had had to have a name. Mother would have said he had a belly 'like our Sam Herbert' and that could well have been his name but Margaret named him Born-so, after a relative of the late 1800s whose head, also, had not been quite erect. Strangers had found him on the pavement outside the pub. Fearing he had damaged his head, they were trying to straighten it causing him to protest loudly, 'Born so, yer bugger, Born so!' That became his nickname and our otherwise healthy calf inherited it.

I am not sure that today's mothers have such a fund of sayings and poetry, predictions and anecdotes, to pass on to their children as ours had. They had been born before the twentieth century had even begun and language was richer.

The next animal excitement was hardly our problem, though we had to temporarily solve it. Our cattle were all acclimatised to life out of doors, before Tim decided to let out his. He has a suckled herd and mothers and calves had been wintered together in his barn. It seemed an opportune time to wean the calves. He took them to a location separate from their mothers and they strongly objected.

Late one Saturday night, he rang to say they had escaped and were running all over Oakworth. He had managed to corner eight of the twelve. If he were successful in getting them into his trailer, could he deposit them in our empty bullock shed?

Farmers with Ifor Williams trailers seem to manage what seems to us an impossible task, but their animals are frequently transported thus. Ours object to being forced into a small trailer, having no previous experience. It was long past dark when we saw the headlights of his Land Rover enter our road but, by the time we had donned coats and Wellingtons, he had managed to deposit eight safely in the barn. His wife and son were still looking for the missing four. We have an increasing respect for the mobile phone though seldom use one ourselves. We take one on holiday, but at home it is never in our pocket. Tim's is and he could track the vicinity of all the searchers. Nearing midnight he brought three more and when we counted them next morning, all twelve were prisoners. Amazingly none seemed to have vandalised gardens as ours have been known to do! In the barn they remained for nearly a fortnight, by which time he hoped they had forgotten their mothers.

When we had a suckled herd we never separated the yearling calves from their mothers and we never had chaos of that particular variety. Forgive me if I too frequently use cattle as role models for humans. In the realms of family stability, it is unwise to split up the nuclear one. Just as things went incredibly wrong when a herd was divided into two, so do things crumble when parents split. Society blames this on the instability of modern youth, though rarely tries to prevent it. Following this recent bovine experience, may I suggest the problem parents and teachers and neighbourhoods are facing, is growing roots earlier than that. I believe, babies and toddlers being put into day care, be it only a temporary separation, might be adding fuel to today's flame. Yet the Government is intent on providing opportunities for such instead of recommending a long, mother/child relationship. They calculate family disintegration and juvenile delinquency, as from the moment of divorce when the example of history suggests it begins when the child, human or animal is separated from its mother. My generation had stay-at-home mothers, no baby-sitting service, no play school, pre-school, no nursery. Motherhood was a job. Fatherhood made men out of boys and the responsibility of providing financial support gave men a role, an important status many are now losing.

So often, burdened with disruptive teenagers, Government looks for new ways to solve problems. The old adage stands firm. 'It is sometimes necessary to look back to go forward!'

I am grateful to those newly weaned calves for their strong objection to being separated from their herd. It is useful material, for me as a teacher, to tote out to those who continually separate the human family. If society wishes to tackle the current childhood, social problems I suggest they begin at the very beginning and, with Spring Watch currently on television, there is no better example than to mirror the nurturing expertise of the animal kingdom.

Sadly our farming practice depends on other people wanting dairy products and on calves, born to dairy cows, being snatched away so that their mother's milk can go elsewhere. Knowing this is not ideal, Margaret keeps her status quo, whatever the cost, and there is no more separation whilst they remain with us. She sells them in batches so that, never again are they forced from their adoptive family group. It is not unusual, and often rewarding, to look at nature and find answers.

For the rest of the year we consider we have too many hawthorn trees but in May, when the blossom is heavy on every bough, we become obsessed with their beauty. They hold their flowers far longer than the Japanese cherries which line the urban streets and are just as, if not more, beautiful. The ash followed the oak so quickly rainfall over summer was unpredictable. In any case, I've lost all faith in that, for the oak came first the previous year and look what flooding followed.

During May, fifty years ago, we had been busy decorating our no longer ruined farmhouse. New frames and glass had been returned to the gaping mullions. The rotten doors had been dragged from their sagging hinges and replaced. Layers of white lime had been scrapped from the walls ready for re-papering. The walled up entrances, to the oldest part of the living quarters recently used for housing animals, had been re-opened and the beautiful inglenook fireplace discovered. There had scarcely been a moment when we had not been decorating, Margaret with a paint brush and I exercising my skills with paste and paper.

Whitsuntide had had to be set aside in order to take the whole Guide Company to High Wray, on the western shore of Lake Windermere. The excitement of our renovation, our thrill of an imminent new life, only ever exceeded our joy of taking children to camp by the barest margin. It had been important to make this week in the Lake District special, for we were planning to take only patrol leaders in the summer, on an adventurous trek among the islands of Tiree, Barra, The Uists, Eigg, Rhum and Skye. What a year 1958 had been.

Fifty years on and, not daring to look forward, we were continually looking back. Not just to the beginning but to fifty years of windblown activity. Seeing Margaret at work, a cottage resident observed, 'When do you have time to have fun?'

'Nearly all the time,' she replied truthfully. No-one has ever really appreciated how much fun our life has been nor how much it still is. Never would I have a face lift. What lines are there are laughter ones never to be erased.

The exquisite whiteness of the May Blossom excited Margaret to visit the DIY store and come home with gallons of Brilliant-White emulsion paint and a few small tins of Brilliant-White gloss. We have a continuing history of Spring Cleaning. Many people have neglected this age-old tradition but we celebrate it every year, Margaret with her paint brush and I with soap and water and ironing board. Having accelerated the process, to beat the arrival of an overnight trio, a booking by phone three days earlier, it was gratifying to welcome them into our beamed and mullioned, sixteenth century farm-house, smelling of new paint and freshly washed curtains. We were pretty exhausted with the extra effort acceleration had caused and we sank into armchairs in our sitting room, listening to the creaking of floor boards in Aunty Mary's room. As a large group was coming the next day, one of our frequent guests had been delegated that special accommodation.

There was a sudden knock on the door. The new man was at the wheel of his car reversing it. His daughter was on the back seat and his drab, middle-aged wife was at our door.

'We're not staying,' she said. 'We like something more modern!'

'It's five hundred years old,' I said.

Our frequent guest said, 'Look what they are missing!'

It happens so rarely, that guests do not like our location, our old house, the white interior of our inside walls and the informality of our hospitality, that it is barely worth a mention other than to say that, in our profession guests have a right to their preferences whilst we, as their hosts can not pick and choose our guests. We must make them all 'feel at home even if we wish they were!'

Next day I had no beds to remake for the large group expected at 11 a.m. I had no washing to do. The new people thought they had found the most idyllic spot in Yorkshire. Their children were playing in the yard, with Meg and Sam at 7.30 a.m.

'What are you going to do today?' I asked.

A pint-sized one answered, 'Everything!'

There is nothing wrong with children. I do not believe in Original Sin. They are born alright. Let's do away with modernity.

Chapter Twenty-one

Pause now upon your path,
And listen to the song echoing from the past.

T HERE WAS AN UNEXPECTED HITCH in booking for our spring holiday. So many positives have to come together when one leaves a business behind. More so when two are concerned. The right moments are limited by season, farming routine, holiday guest bookings and availability of supply staff. All these dictate when we can go but where depends on whether accommodation can be found for us and our two dogs. It is a nightmare activity getting all the eggs into one basket.

We had unanimously and sadly come to the decision that leaving a still competent Dorothy alone for a fortnight was risky. She had been a loyal friend for twenty-two years and, with George, her husband and Joy her daughter, had been left with multiple bookings and evening meals galore. These she and George had stopped when Joy married. For two weeks in spring and two in autumn guests had to be satisfied with bed and breakfast only but the status quo could continue. When George and Harry both died, we felt we could cut our holiday excursions down to one week only. Aunty Mary was too old and inactive to take to Scotland or Wales. For the first two autumn holidays of Dorothy going alone, we were but a few miles away. When, in spring, we ventured to the islands, relatives came to care for their Aunty Mary, Dorothy used the Mistal Cottage and was in charge of the holiday-makers.

After Aunty Mary's death, we organised that our wallers-cum-jacks-of-all-trades, had work on the premises so that Dorothy had emergency help whenever she needed it. In twenty-two years there can be a multitude of such and we were never unaware of what might happen to frighten the living daylights out of all of us.

We were not only loathe to give up our holidays, of which there can not be too many left, but we needed to take the full fortnight in spring. We were not in retirement, like our contemporaries and we'd begun to feel the need for an autumn break to face the winter. Gradually we had introduced Helen and Chris to becoming our second source of supply help and when the floods of 2007 tested Dorothy to near limit it was a unanimous decision to transfer spring duties from her to them, before the limit was actually reached. Is the era of Dorothy over? We never say never. Is the era of my morning seat at the typewriter over? Never is too strong a word for that also. Are our spring holidays in The Hebrides coming to an end? Not yet, God willing, but there was a hitch which caused us to make several phone calls and re-route and re-locate on the journey north.

Having appointed our caretakers and secured the two week booking of our chalet at Luskentyre early, we did not hurry to book nights going and returning at our dog-friendly accommodation in Mallaig. When we did it was to find our hosts were fully booked with a party of students. There being few places where one can take dogs, we were flummoxed as to what we could do. To leave our dogs behind is not an option, even if Dorothy was not to be there with all her pack of show winning collies.

A chance meeting with a village resident, visiting our cousin Freda at the same time as we, alerted us to the possibility of catching an early morning train to Mallaig, via Edinburgh. It could get us to the ferry terminal in time to catch the last boat to Skye. I phoned the Railway and Caledonian MacBrayne and the island Youth Hostel but the latter didn't take dogs. I was determined to find a way, so I phoned the home of the Uig taxi driver we would need to employ, to take us across Skye to catch the Outer Ises steamer. His wife answered the phone.

'Do you know anyone who will take dogs?' I asked. I told her we would need to use a taxi to cross the island as the bus service had a one dog policy and we had two well behaved collies.

'We do Bed and Breakfast,' she replied, 'and we take dogs.' My relief must have been audible over the phone.

WE COULD STILL GO TO HARRIS. I again phoned the Railway and found we need not even go via Glasgow and Mallaig. We could go Edinburgh to Inverness and take the beautiful crossing of the Highlands to Kyle of Lochalsh. The taxi could meet us there. We could cross the bridge to Skye and be taken right to the doorstep of his dog-friendly wife.

Then, and only then, could we get on with the long drawn out winter of 2008.

The final countdown to our much needed holiday began with our annual reluctance to leave so many responsibilities and the need to tick off as many boxes as possible and tie off any loose ends. The two weeks of our absence have to be as trouble free as we can make them. Holiday preparations result in a frantic attempt to double check animals, boundaries, book- ings, cupboards, fridges, freezers, linen etc, etc, *ad infinitum* and the task is monstrous. So, invariably, we wish we were not going and anticipate that a last minute emergency will scupper a calm departure. What it will be can never be predicted, only the certainty that it will come.

It was necessary that we worm the calves before we left, a simple task providing we can tempt them back into the shed and immediately release them through the cattle race. Normally turn-out begins gently in March when calves are let out during the day and come home every evening, for a month or more, learning a routine return to the shed. In 2008 they were released so late, and the spring's almost overnight appearance meant that this daily activity was never rehearsed. We wondered how best to gather untrained animals for just this simple medication. We are not as agile as we used to be and were winter weary. Training we consider to be highly important and this generation of calves had not had their April course. Like children they have to be taught ground rules and these Come Home ones had not been learned.

So Margaret set the wallers to finish the dry stone restoration of the fold, which runs parallel to the south wall of the Five Acre. It begins in the Low Pasture field and ends in the paddock in front of the three shed entrances. Most of the wall had been rebuilt on the Stewardship Scheme and only twenty metres, no more, remained. They had been left because time had run out. The ten years were over. Also more stone had been needed and there had, at the time, seemed more important things to do and on which to spend money, now the 60% grant was over. Margaret decided that a financial opportunity could not be waited for. The men hurried to ferry stone and finish the job and to gate both entrances.

With only days left before our holiday, they finished and it looked beautiful. We had waited many years to afford the re-build of that very lovely, inherited piece of history. Margaret and Sam steered the calves into the Low Pasture and shut the field gate. They grazed all morning then, as predicted, gathered at the gate wanting to come back into the Five Acre where there is water. Instead of opening the field gate she opened the fold one close by and every man jack of them walked up the fold to the paddock enclosure. It was a doddle. They then had no alternative but to enter the bottom shed, a place of which they had familiarity. The round-up was a piece of cake. We re-opened the shed door half way so that exit was confined to the crush race and, as each calf filed through, Margaret squirted the wormer along its backbone. The job, for which we had an appreciative audience, was completed in less than ten minutes.

In the Royal Box, leaning against the yard wall, our long retired Agricultural Merchant watched the operation with amazement. He, like we, remembered the days before Pour-on. To worm cattle, not all that long ago, was a full day's job. The crush had to trap each head in turn and it be grabbed and raised. Each mouth had to be forced open and wormer poured down each throat. Those animals waiting to pass out to pasture soon became aware of what was happening to their peers and each had to be forced into the crush and we were constantly in danger. Whoever invented Pour-on certainly extended our working life by years.

Our wide-eyed spectator was Alwyn Pickles, a keen photographer and DVD expert. He had managed to put Scottish music on our disc of the

1970s films. These had been taken on Harris by Keith Whalley, his after-noon companion, father of one of our Guides and a distant relative on Mother's side. The very quick worming procedure left us ample time for all to assemble in the sitting room, have a cup of tea and watch the no-longer silent film.

Keith said, 'If I hadn't taken those films of camp you'd have forgotten.' We will never forget. We do not need photographs or moving pictures. We do not need *A Song to Sing and a Tale to Tell*. We do not even need to re-unite every year or go to the islands every spring, to remember clearly, every one of those twenty five, character building years which created the family we have all become. Nevertheless, the DVD disc, now with music, is more precious to us than ever jewellery would be and a six minute capture of all our premises, which Alwyn filmed after the tea break, now entertains our guests.

For several weeks a too-large, plastic, circular water trough had been awaiting installation because Margaret feared jostling drinkers might tumble in. Some concrete pipe rings had been located at John Sugden's place, at Dob Hill. Placed in the centre of the enormous tub they would discourage children believing it to be a swimming pool and prevent any bovine accident. There was time, before we left for holiday, to install the tub and plumb it in. It took less than a morning. The wallers seem to be able to do anything speedily.

We appeared to have two days free to get our house, our letting accommodation ready and our minute rucksacks packed in peace, but a letter came from Defra, two days before leaving, containing a form, re Single Payment Entry Level, which needed completion and signing. It, like most ministerial correspondence, was so complicated we needed our consultant's help to fill it in.

Her visit is always pleasant but a valuable morning of our final two days, was lost. Next day, at precisely 8.30 a.m. a Defra inspector rang to say she was to be in the area and could she come to do a routine inspection of our land and paper work re Entry Level.

'We are just going on holiday!' I said. I was horrified. We had little enough time to spare to entertain inspectors.

'What time are you leaving? I can be there in half an hour.'

I gasped. I could not believe what I was hearing. Could she really mean she would come even if we were leaving that morning?

'Well we are not actually leaving until early next morning but you can imagine it's pretty hectic here!'

'It won't take long,' (only half a day) she said. 'I'll be with you in half an hour. I will want to see your Manure Management Scheme and I will need to walk all round your property and acreage to check for any non-compliance. I'll come back immediately on your return from holiday with the necessary inspection results and the form to sign.'

All this for a few pounds Entry Level addition to our diminishing Single

Payments and just when we were already in a flap clearing the way to leave for holiday.

She is a nice inspector who always enjoys a cup of tea having rarely been offered one at her previous call, (do you wonder why). When she left shortly after 1 p.m, I viewed a now untidy desk with some annoyance. I had had to search for that stupid Manure Management Scheme, an elaborate definition of Muck Spreading. Searching brings confusion to otherwise order. Where I replaced it is unknown, should I ever have to find it again!

We got up very early, put the dogs in the Land Rover and released them to follow the vehicle as we sped over the once-was moorland. It would be the only activity they would get that day.

Chris came and we caught the train. We always have to, even if it means something is left undone, (or behind like the lunch box we left on the kitchen table and the two plastic dog plates. The one we could do without, the two were important!) We have to catch that train, come what may, for we have a twelve hour journey with many connections. To have missed the first would have been catastrophic.

We only caught the Edinburgh train by a stroke of luck. Being confused with busy city stations, albeit with little luggage and two well behaved dogs, we took a friend's advice and arranged to have a porter meet each train and just lead us to the next appropriate platform. However, we'd actually caught a train thirty minutes earlier than necessary, to Leeds so the arranged help wasn't there. But it came immediately a railwayman, with a mobile, summoned assistance. We were helped to the lift with courtesy and escorted to Platform 9 with plenty of time.

It was very early in the morning and, though there was promise of a beautiful day, the 'Song of a Morning' we are used to at the start of a holiday, it was nevertheless chilly. The kind man took us to a platform shelter of almost total glass He seated us in front of the door and told us he'd return when the train was due. It was a modern 'greenhouse' with a door which opened automatically every time we leaned forward or passengers passed by. So we re-located to the middle of the room and had the added entertainment of a Departure Screen directly in front of us, the like of which I have never seen before, or since, actually on a platform.

When our train came up on the screen, it said Platform 8C. A lady had entered the waiting room and we asked if she was going to Edinburgh but her destination was London. We couldn't believe it and scrutinised the moving screen, she and we together, then grabbed first one porter and then another, becoming more concerned by the minute. Thank goodness for mobile communication. Our man was finally located and came, with apologies, to hurry us to the lift and across the bridge to Platform 8C and the Edinburgh train. He stayed with us, found us seats with a table and all was well. It would not have been so, had we not been seated in the waiting room opposite a Departure

Screen for, had we missed that first Friday connection, it would have meant returning home, our only hope being that our reservation, and our booked Bed and Breakfast, could be altered to Monday.

From that moment onward every mile of the way was without stress, bathed in sunshine and through a landscape of World Class, truly unbeatable. We were silent. I spent the first lap of the journey remembering fifty years ago when I was only 28 and Margaret 19 and we were travelling northward with a party of seven, on an epic adventure with one wheeled Trike Carts, heading for The Hebrides. Here we were again, heading towards a Caledonian Ferry Terminal. This fifty year milestone was addictive and the romance of the islands as alluring as ever. My excellent Time Machine is capable of backward projection whenever I wish to step into the cubicle.

* * * * * * * * * * * * * * * * * *

1958. From *A Song to Sing and a Tale to Tell*.
Brown Ferguson, Glasgow, first published 1979.

We borrowed the carts from Miss Dorothy Clough, of Steeton Hall whose long life has been in the service of young people. She taught me my camping skills, when I was a child and has been friend and counsellor ever since. The carts were collapsible with one detachable wheel, similar to that on a bicycle, and two pole shafts. They were useful vehicles though they looked somewhat ridiculous and caused much public interest. On them we could strap our bedding rolls, rucksacks, tents and kitchen equipment and we pushed them on Tiree, Barra, South Uist, Eigg and Rhum and Skye.

When we needed to travel by bus we just unscrewed the wheel and unslotted the poles and everything went easily into the boot. When we went on board we took off the wheel and carried everything on, like on a stretcher. It was easy and between us we had a holiday of a lifetime, an adventure never to be forgotten. Had my life offered me more time, I would have repeated this kind of expedition every year, but time for me is limited and when the choice is between fifty and five the fifty must take priority.

If you want to make friends, we have found, the best way is to do something odd, even daft and everyone shows kindly interest and amusement. Do the odd thing with children and you have friends everywhere.

We began the journey on the friendly soil of Tiree and pushed our two wheels from Scarinish, along Gott Bay to Salum. We camped in Happy Valley, on the shore and spent four blissfully happy days wandering about Tiree, accompanied by many of the island children we already knew so well.

We were eight when we journeyed from Yorkshire because one of the fourteen year old Tiree girls, had just spent a fortnight's holiday with us and was returning after her first spell on the Mainland. It had been her unique introduction to trees and trains and cities.

The Trek, 1958.

I had collected Mary two weeks earlier, from the boat in Oban and brought her by train and bus to Yorkshire. She was very composed, only occasionally giving away the fact that this was all as new to her as the moon was to Neil Armstrong. She would not, could not bring herself to cross the unstable passageway between two carriages on the train and when we arrived in Callander she was convinced we had reached Glasgow. On arrival at the bus station in Buchanan Street she was very quiet and when we visited the Ladies she saw no relationship between a disc and a slot and fumbled with her penny.

Mary returned with us to Tiree at the beginning of the trek and when we arrived at the thatched, white cottage which was her home, the table was laid for a full course meal. It was not the first time, nor the last, we had eaten a meal with our good friends Effie and John Lachie. We go to their cottage like going home. They were our first friends on Tiree and Happy Valley belongs to them. Without them there never would have been a first time. It was on their land we planted the acorn which grew into an enormous oak. The island girl, we first knew as a barefooted ten year old, won a scholarship to Oban High School. She graduated from Aberdeen University taking an MA degree. She spent some time teaching in Canada, married a boy from Tiree and they have been living in Hong Kong ever since. (On retirement they returned and have settled on Tiree.)

There were four children in the family, Mary, Ellen, Christine and baby Hughie. There were also four boys at the Post Office and Mary Ann MacLean and wherever we went they were with us and when we slept the last night in John Lachie's clean, whitewashed barn they slept there, too. Our girls did not want to leave and if we had changed our plans and said we would stay the whole holiday on Tiree, I think they would have cheered. But I was silent and we packed our bags and went to Barra.

It would have been more encouraging if the weather had not been so stormy. The *Claymore* tossed all the way across The Minch. When we carried our stretchers down the gangway at Castlebay, on Barra, ours was a bedraggled and dejected party. There is a small waiting room on the pier. It is an incongruous, concrete shed, quite out of place among the Hebridean houses with their peat smoke drifting horizontally and all the conglomeration of fishing tackle, lobster creels and herring boxes.

The waiting room door was open and we dashed inside, out of the rain, stacked our peculiar equipment against the wall and took stock of our position. The first thing we needed was food but long experience on these islands has taught us that you can seldom get anything whilst the boat is in. Almost always the shops are shut so that the owners can go down to the pier to collect further supplies. We waited two hours once, on Jura, in blazing sunshine but then we had the novelty of watching the whisky barrels being rolled up the slope outside the distillery, at Craighouses. We waited for a shop to open on Coll in a similar deluge to the one on Barra. Oh yes, we knew very well that we would get nothing until the boat left for South Uist and there was nothing we could do about it.

We knew, too, that once we left Castlebay we might find no other shop until we reached Northbay, so we waited patiently in the concrete waiting room, glad of its temporary shelter. We spent some time adjusting our equipment, securing our oilskins, stamping our feet to keep warm.

Eventually, heads down into the wind, we ventured outside. The RMS *Claymore* was turning and heading for Lochboisdale. The shops in the Main Street were still closed but by the time we reached the Co-op there were signs of activity and we were able to replenish our larder. Laden with awkward tins and packets and loaves of bread, just unpacked from the steamer, we went back to the waiting room.

We fumbled with the door handle, streams of water running from our sou'westers, finding illegal entry and trickling coldly down our necks. The handle was unyielding, the door was locked. This is something we had not expected on Barra where house doors are not bolted. The one remaining human being on the otherwise deserted pier told us that the piermaster was, 'Away to Norsebay' and suddenly the enormity of our plight could not be disregarded.

We had tins but no opener, bread but no knife. We had no cooking equipment, no tents, no sleeping bags and no personal gear in which to find dry clothes. A crowd began to gather. There was much Gaelic and rattling of the lock but, unlike a station master's room we know, it held firm. We and our kit were parted.

'Well, well, and the man's away to Norsebay,' said one of the men. There was a great deal of Gaelic and our interpreter turned to us. 'They're saying he'll no have gone straight home. He'll be having a strupak right enough.'

He named a small township on the Northbay road. 'They're to take the lorry and go after him for the key.'

Several men climbed onto the lorry. We had brought unexpected and welcome entertainment. Northbay is seven miles away on a road so narrow and winding that we settled down and prepared ourselves for a long delay. The depression which had enveloped us when we left Tiree had gone and the incredible five, Janet, Ann, Toots, Margaret jun. and Foxy were already in high spirits and laughing at our predicament.

A crofter's wife waved to us as she passed on a footpath below. We watched her go to one of the fishing boats and return with half a dozen fish in a string bag. She made a detour and came towards us. She showed anxiety over our plight and could not understand our amusement and lack of concern. She generously offered us the use of her home, wanted to feed us and said we could stay the night.

We could not accept even shelter from the rain whilst men were still dashing round in a lorry, trying to find us the key. We thanked her for the supremely generous offer and have never forgotten the sincerity with which it was made. She walked away slowly and looked back several times.

The pier master was located as our friends had predicted, supping his strupak not far away and when the lorry returned he was with it. The men were delighted with their success and stood around watching whilst we screwed on the wheels and prepared to push the two carts up the steep Main Street. They followed us to the top, waving as we turned west for Tangasdale and we thanked them sincerely. They all stood waving as we set off at a spanking pace, heads bent against the weather, confident once again in the benevolence of the islands and their people. It must have been close on seven o'clock. We decided to cross the island and make camp as soon as we reached the sandy machair, which we prefer. We were all very hungry. We reached the summit of the road in a lather of sweat and rain and after that the downward trek into Tangasdale was easy. The bicycle wheels were running freely and we reached the shore in good time.

We never pitch without permission. For one thing courtesy demands this. For another we generally need to use a crofter's water supply and, especially if we have children with us, we like our presence to be known and accepted. We never know when an emergency will mean we need help. So we asked at a small cottage on the shore, white and thatched, for permission to pitch three small tents on the machair. We were told that the land belonged to a crofter who lived half a mile back on the road. It meant a further delay and everyone was tired by this time. A sea mist obliterated what Margaret and I knew to be one of the most beautiful Hebridean shores. All Barra's magnificence was completely hidden. I did not want to press the youngsters beyond the limit they could go.

'You stay here,' I said 'Flim and I will run back along the road. We won't be long.' They sat down in their oilskins, leaning on an upturned boat, their sense of humour somewhat exhausted.

Margaret and I hurried back up to the house we had been shown. We must have looked like shipwrecked mariners with waterproofs and sou'westers. The rain was dripping from our noses, running down our legs and soaking the socks in our hiking boots. We felt embarrassed to be knocking on someone's door.

A woman opened it and I asked the simple question I have asked so many times. 'Could we please have permission to pitch our tents on the shore and may we fill our water carrier?'

'You are wet,' said the woman, immediately concerned. 'You must come in and get dry.'

We explained that we couldn't, that we had left five girls on the shore and that we were all ready to pitch our tents if that was all right. The woman turned to her daughter and there was a discussion in Gaelic.

'Himself is not at home chust now,' she explained. 'You must come in and get dry and when he comes we will ask him about the tents.'

We told her that there were seven of us and that we were all too wet to go into anyone's house but that as soon as we could pitch our tents we would be all right. We would soon be able to get dry and cook something to eat. To her this was unthinkable. We were wet and must be dried; hungry and must be fed. Tents were quite outside her comprehension.

'Take off your oilskins,' she insisted. 'You must come inside. Himself will soon be back from the hill.'

Her daughter had understood about the teenagers left on the shore. 'Run down to the machair,' she prompted Margaret. 'Bring the others. You can get dry whilst my father comes.'

We were helpless. We had genuinely tried to save this good lady trouble and she had refused to listen. Margaret went down to the shore to collect the others and bring up the carts. There was nothing else we could do.

Never have we felt so wet or so cluttered with oilskins. We left them in a pile outside the door, believing that they could not get any wetter at all. Never have seven pairs of shoes looked so many as they did on the floor of the small entrance porch. We seated ourselves beside the stove, some on chairs and some on the floor and began to steam. We toasted ourselves until we began to tingle and our bare toes to curl up in pleasure.

The two women began to be very active. The daughter was busy in the kitchen and her mother began to fuss around the living room. She scrubbed the wooden table quite unnecessarily and laid a spotless cloth. There was not much conversation. I felt she would have talked if we had had the Gaelic. It was being spoken fluently in the kitchen. The atmosphere, however, was easy. We were in no doubt at all about our welcome.

We watched, intrigued, whilst our hostess lifted a cardboard box from the cupboard and began to unpack a lovely, china tea service from its protective tissue. We were deeply honoured. In England, had this happened, I feel certain we would have been turned away, have received permission to camp and would have already been pitching. Had we had the good fortune to be asked into the kitchen, I think we would have been given mugs which would have been quite suitable for wandering, wet strangers.

But here on this remote island in The Outer Hebrides, on the worst night of summer, the best china was being unwrapped, the newest of delicious scones were being spread with the morning's fresh butter. Fresh cream was being folded into the crowdie, slices of new brown bread were being cut and homemade oat cakes piled on a plate. We have been fed many times on many islands but never more liberally than this, never with more grace and dignity and our hearts warmed to this born hostess.

Himself was slow to arrive and when he did he disturbed the calf which was enjoying a meal of oilskins at the front door. It had eaten a big square out of Ann's long gas cape. When the man came into the house he greeted us as warmly as if we were known and expected guests. Apparently such were far too rare to send away at once. He was much more garrulous than his wife and he completely ignored my request about the tents. Instead he apologised for being unshaven and proceeded to remedy it at once.

'Och, first I must take off the whiskers,' he decided, lathering his face in front of the mirror. 'I do believe the rain will stop. Ach! There is plenty of time, I'm sure!'

He was so obviously enjoying himself. I should have wanted to get the tents pitched and the business of unpacking over, the ground sheets down and my family settled for the night. Instead, like my retinue, all I wanted to do was to sit by the peat fire, within the friendship of this family circle and listen to Himself.

He was the most entertaining host. Having shaved he took his mug of tea, drew up his chair and prepared to enjoy this unexpected and obviously very welcome céilidh. He was full of stories of the island, of folklore and superstition and he held us spellbound. He believed sincerely in second sight and told us stories of lights and premonitions and visions; of life in a crofting community, of treasures washed up by the sea, of shipwrecks during the war and of survivors washed ashore with their dead companions.

When we rose to go he insisted we sat down again and he turned the handle of an old gramophone and played us Gaelic songs. He begged that we would sing and we did and darkness fell and still the gay céilidh went on.

Finally I forced him to talk about tents. 'Well,' he said, 'and I'm sure you could camp by the lochan if it weren't for se sistles.'

'Blow the thistles,' I groaned silently. He took me out to negotiate the land. Across the road, below the house, was a sloping field with a lochan in its hollow. The thistles were pathetic apologies for the Scottish Emblem and were only sparsely scattered.

'This is perfect,' I said.

It was long past midnight and the rain had stopped. Our genial friends stood in the their illuminated doorway and waved both arms in salute.

* * * * * * * * * * * * *

Was there any wonder that we returned so often? That was an extraordinary beginning. Was I going to be occupied all the way with fifty year old memories? If so my journey could only be pleasant. I didn't feel any different. Though grey on top, I am still who I was then and so is my sister. Neither of us has changed. What we were, we still are. We are too easily recognisable not to believe we actually look much the same. We have had no weight accumulation, no hair style make-over. We have never worn make-up, we wear the same sort of casual clothes. Whilst I have to ask, 'Who am I speaking to?' it is never a question I am asked, though I am frequently stopped by school children or their parents I haven't seen for decades.

Travelling is like fruit picking. The mind wanders continually from one thought to another but, unlike harvesting, the view triggers the subject, not the monotony. We were fortunately not on one of these modern express monsters intent only on getting from A to Z as fast as possible. Others in the compartment were wired into lap-tops and music stations or repeatedly phoning to tell friends they were on the train, but we were glued to the glass identifying Northumbrian landscapes, visited so often in the era before Bed and Breakfast made us prisoners to holiday guests. I had made annual visits to my college daughter's home in Wooler. When she had married, Alnwick had become my Easter break. When her husband, Peter, became headmaster at Fenwick I had watched her children grow from babies into teenagers and, when Peter was appointed to another headship in Berwick we, as a family had made it our overnight stop when travelling north. We had taken Guides to camp for three weeks at Budle Bay, near Bamburgh and when Father had been diagnosed with prostate cancer, we had spent several holidays at Fenham-le-moor. It was wonderful. We could see Holy Island and the causeway. We saw Bamburgh Castle and the ancient walls of Berwick and the coastline over the Border, we knew so well. We saw all these places we had once loved. We saw the holiday cottage we had used when the aunts brought our family number up to seven. Nothing had changed. It was beautiful weather. What a lovely island Great Britain is and how empty it really is, how green and fertile. Thank God I have a sister who looks out of the window and doesn't know one end of a computer from the other.

More recently we had been travelling the West Highland Line from Fort William to Mallaig. Most of our wanderings in the Kyle of Lochalsh area had been by car and we found the rail journey from Inverness to the Skye terminal absolutely breath taking. The Islands and Highlands were approaching the end of a nine week drought and it was just beginning to show, with a browning alongside the single track line. Residents were praying for rain.

Immediately we reached Loch Carron we almost rose from our seats to hang out of the window like the children we used to take. We could see the places Margaret and I had walked that year when we could not get to the islands because of a ferry strike. We could pick out the route we had travelled with family in the Land Rover and the cottage, Heron's Flight, at Plockton where we had had such a lovely bed and breakfast for seven.

Our taxi was waiting for us at the station terminal and we crossed to Skye, via the bridge, for only the second time. It is really quite a beautiful bridge and I'm sure that, in the long run, Skye must have benefited though some of the 'over the sea to Skye' romance has been lost. The hour was late and the sun was brilliant in the windscreen, so it was lucky that the roads were relatively empty. We are nervous passengers when others, who do not fear speed, are driving.

We reached our B&B safely feeling like royalty, being transported from platform to door. Mrs MacKenzie, 'Caberfeldh', welcomed us with real island hospitality. Nothing has changed. It is the same wherever we stay. Let it remain so!

Our dogs had been captive for more than twelve hours and our first job was to take them on an urgent investigation of the narrow lane and its interesting roadside amenities. Sam was happy but Meg was not. If there is such a thing as psychic power and if dogs have that ability, I would say Meg was convinced that there was some spirit life in the area. That, or some smell she didn't like, some insect chatter we could not hear.

Normally obedient on the lead she stubbornly refused to move away from the cottage doorstep. I dragged her, forcibly to the grass but she stood with legs firm and would neither go up the road nor down. It was fortunate she had toileted outside the station, for nothing would have made her do so at Shrader. She was happy in the bedroom, stuck her head under the bed and relaxed. Next morning her attitude outside was just the same and, with feminine stupidity, she waited till we reached the pier before she would perform.

There was a moment of panic when the steep, rattling gangway startled Sam and, taking a fear stricken glance through the open sides, he was to drag to the summit. Meg's hair didn't even stand on end. She'd done it so many times. Both dogs were as eager for the sail as the humans returning, and those visiting for the first time. Those just going for the sail, had felt encouraged by the beautiful weather, the blue sky and the calm water which, together, promised a sail to remember. Fifty years ago we would have been on deck, but the MV *Hebrides* does not provide the wonderful outdoor facilities her predecessors had. We'd frightened Sam with one awkward climb, so we sat comfortably in the lounge where our dogs had the luxury of a carpet and the adoring attention of every passerby. So it was the fog siren which first alerted us to the obliteration of absolutely everything outside. Uig had been almost immediately lost from sight. There were no islands, no vista of Cuillins, or MacDonald's Tables and there appeared no destination ahead. We were sailing in a thick, thick soup of unexpected fog and the eerie sound of the foghorn interrupted our journey all the way. Those who had just come for the sail, and were to return without disembarking, would be truly disappointed. Everyone had to be satisfied with socialising with fellow passengers, investigating the various decks and visiting the buffet. Children sat on the carpet stroking our dogs, for the view was non-existent.

An hour and a half later we were suddenly in brilliant sunshine. The loud speaker was calling drivers to the car deck. Scalpay appeared on our starboard and the moonscape of Harris dazzled in sunlight. We docked in the township expecting the scent of peat to drift tantalisingly on our nostrils but to feel a heat making all fires unnecessary.

We had a welcome wait in Tarbert, for our transport was not to come until 2.30 p.m. We left our small amount of luggage in the waiting room, in the car park and strolled down to the quay to watch cars being loaded onto the ferry. We could have gone straight to the mini-market to buy stores because, for the rest of our stay our only shopping would be from the twice weekly travelling van. We knew that no island shop now closes when the boat comes in but we preferred to sit on that seat in the hot sunshine. We bared our arms and rolled our trousers up to the knee and remembered Jura and Coll and that wet arrival in Barra and, believe me, we felt as young as ever.

We were abruptly reminded of our age when the man releasing the hawsers, for the boat to return to Skye, turned, lifted both arms in salute and hurried over to our bench. It was Farquhar who'd been only a boy when we first met him. For us, the most pleasant thing that can happen, as we step onto an island, is that we are recognised. We chatted happily, hearing, almost immediately the re-occurring sound of the siren as The Hebrides was again lost in the fog.

Tarbert being our only opportunity to buy an ice cream, I left Margaret and climbed the steps from the harbour to the Main Street and indulged in a stroll round The Harris Tweed Shop. For a fortnight we had been hunting for treasure in the shape of a gift to send after the birth of a special baby.

We had had to wait until mid-May for news of the safe arrival of Denis's second baby, a boy they had named Jean. It would never have the same pronunciation as mine but I felt honoured and delighted. We wanted to send a gift with a name on it, to convey my pleasure but no little girls are called Jean, these days. At home we'd been too busy to pursue a trail until we had eventually found an answer. The Harris Tweed Shop is full of souvenirs and novelties as well as tweeds and sweaters and there I found a tweed covered photograph album, decorated with baby motifs. It was lovely, but it was pink.

The lady behind the counter said that was no problem for the craftswoman making these, lived in Tarbert and made them to specification. She could produce one in blue and with names Jean and Lucie on the front.

I hurriedly bought ice creams and returned to Margaret. We were all smiles eating our ices and when we had finished we climbed up the steps to the Main Street. Beside The Harris Tweed Shop more steps led down to a sunken garden and shop basement. The proprietor signalled that we could tie the dogs in the garden whilst we confirmed our order and even leave them whilst we went to Murdo's to buy our stores. This we did and left our purchases behind the counter to be picked up when Norman, and our transport arrived. The caring, hospitality of one of the planet's most beautiful islands can never be beaten.

'Thank you, thank you, thank you!' we said repeatedly over our two week sojourn, close to the beach we had camped beside, so many times and which is recorded as one of the ten best in the world. For us that has never been in dispute and it was echoed by those, admitably few, people we met each day as we strolled like teenagers on the clean expanse of white, shell sand. May the rest of the world not find it and crowd it with the litter of modern tourism. However, a few more could benefit from its discovery. If the people we met were anything to go by, the message is being circulated in our own county for we met couples from Huddersfield, Harrogate, Halifax and Leeds. There were at least ten 'tykes' there during that June fortnight and all were, like we, determined to return.

There are toilets now, in the car park beside the cemetery. Neither they nor it, were there when we first met the people of Luskentyre, forty six years ago. They are the first sensible public toilets I have ever seen. The hand basin is within the toilet cubicle so that any germs are washed away before the handle is touched. Even in hospitals, where MRSI bugs prevail, doors have to be opened before the tap can be reached. Today's rules and regulations are extreme but miss the basic principles. I say, 'Well done!' to whoever planned the Luskentyre Loo and I am willing to shower praise on the council workers who tend the twin burial grounds. On an island of exposed rock, populated sparsely by people who do not cremate, burial grounds are, of necessity where, for centuries the wind has laid acres and acres of sand. Each revered plot is tended almost daily and the grass mown with equal care to that of a bowling green. Before man made roads across the island, coffins had to be carried from the east and south and cairns over the route still mark places where the pall bearers put down their load and rested. The islanders have a great respect for their elderly and for their ancestors and are role models for the rest of the country to follow.

Over the fifty years we have had the privilege of knowing the island terrain, we notice more changes in its contours than in its people. The prevailing wind, which occasionally alters our course, finds the sands of the Western Isles easy prey. The dunes of the sixties have been transformed. Where they were high they have disappeared and where they were not they are now majestic. There are 'suicide jumps' suitable for adventurous children (and there must still be some) but they are not in the same location as they were. It takes millions of years to erode rock and only a decade to recreate the dunes.

These are a doggy paradise. Meg and Sam took only minutes to remember the previous year, the chalet, the gate into the footpath leading to the beach. Like children, they dashed ahead to wait impatiently for the gate to be opened and were immediately lost amongst the spiky marram grass. Meg knew exactly where the stream from the lochan, enters the bay but when she returned she was not only wet but green. There had been no recent rain for over nine weeks and, for the first time in Angus's long life-time, algae choked and coloured the almost stagnant pool. At home Meg's ablutions often result in an auburn model. The green she became was attractive but smelly and it was lucky she also liked the sea rinse which followed. Sam had retained his Billy Elliot capabilities, his springbok agility. Spotting a rabbit in the cemetery, he could leap the wall without touching the top stones.

Margaret had brought a ball with a 'tail'. We could hurl it before the wind so that the chasing dogs left scattered footprints everywhere and flurries of sand as they skid to a halt. The sun and the wind together browned skin not usually exposed and, apart for one day of welcome rain, the fortnight remained dry. We would not have grumbled had there been more, for the island was desperately in need. Flowers were late and roadsides were burnt. Not until that first and only wet day, did we see the orchids. At home the weather, too, was behaving for the little Charolais Margaret had brought from the brink.

Apart from the strange behaviour of Meg, in Uig, which was repeated on our return at the end of our holiday, every day was a joy and every mile of the journey a visual delight. The only scar on the expedition happened when the train pulled into our home town station. I hesitated before alighting, as I always do. I held Meg back with one hand and placed the other firmly round the handrail for the gap between train and platform was unusually wide. A kind man, stepping off the train in front of me, turned to offer me help. With his eyes on me, he stepped forward and fell heavily down the, far too wide, gap. Passengers crowded round to help him. It had the potential to be a nasty accident. Where is the Health and Safety Team in places where it is really needed? Had that been a child, would today's strict rules have prevented any adult from assisting. The man, obviously shaken and sore, protested he was all right but when we returned to enquire of the receptionist, on the Monday morning, we heard the man had been to the hospital and had returned to the station to fill in an accident form. We, as witnesses, were allowed to sign. Courtesy is rare, these days. That man was a gentleman worthy of respect and he could have been maimed for life.

Chapter Twenty-two

In this busy world I pray
Grant me each and every day,
Just some moment to be free
To sit alone and just be me.

ONE LADY VISITOR to Luskentyre, alone and wide eyed, had greeted us with, 'This is as near paradise as one can expect to be.' True, but we need work and that is at home. If there is a heaven, its inhabitants must be employed or it won't be paradise. Take Chris, for instance. Our absence from The Currer had gone more smoothly, for our caretaking team, than on several previous years and they may have been lulled into thinking that life here is incident free. Dorothy, who stood in for us so admirably for so long, would tell them it is no such thing. She had coped with an avalanche of guests requiring evening meals, with sick animals, straying cattle, our relatives and an ailing Aunty Mary and, sometimes, with appalling weather.

Chris and Helen had a trouble-free fortnight but paradise is where there is work and Chris invented it. He interpreted his role as that of handyman, re-painting the outside doors, windows and guttering and with hammer and nails and screwdriver he was active all day and every day. People on Harris have built new homes and have a lifestyle far ahead of the 90% of people who live in tenements, streets, terraces and council estates of urban Britain and they have a sensitivity to design and colour so that the outside beauty is matched within.

Hundreds of miles away from home, we always wonder if our five hundred year old, once-was ruin could compete. Returning to it, three weeks ago, in sunshine, newly painted, yard swept and seated among green, Pennine fields, we fell in love with it again for the umpteenth time. Perhaps, had we returned a day later, we would have been less impressed for it was a day more appropriate to November. Four people, from Bombay of all places, arrived in a thick mist. The sheds across the yard were scarcely visible. Apparently we had no cattle at all and a foghorn would have been a fitting reminder of our location.

A high wind was needed to dispel the grey blanket but the weather clerk sent one so strong it stripped the leaves from the trees, tore down branches nationwide and, passing through town next day, we were shocked to see the hanging baskets and flower tubs had been robbed of all their contents.

Wind seems a dominant feature of our country's daily weather chart, since the appearance of the new millennium. Is it that we just notice it more, now that fighting it is more exhausting than exhilarating?

Despite the weather we felt 're-newed indeed, because we'd smelt the Harris Tweed' and now, two weeks into July 2008, I can write this final chapter of our fifty year occupation of The Currer and I can wallow in memories that will bring life to old bones and prepare me for how ever many years lie ahead. May I please have 'work until my life is done and life until my work is done?' May I also have something to do in heaven, if that is my destination and I am not sent back to try harder!

In a little while I will turn back the pages of *We'll see the Cuckoo* to the twelfth of July 1958, for my reader's benefit. I need no reminding of that all important milestone in our history. It is as clear today as it was then.

But first I must put on shoes I so seldom wear and take the dogs up to the intakes and check that the gates are secure. Margaret wants to allow her calves into the Footpath Field. It currently looks like a meadow, so grass-rich are we at the moment. It is a beautifully still and sunny day and I am walking alone which affords me thinking time. Time to be just me. I am leaning on the firm, drystone wall, looking towards the house and buildings and beyond is distant Ingleborough. To the north are the beautiful Dales of Wharfedale, Nidderdale, Wensleydale, Swaledale and Teesdale and to the south lies Calderdale, but Airedale is my dale and it is just lovely. The wind has never succeeded in blowing me away from it permanently, nor ever will.

Little has changed in fifty years. Least of all me. Who I was then, I am now. Others talk about the different stages of human life, as if childhood houses a different being and teenage is inevitably turbulent. I experienced no life changing twenties, no mid-life crisis followed by a well deserved retirement. I have not travelled any of that changing journey through my life. I have felt to be just me all the time. I have not altered course, changed my lifestyle, my hair-do, my ideas, altered my priorities, lost or regained my faith so I must be the most uninteresting lady to pick up a pen. From where, oh where has come the material for four books about one small hilltop farm in Yorkshire?

I have not changed and neither has Margaret or our landscape, our outlook over the valley. There are a few more houses and a well kept golf course, but in August heather purples the slopes of Ilkley Moor just as it always has, before and since the Roman invasion. The trunk road along the valley is hidden and can only be heard if the wind is from the north. Heather and bracken and bilberry have gone from the plateau above the intakes but still grow healthily on The Rough. The silver birch saplings of the seventies, are trees now and those I planted below the feeding bay have reached above roof height and can be seen from our front room window. The Scots pines we planted behind the house, before Father died, have thirty five years of growth, and whereas trees in the hollow, reputedly said to belong to Jimmy, were sparse in 1958, they are plentiful in 2008.

A road has connected us with Moss Carr for forty nine of the fifty years we have been here. We laid the foundations so well that, though on a steep hill, they have moved not one inch and neither the elements nor the heavy lorries, bringing fodder or taking animals to market, have succeeded in eroding it.

The same variety of meadow flowers are found everywhere, colouring the pastures at my feet as they always did and the cow paths take the same route as when we were bare footed children. A moving herd still follows the same track, decided by their ancestors long before we were born.

The stones of this dry wall on which I lean, were unearthed by the monks of Rievaulx Abbey, before the Dissolution of the Monasteries and today they are warmed by the same sun which is infinitely older. I do not want hedges, or ditches or fences. I want walls. Our skilled workers have restored them admirably. The trees on the skyline, rooted in the composted soil of St Ives, have grown in the last five decades and the ash saplings which appeared accurately spaced when the New Age Travellers departed, are thriving on the green roadside of Altar Lane.

This is our land and we are proud of it. We had farmed it twenty nine years before we came to live in that house below me, ruined no longer, surrounded by its more recent cluster of barns and sheds and corn tower. For six months at the beginning of 1958, we had rapidly made the dwelling habitable, growing more and more attached to it as the days and weeks went by. We had neither money nor inclination to make of it a Grand Design. Outside and inside it has remained the Sixteenth Century, humble home of ordinary working people. Covenanted to The National Trust, in perpetuity, hopefully so it will remain.

And now, for those who may have forgotten, unlike us who never will, I will briefly turn back the pages of my memoirs. Margaret and I had already been a week in the empty house before the real removal to The Currer. After the installation and the lighting of the Aga, we had brought sleeping bags and kept the precious 'new buy' company.

* * * * * * * * * *

July 1958.

During the week that followed we lifted our threadbare carpets and brought them on the tractor to lie like ridiculous pocket handkerchiefs on the floors of The Currer. The real removal, on the following Friday, had all the ingredients of a first-rate cartoon. We hired a small, open lorry and prayed for a fine day. It was essential that the ground should remain firm in the First Intake and the Footpath Field, for there was no way that a small lorry could come down the cart track in Currer Lane. The ruts, mutilated by tractor wheels, were deep and wide. Stones had rolled from the parallel walls and become overgrown and presented hidden dangers. The hillside was slipping at the bend and generously spilling its clay into the track. In wet weather it was a quagmire and in the sun the clay ruts hardened into miniature cliffs. The only possible way, for any normal vehicle, was through the field.

I missed the removal for there is no clause which says a teacher can have a holiday to remove her belongings less than a mile. So, whilst everyone else was there to see the funny side, I was teaching the 3 Rs. The lorry had to make two journeys; both were precarious. Mother went with the first load and was there to organise the distribution of the incredibly few contents. Conforming absolutely to character, she saw the hot oven and started to bake. When I came home from school there was a lovely smell and a batch of newly baked scones on the table. Mother has an obsession about having her cake tins full. She loves to bake and it is as good as a tonic for her to do so. Seldom would a guest arrive here and find the cupboard bare.

And so a new life began at The Currer, a life of living next to a barn and animals being our nearest neighbours; a life of trimming Tilley Lamps and filling them with paraffin, of carrying all the shopping across five fields and ironing with a flat-iron. My early impressions were all olfactory. The smell of new-mown grass whilst still wet with dew, the sickliness created by the new hay stacked in the barn so close to the house that the smell penetrated the west wing bedrooms and competed with the soap and talcum in the bathroom. There was a constant fragrance of wood smoke from the sitting room fire, paraffin lamps and snuffed-out candles. Mother baked perpetually, and nothing smells nicer than new baked bread and currant teacakes.

I began to love the early morning walk across the fields. By the time I reached the bus stop I felt so healthy I ignored it and walked down the snicket, past the church and took the steep, cobbled way through the wood.

My energy knew no bounds. There were evenings when I walked the three miles from my school over by The Gormless, John Brown's Lane and Fairfax Pinnacle. I bragged I could do the three miles quicker that way. I loved coming home in the dark and had no fear of the fields or Currer Lane. The latter I preferred for it afforded a better view of the valley lights, a truly wonderful display.

More especially I learned to love the dawn. The early morning time is my time. Margaret is difficult to move in the morning and can stay up until long after midnight. This makes us a very good partnership for one or other of us is about, for eighteen hours of each day. At dawn there is often a mist which lies in the valley like a huge, white lake. It creeps up the hillside and escapes through the funnel of Jimmy's Wood, follows the stream in the Dyke Field and misses the house. It is a friend for it brings a beautiful day. The early morning is alive with the song of lark, peewit and blackbird, wrens hunt for insects in the stable wall and only the north wind picks up the metallic sounds of the Twentieth Century. Mother became vocal that first, sun-filled July. Making her beds with heat shimmering on the counterpane she would open the mullioned windows and sing.

My father's part in installing his family in the farmhouse was the major one. He was the pillar of strength which kept us all going and to whom we all turned for advice. He had a fantastic optimism, was always sure that, 'Summat 'ud turn up', and he worked like a young man to achieve a green and pleasant land. Now other people do not know, or have forgotten, what these acres looked like: fields carpeted with crowberry, the bent turf full of rushes and cotton grass, with bracken and bilberry. Others do not remember the ruin at the foot of Currer Lane but we do and that is why I write.

We'll see the Cuckoo

* * * * * * * * *

I have returned from my meditation, leaning on the drystone wall, alone with my memories. They are many and they are golden on this, July 12th, the 50th anniversary of our removal to The Currer; Mother, Father, Harry, Margaret and me. We have known great happiness. As is the way of things, we have also known bereavement. Our close family is reduced to two, stoic ladies, still satisfied with our life, here on this, now fertile Pennine ridge. We grieve the loss of loved ones, the lack of freedom for today's children and are sadly aware there are fewer and fewer birds. This is noticeable too, even on the islands. This year, dare I say it, we had to go to Harris to hear the cuckoo!

We have had to work endlessly, for money has never been plentiful, land and animals need constant attention and caring for others, though rewarding and enjoyable, is time consuming.

We have braved the storms, being blown by the winds of weather, of fortune and of change, yet we would do it again, given the opportunity. Unfortunately the spiritual draught from heaven propels everything forward. Joan Entwistle reminds us that, 'Life is not a rehearsal.' There are no repeats but enjoyment of it, we have proved, can be continuous.

I am laying the table for we are expecting the imminent arrival of Sally and Geoff Heddle, briefly returning to Kent to visit friends and family. The Currer is the second of two stops on their way from The Orkneys. Sally was already confined to a wheel chair when they first started to come here, on holiday, over twenty-five years ago. She and Geoff are the most creatively active of all our friends and having already celebrated their Golden Wedding anniversary, are relocating from Kent to their newly built house on an Orkney shore. They are adventurous role models for all who know them and their short stay will remind us that every end has a new beginning.

The Currer from the meditation wall.

Reading this manuscript Margaret's respectful comment was,

'For all of fifty years, we've not done a bad job. We've given it our all.'

True, but we must keep our hands steady on the tiller and continue to trust the wind to blow us in the right direction. We must trim our sails if necessary, and be ever appreciative of the setting sun. As I lay the cutlery it is painting golden The Currer landscape as far as I can see.

With gratitude I quote,

> When yesterday is already ours,
> what more can we ask?
>
>   from Cadfael